Introduction to Organizational Behaviour

Helga Drummond

Professor of Decision Sciences, The Liverpool Institute of Public Administration
and Management, The University of Liverpool

UNIVERSITY PRESS

OXFORD
UNIVERSITY PRESS

Great Clarendon Street, Oxford OX2 6DP

Oxford University Press is a department of the University of Oxford.
It furthers the University's objective of excellence in research, scholarship,
and education by publishing worldwide in

Oxford New York

Athens Auckland Bangkok Bogotá Buenos Aires Calcutta
Cape Town Chennai Dar es Salaam Delhi Florence Hong Kong Istanbul
Karachi Kuala Lumpur Madrid Melbourne Mexico City Mumbai
Nairobi Paris São Paulo Singapore Taipei Tokyo Toronto Warsaw

with associated companies in Berlin Ibadan

Oxford is a trade mark of Oxford University Press
in the UK and in certain other countries

Published in the United States
by Oxford University Press Inc., New York

British Library Cataloguing in Publication Data
[Data available]

Library of Congress Cataloging in Publication Data
[Data available]

ISBN 0-19-878217-9

Typeset in OUP Swift
by RefineCatch Limited, Bungay, Suffolk
Printed in Great Britain by
The Bath Press, Bath

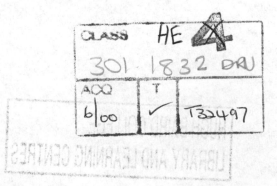

For August and Frida Stark

Mind is the forerunner of everything.
Mind is sovereign.
All things are generated by mind.

(Dhamnapadi Verse 1)

Contents

List of Figures

Acknowledgements

I wish to thank the following people: David Musson of Oxford University Press who suggested the idea of writing this book and Brendan George who subsequently saw it through to production.

David Collins who read the text in draft form and who generously contributed ideas and insights.

Rhona Wilson-Owens for permission to quote from her unpublished work.

Chris Allinson (who taught me Organization Behaviour longer ago than either of us would care to remember), for access to specialist references.

My colleagues in the Institute of Public Administration and Management in Liverpool for their unfailing warmth and good humour. I am especially grateful to Helen Bird, Michael Keighley and Rachel Silcock for their assistance.

Janet Beale for proofreading the manuscript. The remaining errors are mine.

Introduction

The Torah speaks about four sons: one who is wise and one who is contrary; one who is simple and one who does not even know how to ask a question.

(The Passover Haggadall, in Wiesel *The Fifth Son*)

THIS book is intended to provide an introductory text to the subject of Organization Behaviour. It is aimed at undergraduate and postgraduate students working on degree level courses in management. More specifically the objectives are:

- To explain key concepts, theories and ideas in the Organization Behaviour literature.
- To highlight the underlying assumptions and ideological implications of the Organization Behaviour literature.

Some of the topics are familiar: motivation, leadership, or workplace stress for example. Others, including metaphoric thinking, paradox, contradiction, ambiguity and symbolism are relatively new. They are included because they form part of an emerging vocabulary in Organization Behaviour which holds the potential to enhance our understanding of organizations.

To be more precise, the subject matter is approached from three intellectual standpoints:

1. managerialist
2. interpretive
3. critical.

The *managerialist* (sometimes called functionalist) literature is concerned with supporting the economic goals of the organization. The emphasis is upon prediction and control. For example:

- What motivates people?
- What style of leadership works best?
- How can an organization's culture be changed?

The managerialist literature assumes reality is a concrete entity. A key presumption is that organizational effectiveness rests upon clear communications, carefully defined lines of responsibility and the like.

In contrast, the *interpretivist* literature sees reality as a socially constructed entity. In this view, ambiguity, paradox and contradiction are not aberrations, but part of the natural experience of organizations. The emphasis is upon understanding the subtleties and dynamics of organizational life. For example:

- How do shared meanings arise?
- How do status divisions arise and operate?
- How do people express unity and hostility?

Critical theorists believe that reality is very real. According to critical theorists, people have only a marginal amount of freedom to define and shape their existence. Critical theorists regard management science as bogus, a means of legitimizing economic exploitation. In a nutshell, critical theorists are primarily concerned with:

What is not?

Critical theorists see much of the Organization Behaviour literature as unreflective and unemancipatory because it takes the existing order for granted, and is inherently gender biased. For example, critical theorists would argue that far from empowering people, modern management techniques such as transformational leadership merely reproduce existing power relations.

Learning Outcomes

THE key learning objectives which I seek to achieve are as follows:

1. To highlight the complexities, ambiguity and potentially paradoxical nature of organizational life.
2. To highlight the ideological implications of the Organization Behaviour literature.
3. To highlight the relevance of the wider society to students of Organization Behaviour.

Academics are sometimes accused of living outside the real world. Yet where is the real world? Is it the world of the 'Flaming Ferrari' investment banker wondering how to spend their £1 million bonus? Or is it the world of the Job Centre conscript packing boxes into a supermarket cold store for £3.60 an hour? Or is it the volunteer worker on a preserved steam railway lighting the gas lamps on a foggy November afternoon?
   An assumption implicit in the present text is that:

■ there is not one world, but,
■ many different worlds.

I have tried to represent a selection of different worlds in the text. We shall meet a diversity of people including the enthusiastic research engineer employed by Hewlett-Packard, a disgruntled gas fitter, and the beleaguered parish council clerk dutifully minuting the incident of a plastic bag blown into a hedge.
   A further assumption that has shaped my teaching and learning objectives is that what matters most is:

knowing the limits of one's knowledge.

I could have said more on every topic. For example, the coverage of motivation and leadership in Chapter 3 could list more theories and ideas. Likewise, I could have gone into more detail on managing culture in organizations. Instead I have tried to show how precarious is our knowledge.

To further this objective, every chapter of the present text is punctuated with pauses which invite the reader to reflect upon some aspect of the subject matter. Sometimes I suggest answers or explanations. Other times I leave it to the reader's judgement and imagination. The aim is to show that our theories and concepts and ideas are at best partial. The same applies to the questions for discussion which appear at the end of each chapter. I have used these to discourage rote learning and to unsettle any illusory sense of certainty which comes from reading a textbook.

Another important assumption which underscores the present text is that:

there is not one 'true' level of understanding but many levels of understanding.

Edward De Bono (1995) has suggested that our approach to knowledge is too adversarial, too orientated to the search for a truth at the expense of seeing other potentially plausible possibilities. As the philosopher Niels Bohr said, the opposite is often a profound truth also.

Personal Influences on the Text

EVERY author brings their own values, prejudices and enthusiasms to their work. This applies particularly to a subject like Organization Behaviour which is intellectually rich, challenging, and controversial. In my case, one important influence was seeing *The Pity of War* performed by Peter Florence. Florence takes the part of Wilfred Owen. The script is derived from Owen's poetry and letters. At one point Florence reads a letter written by Owen to his sister. The letter is dated 8 May 1917. The address is Casualty Clearing Station. The purpose of the letter is reassurance:

You know it was not the Bosche that worked me up, nor the explosives, but it was living so long by poor old Cock Robin (as we used to call 2/Lt. Gaukroger), who lay not only near by, but in various places around and about, if you understand. I hope you don't. (Wilfred Owen, *Collected Letters*, p. 509)

Hearing Florence articulate those words, 'I hope you don't,' brought home to me that we probably understand very little of what we see, hear and experience in organizations. We may think we understand, but in fact rarely do we look below the surface.

Another assumption which is reflected in the present text is that students of Organization Behaviour can and should concern themselves not only with productivity and product quality but also with:

the value of what is produced.

As a housewife, I find it prudent to shop in Leeds market where fruit and vegetables are astonishingly cheap compared with supermarket prices. There is a very different side to Leeds market, however. One vivid memory is that of a pensioner shakily parting with the sum of £2 in exchange for a pen marketed in a presentation box. The pens are an example of what William Morris (1934) called the deliberate manufacture of wants, goods which cost more to sell than they do to produce. Society dignifies and even reveres business. It does no harm to remind ourselves that many modern executives are not far removed from Groucho Marx's celebrated Doctor of Divinity hawking can openers as a sideline (Marx 1995).

Another important point is that:

Organization Behaviour does not exist in text books but 'out there'.

One morning I arrived at the market early. Most of the traders were just getting ready for business, sliding up the metal shutters of their stalls. Passing by a cafe, I noticed a youth dressed in an apron easing the contents of a catering size tin of a substance known luncheon meat on to a work surface. The pink mass of processed meat, gristle, salt, water, stabilizer, emulsifier and anti-oxidant slid forth in a solid mass.

Watching the youth going about his work, I wondered what motivated him. I realize now that it was a silly question. Motivated or not, he would do the job and do it adequately anyway. The mere fact that I asked it underscores the viewpoint espoused by critical theorists that motivation has become a substitute for meaning.

Later that morning I passed by the cafe again. This time I noticed a woman sitting at one of the formica-topped tables. She wore a shapeless brown and white herringbone-style coat. She was smoking a cheap cigarette while spooning white sugar into a cup of tea stewed from the cheapest of teabags. It was the lines on her face that caught my attention and the preoccupied look. The Organization Behaviour literature reduces emotion in a clinical fashion. To the extent that it has anything to say about that face, the literature would reduce to a theory linking socio-economic status, and nicotine abuse to stress. The theory may well be valid. However, knowing the limits of one's knowledge requires a willingness to consider:

- not only what theories reveal, but,
- what they conceal.

The woman's face is a story. That story is as relevant to our understanding of organizations and the wider context as any textbook. What has she seen?

An important theme of social-constructionism is that management information, that is, audit reports, accounts, and the like:

are not mirror reflections of reality, but, creations which become reality.

This was brought home to me during a performance of the Marx Brothers' *Animal Crackers* at the Royal Exchange theatre in Manchester at Christmas 1995—shortly before the theatre was wrecked by an IRA bomb. As the final scene draws to an end, a light shines above the darkened stage and illuminates a photograph of the three originals. Only then do we remember that we have not been watching the Marx Brothers at all, but a performance that has become the Marx Brothers. The picture is simultaneously sentimental and chilling. We have been watching dead men. The lights go down. The stage empties. Finally, Harpo, Chico and Groucho reappear and settle down in the straw for a game of cards. Harpo speaks for the first and last time. The play ends with one word, 'hearts'.

That final gesture seems to have presaged the death of Diana Princess of Wales in a car crash in August 1997. Later in this book I refer to the images of flowers and long queues of people waiting to sign books of condolence as an example of the partiality of metaphor. The image depicts the 100,000 or so people who felt moved to act. However, it eclipses the 100 *million* or so who went about their business as usual.

Yet I should add that I was in Manchester on the day of the funeral. I was struck by the subdued atmosphere in a city normally busy and jostling. My journey home took me through Albert Square and past the memorial decked with flowers and other artifacts of mourning. For all my scepticism about the media and the creation of collective sentiment, I remember relighting one of the candles which had blown in the wind and rain and sitting up a white Teddy bear which had also been blown about. My interest in organizational symbolism probably stems from a personal belief that science and rationality can only take us so far.

Structure of this Book

CHAPTER 1 sets the stage for what follows. It starts from the seemingly mundane question, 'what is an organization?' The purpose of the chapter is to highlight dimensions of complexity which may lie behind the seemingly obvious. The chapter begins by explaining the metaphorical nature of knowledge and how we use metaphors to make sense of the world. For example, ideas are 'buried'; decisions return to 'haunt' us, plans disappear into 'black holes' from which they never emerge.

It is emphasized that metaphors are not mere literary embellishments to make conversation more interesting but a reflection of something deeper. In the context of Organization Behaviour, the 'something deeper' concerns how our theories and ideas are influenced by mechanical imagery and linear intuitive thinking.

Part of the purpose of this chapter is to show how such thinking patterns obscure the potentially paradoxical and ambiguous nature of organizations. Particular attention is paid to the notion of rationality as it underscores much of the organizational literature. Rationality means calculation of the most appropriate means of achieving a particular objective. We see in Chapter 1 how:

- rationality may be driven by emotional impulses, and,
- how rationality can descend into absurdity.

The second of these two themes reappears in Chapter 7 which examines decision making in organizations.

Chapter 2 suspends judgement about the darker forces which may lurk behind rationality, and examines the work of the arch-proponent of industrial efficiency,

F. W. Taylor. Taylor's contribution to the organizational literature comprises a set of prescriptions for the management and control of work known as 'principles of scientific management'. Taylor's influence is visible in modern day management practice including time management, productivity targets, and, the so-called 're-engineering movement'. For example, many call centres are run on Tayloristic lines which may explain why the media often refer to them as the new satanic mills.

Chapter 3 focuses upon the behavioural approach to management, that is, the so called 'human factor' which Taylor largely ignored. Taylor assumed people could be motivated by a combination of material rewards (known as piecework) supplemented by surveillance and sanctions. The central assumption of the behavioural approach to management is that instrumental control is inadequate. If people are to be truly motivated, management must ensure that they are happy and satisfied.

Yet as we shall see:

- there is very little evidence to support this proposition,
- yet we continue to teach the theory.

The chapter ends with a discussion of this apparent absurdity. It should become obvious why my preoccupation with the motivation of the youth opening the tin of luncheon meat is indeed a narrow and possibly unhelpful question.

Chapter 4 focuses upon more recent developments in management techniques and philosophy. Such developments include, 'total quality management,' new-wave manufacturing and business process re-engineering. For example:

time is not only money, it is now a competitive weapon.

Particular reference is made to the work of Edward Deming and the implications of Deming's ideas for managing people in organizations. A central question is whether Deming's ideas are new, or basically Taylorism rescored in a different key.

Chapter 5 is about power in organizations. The previous three chapters are prescriptive. This is, they suggest:

how organizations should be (according to managerialist philosophy).

In contrast, the discussion on power concerns:

how organizations really are.

Mechanical imagery depicts organizations as static machine-like entities operating in a steady and predictable manner. Likewise, the metaphor of bureaucracy suggests that people in organizations are bounded by rules, job descriptions and organization charts.

Part of the purpose of Chapter 5 is to highlight the limits of this assumption. This chapter emphasizes the subtle shifts, and the unpredictable twists and turns whereby power relations are shaped and how people may become more or less powerful than their formal role prescription suggests. We also see how ambiguity can mask resistance.

Another important theme of Chapter 5 is that the supreme exercise of power is that which is invisible. For example, the most invidious acts of discrimination on grounds of sex, race and sexual orientation may result not from individual misconduct, but from 'taken for granted' assumptions about what is appropriate.

Chapter 6 continues the theme of organizational reality as it focuses upon politics and political behaviour. This chapter explains how things in organizations are not always quite what they seem. It also describes the tactics which people may use to advance their interests. A question which arises is:

- do politics undermine organizations, or,
- are politics essential to organizations?

Chapter 7 focuses upon decision making in organizations. This chapter builds upon the themes of metaphorical thinking and paradox and contradiction introduced in Chapter 1. The decision sciences literature sees organizational outcomes as flowing from 'decisions', that is, clear-cut choices between alternatives. I take a different perspective. My purpose is to show how that the notion of 'decision' is basically a metaphor. It highlights conscious choice, but obscures how organizations can become involved in ventures, or change strategic direction without anyone apparently having made a decision! We shall see that frequently, decision making:

- is not about deciding what to do, but,
- deciding what has already happened.

Metaphorical thinking also enables us to see into the heart of a paradox, namely that decision makers' information may be both:

- factually correct, *and*,
- a dangerous illusion.

Chapter 7 also examines how people cope with risk and uncertainty. It is emphasized that for all our sophisticated mathematical techniques and computing power, the ultimate arbiter is chance.

Chapter 8 concerns occupational stress. This chapter highlights the cost of organizational life. We see how work can undermine physical and mental health. For example:

1. How environmental factors such as noise can cause stress without people necessarily being aware of it.
2. How tiredness increases risk-taking, and,
3. How factors outside the workplace can exacerbate tension.

The discussion also attempts to draw back from the clinical managerialist literature and to see stress from a wider cultural and political angle.

Chapter 9 focuses upon organizational culture. Until fairly recently, management texts emphasized technology, process planning, communications structures and procedures, spans of control and the like. Indeed, the 'total quality management' literature and its derivatives largely assumes that organizational effectiveness is an engineering problem. The concept of culture highlights the intangible dimensions of organizational life.

In the present text, culture is examined from two intellectual standpoints. These are:

1. Culture is something an organization *has*, and,
2. Culture is something an organization *is*.

The managerialist literature treats culture largely as the property of management. In this view, the central challenge of management is to create an appropriate organizational culture. The present text pays particular attention to the so called 'excellence' literature and the espoused links between values and product quality.

Yet we shall see that the soaring optimism and transcendent language of excellence conceals a sinister purpose. The behavioural approach to management described in Chapter 3 assumes a basic consensus between managers and the managed, which managers occasionally upset by their insensitive behaviour. An invidious twist of the excellence literature, however, is that it attempts to link people's sense of self worth to their attitudes to work. In plain language, 'excellence' implies that:

if you do not love the product, (including the tawdry pens destined for Leeds market), there is something wrong with you.

When we come to examine culture as something an organization *is*, we leave behind the terra firma of prediction and control and travel across quicksand.

This section continues the notion of metaphorical thinking and builds upon the themes of power and politics. Seeing culture as something an organization *is*, helps to illuminate the limits of managerial control. We shall see, for example, that organizational activity may not be governed by rules so much as negotiated between parties. Likewise, organizational arrangements may be dictated not by operational needs so much as status claims. Moreover, we shall catch a glimpse of some of the dimensions of complexity surrounding organizational life.

More specifically, mechanistic thinking treats organizational events as one-dimensional. We shall see that what may appear as straightforward can be vested with multiple meanings. For example, mechanistic thinking sees:

either unity *or* division.

In Chapter 9 we see how the same event can express,

both unity *and* division.

Chapter 10 builds upon the theme of culture by examining the symbolic life of organizations. Symbolism brings us back almost to where we started. Instead of seeing the organizations as comprising buildings, offices, car parks, rule books, meetings and other forms of purposeful activity, we see these as symbol systems. Chapter 10 invokes the metaphor of text, the organization is studied as if it were a living document. Even the Christmas party assumes a deeper significance than surface appearances might suggest. Indeed, such is the power of symbolism that we can comfort ourselves with the knowledge that we will look better dead than we ever did alive!

It is more than that, however. In this chapter the veil of rationality is lifted. Notions of strategy, policy, business plans, projections and so forth are stripped away to reveal primitive fear, superstition and the suspicion of witchcraft.

Chapter 11 reverts to everyday reality. This chapter comprises a guide to writing essays and preparing for examinations in Organization Behaviour. Personal tuition is becoming a luxury in higher education. This chapter was written particularly to assist the student who has limited access to tutorial support.

The same applies to Chapter 12 which comprises a guide to researching and writing a dissertation or similar project. Although this chapter offers some general guidance, it is mainly orientated to Organization Behaviour. It contains ideas for generating topics, advice upon how to conduct research and how to maximize the prospects of success.

Chapter 1
What is an Organization?

Think of our organization as one big happy family

I doubt if any camera could capture my inner beauty.

(Groucho Marx, *The Groucho Letters*)

ITALO Calivino's novel *The Castle of Crossed Destinies* tells of a group of travellers who meet in a castle and inn. Deprived of the power of speech, the travellers tell their respective stories by setting out tarot cards on the table. For example, 'Roland Crazed with Love':

He set down the figure of the *King of Swords*, which attempted to render in a single portrait his bellicose past and his melancholy present . . .

Now he pointed to the *Queen of Swords*. In the figure of this blond woman who, among sharpened blades and iron plates, proffers the elusive smile of a sensual game, we recognized Angelica, the enchantress . . . and we were convinced that Count Roland was still in love with her.

After that came . . . the *Ten of Clubs*. We saw the forest open . . . The whole wood seemed to say to him: 'Go no farther! . . . The forest of love, Roland, is no place for you! You are pursuing an enemy from whose snares no shield can protect you. Forget Angelica! Turn back!'

The next card laid out by Roland, however, is *The Chariot* driven by the sorceress holding the reins of two white horses:

This was how Roland's raving imagination conceived Angelica's enchanted entrance into the forest. Wretched man! He did not yet know that in the deepest part of the thicket Angelica and Medoro were meanwhile united in a soft, heart-rending embrace. It took the Arcanum (tarot card) of Love to reveal this to him. (Calivino, 1978, pp. 28–29)

Imagine yourself as a traveller. Which cards would you select to tell your story?

This chapter concerns the metaphors or images (cards) we use to understand and think about organizations. Usually we invoke words like 'machine' or 'bureaucracy'. Yet sometimes words like 'madhouse' or 'circus' seem more appropriate. Indeed, many large organizations unwittingly function as 'sinks' for the purposes of money laundering (Robinson 1998). This chapter explains how the images we use (often unconsciously), exert a profound impact upon 'what' we see, and 'how' we see. The issues addressed in this chapter include:

Key Issues

- What is an organization?
- Is rationality irrational?
- Do we *describe* reality or *create* it?
- Do managers impose order upon chaos or create chaos in the name of order?
- Does science lead us to the truth or take us further away?

1.1 What is an Organization?

THE art of teaching involves two challenges. These are:

1. Making that which seems complex simple, and;
2. Highlighting the complexity of that which seems simple.

The question, 'what is an organization?' may seem simple. For example:

An organization is the rational coordination of activities of a number of people for the achievement of some common explicit purpose or goal, through division of labour and function, and through a hierarchy of authority and responsibility. (Schein, 1980, p. 15)

Likewise, Hall (1987 p. 40) defines organizations as possessing, 'A relatively identifiable boundary . . . ranks of authority, communications systems, and membership-coordinating systems.'

Note the words, 'goal', 'function', 'authority' 'responsibility' and 'boundary'. We will return to those themes later in this chapter. Here it is sufficient to note that such definitions basically imply that:—

- organizations exist for a purpose, and,
- they can be known through a structure of job descriptions and organization charts (e.g. Brown 1960, Katz and Kahn 1966).

This chapter is less concerned with what these assumptions reveal about organizations and organizational life, than with what they conceal. In order to see what they conceal it is necessary to step back a little and examine the basis of our knowledge.

1.1.1 The role of metaphor

Let me begin by reformulating the question. Instead of asking what an organization is, consider:

'an organization is like—what'?

Crucially, whether we say an organization is like a machine, a bowl of spaghetti, or even a tin of beans, we invariably invoke a *metaphor* in order to describe it. A metaphor is a constructive falsehood, that is, a linguistic device which enables us to understand one phenomenon through the medium of another (e.g. Brown 1977, Morgan 1980, 1983). Figure 1.1 lists some familiar metaphors. Metaphors are not literally true. For example, a computer does not literally contract a virus. Yet the falsehood is constructive because it enables us to conceptualize the potentially contagious nature of electronic corruption.

Metaphors play a crucial role in enabling us to understand the world. Indeed all

Figure 1.1 Examples of metaphors

'The computer has a *virus.*'

'The system has *crashed.*'

'This place is a *madhouse.*'

'We don't have the *machinery* to pay your expenses.'

'Our plans have *backfired.*'

'Time is *money.*'

knowledge is metaphoric. Words such as cancer and depression are basically metaphors invoked to enable us to conceptualize 'something else'. Likewise, 'We talk of "Death" for convenience, but there are almost as many different deaths as there are people,' (Turner 1996, p. 92, citing Proust).

1.1.2 The logic of metaphor

A vital point to remember, is that:

all metaphors are partial.

Figure 1.2 illustrates the point diagrammatically. Note that if there is too much correspondence the metaphor is redundant (Lakoff and Johnson 1980).

To say 'software is like software,' for example, tells us nothing about software. The same applies where there is too little correspondence. For example, to say 'software is like jelly' is unhelpful because there is hardly any connection between the two. Whereas to suggest that software is the 'engine' that drives a computer system enables us to grasp the role of software in computing technology.

Another vital point to remember is that since all metaphors are partial:

no metaphor can fully explain a particular phenomenon.

For instance, 'the mind is a machine' is a useful metaphor in highlighting the mind's analytical and computational abilities. The metaphor is partial because it eclipses the mind's creative and intuitive powers (Lakoff and Johnson 1980). Likewise, we can say, 'life is a journey', or, 'life is suffering'. Each metaphor resonates with our experience yet each misses something that is important in understanding the meaning of life.

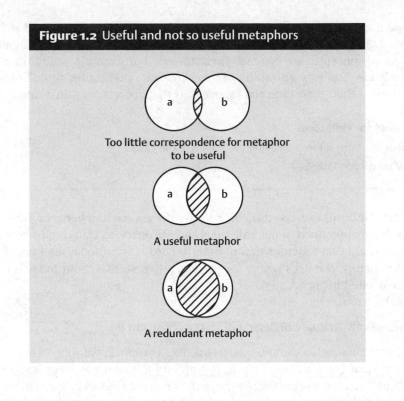

Figure 1.2 Useful and not so useful metaphors

1.1.3 Metaphor and understanding

The issue is important because the choice of metaphor shapes:

- *what* we see, and,
- *how* we see.

For instance, do we see insanity as illness, or as an extreme form of social distance? If we see the Nazi holocaust as an historical event we can describe what happened. Yet if we conceptualize the holocaust as a 'window' we can go a stage further and see how the destruction of millions of people was enabled (Bauman 1989). If we see housing estates with high unemployment and high crime rates as 'problem areas', the solution is seen in the bulldozer and wholesale dispersal of residents. Yet if we conceptualize those estates as 'frustrated communities' the solution is seen in organizing self-help and other initiatives aimed at releasing people's creative potential (Schon 1993).

> **Pause for reflection**
> Imagine time.
> What do you imagine?

A good illustration of the power of metaphor in shaping our thinking is to imagine time. Most people would think immediately of a clock. The clock is a metaphor which allows us to conceptualize time in a certain way. For example, study time, leisure time, bedtime. You may also think of marking time, playing for time, of ideas that were ahead of their their time and innovations that are a race against time.

Pause for reflection

Imagine time without invoking the notion of the clock.

What do you imagine?

You may find this exercise difficult because the association between time and the clock is deeply ingrained in our conscious and unconscious thinking patterns. Yet St Augustine had a very different view of time, 'O Lord . . . your today does not give place to any tomorrow. Nor does it take the place of any yesterday. Your today is eternity.' (*Confessions*, cited in Turner 1996).

Crucially:

metaphors both facilitate understanding and constrain it.

Many metaphors are so commonplace that, like the clock, we forget they are metaphors and treat them as literal truths (Lakoff and Johnson 1980). For instance, until recently physicists conceptualized time in the image of the clock. Stephen Hawking's genius was to see the constraints implied by the choice of metaphor. The clock depicts time as moving forwards.

Hawking asked himself, 'If time could be seen as moving backwards as well as forwards, what possibilities might that suggest?'

Reconceptualizing time was the precursor to the 'discovery' of so-called 'black holes' (Hawking 1988).

1.2 Metaphors and Organizations

1.2.1 The obvious? Organizations and machine bureaucracies

The same logic applies to the metaphors we invoke to conceptualize organizations. Just as an aircraft assumes the metaphor of a bird, many organizations (but not all) asssume the metaphor of bureaucracy. Bureaucratic organizations are characterized by:

- Functional specialization or division of labour.
- Hierarchical command or authority.
- Reliance upon written rules and procedures.
- The rational application of rules and procedures (Weber 1947).

While far from advocating bureaucracy, Weber predicted that bureaucratic organization is inevitable because it is a technically superior form of organization. According to Weber, bureaucracy offers:

Precision, speed, unambiguity, knowledge of the files, continuity, discretion, unity, strict subordination, reduction of friction and of material and personal costs. (Gerth and Mills 1991, p. 241)

Later in this chapter we shall see that bureaucratic structures may not be as efficient as Weber suggests. The issue here is the mechanistic thinking which underlies the notion of bureaucracy.

Mechanistic thinking sees organizational effectiveness as a technical problem (e.g. Smircich 1983a).

Mechanical imagery assumes that organizations exist as instruments for task accomplishment. The organization is depicted as consisting of multiple parts to be designed and meshed into fine tuned efficiency, hence allusions to the organizations as 'a well oiled machine', and 'running smoothly' (Smircich 1983a). Significantly, Ray Krock's book on the story of McDonald's is entitled *Grinding it Out*. Likewise, the implementation of the holocaust became a problem of technological efficiency pursued to 'final solution' (Bauman 1989).

Mechanistic thinking is reflected in questions such as what is the optimum span of control, what pattern of delegation works best, how can work be designed to maximize productivity? Chapters 2 and 4 explore the impact of mechanical imagery in more detail. The present chapter is less concerned with what mechanistic thinking reveals about organizations and more concerned with what it conceals.

1.2.2 Bureaucracy as metaphor

In *The Castle of Crossed Destinies* referred to earlier, the tarot cards function as metaphors whereby one phenomenon, in this case a person's life story, is understood through the medium of another, that is, the symbolism of the tarot. Bureaucracy is understood through organization charts, job descriptions, procedural manuals and other such devices.

Yet as Brown (1960) perceptively notes, there is often a wide discrepancy between how the organization appears on paper, and how it works in practice. For example, employees are sometimes unsure what their job is or who they report to. The organization chart may show that manager X is in charge. Yet manager Y appears to have taken control. Employees may be asked to undertake work outside their job description. In other words:

the trappings of bureaucracy typically say more about what *should* be, than what really *is*.

Metaphoric thinking enables us to take Brown's observation a stage further. A map of the London Underground may be accurate but it is not the London Underground. The map may help us find the correct route to our destination, but, as anyone who has ever taken a wrong turn at one of the larger stations knows, it says nothing about the labyrinth of tunnels and escalators. Nor does it give any impression of the sights and sounds of the underground, the warm fusty smell, the rattle of trains and the queues at the ticket machines and the crush at the ticket barriers. The same applies to organization charts, job descriptions, procedural manuals and the like. They too are metaphors. They are informative as far as they go, and yet inherently limited, depicting reality in a particular way. We can best see what is concealed by examining different metaphors of organization.

1.2.3 The not so obvious? Organizations as psychic prisons

Gareth Morgan's *Images of Organization* first published in 1986, was an important landmark in organization theory. Morgan suggests that organizations can be seen as 'brains', as 'flux and transformation', as well as from more familiar mechanistic, systems, power, political and cultural perspectives discussed later in this book. In order to demonstrate the revelatory power of invoking different metaphors, let us briefly examine Morgan's most controversial proposition, namely the notion of organizations as psychic prisons.

All good 'blockbuster' novels are shot with emotional tension. An airplane heads for disaster as control tower staff squabble among themselves. A bank totters as the chief executive is embroiled in a sexual scandal. A vital discovery made by a brilliant junior medical scientist is suppressed by jealous senior colleagues. Such incidents are by no means confined to paperback novels.

Morgan (1996a) has coined the term 'psychic prison' in order to capture the psychosexual dimension of organizational reality. Morgan's image of organizations as psychic prisons reverses the assumptions implied by the machine metaphor. Mechanistic thinking sees emotion as irrational, as undermining operational efficiency:

[Bureaucracy] develops the more perfectly the more bureaucracy is 'dehumanized', the more completely it succeeds in eliminating from official business love, hatred, and all purely personal, irrational and emotional elements which escape calculation. This is the specific nature of bureaucracy and it is appraised as its special virtue. (Gerth and Mills, 1991, p. 216)

By contrast, the psychic prison metaphor suggests that:

our ideas about what constitutes efficiency are basically sexual.

Morgan writes:

As we examine the bureaucratic organization . . . we should be alert to the hidden meaning of the close regulation and supervision of human activity, the relentless planning and scheduling of work, and the emphasis on productivity, rule following, discipline, duty, and obedience. The bureaucracy is a mechanistic form of organization but an anal one, too. Not surprisingly, some people are able to work in this kind of organization more effectively than others. (Morgan 1996a, p. 225)

Morgan further suggests that anality as a repressed form of sexuality has shaped the nature of many organizations which we would recognize as bureaucracies. Moreover, sexuality may lurk behind other forms of organization. Morgan continues:

Take, for example, the more flamboyant, flexible, organic, innovative firms now making such an impact on the corporate world. These organizations often call for a creative looseness of style that is quite alien to the bureaucratic personality. Freudian theory would suggest that the corporate cultures of these organizations often institutionalize various combinations of oral, phallic and genital sexuality. (Morgan 1996a, p. 225)

1.2.4 Implications of the psychic prison metaphor

The psychic prison metaphor thus implies:

- organizations are driven by both rational and irrational forces,
- rationality is often irrationality in disguise, and,
- the irrational undercurrents of organizational life significantly influence organizational outcomes.

For example, Morgan suggests that high regard for a leader or role model may actually be prompted by unconscious anxieties and aggressions. Likewise, organizational initiatives such as mergers, takeovers and downsizing initiatives may be objectively defensible yet actually motivated by what Morgan (1996a), calls 'the hidden dimensions of everyday reality', (p. 245). (For an interesting analysis of an actual case see Kets De Vries and Miller 1987.)

Emotional influences are seldom made visible because they are regarded as irrational and therefore illegitimate. In practice, emotion is usually hidden beneath a veneer of rationality, as in the use of coded language. In Chapters 6 and 10 we see how business plans, costs benefits analysis, project planning techniques and so forth serve to create the appearance of rationality where none exists. Emotion impacts at all levels of organizational activity, not just at the strategic apex. For example, some Job Centre clerks prosecute their duties with distinct vigour. It is as if they secretly enjoy their power to discomfit claimants and force them into low paid and uncongenial jobs. One senior manager I know of admitted to being jealous of a subordinate who appeared in a superior suit on the day of a royal visit. The subordinate was promptly despatched on an errand to the other side of the city.

Moreover, suggests Morgan (1996a), when emotional undercurrents do erupt in aggressive outbursts, displays of greed and so forth, they are soon rationalized, punished or otherwise explained away. We apologize, we claim that we are under pressure, that our behaviour was out of character—almost as Churchill once said of Jane Austen's novels:

What calm lives they had, those people! . . . Only manners controlling natural passion so far as they could, together with cultured explanations of any mischances. (In Churchill, Winston, *Closing the Ring*, vol. V. of *The Second World War*, London, Cassell, 1950, p. 425)

Jane Austen's world may seem far removed from the pressures of modern day living. Or is it that the literature upon workplace stress described in Chapter 8 basically attempts to rationalize and explain away antisocial behaviour?

The point is, says Morgan, no matter how much we explain and rationalize, 'We do not get rid of those repressed forces lurking in the shadow of rationality' (Morgan 1996a, p. 246, see also Burrell 1998).

Emotional forces are not necessarily sinister or destructive, however. Whereas the machine metaphor equates organizational efficiency to the repression of emotional influences, the psychic *prison* imagery suggests a different challenge. That is, how to release and make productive the psychic energy underscoring organizational life (Morgan 1996a). The popular management literature has grasped the possibilities to an extent. Managers are urged to create a passion for excellence, to be obsessive about quality, and to kindle excitement. Yet the literature sees mainly the potentially productive side of obsessional behaviour. Obsessions can be destructive. For example, Henry Ford's unshakeable belief that everyone wanted a low cost uniform car, and IBM's iron belief in the future of mainframe computers (Crainer 1995). Another feature of the popular literature is that it refers only to culturally acceptable obsessions. What of the creative potential of darker forces?

Organizations as psychic prisons has been criticized as the weakest of Morgan's metaphors. For example, Mangham (1996), argues that metaphor lacks credibility because few people have any experience of organizations as psychic prisons. I suggest that if the metaphor stretches credulity it is because it forces us to recognize a dimension of organizational life that is the very opposite of what the literature conditions us to expect.

It is also a disturbing image because it implies that organizational life is driven by forces which are beyond reason. By themselves, incidents pertaining to the suit and the behaviour of the Job Centre clerk are trivial. Yet if we stand back and imagine the bigger picture, then what they highlight is an emotional undercurrent of organizational life that we know comparatively little about (e.g. Burrell 1984, Hatch and Ehrlich 1993, Hatch 1977, Quinn 1977).

Mechanistic thinking focuses upon the machine-like elements of organization. The psychic prison metaphor illuminates the 'seething and the teeming' that may lie just beneath the apparently calm and ordered surface. To mix metaphors, conventional thinking revolves around the 'mind of the strategist' with all its connotations of high analytical and scholastic competence. The psychic prison metaphor forces us to recognize that beneath the blue pinstripe, lurks a baby in nappies.

1.2.5 One best metaphor?

> **Pause for reflection**
> Paint your autobiography in one colour only.

I imagine that you may find this exercise difficult and frustrating. Can one colour adequately depict the twists and turns of fate, the moments of chance and mischance, the shades of light and darkness that have shaped your destiny?

Much the same applies to organizations. As all metaphors are partial, logically:

in order to understand organizations it is necessary to study them from a variety of perspectives (e.g., Burrell and Morgan 1979, Gioia and Pitre 1990, Morgan 1990).

In theory there should be no limit to the number or types of metaphor invoked to study organizations. Nor are we confined to a single metaphorical lens. We can counterpose metaphors rather like combining filters on a camera. For example, we can see:

power in organizations (red lens),

or, we can see:

stress in organizations (blue lens)

or, we can see:

power *and* stress in organizations (red and blue lens)?

If we view stress through a single conceptual lens we may see it as a medical problem largely related to home and family pressures and inappropriate lifestyles. If we combine conceptual lenses, however, stress emerges as a facet of economic exploitation and inequity and the disproportionate burdens placed upon women.

In practice, we regularly blend metaphors in order to make sense of our world (Mangham 1996, Turner 1996). For example, people in organizations speak of 'lifting the lid off a can of worms', of ' "it" having hit the fan', and 'square pegs in round holes'. Much of the cross-referencing in this book involves mixing metaphors. For instance, part of the literature on organizational culture mingles images of power and politics.

1.2.6 Invent your own metaphors?

Our ability to generate metaphors and engage in metaphoric thinking is constrained only by the limits of the human imagination. Indeed, part of the fun of metaphoric thinking is that you can invent your own images of organization. Gareth Morgan (1993) describes the technique as 'imaginization'. Imaginization involves seeing the organization as if it were something else and mapping out the similarities.

The purpose of invoking novel metaphors is to highlight previously unseen features of organization (Chia 1996), that is:

■ to see the familiar differently, and,
■ to prompt new patterns of thinking.

For example, Morgan (1993) suggests that 'imaginizing' the organization as a spider plant can highlight the potentially pervasive nature of organizations and the dangers of unplanned growth.

> **Pause for reflection**
> Management is like—what?

Metaphoric thinking can enable us to see our assumptions for what they are, and to see the extent to which they condition our thinking. What do you imagine when you imagine management? More importantly, why do you imagine management in a particular way? You might have jotted down words like 'control', 'direction'—are they the only possibilities? How does the word 'nurturing' change your perceptions of what might be? Mechanistic thinking partly explains why much of organization theory is gender blind (e.g. Acker 1992, Burrell 1984).

1.3 From Metaphors to Metaphoric Thinking

1.3.1 Why bureaucracy?

Bureaucracy may seem like an old fashioned word. Yet bureaucracy continues to be a highly influential template for designing and managing organizations. Ritzer's (1993) fascinating essay entitled the 'McDonaldization of Society' suggests that a wide spectrum of modern organizations are designed to facilitate efficiency, calculability, predictability and control—not least 'fast food' restaurants. For example, the seats in 'fast food' restaurants are designed to subtly control behaviour. The calculation is that by making the seats uncomfortable, people will be disposed to eat quickly and leave. Ritzer sees a similar trend in higher education. According to Ritzer, education is becoming almost as standardized as hamburgers. For example, McUniversity employs multiple choice tests because they are cheaper to mark than essay-style examination scripts.

1.3.2 Designing organizations as biological organisms

Another influential metaphor is the notion of the organization as a biological organism, often referred to as systems theory. From a biological perspective, survival is the organizational imperative. From a systems perspective the key to survival is the organization's relationship with the environment. More specifically, survival is seen as critically dependent upon the organization's ability to adapt, to change, and to renew itself (e.g. Hall 1987). In other words, whereas mechanistic thinking sees technical efficiency as all important, the biological metaphor points to the importance of strategy and the regulation of organizational subsystems.

Although Weber regarded bureaucracy as supremely efficient, bureaucratic structures are ill attuned to operating in turbulent environments (e.g. Toffler 1970). Bureaucratic decision-making procedures and hierarchical structures are apt to hamper innovation and discourage risk taking. The biological metaphor is at the root of so-called organic approaches to management (Burns and Stalker 1961). Organic approaches to management stress flexibility and fluidity. Meetings play a central role in sharing intelligence, identifying and solving problems and coordinating work. Where bureaucratic organizations rely upon rigid job descriptions and compartmentalization, organic structures are characterized by *ad hoc* arrangements. One feature of such structures is the use of cross-functional project teams assembled to work on a particular project and subsequently dissolved or reformed to meet a new need. In organic organizations jobs may be allowed to shape and reshape themselves as circumstances require.

An interesting refinement of the biological metaphor is Weick's (1976) notion of 'loose coupling' as a basis for organizational design. As the term suggests, loose coupling implies a significant amount of autonomy for organizational sub-units. For example, many department stores are loosely coupled organizations. Different counters, perfumes, leather goods, and so forth are usually owned by different companies, that is, shops within a shop.

1.3.3 Designing organizations as loosely coupled systems

Whereas tightly coupled systems are characterized by a high degree of interdependence between organizational sub-units, loosely coupled organizations are relatively cheap to run because their relative autonomy requires fewer resources for control. In the case of department stores, for example, each 'counter' is responsible for most of its own marketing and recruitment. Loosely coupled organizations are also less vulnerable to environmental turbulence because if one part of the business declines the damage is confined to that particular segment. For instance, if the chocolate counter defaults, the organization as a whole is unlikely to be jeopardized. Another interesting example of loose coupling is the recent decision by a UK railway company to employ passengers as part-time guards.

1.3.4 Better by design? Metaphoric thinking inside organizations

Pause for reflection
What is a university library?

Metaphoric thinking can also be applied to designing and managing organizational activities. For example, a hotel can be designed as a 'sleeping factory' or as 'home from home'.

Some hospitals exhibit more concern for monitoring the urine of terminally ill patients than they do for providing psychological and spiritual care. Likewise, Garud and Kotha (1994) have observed that production systems based upon specialist division of labour and hierarchical control are incapable of meeting modern day demands for speed and flexibility. They suggest that the human brain is a more appropriate metaphor for designing manufacturing systems in order to achieve self-organizing capability.

Many university libraries could improve the service to students and staff if they reconceptualized their role in the light of changing technology. Hitherto, libraries have been seen as mainly repositories of books and papers. What root metaphor might be appropriate for the future?

1.4 Metaphoric Thinking and Understanding Organizations

1.4.1 Jazz musicians and organization theory

Metaphoric thinking can shed new light upon organizational life. For instance, bureaucracy depicts people in organizations as *constrained* by rules and regulations. Yet Gouldner (1954) notes that one of the paradoxes of bureaucracy is that rules and procedures intended to regulate conduct are apt to result in minimum standards being observed. We can see further into the heart of this paradox if we 'imaginize' organizational structure as improvizational jazz, 'Jazz musicians . . . do not accept their structures as given. They believe that the appropriate attitude to structure is one of finding out what you can get away with' (Hatch, forthcoming).

The jazz metaphor highlights the potential subtleties and ambiguity of human behaviour. Ostensible rule observance may border upon recalcitrance. While appearing to stay within boundaries, people are forever testing these. People over-spend budgets slightly. They transfer monies between accounts hoping that the auditors will not notice. If challenged they will claim the rules are unclear, or that a clerical error has been made. People break deadlines by a few days. They miss a few meetings. That is, literally seeing what they can get away with.

Mechanistic thinking presupposes that clear rules and appropriate control mechanisms can prevent risk and danger. The jazz metaphor enables us to see the limits of this assumption as it illuminates the grey area that exists between propriety and impropriety.

It is more than that, however. Mechanistic imagery depicts the organization as static, like a free-standing machine. The jazz musician highlights the dynamics of organization.

As boundaries stretch and reform, as custom and practice modifies rules and relationships, so the organization obliquely develops and changes in ways that are difficult to control.

1.4.2 The chimpanzees' tea party: Paradox and contradiction in organizations

> **Pause for reflection**
> *Customer:* 'Why haven't you got a dart board in this pub?
> *Bar tender:* 'No darts'.

Mechanistic thinking is based upon linear and intuitive assumptions about the nature of organizational life (Cameron and Quinn 1988, Quinn and Cameron 1988). For example, 'common sense' suggests that control is preferable to anarchy, and more control is preferable to less. While such assumptions are not necessarily wrong, they are not universally correct either. Metaphoric thinking can enable us to see their limits by illuminating the existence of paradox and contradiction in organizations.

The point is best illustrated by invoking an unconventional metaphor of organizational life. Instead of seeing organizational activity as comprising an ordered and logical sequence of events, let us 'imaginize' it as a chimpanzees' tea party (Drummond and Kingstone-Hodgson nd). The 'chimpanzees' tea party' was an attraction once offered by zoos to entertain young children. A group of chimpanzees are seated at a table. The table is arranged as if it were indeed a real tea party. Mats are provided, food is served upon plates and drink is poured into cups.

The chimps have other ideas, however. They tip their cups upside down, spill their orange juice on to the ground, bang their plates on the table scattering the food far and wide, and wear the table mats on their heads. In fact, they do almost anything except eat their tea in an orderly fashion.

Mechanistic thinking equates organizational efficacy with control. For example, we refer to 'run-away projects' and 'projects spiralling out of control'. Again it is not what this assumption reveals that is significant but what it conceals, namely:

the opposite may also be true.

That is, control can destabilize an organization. In the chimpanzees' tea party a keeper stands by with a broom and a large waste disposal bag. Never does the keeper attempt to direct the chimps. At best, the exercise would be futile. More likely, pandemonium would ensue.

This insight raises a question, namely:

Do managers sometimes create chaos in the name of order?

Mintzberg (1973) has observed that an important function of management is 'disturbance handling'. A problem erupts, the manager intervenes to restore equilibrium, sometimes known as 'fire-fighting'. The tea party metaphor suggests that managerial intervention can create the opposite of what was intended. Far from restoring equilibrium, managers may make matters worse by interfering. Figure 1.3 contains some more examples of paradoxical thinking.

More importantly, the tea-party metaphor suggests that the notion of disturbance is one sided. Although much food and drink is spilled, the chimps do actually eat their tea albeit after a fashion. Whereas the manager's task is usually seen as:

imposing order *upon* chaos,

the tea party illuminates the notion of:

order *within* chaos (Brown 1977).

Figure 1.3 Examples of paradoxical thinking

'Make haste slowly.'

'More haste, less speed.'

'Organized chaos.'

'I am lost, yet I know exactly where I am.'

'Busy doing nothing.'

'The more I find out, the less I know.'

Western management philosophy is goal driven, 'management by objectives', for example (e.g. Drucker 1954). The tea-party metaphor highlights a very different possibility. Specifically, the behaviour of the keeper suggests that sometimes managers may achieve more by adopting the Eastern philosophy of 'going with the flow'. 'Going with the flow' implies harmony, blending with other people's pace and ideas rather than imposing one's own. It is the difference between the architect who places footpaths where people actually walk and the architect who dictates the route only for people to walk across the grass anyway. Likewise, Western management philosophy equates strong leadership with aggression. For example, proponents of the re-engineering movement depict managers as 'blasting' their way through obstacles (see section 4.3.4). By contrast, Eastern philosophy is based upon the analogy of removing stones from the river (Eisenhardt and Westcott 1988).

1.4.3 More is better? The limits of mechanistic thinking

Another assumption implied by 'more is better' logic is that good management rests in clear communications, and clearly defined lines of responsibility, the clearer, the better. For example, *'Channels of communication should be definitely known'; 'the line of communication should be as direct or short as possible'* (and not) *'interrupted during the time when the organization is to function'*, (Barnard 1938, pp. 177–9, italics in original).

Barnard's advice implies that ambiguity is dysfunctional. Indeed, ambiguity can undermine organizations. For example, role ambiguity (the individual is not certain what their job is) has been linked to stress (see section 8.3.2).

Metaphoric thinking allows us to see another possibility, however. Returning to the jazz metaphor, 'Jazz musicians see ambiguities as empty spaces into which they can insert their ideas and have influence on the way a tune is played' (Hatch, forthcoming, p. 21).

In other words, the jazz metaphor suggests that eliminating ambiguity (if, indeed, ambiguity can be eliminated) can also create problems by stifling creativity and initiative and make people feel powerless. Powerlessness is also associated with stress; for example if an individual is unable to resolve conflicting role requirements (see section 8.3.2), and it can be alienating. We shall see in Chapter 4 that 'total quality management' programmes are designed to eliminate ambiguity by specifying exactly what must be done, where, when and by whom. By imposing control they risk destroying the responsible autonomy and self-organization which already exist in the organization.

1.4.4 Metaphoric thinking and playing games with reality

Mechanistic thinking assumes a monochromatic view of reality. In this view a table is a table. By contrast, metaphoric thinking can illuminate the potentially prismatic nature of that which we call 'reality'. For instance, a table is simultaneously a collection of atoms (Wisdom 1965).

Estate agent's property guides are a good example of the prismatic nature of reality. Estate agents typically highlight the selling points of a house. The surveyor's report basically constitutes a metaphoric redescription of the house (Brown 1977, 1989, Hobbs 1988, Rorty 1989). Character and old-world charm give way to damp and dry rot. Both accounts may be factually correct yet the contrast may be such that it is difficult to believe that they refer to the same house!

We shall see in Chapter 6 how political activity in organizations often involves metaphoric redescription. 'Failure' is redescribed as 'success'. Reputations are rehabilitated or discredited. For example, President Clinton has undergone a metaphoric redescription in the light of his relationship with Monica Lewinsky. Prince Charles has recently attempted to achieve a metaphoric redescription of his public persona.

Metaphoric thinking allows us to see further still, that is:

we do not *describe* reality so much as *create* it (e.g. Berger 1972, Berger and Luckman 1966, Rorty 1989, Schon 1993).

> **Pause for reflection**
> An authoritative estimate suggests that if the members of the British armed forces killed in the First World War returned, assuming they marched four abreast, it would take them three days to pass the Cenotaph (Dyer 1995).
> What does this statistic mean?

We can interpret the statistic in many different ways. In organizations people refer to deeds and decisions returning to haunt them. What does the spectre of the returning dead signify? Do they return proud and immaculate in dress uniform? Or do you picture them caked in mud, bodies swarming with lice, marching in sullen silence?

Metaphoric thinking enables us to see that what may seem like neutral description is actually deliberate creation. For example, accountants are commonly perceived as 'bean counters'. Yet accountants do not slavishly mirror the financial reality of organizations so much as invent it (Alvesson and Willmott 1996). For example, the accountant decides how the depreciation is calculated and whether items on order are booked as 'sales' or whether 'sales' include only those transactions for which payment has been cleared.

When we see the metaphoric nature of information we can begin to appreciate why things are not always what they seem in organizations. For example, we can begin to understand why an organization can have a healthy balance sheet and yet be on the verge of collapse, and why projects can be declared 'completed' while still under construction.

1.5 Organization: Using Metaphors to Understand Metaphors

A further twist in the discussion is that the notion of organization is itself a metaphor, a figurative device to enable us to understand 'something else' (Smircich 1983a). Recall that metaphors prefigure the ground of thought. The notion of organization predisposes us to focus upon order and orderliness (Smircich 1983).

1.5.1 Railway tracks, cart wheels and the limits of rationality

Notions of order and orderliness can lead us to assume that the world is a much more rational place than it really is. For instance, most of the world's railway tracks are built to a gauge of four feet and eight-and-a-half inches. This is not because it is the optimum width for a train. The measure was copied from the standard width of cart wheels. A more recent example concerns Microsoft's increasing domination of the office software market. Whether Microsoft's ascendancy is due to technical superiority of 'Windows' is a matter of opinion. We return to this point in the chapters on power and organizational culture.

Notions of orderliness can lead us to believe that the organization is in control—almost to the point of assuming the existence of an organizational deity. For example, a manager recruits a new employee and assumes that 'someone in Personnel' will check that person's antecedents and qualifications. I once learned a salutary lesson on a visit to a salaries office. There was a pile of boxes on the floor. The boxes were stuffed full of forms with applications for employee pension entitlements, 'We don't know where they've come from,' said the clerk, 'they just arrived.' I would not be surprised if they are still there!

Rationality means calculation of the most appropriate means of achieving a particular objective (Gerth and Mills 1991). Mechanistic 'more is better' logic implies that the more perfect the bureaucracy, the more efficient the organization. Once we become conscious of organization as metaphor, we can see another side of rationality. We shall see in Chapter 7 that rationality can produce some bizarre effects known as the 'irrationality of rationality' or 'paradox of consequences' (Ritzer 1993, Watson 1995) (see section 7.9.6 especially).

One such paradox is what Gouldner (1954) calls bureaucratic sabotage whereby conscientious observance of the rules (work to rule) creates chaos. Electronic mail is quicker and cheaper than conventional post. It is thus a more rational mode of communication. Yet paradoxically, stiff note paper and a fountain pen are a better investment for gaining attention (Jackson, T. 1995). Moreover, the speed and ease of electronic communication increases the risk of impulsive action. Anecdotal evidence suggests that managers are increasingly spending time repairing social relations damaged by hasty, ill-considered and intemperate electronic communications.

1.5.2 Metaphoric thinking and the limits of control

Where does an organization begin and end? Notions of order and orderliness imply the existence of boundaries. Yet the notion of boundary is a metaphor. The issue may appear fanciful. I suggest that it is profoundly important because the notion of boundary implies we know where an organization begins and ends. Such knowledge may be comforting but misleading.

For instance, when the late Robert Maxwell sold Pergamon Press the purchasers thought they had bought a thriving concern. It was only as they unwrapped their purchase that they began to wonder what exactly had they bought:

The new managers . . . did not open any champagne bottles. . . . No one was sufficiently tactless to speculate about just why they found themselves managing a company which employed over 2,500 people, which had just lost its key personnel, and whose financial status was in dispute, although it definitely had no money in the bank. (Bower 1992)

Likewise, most large organizations such as IBM and the UK clearing banks actually comprise many different organizations. For example, the senior manager of a UK clearing bank once said, 'We don't actually know what we own.'

Yet we take comfort in large organizations. Their very size is reassuring. We may feel safer dealing with them precisely because they are large. Metaphoric thinking enables us to see that such organizations may not be as stable as they seem. Why do we imagine boundaries? Would 'universe' be a more appropriate metaphor?

1.6 Discussion

1.6.1 The limitations of metaphoric thinking

> **Pause for reflection**
>
> A millionaire's son returned home from university where he was studying philosophy and sociology. The son contemplated the fine mansion, the gardens, the collection of *objets d'art* and said, 'Dad, you know, you don't really own any of this.'
>
> Later that day the son asked his father if he could borrow the car to take his girl friend out for the evening.
>
> What, do you imagine, was the father's reply?

The father said, 'No! Go drive your head round the block' thus identifying a prime weakness of metaphoric thinking, namely material reality. I imagine few commuters muse upon the metaphoric status of the London Underground map. Likewise, for most people it is irrelevant how organizations are conceptualized. Whether the organization is depicted as a machine, a system, or even as a pair of socks, what matters is the salary cheque. The gas bill may be an abstraction but it still has to be paid. Moreover, in practice, people have little power to construct reality (e.g., Clegg and Dunkerly 1980, Morgan 1996b). We shall see in section 5.3.1 how the most fundamental exercise of power rests in the unquestioned assumptions which we call 'reality'.

1.6.2 Too many metaphors?

Another issue concerns the role of metaphors in organization science. While metaphoric thinking is limited only by the human imagination, that is not to suggest that 'anything goes'.

Metaphors can be misleading if we ignore their limitations (Tsoukas 1993), or, if we become seduced by their sheer novelty regardless of their analytical potential (Pinder and Bourgeois 1982, Bourgeois and Pinder 1983).

Pinder and Bourgeois suggest that metaphors are too vague to possess any real scientific value because metaphorical insights cannot be falsified and there are no standard rules for creating or interpreting metaphors. According to Pinder and Bourgeois, the exercise of creativity implied in generating metaphors introduces ambiguity. Perhaps Pinder and Bourgeois had in mind the following quotation:

Hamlet: Do you see yonder cloud that's almost in shape of a camel?
Polonius: By th'mass, and 'tis like a camel indeed.
Hamlet: Methinks it is like a weasel.
Polonius: It is backed like a weasel.
Hamlet: Or like a whale.
Polonius: Very like a whale.

(William Shakespeare, *Hamlet*)

Pinder and Bourgeois call for an organizational literature that is 'precise . . . predicated on scientific grounds', utilizing literal language wherever possible based upon a 'formal lexicon of language dealing with organizational phenomenon and characteristics' (Pinder and Bourgeois 1982, p. 650).

Critics have suggested that Pinder and Bourgeois's views are contradictory as they invoke metaphors in order to oppose metaphors (e.g. Clegg and Gray 1996, Morgan 1983, Smircich 1983). Morgan (1983) argues that forcing organization theory into lexicons, literal language and precise formulations is a retrograde step. Moreover, says Morgan (1983, 1993), there is no such thing as literal language. Literal is itself a metaphor. Indeed, who defines the language in the first place and who decides that it is literal? Indeed, all knowledge is ultimately metaphorical (see Winner and Gardner 1993).

Pinder and Bourgeois's cautioning against the careless proliferation of metaphors seems justified. Some metaphors are more useful than others. The value of a metaphor depends upon the number of connections that be can generated from it (Lakoff and Johnson 1980, Tsoukas 1991, 1993) and the richness of insight stimulated. Pinder and Bourgeois also have a point when they suggest that invoking more and more metaphors does not necessarily advance organization theory. Novelty is not synonymous with depth and profundity of insight. For example, an organization could be 'imaginized' as a tube of toothpaste or as a football but I doubt whether it would lead very far.

Yet Pinder and Bourgeois may not be altogether justified in warning against metaphors becoming increasingly divorced from the subject of study, that is, organizations. The alternative viewpoint suggests that the more remote the metaphor from the subject of study, the greater the potential to stimulate new insight. For example, Lakoff and Johnson (1980) suggest that the metaphor, 'A woman without a man is like a fish without a bicycle' is so incongruous that it makes the point about women's independence in an extremely lucid fashion. The whole point of engaging in metaphoric thinking is to discover unsuspected linkages.

1.6.3 Not enough metaphors?

Metaphors may or may not be scientific. Yet is empirically based science the only route to understanding the reality we live in? (Chia 1996, Grant and Ostwick 1996). In the Introduction to this book I suggested that our intellectual tradition assumes the existence of a universal truth—hence Pinder and Bourgeois's (1982) emphasis upon precision and formality.

Morgan (1983) has suggested that we need to change our philosophy of science. That is:

> We replace the view that scientific knowledge is in some sense "foundational" with the realization that science may be able to generate many different and perhaps contradictory knowledges about the same phenomenon, all of which may have some merit. (Morgan 1983, p. 606)

In other words, the cloud can be seen as a camel *and* as a weasel *and* as a whale. Perhaps, and yet maybe our interest in metaphor reflects the limits of scientific knowledge however we define it, in understanding organizational life (Chia 1996). For instance, I doubt that the lexicon envisaged by Pinder and Bourgeois would contain words such as 'evil', 'hell', 'madhouse' and 'crazy' though they reflect a dimension of organizational life which may transcend science and which we have barely begun to probe.

1.6.4 Metaphoric thinking and the limits of understanding

Perhaps the most important feature of metaphoric thinking is that it helps us to recognize that we can never see or understand the whole of anything. Groucho Marx's flippant remark about the inability of any photograph to capture his inner beauty is profoundly insightful. We may think we know the man from the photograph, just as we may think we know the organization from the organization chart. Yet our knowledge is an illusion. Metaphoric thinking can save us from the trap of over-confidence by making us more aware of the limits of our understanding. *Quod petis umbra est*, 'what we seek is but a shadow'.

Summary

1 This chapter has focused upon the role of metaphors and metaphoric thinking in understanding organizations.

2 Metaphors are constructive falsehoods, that is, linguistic devices which enable us to understand one phenomenon through the medium of another, 'computer virus', for example.

3 All metaphors are partial. They illuminate certain facets of a particular phenomenon while concealing others.

4 Since all metaphors are partial, logically no metaphor can fully explain a particular phenomenon.

5   The choice of metaphor shapes *what* we see, and, *how* we see.

6   Some metaphors are so commonplace that we forget they are metaphors.

7   Metaphors both facilitate understanding and constrain it.

8   The most common metaphor deployed to understand organizations is the image of the machine or bureaucracy.

9   Yet we can see organizations in many different ways, for example, as biological systems, political systems, cultures, and as psychic prisons.

10   The purpose of exploring new metaphors of organization is to generate new insight and prompt new questions. For instance, the psychic prison metaphor highlights the hidden forces lurking beneath the calm surface of rationality.

11   In practice, we blend metaphors in order to shape understanding and perception.

12   Metaphoric thinking can be invoked to design organizations. For instance, we can envisage organizations as 'loosely coupled systems', and configure production systems as 'brains'.

13   Metaphoric thinking can illuminate the subtle dynamics of organization and the existence of paradox and contradiction. For instance, mechanistic thinking sees order imposed *upon* chaos. Metaphoric thinking illuminates order *within* chaos.

14   Metaphoric thinking enables us to see that in *describing* reality we are actually *creating* it.

15   The notion of organization is itself a metaphor.

16   Metaphoric thinking has been criticized as unscientific.

17   Yet is science the only route to understanding organizations and organizational life?

18   Metaphoric thinking helps us recognize the limits of our understanding. We can never see the whole of anything.

Questions for Discussion

1   What is an organization?

2   'Organizations do not exist.' Prove this statement.

3   How can metaphors and metaphoric thinking facilitate the management of organizations?

4   What features of organization do the following images suggest:
- the charge of the Light Brigade,
- a dog's breakfast,
- Laurel and Hardy,
- black holes?

5   What are the strengths and weaknesses of imagining an organization as:
- a scripted play,

   - a bowl of spaghetti,
   - a mad-house?

6 Invent your own metaphor for understanding organizations.

7 Imagine you have won a lottery 'jackpot prize' of £25 million. You intend to use part of the money to establish a charity to assist indigent university students.

How could metaphoric thinking facilitate the task?

8 Are metaphors necessary?

Further Reading

- Chia, R. (1996) 'Metaphors and Metaphorization in Organizational Analysis: Thinking Beyond the Thinkable' in D. Grant and C. Ostwick (eds.) *Metaphor and Organizations*, London, Sage.

- Lakoff, G. and Johnson, M. (1980) *Metaphors We Live By*, Chicago, University of Chicago Press.

- Morgan, G. (1980) 'Paradigms, Metaphors and Puzzle Solving in Organization Theory', *Administrative Science Quarterly*, 25, 605–622.

- Morgan, G. (1983) 'More on Metaphor: Why we Cannot Control Tropes in Administrative Science', *Administrative Science Quarterly*, 28, 601–607.

- Morgan, G. (1993) *Imaginization*, London, Sage.

- Morgan, G. (1996) *Images of Organization*, London, Sage.

- Quinn, R. E. and Cameron, K. S. (1988) 'Paradox and Transformation', in R. E. Quinn and K. S. Cameron (eds.) *Paradox and Transformation: Toward a Theory of Change in Organization and Management*, Cambridge, Mass.: Ballinger.

Chapter 2
Scientific Management

'THOMAS GRADGRIND, Sir. A man of realities. A man of facts and calculations. A man who proceeds upon the principle that two and two are four, and nothing over . . . . With a rule and a pair of scales, and the multiplication table always in his pocket, Sir ready to weigh and measure any parcel of human nature, and tell you exactly what it comes to.'

(Charles Dickens, *Hard Times*)

WHY does a clock keep ticking? The previous chapter introduced the notion of metaphor as a device for conceptualizing and understanding organizations. In essence, it was suggested that organizations are a construction of the human imagination. It was further suggested that metaphoric thinking can reveal dimensions of organizational life which are obscured by more conventional linear intuitive thinking patterns, notably the potentially paradoxical and ambiguous nature of organizations.

The present chapter examines the work of F. W. Taylor. Taylor would have got on well with Charles Dickens' fictional Thomas Gradgrind. Taylor was likewise a man of realities, of facts and calculations. In Taylor's estimation, one and one invariably made two. I doubt whether Taylor would have had much sympathy with the idea of applying metaphors and metaphoric thinking to management. Taylor would probably have regarded metaphor as the province of poets, and certainly remote from the needs of management. In Taylor's view organizations need clearly articulated objectives, sharp divisions of labour, specified hierarchies and responsibilities, and formalized systems of control.

Yet although Taylor prided himself in calling a 'spade' a 'spade', he might have been surprised to learn that his philosophy of management is underscored by metaphoric thinking. Taylor's work is described later in this chapter. Here it is sufficient to note that Taylor's philosophy is founded upon mechanical imagery. Taylor viewed organizational effectiveness as an engineering problem. Moreover, like the fictional Gradgrind, Taylor saw people as near-automatons, potentially troublesome perhaps, but basically programmable given proper supervision and appropriate incentives. In Taylor's eyes, the existence of contradiction and ambiguity in organizations were signs of managerial weakness, something which could and should be eliminated. Taylor's work is basically a recipe for achieving clarity and control.

It was suggested in the previous chapter that the image of organizations as machines exerts a powerful hold over our thinking. Taylor's ghost continues to walk. Although Taylor's ideas continue to inform management theory and practice, that does not necessarily mean that they are good ideas or applicable in every situation. We discussed some of the limitations of mechanistic thinking in Chapter 1. The present chapter begins by describing Taylor's precepts. We then examine their implications.

You may have turned to this chapter because you felt it was *time* you did some work. You may have *planned* to spend an *hour* reading. Your *timescale* for completion of note taking may depend upon other *priorities* and *objectives*. Yet in pre-industrial society, time counted for little. People generally worked as daylight permitted. If an artisan (or a student) decided to spend an afternoon fishing instead of working, that was their choice. In industrialized societies such freedom is rare. Our lives are dominated by time. Alarm clocks announce it is 'time' to get up. We have to be at work by a certain time. Executives plan their diaries. They attend courses on how to manage their time—why?

F. W. Taylor pioneered a technique known as 'scientific management'. 'Scientific management' stresses careful planning, measurement, timing and monitoring of work as a precursor of industrial efficiency and harmony. Taylor's ideas have also provoked controversy. Critics have argued that Taylor's science was bogus and a smoke screen for economic exploitation. According to critics, Taylor's primary aim was to disempower and dehumanize the worker by destroying pride and pleasure in work. Whatever our views, Taylor's ideas are important because they continue to inform the production of goods and services today. The issues addressed in this chapter include:

Key Issues

- What is mass production?
- What new problems did mass production create?
- Is 'scientific management' scientific?
- Is 'scientific management' efficient?
- Is 'scientific management' a form of madness?

2.1 What is Mass Production?

BEFORE the industrial revolution goods were produced by hand. People usually specialized in a particular trade, barrel makers, wheelwrights, weavers and so forth. Production was controlled by organizations known as guilds. Guilds were basically cartels. They regulated the price of goods and controlled entry to the various trades (Kieser 1989). Guilds were also socially important. In those days starvation was a very real possibility. Guilds provided a form of social insurance. They helped members to get started in a trade and helped to maintain those unable to work (Rickert 1949). The guilds also controlled quality standards. Hand crafted goods were expensive. Accordingly, miscreants were swiftly and severely punished. For instance, a certain Katherine Duchewoman was found guilty of substituting linen for wool. She was sentenced to the pillory and to have the offending tapestry burned before her eyes. Likewise one

John Penrose, convicted of selling unwholesome wine, 'Was forced to take a draught of the same and have the remainder poured over his head' (Rickert 1947, p. 23).

The invention of steam power in the eighteenth century opened up new possibilities for mechanizing production with corresponding gains in productivity. People began to congregate under one roof in order to harness the new power. Such organizations became known as manufactories and later as factories. Initially people worked independently or in small cooperatives. Gradually, however, people began to work for those who owned the machinery and factory buildings. The guilds crumbled. A new era of hired labour began.

2.1.1 Why is mass production more efficient than craft production?

The advent of steam power was only the beginning. There followed Adam Smith's 'invention' of the *division of labour*. Hitherto a pin maker, for example, would undertake the task from start to finish. Using this method production seldom exceeded one pin per day. Smith's treatise published in 1776 argued that productivity could be increased by dividing the labour into eighteen discrete stages as follows:

One man draws out the wire, another straights it, a third cuts it, a fourth points it, a fifth grinds the top for receiving the head; to make the head requires three distinct operations . . . (and so on). (Smith 1983, p. 110)

According to Smith the economies achieved by the division of labour stemmed from three factors as follows:

1. The increased dexterity of each workman.
2. Time savings in passing from one operation to another.
3. The invention of machines which shorten and facilitate labour.

Smith suggested that his method would enable a small manufactory to produce twelve pounds of pins in one day, provided they exerted themselves, that is.

2.1.2 What problems did mass production create?

The industrial revolution and the subsequent emergence of the factory system resulted in fundamental changes in society and in the nature of work itself. The division of labour requires careful coordination for its effectiveness. Yet the factory owners were faced with a work force accustomed to self-direction. Moreover, once a person would sell their finished goods in the market. Now a person sold their labour. To be more precise, factory owners purchased, '*Not an agreed amount of labour, but the power to labour over an agreed period of time*' (Braverman 1974, p. 54, author's italics).

How could the factory owners ensure that their purchase was converted into productive effort (e.g. Knights and Willmott 1990)? From their point of view, it was a vital question. It still is. Let me now express the problem in a more rigorous manner.

2.1.3 Organizations and transactions costs

When people worked independently or in small cooperatives, a market mechanism sufficed to regulate exchange. Markets are efficient because they enable business to be conducted without the costs of employing people and paying other people to manage them. Under the new conditions, however, the market mechanism became too cumbersome. It is difficult to coordinate a factory comprising hundreds of individual and independent contractors. It made economic sense, therefore, to create a different contractual relationship, that is, to employ people (Ouchi 1980).

Employment contracts have the advantage of flexibility. Unlike, say, a spot contract to buy a specific quantity of a commodity at a specific time, the precise requirements are undefined. Take the work of a dental receptionist, for example. It is impractical to pay the receptionist according to the number of calls answered, patients received, letters typed and so forth. It is simpler and cheaper to buy the person's time.

The fundamental problem of management is that organizational and individual objectives differ. Whereas the organization may be interested in maximizing output and minimizing cost, the individual employee may have other priorities. The problem for the organization is how to eliminate opportunism. The early factory owners resorted to coercion. Employees were sometimes locked inside factories. Unscrupulous owners turned back clocks in order to extract further effort from workers who might already have worked twelve hours or more (Marx 1976). Unsurprisingly, industrial relations were often marked by conflict. 'In a word, oppressor and oppressed, stood in constant opposition to one another' (Marx and Engels 1976, p. 79).

One of the earliest and most influential proponents of a systematic approach to management was a man known as Frederick Winslow Taylor. Taylor's ideas for reducing conflict and eliminating opportunism centred upon a technique known as 'scientific management' (Taylor 1947). Let me now explain Taylor's ideas.

Pause for reflection

'Work expands to fill the time available.'

(Parkinson's law)

How far is this statement consistent with your experience?

2.2 What is Scientific Management?

FREDERICK Winslow Taylor (1865–1915) is regarded as the founding figure of management philosophy. Taylor was born into a middle-class family who lived in Philadelphia, USA. Taylor originally trained as a lawyer, but, having damaged his eyesight in studying, sought work which did not involve overmuch reading and writing. Taylor did a variety of jobs in industry. He began as an apprentice pattern maker. He then became a labourer in the Midvale Steel Company. Taylor subsequently progressed to a variety of roles including timekeeper, foreman and ultimately, chief engineer.

Taylor became concerned about the continuous acrimony between management and the workforce. According to Taylor, such conflict was needless. Taylor believed that it was caused by a misperception. Management and workers believed that their interests were incompatible. Management wanted higher production and lower costs. Both parties assumed that this could only be achieved at the expense of the workforce. The workforce resorted to output restriction known as systematic soldering in order to protect themselves from redundancy. Taylor believed that such practices were a prime source of conflict.

Taylor's starting point was that the interests of management and the workforce were not necessarily incompatible. Taylor suggested that increases in productivity coupled with reduced cost could lead to mutual prosperity including higher wages for the workforce. Taylor called this the 'mental revolution' that was the essential prerequisite of 'scientific management'.

According to Taylor, output could be increased not by requiring operatives to work harder, but by showing them how to work more efficiently. 'Scientific management' centres upon planning and control of work. Figure 2.1 summarizes Taylor's ideas.

The key points of Taylor's ideas are:

1. Work as a science.
2. Scientific selection and training of the workforce.
3. Combining science and the scientifically trained worker.
4. A clear division of labour whereby managers plan and coordinate work and workers execute directives.

Each of these points is now described in detail.

2.2.1 First principle: create a science of work

According to Taylor creating a science of work involves:

■ discovering the '*one best way*' of performing tasks, and,
■ determining the *correct time* for the performance of each task.

Figure 2.1 A summary of Taylor's principles of scientific management

1 Create a Science of Work	2 Scientifically Select and Develop the Workforce	3 Bring Science and the Scientifically Trained Worker Together	4 Institute an Equal Division of Labour
Experiment to discover: ■ best tools ■ best machines ■ best sequencing of operations. Determine the correct time for the accomplishment of tasks. Classify and index time study data. Lodge data in files.	Select only 'first class' employees. Train employees in 'one best way' of working. Seek out employees 'good points' as a basis for development. Institute systematic observation of employees and collection of performance data.	Institute functional management. Institute functional observation. Assign each employee to a clearly defined task. Institute rewards for task completion and penalties for failure. Allocate rewards on an individual basis. Provide rapid feedback on earnings achieved.	Institute a centralized planning department. Management to be responsible for: ■ discovering the 'best ways' of task accomplishment. ■ planning operations to ensure timely availability of materials, tools and work instructions.

'One best way'

Taylor recommended that organizations conduct careful and detailed experiments in order to identify the most efficient, that is, fastest, means of accomplishing work. Much of Taylor's time was spent studying shovelling. Taylor performed detailed calculations in order to discover which size of shovel was best, the correct amount of iron to be loaded on to the shovel, and the most efficient technique of bodily movement. Taylor's ideas extended to production planning. He urged managers to analyse the layout of factories and workshops in order to optimize the sequencing of operations and to eliminate losses caused by coordination failures.

Controlling time

Taylor observed that managers knew little about the work which they controlled. Such knowledge as management did possess was vague or unreliable and seldom committed to writing. Hardly surprising, said Taylor, that workers could deceive management over how fast work could be accomplished. Taylor said that management must know what a proper day's work comprised. Moreover, that knowledge must reflect careful observation, recording and tabulation.

Taylor's solution was to time 'first class' (highly efficient and compliant) operatives while they were working fast. Taylor further recommended that each task be broken down into its constituent elements and each element timed, retimed and averaged in order to establish what constitutes a 'fair' day's work. For example, the elements of loading pig iron comprised:

(a) picking up the pig from the ground or pile (time in hundredths of a minute); (b) walking with it on a level (time per foot walked); walking with it up an incline to car (time per foot walked);' [and so on]. (Taylor 1947, p. 48)

The resultant observations, said Taylor, should be classified, indexed and lodged in files. Taylor envisaged that the files would be used both for immediate control, and as a data bank of standard time allowances for similar operations.

An incentive system

The time study data was used to calculate piecework rates. Under a piecework system operatives receive a specific payment usually known as a 'price' for each unit of output achieved. Taylor believed piecework held the key to industrial harmony as it provided workers with an opportunity to earn more money by increasing their output. Otherwise, said Taylor, what incentive did a conscientious worker have, if less productive colleagues were paid the same amount?

2.2.2 Second principle: scientific selection and development of the workforce

Taylor urged managers to match workers to the tasks for which they were best suited. Taylor further recommended that organizations conduct detailed observation and analyses of an individual worker's strengths and weaknesses and select 'first class' operatives only. When questioned about the social implications of such selectivity, Taylor replied that it should always be possible to discover what tasks an individual can accomplish in a 'first-class' manner (Taylor, 1947).

Scientifically selected operatives should then be thoroughly trained in the 'one best way' of executing their allotted tasks. Should a worker's performance subsequently fall below standards, they should be retrained. For example, said Taylor, a worker might forget how to shovel properly. Taylor stressed that training should be undertaken systematically. It should be approached in the spirit of helping and teaching workers as well as inculcating obedience and conscientiousness. Taylor also envisaged that training would enable workers to realize their potential:

The labourer who before was unable to do anything beyond, perhaps, shovelling and wheeling dirt . . . , is . . . taught to do the more elementary machinist's work . . . The cheap machinist . . . is taught to do the more intricate and higher priced lathe and planner work, while the highly skilled and more intelligent machinists become functional foremen and teachers. And so on, right up the line. (Taylor 1947, p. 42)

Taylor saw the ultimate aim of such development as enabling the operative 'To do the highest and most interesting and most profitable class of work for which his abilities fit him, and which are open to him in the particular company in which he is employed' (Taylor 1947, p. 42).

Pause for reflection

The 3Com Palm III Organizer can store the following information:

- 1,500 'to-do' items,
- 1,500 memos,
- 200 e-mails,
- 6,000 addresses,
- 5 years of appointments.

Write a report to F. W. Taylor explaining how this level of capability could be improved.

2.2.3 Third principle: bring science and the scientifically trained worker together

Taylor advocated specialization. Each operative should be assigned as few tasks as possible and preferably one only. Furthermore, said Taylor, the day's task must be clearly defined. Taylor urged managers to compile instruction cards for each operation. Such cards should specify:

1. The details of work;
2. The time allowed for each operation;
3. The piece rate paid for completing the task within the specified time; and,
4. The name of any supervisor available to give special direction.

The instruction card should be both precise and detailed. For example, it should indicate which drawings an operative should refer to. Administrative details such as cost order numbers should be specified. The card should also direct exactly how the work should be performed. For example, where to start each cut, the number of cuts required the exact depth to be cut, the tools to be used for each operation and the manner in which the tools are to be used. Everything needed to undertake the work (tools, equipment, materials and so forth), should be made readily available.

Taylor recommended that operatives receive daily written notification of the previous days' earnings in order to demonstrate the relationship between effort and earnings. Wherever possible, said Taylor, rewards should reflect individual performance. Taylor also envisaged penalties for failure. Surveillance and inspection feature prominently in 'scientific management'. Taylor urges supervisors to maintain elaborate records of operatives' 'good' and 'bad' points. Taylor further recommended that inspectors sign printed cards daily to confirm the work done by each operative. The card should indicate which tasks have been performed satisfactorily by the operative and list in detail those elements of the operatives' performance that are unsatisfactory. The recalcitrant are referred to the shop disciplinarian who applies an appropriate remedy and 'sees that a complete record of each man's virtues and defects is kept' (Taylor, 1947, p. 103).

2.2.4 Fourth principle: an equal division of labour

Taylor's vision of management was clear. It can be summarized as follows:

- managers 'to think', and,
- workers 'to do'.

Taylor advocated centralized control. One department should be responsible for all planning and coordination of work. Those responsibilities should include work scheduling, discovering the 'one best way' of accomplishing tasks, issuing work instructions, and ensuring that the correct materials, tools and other facilities were available as required.

Taylor recognized the cost implications of his ideas. He noted that the development of new standards requires much time, patience and systematic application of effort by management. Taylor regarded such activities as a means of eliminating waste. The aim of planning and coordination should be to minimize waste accruing from factors such as lost machine time, misapplied effort, and stoppages caused by delivery of wrong quantities and other co-ordination failures.

2.2.5 Taylor's ideas today

Taylor's ideas were subsequently developed by others. Two prominent disciples were Henry Gantt and a husband and wife team known as the Gilbreths. Gantt made Taylor's ideas cheaper to apply by using less detailed time study. He also modified Taylor's piecework incentive system by combining set day rates with bonus payments (Gantt 1919). This arrangement continues to provide a popular alternative to piecework. The Gilbreths applied Taylor's ideas to bricklaying (Gilbreth 1908, Gilbreth and Gilbreth 1916, Spriegel and Myers 1953). They reduced the number of movements from eighteen to five. Unlike Taylor the Gilbreths' calculations incorporated an allowance for human fatigue. The Gilbreths also considered the organizational value of social facilities at work, thus anticipating the so-called 'human relations movement' latterly known as the behavioural approach to management (see Chapter 3).

Taylor's ideas are also seen in management techniques which are still in use today. Such techniques include work-study, ergonomics (a branch of knowledge concerned with the relationship between workers, their environment and machinery) and operations research. Taylor's influence is also seen in more recent developments such as 'total quality management', 'just-in-time production', and business process re-engineering (see Chapter 4). All of these techniques aim to optimize efficiency by eliminating waste.

Many organizations today practise surveillance in a manner of which Taylor would have approved (see Drummond 1995, Sewell and Wilkinson 1992 a,b). In some organizations surveillance cameras, electronic pads, and sensors capable of detecting the most minute deviation from stipulated working methods have largely supplanted human supervisors. Computers have replaced shop disciplinarians. Organizations can now hold data files on each operative. Computers enable organizations to collect statistics on almost every aspect of an operative's performance including adherence to quality standards, conformity to standard times, achievement of production planning targets and absenteeism. Whereas Taylor centred upon the worker as an individual, some modern organizations invoke group pressure to procure compliance. For example, Sewell and Wilkinson (1992b, p. 105) report instances of such data being prominently displayed and discussed intensely at daily team meetings.

Likewise, supermarkets train cameras upon check-out assistants in order to monitor their behaviour. Call centres have been dubbed the 'new satanic mills' of the industrial era. Call centre employees work to targets which require them to deal with a specific number of enquiries per hour. They may have sales targets known as 'hit rates'. Supervisors listen in to calls to monitor performance. Employees are expected to reach targets without hurrying customers.

Although Taylor's ideas were developed for shop floor workers, they have been applied to many types of work. Some offices are organized along Tayloristic lines whereby one clerk stamps a form, another logs it, another checks the details and so forth. The principle of issuing work instructions is seen in the scripted conversations which sales staff and receptionists of banks, insurance companies, estate agencies and other service organizations are expected to recite, such as, 'Good Morning. Direct Debit Insurance Company. This is Mark speaking. How may I help you?'

Such conversations are often recorded and monitored by supervisors. Staff may be appraised both upon the quantity of calls made or received and conformity to the script.

Taylor's principles have also been applied to work requiring the application of interpersonal skills. Many airlines, for example, require cabin staff to greet passengers with a warm welcome:

A young businessman said to a flight attendant, 'Why aren't you smiling?' She put her tray back on the food cart and said, 'I'll tell you what. You smile first, then I'll smile.' The businessman smiled at her. 'Good,' she replied, 'Now freeze and hold that for fifteen hours.' (Hochschild, 1983, p. 127)

Similarly, staff employed in 'fast food' outlets are not only appraised upon instrumental task elements such as whether the proper amount of ice is served with drinks, and whether containers are double folded; supervisors also monitor whether they greet the customer with a sincere smile and make eye contact (Morgan 1996).

2.3 Discussion

METAPHOR means the association of one thing with another. Recall that Taylor associated organizational effectiveness with engineering. Taylor's ideas have their strengths. Any one who has ever employed a disorganized builders' firm or stood at the back of a queue while a clerk rummages for papers will appreciate the benefits of a systematic approach to work. You too may recall occasions when you could have accomplished something in a fraction of the time had you been better organized.

We saw in Chapter 1, however, that metaphors are inherently partial. They structure thinking and may facilitate the generation of ideas and insights, but they also constrain thinking and creativity. For example, you may be one of those people who has to write ten pages of whatever comes into your head before starting an essay. In theory it is the wrong way to go about it. Yet it works for you. Likewise, sometimes you have to really mess a room up, that is, create worse inefficiency, before you can tidy it.

The constraints implied by a particular metaphor are best seen by going beyond it.

For example, we shall see in Chapter 4 how 'total quality management' mixes mechanistic and cultural metaphors of organization to create another view of organizational effectiveness. When we consider organizations as cultures in Chapter 9, we see something different again. The cultural lens reveals the limits of managerial power and even the possibility of 'no go' areas of organizations (see especially section 9.6).

Taylor, like the fictional Thomas Gradgrind, saw reality as a concrete entity. Taylor too might have been willing to weigh and measure human nature, and to believe in the results. When we examine the behavioural theories of management outlined in the following chapter we will see that is more or less what occupational psychologists have tried to do.

The epicentre of Taylor's world, however, was not people but production. Taylor saw the organization as represented by buildings, machines, tools, instruction cards and the like. Chapter 10, which focuses upon the metaphor of symbolism, reveals a dimension of organizational life which Taylor largely missed. For example, Taylor saw actions as having *instrumental* consequences. His mechanistic frame of vision did not allow him to see that they can have *expressive* consequences as well. Part of the impetus to the so called 'human relations movement' described in the next chapter was the recognition that proverbial man does not live by bread alone.

We saw in Section 1.1.3 that some metaphors are so commonplace that they seem literal—the association of time and the clock, for example. Yet since metaphors are human constructions, the choice of metaphor is by no means absolute. There are no right or wrong metaphors, only that some metaphors are more useful than others. Recall also that we can obtain a more holistic view of things by counterposing different metaphorical lenses. However:

Taylor's 'one best way' assumption presupposes a single metaphorical lens.

In other words, Taylor's approach not only seeks to narrow rather than expands the possibilities, it can bind organizations to policies and practices which have outlived their usefulness. For example, the notions of 'strategic management' and 'organizational structure' are underscored by 'one best way' logic. Moreover, strategy making is still equated with the formulation and articulation of highly specific plans which are then implemented, and whereby 'structure' follows strategy. When we examine power, politics and decision making in subsequent chapters we shall see, 'it ain't necessarily so'.

Metaphors, it was suggested, may be more or less useful. The question is, useful for whom? We shall see in Chapters 5 and 6 which focus upon power and politics that the choice of a particular metaphor can serve vested interests. Moreover, the most invidious exercise of power often rests in the 'taken for granted' metaphors.

Let us now consider in more detail the implications of Taylor's ideas and the interests served by his approach to management.

2.3.1 Is 'scientific management' scientific?

Let me now discuss some of the implications of Taylor's principles of 'scientific management'. The application of Taylor's ideas provoked considerable hostility in the USA. Although 'scientific management' led to increases in productivity, those increases were not reflected in higher wages and the development of the individual as Taylor had envisaged. Instead, the opposite happened. Recall that Taylor advocated dividing work into its simplest elements, known as *deskilling*. The less skill a task involves, the lower the remuneration commanded by the work, and, potentially, the greater the monotony. The resultant hostility culminated in a strike at Watertown Arsenal. The strike prompted a committee of the House of Representatives to investigate Taylor's methods.

Taylor presented his case in person to the committee (he did nearly all of the talking). Taylor maintained that properly applied, the techniques of 'scientific management' could improve efficiency and harmony. The committee concurred. However, Congress subsequently banned Taylor's methods in the defence industry in wartime (Huczynski and Buchanan 1991).

> **Pause for reflection**
> Design the most inefficient factory imaginable.
> How would it operate?

A prominent critic of 'scientific management' is Henry Braverman. Braverman's thesis entitled 'Labour and Monopoly Capitalism' was published in 1974. According to Braverman, Taylor's central objective was control. Braverman notes that the verb to manage is derived from the Latin *manus* which originally meant to train a horse in its paces (p. 67). Braverman argues that Taylor saw things mainly from the industrialists' viewpoint, and not the workers'. Braverman suggests that Taylor saw 'the problem' of management as being how to control and extract effort from a potentially recalcitrant work force.

According to Braverman Taylor's real purpose was to promote economic exploitation by:

1. Creating an impression of scientific objectivity in order to justify production targets.
2. Reserving planning and coordination for management known as separating conception from execution.
3. Subdividing tasks in order to cheapen and disempower the workforce known as de-skilling.

Each of the three strands of Braverman's thesis is explained below.

2.3.2 A bogus science?

Taylor's authority rests upon the claim that his methods are scientific and therefore incontrovertible. When Taylor gave testimony to the congressional committee he insisted that it was inappropriate to describe his work as a task or piecerate system. Taylor insisted that it be called 'scientific management' (Taylor 1947, p. 7).

According to Braverman, however, the experiments which underpin Taylor's time study calculations were false. Braverman argues that Taylor's approach to experimentation fell far short of the rigour required by true scientific enquiry, 'Such records and estimates as he did produce are crude in the extreme . . . his various "experiments" . . . were not intended as experiments at all, but as forcible and hyperbolic demonstrations' (Braverman 1974, p. 89).

Recall that an essential precondition for exchange is a mutual perception of fairness (see section 2.1.3). According to Braverman, Taylor's notions of 'a fair day's work' were far from fair. They reflected the maximum an operative could produce without actually injuring their health. Why that should be the base target is never explained, says Braverman.

2.3.3 Separating conception from execution

According to Braverman, Taylor's purpose was to transfer knowledge about working methods from operatives to management. Knowledge is power. According to Braverman, removing all brain work from the shop floor reduces workers to the level of animals. It is not the instruction cards themselves that are important, says Braverman, so much as the monopoly over knowledge which lies behind them. 'Labor itself has become part of capital' (p. 116).

2.3.4 De-skilling

Taylor encouraged managers to practice human resource development. Braverman argues that de-skilling undermines this objective. The division of labour was not Taylor's invention. However, according to Braverman, Taylor perfected the technique by breaking down tasks to render them as short and simple as possible. Braverman suggests that Taylor deliberately intended to cheapen and disempower the worker by decreasing their skill (de-skilling) and increasing their output. Moreover, says Braverman, increased output was seldom matched by a proportionate increase in wages.

2.3.5 Is 'scientific management' efficient?

Does 'scientific management' lead to optimal efficiency as Taylor claimed? The limitations of Taylor's ideas include:

1. Neglect of human and social aspects of organization as a means of promoting efficiency.
2. Questionable assumptions about the nature of motivation.
3. Piecework may encourage rather than prevent output restriction.
4. De-skilling can lead to inflexibility and waste.

> **Pause for reflection**
>
> An international credit company seeks to recruit a Director of Management Development. Applicants must possess:
>
> > Proven experience in organization change, competency development and talent gap analysis. The ability to design and implement tools, processes and development interventions which support organization and management effectiveness objectives is essential.
>
> Comment upon this advertisement.

2.3.6 The limits of engineering

What is missing from Taylor's work? Recall that Taylor was an engineer. He equated organizational effectiveness with scientific efficiency (see Mills and Tancred 1992, Morgan 1996). Taylor saw little productive potential in social relationships. Talking, for example, was seen by Taylor as a wasteful activity, something to be discouraged. Yet talking can serve a useful purpose by oiling the social wheels of organization. Effective social relations can be critical in coping with breakdowns and other engineering failures. Likewise, humour and the cracking of jokes can play an important role in sustaining an organization when conditions are stressful (Hatch and Ehrlich 1993). We will return to these points in Chapter 9 when we examine the cultural dimension of organization.

2.3.7 A mechanistic view of the world

Like the fictional Thomas Gradgrind, the emphasis in Taylor's writings is upon rote learning and concrete fact. Taylor's view of leadership was highly instrumental, reminiscent of 'transactional leadership' (see section 3.4.5). Although Taylor makes some reference to leaders coaching and encouraging workers, the emphasis is upon monitoring and regulation. There is no reference to words such as inspiration and charisma.

Taylor seems to have assumed that effective organization is largely a matter of engineering. Moreover Taylor's view of engineering is limited to measurement, analysis and calculation. Look again at the job advertisement in section 2.3.5. It might have been written by Taylor's ghost. Creativity, inventiveness and aesthetics are excluded from Taylor's conceptualization of engineering. Yet these factors are potentially crucial in enabling organizations to innovate.

2.3.8 Does piecework encourage output restriction?

Taylor assumed that piecework incentives would discourage opportunism because workers would be motivated to maximize their earnings. Yet evidence suggests that people sometimes ignore economic logic. Studies undertaken in the UK (Cunnison 1963, Lupton 1963) and in the USA (Dalton 1948, Roy 1952, 1954) have shown that piecework does not necessarily prevent output restriction. Indeed, it may actually encourage it. Recall that Taylor timed work by observing operatives in action, and not according to any absolute standards. Moreover, Taylor apparently admitted that the stop watch involved an element of guess work (Thompson and McHugh 1995). Taylor tacitly assumed, however, that any inaccuracies would reveal themselves in exceptionally high earnings.

Not necessarily. Roy (1952), for example, observed that workers covertly held back on jobs with easy timings. Roy describes a conversation with a fellow worker, a man called Starkey, 'Don't you know,' cried Starkey angrily, 'that $1.25 an hour is the most we can make, even when we *can* make more!'

Roy suggested that surely it made financial sense to produce more work and earn a bonus accordingly. Starkey replied:

'Yes! They'd pay me—once! . . . And they'd retime this job so quick it would make your head swim! And when they retimed it, they'd cut the price in half! And I'd be working for 85 cents an hour instead of $1.25.' (Roy 1952, p. 430)

Starkey apparently spoke from experience. Before, workers had competed playfully with each other to see how much they could produce. The price was indeed cut in half.

Roy concluded that output restriction was part of the unwritten social code aimed at defying management. The cost to management was substantial. Roy estimated he lost 1.39 hours out of every 8 worked. In other words, the plant was working at under 80 per cent capacity. Taylor would have spun in his grave!

2.3.9 Is 'scientific management' wasteful?

It was suggested earlier that de-skilling can demotivate people. Another potential negative consequence of de-skilling is inflexibility. The fewer tasks operatives are trained to perform, the greater the constraints upon deploying labour. How useful is it, for example, if a supermarket security guard is trained to restock shelves and operate checkouts, or if a carpenter is trained to undertake painting as well as joinery?

Taylor's methods involve high transaction costs. Transaction costs are those activities required to satisfy each party to an exchange that what is given and received matches expectations (Ouchi 1980, p. 130). Work study timings, instruction cards, supervision, maintaining performance records and so forth represent cost. Taylor regarded such expenses as ultimately justifiable. In practice, organizations often resorted to short cuts in order to save money. For example, old time study calculations were often adapted to new tasks. Instead of measuring say a new building in order to calculate cleaning times, management might utilize data from another building of similar dimensions. The cumulative effect of such practices can be costly.

Taylor recognized that work methods could be improved. He also conceded that production planning might need to incorporate workers' idiosyncratic preferences. However, the emphasis in Taylor's work is clearly upon 'one best way'. Trist and Bamforth's (1951) study of the mechanisation of the UK coal industry shows how notions of 'one best way' can rebound upon engineers.

Hitherto, coal mining resembled a craft industry. Autonomous working groups took responsibility for extracting a seam. The new 'longwall' method ('one best way') created a division of labour with one shift preparing the seam, another removing the coal, another carrying out follow-up work. The 'longwall' method was intended to boost productive efficiency. Production, however, was undermined by the social and psychological tensions created by the new arrangements.

Trist and Bamforth's study highlights the notion of:

socially ineffective systems,

and their consequences. For example, the new system involved a division of labour which accentuated status differences and tension between high and lower status employees:

As the lowest paid and lowest prestige group . . . doing the least skilled task, gummers are both an outcast and scapegoated group. Their work is arduous, dangerous, dusty—and awkward. Hostility in them towards the 'the system' and other face workers is almost inevitable and is most easily displaced on to the fillers, whom they never see but can severely annoy. . . . A system that puts this power of interference into the hands of a potentially disgruntled, scapegoated group with no means of controlling it, fosters the hostile tendencies almost inevitably present. (Trist and Bamforth 1951, p. 33)

Many more studies could be cited of the alienating effects of monotony, inadequate social interaction and so forth. We shall return to this issue in Chapter 3 when we discuss job satisfaction. We shall also see in Chapter 8 when we discuss occupational stress that efficiency gains may be offset by stress related illness. For instance, evidence suggests that highly repetitive jobs lead to dissatisfaction, poor mental health, a low sense of accomplishment and personal growth (Melamed, Ben-Avi, Luz and Green 1995).

2.3.10 Is 'scientific management' a form of madness?

Mechanization and systematization have led to vast increases in production. In medieval times a chicken cost twenty pence (Rickert 1949). Today a factory-farmed chicken with a much higher meat to bone ratio than its medieval counterpart can be bought for under £2. There may be another price to pay in human health and animal welfare. Yet the increase in productivity is undeniable. Moreover, it could be argued that control systems do at least bring clarity and predictability—both conducive to organizational effectiveness (see Farkas and Wetlaufer, p. 119).

Although Braverman (1974) argues that Taylor's principles hold the potential to achieve virtually absolute control over the worker, we have already seen that in practice, control may be far from absolute. Indeed, 'scientific management' can benefit the workforce. According to Roy (1952, 1954), piecework:

- imparts a measure of control to the workforce,
- provides an outlet for aggression against management, and,
- enables the enjoyment of playing a game and earning approval from colleagues.

I would also add:

piecework and other numerical targets reduce ambiguity.

The implications of targets are discussed in section 4.2.10. Suffice to note here that targets mean that an employee knows what is expected of them. As such, targets can protect an employee against managerial arbitrariness.

Where does it end, however? Weber (1947) saw routinization and mechanization as ultimately destructive, that is, as eroding the spirit and capacity for spontaneous action. Braverman (1974) recounts the story of a manager analysing the placement of office water fountains. The manager discovered, presumably to his horror, that staff walked a total of 50,000 miles each year just to fill their cups. Another office manager solemnly suggested that if the correct pens and paper were used, the blotter and all the useless motions involved in blotting could be eliminated.

Consider also the popular anecdote of the work study engineer who attended a concert. The engineer observed that the drums were played only three times during the performance, and that the horns were underutilized to a tune of 50 per cent (Huczynski and Buchanan 1991).

Pause for reflection

Imagine a concert with Taylor in charge.

How might it function?

Yet Taylor might have retorted that, with a little more efficiency, Schubert's Eighth Symphony would have been finished! Efficiency is not necessarily destructive. For instance, funding restrictions in the UK has prompted a revival of chamber music, hitherto eclipsed by the large, expensive to stage, symphonic pieces.

Another issue is the intensity with which mechanization and systematization are pursued. Thompson (1967) has suggested that the industrial revolution led to a fundamental change in the significance of time in people's lives. Calculators, lap-top computers, videos, televisions, radios, microwave ovens and mobile phones incorporate clocks. We saw in the discussion on organizations as psychic prisons (see section 1.2.4) that rationality is potentially a form of repressed sexuality. Morgan (1996) suggests that Taylor's obsession with measurement and control is a prime example. Morgan further suggests that the same pattern is evident in the way we organize our lives.

We expect trains, buses and airplanes to run 'on time'. We apologize when we are 'late' for a meeting or other engagement. We set ourselves targets. We draw up lists of tasks which must be completed 'on time'.

Obviously, there is something to be gained by organizing one's time and schedule of tasks. (This point is emphasized in Chapters 11 and 12 which deal with study and research techniques). Moreover, Taylor did not invent time management. For example, the monasteries operated elaborate systems of production planning and control in order to maximize the time for prayer (Kieser 1987). Likewise, the diarist Samuel Pepys used a form of 'Filofax' to compile 'to do' lists (Ollard 1984).

Surely it is a question of degree. Is it better to set one objective and achieve it than to start ten projects and finish none? Likewise, what are the long-term consequences if managers are continuously preoccupied with issues which are urgent as distinct from those which are important? Even if we live long enough to get through the 1,500 tasks stored in our personal organizer, the likelihood is that 1,495 of these were not worth doing anyway.

We shall see when we examine the role of symbolism in organizations in Chapter 10 that executive diaries, palm computers, mobile phones and the like may be more important for what they signify than their practical utility.

2.3.11 Is 'scientific management' economically optimal?

It was suggested in section 1.4.2 that the machine metaphor of organization implies linear intuitive patterns of thinking. Such thinking is inherently one sided because it obscures more complex possibilities. For instance, recall that Taylor saw ambiguity as undesirable. Indeed, we shall see in section 8.3.2 that ambiguity can be stressful. We saw in section 1.4.3, however, that if we invoke a different metaphor organization, namely the notion of the jazz player, we see ambiguity in a very different light, that is, as a prerequisite of creativity. Ambiguity provides the 'empty spaces' into which people in organizations can insert their ideas.

That is not to suggest that ambiguity is 'good' as distinct from 'bad'. (Only linear intuitive thinking may lead us to assume that if something is not invariably good it must be bad.) Invoking different metaphors enables us to see ambiguity as an inherent issue of organization. When we invoke different metaphorical perspectives we see that ambiguity as desirable or undesirable depending upon the situation, or, as question of balance, perhaps as trade off over and under control. Metaphorical thinking enables us to see that ambiguity is not a problem which can and should be 'fixed' once and for all. Taylor offers answers, 'one best way'. Metaphoric thinking enables us to see that:

- the question may be more important than the answer,
- if indeed there is an answer (see also section 7.2.1).

Taylor's ideas on motivation are likewise informed by mechanistic thinking. Taylor assumes that effort is directly proportional to the scale of the reward. Yet as Roy's (1952, 1954) work, for example, implies, cultural forces can lead to output restriction. Moreover, Taylor had little to say about the quality of what was produced. For example, public concern over food safety has led to the exposure of poor hygiene in some abattoirs, such as the fact that regulations requiring careful removal of spinal cords of cows and other potentially dangerous offal are often flouted. Is it any coincidence that many abattoirs use piecework incentive systems? We return to this point when we discuss the implications of 'total quality management' philosophy for Organization Behaviour.

Taylor's machine-like notions of time can harm organizations in more subtle ways. Although Taylor's ideas were developed for the shop floor, many professional organizations have seen fit to utilize Taylor's principles. For example, some professionals are evaluated according to amounts billed to clients. A casual word in a corridor with a colleague may be recorded as one unit of time, that is, fifteen minutes. Given that firms may be charging £350 an hour for their services, this practice makes the fee earner appear highly productive but at the possible expense of prompting the client to change firms.

Taylor's concrete 'no nonsense' view of the world led him to adopt a polarised vision which obscured more complex realities. Taylor saw either:

order *or* chaos, subservience *or* resistance,

but never,

order *within* chaos, unity *and* disunity existing simultaneously (see section 9.6).

In other words, the idea of organizations as held in dynamic tension escaped him. The issue is important because if managers attempt to control what they cannot control, they create a fundamentally unstable situation. Such are the limits of the machine metaphor of organizations.

Finally, Taylor suggested that the key to eliminating industrial conflict was to increase the general prosperity. In some countries, this century has seen living standards improve. Yet do our televisions, telephones, videos and other consumer goods represent affluence or poverty? According to Marx, the payment of wages in the nineteenth century bore no relation to profits. Payment said Marx, 'Is restricted, almost entirely, to the means of subsistence that he requires for his maintenance, and, for the propagation of his race' (Marx and Engels 1976, p. 87). According to Marx, industrialization transformed labour into a commodity, 'exposed to all the vicissitudes of competition, to all the fluctuations of the market' (Marx and Engels 1976, p. 87).

What has changed?

Summary

1 The industrial revolution prompted the emergence of the factory system as the principal means of producing goods.

2 The factory system is characterized by mechanization and division of labour.

3 The factory system created new problems of coordination and control. An important issue for organizations involves converting the purchase of labour power into productive effort.

4 According to F. W. Taylor, the key to industrial harmony lies in increasing the general prosperity. Such increases can be achieved not by working harder, but by working more efficiently.

5 Taylor's recipe for efficiency is embodied in his four basic principles of 'scientific management'. These are:

- create a science of work,
- scientifically select and develop the workforce,
- bring science and the scientifically trained worker together,
- institute an equal division of labour.

6 Taylor's ideas are still in use today. They are seen in ergonomics, work study, and operations research.

7 Taylor's ideas are also seen in the service industries. They are sometimes applied to the emotional aspects of work.

8 Taylor's ideas have provoked controversy. It has been argued that Taylor's 'science' was bogus. Allegedly his real purpose was to control the workforce and extract maximum productivity by:

- monopolizing knowledge over work,
- depriving the worker of control over how work is performed,
- separating conception from execution,
- de-skilling.

9 Taylor assumed that organizational effectiveness required a combination of:

- engineering,
- a monetary incentive system known as piecework, and,
- careful surveillance and monitoring of the workforce.

10 Taylor saw no productive potential in social relations, charismatic leadership or human creativity and emotion. The emphasis is upon engineering and 'the one best way'.

11 Evidence suggests that 'scientific management' may not optimize efficiency. Output restriction can occur despite piecework incentives and controls. Piecework may even encourage output restriction.

12 Taylor's methods may result in waste and inflexibility. They also involve high transaction costs.

13 Far from disempowering the worker, piecework may facilitate control, not least by reducing ambiguity.

14 Taylor's influence is also seen in the way many people conduct their lives. 'Scientific management' can lead to productivity gains. Those principles can also undermine organizations.

Questions for Discussion

1 'All this emphasis on producing—that is all right for a cow, but not for a human being.' (Siegmund Warburg cited in Reich 1980, p. 177)

Discuss.

2 How far are the principles of 'scientific management' useful today?

3 Is the application of 'scientific management' techniques more likely to prompt output restriction that prevent it?

4 A theatre manager has read a book about Taylor's ideas. The manager is considering adopting Taylor's principles.

Advise the manager.

Further Reading

- Braverman, H. (1974) *Labour Monopoly Capital*, New York, Monthly Review Press.
- Knights, D. and Willmott, H. (1990) (eds.) *Labour Process Theory*, London, Macmillan.
- Ouchi, W. G. (1980) 'Markets, Bureaucracies and Clans,' *Administrative Science Quarterly* 25, 129–41.
- Taylor, F. W. (1947) *Scientific Management*, New York, Harper & Row.
- Thompson, P. and McHugh, D. (1995) *Work Organizations: A Critical Introduction*, London, Macmillan.

Chapter 3
Motivation and Leadership

'I plan to stay with my present firm because I do not feel obliged to "trim" personal or ethical standards in order to make a living . . . The firm's ethos is the pursuit of excellence.'

(Assistant solicitor)

'Everything has to be bang on. Its a case of "sit there and do it. *Don't* use your initiative." Fortunately the job's only until April. If I last until then, I'll be brain dead.'

(Bank clerk)

'One incredibly satisfying project was an infra-red application. My work became an industry standard. Yes I could make a lot more money . . . . A friend of mine joined Kleinwort Benson for three times my salary. But he's basically fixing other people's computers. That's not a job for someone with a Ph D.'

(Research and development engineer)

'There are plenty of leadership styles! If he'd just try one of them!'

(Disgruntled assistant manager)

WORK, observed Oscar Wilde, is the curse of the drinking classes. Organizations exist to facilitate productive effort. Organization theorists have devoted considerable attention to the question of how to lead and motivate people to work harder and better. This chapter examines the main theories of motivation, job satisfaction, organization commitment and leadership. The discussion also considers some of the assumptions and ideological implications that lie behind the various theories and research studies. The issues addressed in this chapter include:

Key Issues

- What motivates people?
- Is job satisfaction important?
- Who are the highly committed employees?
- Which leaders are the real 'movers and shakers' of the world?
- Do happy and satisfied workers perform better?
- Do leaders make organizations successful or do organizations make leaders successful?
- If our theories are wrong, why do we go on teaching them?

3.1 Managing Behaviour in Organizations

Do people like work? According to McGregor (1960) the answer may be either 'yes' or 'no'. McGregor depicted managers as embracing one of two contrasting assumptions. Managers who subscribe to 'Theory X' assume that people are inherently disinclined to work. In contrast, managers who subscribe to 'Theory Y' assume that work is a natural and potentially pleasurable activity.

Note that McGregor does not suggest *what* motivates people. McGregor's contribution to the organizational literature is to provide a model whereby managers can examine the assumptions they make about people and how those assumptions affect their approach to management.

We saw in Chapter 2 that F. W. Taylor had no doubts about how to manage behaviour. Taylor basically subscribed to the so-called 'Theory X' of motivation, that is, that people are fundamentally lazy and must therefore be enticed, driven or bullied into productive effort (McGregor 1960). Taylor viewed motivation mainly as a matter of combining carrot and stick, that is, providing a system of incentives to motivate, and a system of controls and punishments to discourage the potentially recalcitrant.

During the 1930s, organization theorists broadened their approach to work motivation. A new set of assumptions gained credence, known as 'Theory Y' (McGregor 1960).

'Theory Y' is diametrically opposed to 'Theory X'. 'Theory Y' states that people need to work for social reasons as well as economic ones. Moreover, far from being inherently lazy, most people are capable of enjoying work and take pride in doing good work. In other words, it began to be assumed that people would be more productive if they could be kept happy in work. This became known as the human relations or behavioural approach. (Both terms are used interchangeably hereafter.)

3.1.1 The Hawthorne Studies

The behavioural approach to management was prompted by the so-called Hawthorne Studies. A group of researchers at the Hawthorne plant in America were experimenting in 'scientific management' tradition with the effects of lighting upon productivity. The experiments were conducted with two groups of female workers. One group worked in a test room where levels of illumination were varied experimentally. The second group, a control group, worked under normal lighting conditions.

The Hawthorne researchers were surprised to discover that productivity increased in both rooms, even when illumination was lowered to the point of near darkness. Employees were then interviewed about their job attitudes including supervision and working conditions. The researchers subsequently attributed increased production to a change in 'mental attitude' resulting from the special attention paid to both groups generally, and in particular, to more friendly methods of supervision such that, 'In the new "relaxed" relationship of confidence and friendliness . . . practically no supervision is required' (Carey 1967, p. 405 citing Roethlisberger and Dickson). This became known as the 'Hawthorne effect'.

However, when the researchers attempted to replicate the Hawthorne pattern with a group of male workers (known as the Bank Wiring Room study) the result was very different. Far from increasing their output, operatives kept production well below work study targets. The researchers concluded that output restriction was caused by fear of unemployment, fear of raising standards, a desire to protect slower workers, and managerial acceptance of the situation (Roethlisberger and Dickson, 1939).

Later in this chapter we will see a different side of the Hawthorne studies. Here it is sufficient to note that the Hawthorne studies pointed to the role of the 'human factor' in production, including the supervisory climate and informal group pressures.

Pause for reflection
Describe perfect work.

3.2 What Motivates People?

MOTIVATION is central to the behavioural approach to management (e.g. Pinder 1984). The word 'motivation' derives from the Latin word *mouvre* which means to 'move'. Organizational theorists have mainly concerned themselves with how to motivate people to worker better and harder. Motivation theories centre upon the following variables:

1. Needs
2. Goals
3. Expectancies
4. Self-efficacy
5. Fairness
6. Job design
7. Social influence
8. Dispositional factors.

Each of these is now discussed in turn.

3.2.1 Maslow's theory of human needs

Need theories assume that people possess or acquire innate needs which they are moved to satisfy. Abraham Maslow's (1954) theory is the best known of these. Figure 3.1 summarizes Maslow's predictions.

According to Maslow, physiological needs, food, shelter and sex, are the first order of the day. Physical and psychological safety is the next level of need. Love needs refer to social belongingness, needs for affection and affiliation. Esteem needs concern both self-esteem and esteem from others. Esteem needs include need for power, achievement, and status. Maslow suggests that satisfaction of self-esteem promotes self-confidence, feelings of worth and of being useful. Conversely, deprivation produces feelings of inferiority, weakness and helplessness. Self-actualization, that is, realization of one's potential, is the ultimate human need.

According to Maslow, motivation is a dynamic entity. Unsatisfied needs generate tension within the person which drives them to satisfy the need thus reducing the tension. The key to Maslow's theory is that:

once a particular level of need is satisfied, it ceases to be a motivating force. The individual then seeks a higher level of need satisfaction.

For example, according to Maslow, if the house burned down, basic needs which most of us take for granted suddenly become imperative. Maslow's theory also implies that money's power to motivate is limited.

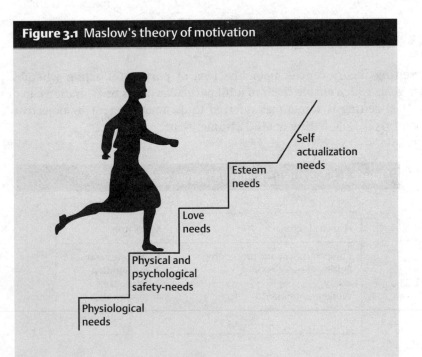

Figure 3.1 Maslow's theory of motivation

3.2.2 Herzberg's two factor theory

Maslow's is a general theory of human motivation. While it may be relevant to organizational life, it was not developed for that context. By contrast, Herzberg's theory is specifically concerned with work motivation. Herzberg's theory was derived by asking accountants and engineers to describe work related incidents which made them feel particularly good or particularly bad, known incidentally as the critical incident technique (Herzberg, Mausner and Snyderman 1959).

Figure 3.2 summarizes Herzberg's findings. Motivation, suggests Herzberg, is generated through satisfaction of higher order needs, that is, by providing opportunities for achievement, recognition and personal growth. Although so called hygiene factors are important, they do not motivate. Their absence, however, implies poor working conditions, incompetent or abrasive supervision which can create extreme dissatisfaction.

Herzberg implies that the opposite of job satisfaction in not dissatisfaction, but, subtly different:

no satisfaction at all.

Moreover, the opposite of job dissatisfaction is not satisfaction but again, subtly different:

no dissatisfaction.

3.2.3 Goal setting

Goal setting theory centres upon the idea of purposeful action whereby people choose goals which enable them to fulfil particular needs or aspirations. In organizations, goal setting is sometimes referred to as 'management by objectives' (MBO) Drucker (1954). Goal setting or MBO assumes that:

Figure 3.2 Herzberg's theory of human motivation

Hygiene Factors	Motivators
Company policy and procedures	1. Achievement
Quality of supervision	2. Recognition
Salary	3. Work itself
Working conditions	4. Responsibility
	5. Advancement

- Goals encourage strategic thinking, attention to management, and the formulation of action plans.
- Goals regulate efforts that is, they enable employees to order priorities and plan their time.
- Goals encourage persistence, despite obstacles.

Always provided that:

- Employees are committed to the goals.
- The goals are clear.
- Above all, the goals are challenging but not too difficult.

Evidence suggests that difficult goals are more motivating than easy ones, provided they are not too difficult. Moreover, specific goals are more motivating than general goals (Locke and Latham 1990, Mitchell 1997). For example, a target of reducing product failures or hospital waiting lists by a specific percentage is more motivating than a mission statement emphasizing service and satisfaction.

Pause for reflection

1. Try and recall an event in your life which went well. It may have been a job interview, a romantic encounter, passing a driving test, cooking a meal or even just solving a crossword puzzle.
2. Jot down a list of adjectives associated with the event, 'well organized', 'optimistic', 'determined' and so forth.
3. Delete the least important adjectives and any which are overlapping.
4. Try and reduce the remaining adjectives to a maximum of three by focusing upon the most important.
5. Now convert these into a personal slogan for success. For example, 'energising for results', or, 'planning, planning and more planning'.

3.2.4 Self-efficacy

You may have experienced that uncanny feeling of impending success. The exercise in section 3.2.3 is intended mainly for fun though it may enable you to predict your own prospects rather like studying form in horse racing. You may also be familiar with the opposite intuition suggesting failure is inevitable. Such emotions are known to behavioural scientists as perceived self-efficacy. Self-efficacy theories of motivation predict that:

performance depends upon self-belief.

More specifically, if we believe we can succeed, we are more likely to pursue difficult goals and to commit ourselves to the challenge (e.g. Sanna and Pusecker 1994).

3.2.5 Expectancy Theory

Goal-based theories link motivation to what we *want* to do. Self-efficacy theories link motivation to what we think we *can* do. Expectancy theory links motivation to the perceived *consequences* of our actions. More specifically, expectancy theory suggests that motivation is a function of three factors (Vroom 1964). These are:

1. Expected outcomes,
2. The extent to which outcomes are valued by the individual, and,
3. The estimated probability of attaining those outcomes.

Expectancy theory suggests that the strength of an individual's motivation reflects a complex but rational weighing of preferences, priorities and probabilities. For example, if you expect that obtaining a good degree will lead to a good job, and if obtaining a good job is important to you, expectancy theory predicts that you will work exceptionally hard to obtain the requisite qualification.

> **Pause for reflection**
>
> A solicitor is proposing to establish a so-called 'radical' practice whereby clerks and receptionists receive the same pay as qualified solicitors.
>
> What problems might the founding partner anticipate?

3.2.6 Outcome Theories

Outcome theories of motivation link the results of behaviour and subsequent performance. Two such theories of motivation are:

1. equity, and,
2. procedural justice.

Equity theory states that people strive for fairness in social exchange relationships (Adams 1963, 1965). Equity theory rests upon two elements, namely:

1. inputs, and,
2. outcomes.

Inputs refers to mental and physical efforts, the exercise of skill, qualifications, experience and the like. *Outcomes* refers to salaries, recognition, fringe benefits, seniority rights and the like.

Equity theory suggests that people engage in constant comparisons of whether their inputs and outcomes match those of comparable others. The key to equity theory is the notion of:

ratio.

An individual perceives their situation as equitable where:

the ratio of inputs to outcomes is equal to that of a comparable coworker.

Where A believes that their inputs are comparable with B's, and both A and B receive the same pay and benefits, equity exists. However, if A perceives that their skills, efforts and so forth exceed B's, yet B receives the equal or greater pay and benefits, A may perceive the situation as inequitable.

Equity theory is derived from Festinger's (1957) theory of cognitive dissonance. According to Festinger, people strive to maintain consistency between beliefs and behaviour.

A situation of perceived inequity creates a mis-match between beliefs and behaviour. Equity theory states that such inconsistency will prompt the individual to restore equity. Equity may be restored by:

- altering inputs, or,
- by altering outcomes.

Perceived inequity may prompt the individual to reduce their efforts or demand a pay review. Alternatively the individual may distort inputs or outcomes cognitively, that is, persuade themselves the situation is equitable or change the object of comparison. Another possibility is to act upon the other person to alter their inputs or outcomes. For example, we shall see in Chapter 9 how organizational sub-cultures can be more effective than management in pressurizing colleagues who are perceived as not pulling their weight. Ultimately the individual may leave the field, that is, leave the organization or withdraw psychologically. Alternatively, the individual may force the other party to leave the field.

Interestingly, theft and 'fiddling' in organizations may be a means of altering outcomes. For example, an employee may feel that the odd 'dodgy' over-time or expenses claim constitutes due recompense for a myriad of smaller unclaimed benefits.

Perceived inequity can also arise where the individual perceives that the ratio of inputs to outputs is distorted in their favour. For example, in the case of the radical solicitors' practice the objections to an equal pay structure came not from the solicitors but the clerks. The clerks sought to reduce outcomes because they felt embarrassed receiving the same pay as professionally qualified colleagues. Such cases may be exceptional however, there is more evidence to support the prediction for under-reward than over-reward (e.g. Mowday 1991).

3.2.7 Procedural justice

Equity theory suggests that an individual's perception of the situation is all-important. More recent research suggests, however, that it may not be perceived inequity that causes tension, so much as the manner in which inequity was created. In other words, process may be more important than outcomes.

More specifically evidence suggests that:

negative reactions to perceived under-payment are less pronounced if the person believes that the decision process was fair (e.g. Pfeffer and Langton 1993).

For example, a job evaluation exercise may have concluded that the work of technician A is more complex than that of technician B. Theories of procedural justice suggest that although technician B may disagree with the resultant outcome, perceived inequity is likely to be reduced if technician B accepts that the job evaluation exercise was fair and thorough.

3.2.8 Job design

Theories of job design link job satisfaction and motivation. Job satisfaction refers to:

A pleasurable or positive emotional state resulting from the appraisal of one's job or job experiences. (Locke 1976, p. 1300)

Job design theories assume that people will work harder and longer if their jobs yield pleasure and satisfaction. Herzberg (1968) suggested that organizations should design jobs to facilitate achievement, recognition, and responsibility—known as job enrichment. (Two other job design techniques are job rotation and job enlargement. Job rotation involves changing tasks in order to reduce fatigue and monotony. Job enlargement involves adding tasks to make work more interesting.)

The best known contribution to job enrichment is Hackman and Oldham's (1980) Job Characteristics Model. According to Hackman and Oldham, job satisfaction depends upon five factors. These are:

1. *Skill variety*, that is, whether the job involves a variety of tasks or requires an employee to utilize a variety of skills and abilities.
2. *Task identity*, that is, whether an employee can pursue a task from beginning to end, and whether work results in a visible end product.
3. *Task significance*, that is, the extent to which the employee's performance affects other people in the organization, customers, clients, contractors, suppliers and so forth.
4. *Autonomy*, that is, the extent to which the employee can plan their own work and choose their own working methods.
5. *Feedback*, that is, the extent to which the individual receives clear and direct information about their performance.

According to Hackman and Oldham, the higher a job scores upon each factor, the greater the motivating potential. Conversely, jobs with the lowest scores are prime candidates for redesign.

> **Pause for reflection**
>
> A technician is employed by a university library as part of a project to restore an important collection of books and manuscripts dating from approximately 1700 to 1920.
>
> The work involves deciding upon the requisite chemical treatments and utilizing these. The work is extremely painstaking as many of the documents are fragile and each page requires individual treatment.
>
> Analyse the potential sources of job satisfaction.

Job design theories of motivation assume that:

- people share the same basic needs, and,
- those needs may be satisfied by objective job characteristics.

It may seem trite to point out that people are not all the same. The evidence suggests that job satisfaction is influenced by a variety of personal factors including age (Clark, Oswald and Warr 1996).

Physical and mental capabilities can also influence motivation levels (for a discussion see Staw 1986). Indeed Hackman and Oldham (1980) subsequently recognized that some people simply do require opportunities for personal growth and development from their jobs or careers.

3.2.9 Social Influences

Job design theory further assumes that job characteristics exist as concrete entities. Yet we saw in the Introduction to this book that reality is a malleable entity. Social influence theory suggests that job characteristics such as the style of supervision or conditions of the workplace:

- are not given, but,
- constructed (see Salancik and Pfeffer 1978, O'Reilly and Caldwell 1979).

Perceived job characteristics may be a product of the prevailing beliefs, values and meanings of the workplace (Pearson and Chong 1997). For example, routine tasks can appear significant if the end product is perceived as socially important. Salancik and Pfeffer suggest that company newspapers, uniforms, titles and so forth serve to provide meaning, importance and justification to work activities. Money too can influence perceptions—such is the symbolic significance attached to high reward. In other words, social influence theory suggests that job satisfaction is potentially a cultural phenomenon.

3.2.10 **Dispositional factors and job satisfaction**

When a visitor suggested the technician's job must be fascinating (see section 3.3.6) the technician replied, 'Actually, a lot of it is very boring because it's very slow and you're applying the same techniques nearly all the time.'

This may seem a surprising reaction to a job which is both socially valuable and affords considerable autonomy.

Dispositional theory focuses upon the link between the person and job satisfaction. For example, evidence suggests that people with a tendency to complain about life in general are more dissatisfied with their job in particular (Judge, Locke and Durham 1997 citing Weitz, see also Staw 1986).

Dispositional theory focuses upon factors such as self-esteem, self-efficacy, neuroticism and evaluations of the world as dangerous, malevolent and unjust. Although evidence suggests dispositional theory is relevant, it is unclear precisely *what* dispositions influence job satisfaction and *how* job satisfaction is influenced. In a review of the literature, Judge, Locke and Durham (1997) hypothesize that positive mental states are likely to be conducive to job satisfaction and vice versa.

All of the foregoing theories of job satisfaction are potentially relevant but all are partial. Suffice it to note that:

evidence consistently shows that job attributes, namely, scope, autonomy and variety are conducive to job satisfaction, regardless of individual differences. (Judge, Locke and Durham 1997)

3.3 **Beyond Motivation: Organization Commitment**

O**RGANIZATIONS** require more than hard work from employees. Organizations suffer loss if expensively trained and knowledgeable employees decide to leave, or, if employees harbour resentment towards the organization, or secretly hold the organization in contempt.

Another motivational concept which has attracted considerable research interest is organization commitment. Organization commitment concerns an individual's psychological attachment to the organization. A committed employee is one who:

- has a strong desire to remain a member of the organization,
- is willing to exert high levels of effort on behalf of the organization, and,
- believes in the values and goals of the organization (Cook and Wall 1980, Meyer and Allen 1997, Mowday, Porter and Steers 1982).

Organization commitment is associated with a long list of potentially desirable outcomes and behaviours. Evidence suggests that more committed employees experience greater job satisfaction, are more cooperative (known as exhibiting citizenship behaviour). Committed employees are less likely to leave the organization. Their rates of tardiness and absenteeism are also lower (Becker 1992, Mathieu and Zajac 1990, Meyer and Allen 1997).

Pause for reflection

How would you feel about joining an organization which is prepared to offer you a 'job for life'?

3.3.1 Forms of commitment

Figure 3.3 summarizes three types of commitment (Allen and Meyer 1990).

Affective commitment refers to emotional attachment to the organization. Employees who score high on affective commitment are likely to identify strongly with the organization and exhibit a deep sense of involvement with the organization. Such employees stay with organization primarily because they *want* to. By contrast *continuance commitment* refers to employees who *need* to stay. For example, to pay off a student loan. *Normative commitment* refers to a perceived obligation to remain with the organization. Normatively committed employees feel they *ought* to remain. For example, if the organization has invested time and money in training the employee.

Most employees probably experience all three forms of commitment to some extent. Employees who score relatively high on affective commitment (want to stay) exhibit the strongest pro-organizational attitudes and behaviours. The reverse applies to employees scoring high on continuance commitment (needing to stay). High continuance commitment may mean relatively poor performance, unwillingness to

Figure 3.3 Forms of commitment

AFFECTIVE	'Want to stay'
CONTINUANCE	'Need to stay'
NORMATIVE	'Ought to stay'

exceed the call of duty and a greater likelihood of dysfunctional behaviours (Meyer and Allen 1997).

3.3.2 Who are the highly committed employees?

The correlates of organization commitment are similar to those associated with job satisfaction. Commitment correlates positively with job challenge, degree of autonomy, the variety of skills an employee is required to display, and, participation in decision making. Commitment is also related to organization dependability, feelings of personal importance to the organization and fulfilment of expectations (Mowday et al. 1982, Mathieu and Zajac 1990, Meyer and Allen 1997).

Interestingly, evidence further suggests that affective commitment is positively and consistently related to perceived efficacy (Mathieu and Zajac 1990). In other words employees are most likely to want to stay with the organization if they feel competent and that they are allowed to do a good job.

Taken together, research basically suggests that commitment is related to fulfilment of higher order needs. Interestingly, much the same goes for volunteer workers (Daily 1986).

3.3.3 Commitment destroyed

The reverse is also true in that frustration and disappointment with the organization can destroy an employee's commitment. Evidence suggests that stressful work experiences including role conflict (incompatible obligations), role overload, (too many obligations), and role ambiguity (obligations unclear) can damage affective commitment (Mathieu and Zajac 1990).

Perceived injustice can also harm affective commitment particularly when it comes to 'downsizing'. Organizational 'downsizing' involves abolishing whole layers of organization and managing with fewer people. 'Downsizing' typically increases the burden upon those who remain thus placing a premium on commitment. Evidence suggests that 'downsizing' particularly depresses commitment where:

- survivors had a close personal or working relationship with the victims, and/or,
- survivors perceive that the exercise was unfair.

'Downsizing' is likely to be perceived as unfair if selection for redundancy reflects office politics rather than operational need, or if victims received inadequate redundancy pay and help in finding another job (Meyer and Allen 1997). Conversely, high commitment can mitigate the effects of stress following drastic reorganization (Begley and Czajka 1993).

Evidence further suggests that:

disappointment with the organization generally affects the most highly committed. (Brockner, Tyler, and Cooper-Schneider 1992)

Equity theory would suggest that people who have invested their entire being in the organization expect more in return. (See also Randall 1987, below).

3.3.4 Continuance commitment

Continuance commitment (needing to stay) results from two factors, namely:

1. accumulated investments, and,
2. perceived alternatives.

Generally speaking, the longer an employee remains with an organization (or in a particular profession or career), the greater the cost of leaving. Employees tend to accumulate pension rights and long-service privileges. Such 'side-bets' (Becker 1960) as they are known, can restrain employees from changing course. (See section 7.4.1 for a further discussion of 'side-bets'.)

  Employees may also consider themselves bound to an organization through lack of perceived alternatives. For example, an unhappy interview with another firm may convince an employee that changing jobs would be like jumping from the proverbial 'frying pan'. Likewise repeated rejections from other organizations may lead an employee to conclude that there is no prospect of finding alternative employment (Meyer and Allen 1997).

3.3.5 Normative commitment

Comparatively little is known about how normative commitment (perceived obligation to stay) develops. Such evidence as exists points to cultural congruence and socialization (Meyer and Allen 1997). For example, normative commitment may be enhanced where coworkers clearly exhibit a positive attitude towards the organization (Mowday et al. 1982).

3.3.6 Organizational versus professional commitment

In practice, employees may experience multiple commitments, including coworkers, top management, work group, department, trade union, and professional association, (Reichers 1985). Gouldner (1957) coined the terms 'cosmopolitans' and 'locals' to distinguish between employees whose primary commitment is to the organization and those whose commitment lies elsewhere.

  'Locals' identify with the organization. 'Cosmopolitans' mainly identify with a group outside the organization and judge their standards of performance according to that reference group. For example, doctors, solicitors, architects, surveyors and chartered accountants are ultimately accountable to their professional association for their performance. As employers, hospital managers can choose to overlook a doctor's misdemeanours but the General Medical Council has the last word.

The notion of multiple commitments implies the possibility of conflicting loyalties and priorities. For instance, some solicitors *are* required to trim professional standards in order to meet the firm's strictures on cost effectiveness.

A question posed by organization theorists is:

does professional commitment take precedence over organizational commitment?

Reicher's (1985) review of the evidence suggests that employees rarely see themselves as distinctly 'cosmopolitan' or 'local' but usually relate to a variety of reference groups. More recent research has shown that professional and organizational commitment are positively correlated (Wallace 1993). In a study of corporate lawyers, Dias De Oliveira (1996) observed that professional commitment is higher than organizational commitment in the early career stage. By mid- and late-career stages, however, this difference disappears. Both forms of commitment are age related, though interestingly the attainment of partnership by itself does not appear to enhance either professional or organizational commitment (see also Drummond and Dias De Oliveira 1996).

In a recent review of the literature, Meyer and Allen (1997) conclude that professional and organizational commitment are potentially complementary. A study of engineers suggests that high performers may be more committed to *both* their organization and to their profession. By contrast, poor performers may be less committed to the organization yet strongly committed to their profession (citing Bough and Roberts). The evidence is conflicting, however. It is observed that the more dedicated nurses, that is, those who read professional literature and attend conferences regularly, exhibit greater commitment towards their profession but not their organization (citing Meyer et al.).

3.4 Leadership Theory

So far this chapter has referred to motivational theories and the procurement of organization commitment. Yet who is to motivate and stimulate commitment? Another concept which has captured particular attention in the organizational literature is leadership. Managerial leadership may be defined as:

Influencing task objectives and strategies, influencing commitment and compliance in task behaviour to achieve these objectives, influencing group maintenance and identification, and influencing the culture of an organization. (Yukl 1989, p. 253)

In other words, the leaders' task is two-fold, that is, to ensure that organizational objectives are accomplished while sustaining the people charged with accomplishing those objectives. (F. W. Taylor was mainly concerned with the former.)

Pause for reflection

Imagine that you have been invited to participate on the selection committee for senior management appointments to a major retailer such as Marks and Spencer. Each member of the panel will focus upon different aspects of the job. Your task is to judge the candidates' leadership skills.

Assume that trading conditions for the next few years will be difficult.

1. What will you look for and why?
2. Would your criteria change if trading prospects were good?

Leadership has attracted considerable attention because it is assumed that leaders have a critical impact upon organizational effectiveness. For instance, in December 1998 the UK government announced plans to instigate a college of leadership for head teachers. Also in 1998, the *Financial Times* newspaper commented:

James Crosby confesses to playing tennis so badly it counts as 'dangerous' . Shareholders will hope he has a stronger grip on the corporate game as he prepares for the biggest match of his life as chief executive of Halifax. (Brown-Humes 1998)

Research into leadership has focused upon the following questions:

1. Are leaders born rather than made?
2. Do effective leaders require a particular style?
3. Should leaders match their style to subordinates' motivation?
4. Should leaders concentrate upon empowering others?

Each of these issues are now discussed in turn.

3.4.1 Are leaders born? The trait approach

The trait approach links leadership and personality. Trait theory starts from the assumption that leadership abilities are innate. The individual either has or does not have what it takes to be a leader.

Trait research focuses upon identifying the personal characteristics which distinguish leaders from non-leaders. In a nutshell, the results of work extending over half a century are patchy though there is reasonably consistent evidence to suggest that leaders are marked by intelligence, self-confidence, desire for power, integrity and sociability (Bass 1990).

3.4.2 Do effective leaders require a particular style?

Trait theory focuses upon who leaders *are*. By contrast the style approach concentrates upon what leaders *do*. More specifically, the style approach concerns the balance between the leader's:

concern for people, and,
concern for production,

known respectively as 'consideration' and 'initiation' structure (Stogdill 1974).

Leaders with high concern for people trust their subordinates, place considerable emphasis upon fostering group relations, exhibit flexibility in making decisions and encourage high standards. Leaders with high concern for production are more concerned with targets and achievement. Such leaders are apt to be highly directive. They set the tasks, specify the methods to be used, dictate timescales for completion and so forth.

The so-called managerial grid (Blake and Mouton 1985) identifies five styles of leadership as follows:

1. *Authority compliance*—high concern for production, low concern for people, that is, results driven management.
2. *Team management*—strong emphasis upon both people and production, proclaimed as the ideal management style.
3. *Country club management*—high concern for people, low concern for production, that is, 'don't rock the boat'. 'Country club' sometimes distinguishes company chairmen from their more results-driven chief executives.
4. *Middle of the road management*—moderate concern for people and production. Such managers are usually pragmatists believing that management is the art of the possible.
5. *Impoverished management*—low concern for people or production. Such managers typically appear withdrawn and apathetic. Impoverished management is frequently seen where a manager has lost interest in the job for some reason. For example, if they have been disappointed with the organization or have simply been in the job too long. Impoverished management sometimes occurs where a leader is responsible for several departments and takes a strong interest in some at the expense of neglecting others. In the more recent literature impoverished management is sometimes referred to as 'laissez faire' (Bass 1985).

Research into style theory aims to identify a 'one best way' approach of combining task and relationship behaviours which will work in any situation.

Pause for reflection

A recently appointed head teacher of a junior school has a problem. The previous head teacher, who had been in post for thirty years, behaved as an autocrat. The new head teacher has tried to introduce a participative style of management, but has been surprised and dismayed by the hostile reaction from staff.

Advise the head teacher.

3.4.3 Does effective leadership depend upon the situation? (Contingency approach)

Imagine that you are seated in a crowded concert hall. Smoke is beginning to drift from under the stage, growing denser by the second. A flame flickers then disappears. Should you call a meeting to decide whether to evacuate the hall?

Trait theory and notions of leadership style ignore situational variables. Contingency theory attempts to remedy this weakness by linking the leader's personality and style to the situation (that is, contingencies). In a nutshell, contingency theory suggests that:

- production orientated leadership is most effective in situations of high control *and* low control, whereas,
- people orientated leaders are more effective in moderate control situations (Fiedler 1967, Fiedler and Garcia 1987).

3.4.4 Path-goal theory

So far, the discussion has ignored the disposition of followers. Path-goal theory (House 1971, House and Mitchell 1974) attempts to link leadership to followers' motivation. Path-goal theory is derived from expectancy theory (see above). The assumption is that subordinates will be motivated if they believe they can perform the work (tread the path) and that performance will lead to worthwhile outcomes (goal achievement). The leader's task is to:

- choose a style that matches subordinates' motivational needs, and,
- the demands of the task.

Path-goal theory predicts that *directive* leadership works best where subordinates are themselves authoritarian, and where the task demands and organizational rules are ambiguous. This is because directive leadership defines the path. A *supportive* nurturing style works best where the work is frustrating or repetitive as it provides a sustaining 'human touch'. *Participative* leadership works best where tasks are ambiguous and where employees need to work autonomously and thus require a high level of control. This is because participation helps clarify the path without being overly directive. *Achievement* orientated leadership whereby the leader challenges subordinates to perform at the highest level possible, also works well where tasks are ambiguous. This is because leaders who set challenging standards increase subordinates perceived self-efficacy (see above) thus creating self-fulfilling prophesies.

3.4.5 Empowering subordinates: transformational leadership

The foregoing theories of leadership are basically *transactional*. That is, they focus upon exchanges or bargains between leaders and followers whereby followers are rewarded materially or symbolically for achieving predetermined goals or targets. The emphasis remains upon control and direction.

According to Bass (1990), transactional leadership achieves a negotiated level of performance. By contrast, says Bass, 'The real movers and shakers of the world are *transformational*' (p. 23, italics added).

Bass's theory of transformational leadership builds upon Burn's (1978) classification of transactional and transformational political leaders. The theory of transformational leadership is that by developing, challenging, intellectually stimulating and inspiring, the leader can prompt followers to transcend their own interests in favour of a higher purpose.

Whereas transactional leadership procures compliance, transformational leadership engenders empowerment. Transformational leadership works by raising subordinates' aspirations, thus empowering them to reach high goals which would otherwise have seemed unattainable. Empowerment is achieved by promulgating vision, building trust in the vision and helping others to achieve it.

More specifically transformational leaders score high upon:

1. *Charisma*—the ability to engender pride, trust and respect.
2. *Inspiration*—transformational leaders create high expectations, function as role models, and manipulate symbols in order to engender enthusiasm, commitment and a sense of higher purpose.
3. *Individualized consideration*—transformational leaders exhibit high attention to, and respect for subordinates.
4. *Intellectual stimulation*—transformational leaders continuously challenge and stretch followers.

Transformational leadership theory assumes that the leader succeeds by attending to subordinates' needs and growth potential. In this view, leadership emerges through interaction between leader and subordinates. Above all, however, transformational leadership attempts to motivate followers to rise above their own self-interests for the good of the organization.

3.5 Discussion

THE present chapter has focused upon the behavioural approach to management. The subject matter of the present chapter may seem remote from the theme of metaphoric thinking introduced in Chapter 1. Recall, however, that metaphors can become so commonplace that they seem literal (see section 1.1.3). This observation is highly relevant to notions of leadership, motivation, job satisfaction and commitment. We are apt to forget that these too are metaphors, that is, human constructions which are used to explain organizational life. We may talk of *measuring* commitment, or job satisfaction or leadership style. Yet our measures are mere words which attempt to stand surrogate for 'something else'.

We use the metaphors to rationalise organizational life. Managers may not see themselves as 'leading' or 'motivating'. Employees may not be conscious of high, low or medium levels of job satisfaction. The metaphors are an attempt to create meaning.

Like all metaphors:

our notions of leadership, commitment and so forth both facilitate and constrain knowledge.

An important constraint is that the material contained in the present chapter is what is known as 'bog standard'. It is part of the received literature of organization behaviour. It allows us to see organizational life in a particular way. The question is, what do we miss?

The constraints become more obvious when we consider the metaphor of science that lies behind notions of motivation and leadership. In my experience, one of the biggest frustrations students experience in studying Organization Behaviour is that the subject fails to live up to promise. For example, we can read everything there is to read about motivation, yet still have no idea of what motivates someone.

Recall that all metaphors are partial. Organization behaviourists examine emotion via a clinical lens. By adopting a clinical mode of enquiry, they emerge with a clinical answer. We saw in Chapter 1 that language is not merely descriptive but ontological. Language structures thought patterns and frameworks of knowledge. For example, contrast the sterile language of 'expectancies', 'inputs' and 'outputs' with the following extract from Lytton Strachey's biography of Queen Elizabeth I:

The lion heart, the splendid gestures—such things were there, no doubt . . . The sharp and hostile eyes of the Spanish ambassadors saw something different. . . . They had come into contact with those forces in the Queen's mind which proved incidentally, fatal to themselves, and brought her, in the end, her enormous triumph (p. 13).

I doubt whether there is anything in the organizational literature, far less the present chapter, capable of offering such insight. It could be argued that Strachey's observations are highly subjective and therefore scientifically unsound. Such argument resonates with the calls for precision, formal lexicons and so forth discussed in section 1.6.2. To define one language as legitimate is to exclude another. For example, there is little room in the formal lexicon of organization behaviour for words like 'evil', 'madness' and 'folly' though they are real enough to those who work in organizations. Likewise, the phenonemon of 'bullying' in organizations has begun to capture attention. Bullying is potentially a metaphoric reconstruction of a glamorized activity known as leadership.

If anything, Strachey's passage is a reminder of the limits of science in understanding organizations and people in organizations. The proverb teaches 'there's now't so queer as folk'. Yet science attempts to reduce human behaviour to hypotheses and predictable trajectories. Emotion, by definition, is irrational. behavioural research seeks to rationalize the irrational.

Perhaps the biggest weakness of our theories is:

they don't work.

The central tenet of behavioural literature is that motivation is the key to productivity. Yet according to Guest (1990) human relations ideas have never been taken seriously in the UK. Likewise, Staw (1986) suggests that the theories examined in this chapter have been oversold.

One possible reason for the doubtful credibility of the behavioural approach to management is that extensive (and expensive) programmes of research have yet to identify any real evidence to support the central assumption that happy workers are more productive. Moreover, successive studies have yet to substantiate most of the various theories described earlier in this chapter.

More specifically, the evidence for need theories is weak. Needs, it seems, are only tenuously related to action (for recent reviews see Mitchell (1997) and Weiss and Cropanzano 1996). While evidence suggests job design can enhance job satisfaction, there is little to suggest that satisfied employees perform better (Mitchell 1997). The same applies to employees who score high upon affective commitment (Meyer and Allen 1997, Mathieu and Zajac 1990).

Nor is there any firm evidence of links between leadership traits, styles and organizational effectiveness (Bryman 1996, 1992, Northouse 1997). It appears that there is no 'one best' way to lead, even when situational factors are considered. While charisma and inspiration are the two most important dimensions of transformational leadership in influencing performance, transformational leadership is by no means a passport to success. Evidence suggests that transformational leaders are restricted by environmental constraints and organizational history (Bryman 1996).

Pause for reflection

Your computer has failed. The machine is vital for meeting a course work deadline. Who would you prefer to repair it:

■ a technician who seems bored and apathetic, or,

■ an enthusiast who seems as if they can hardly wait to begin taking the machine apart?

Explain the reasons for your choice.

My guess is that you would probably prefer the enthusiast to carry out repairs. Yet if the research evidence is correct, there is nothing to choose between them! One possible explanation for negative findings concerns how performance is measured. Researchers typically focus upon productivity rates. If performance is defined more broadly to include factors such as cooperation, attendance, and diligence, then satisfaction is relevant especially over the longer term. For example, Griffin (1991) reports upon a job enrichment exercise in a bank which took two to four years to show results. Moreover, the converse applies in that dissatisfaction is associated with negative outcomes such as with turnover, absenteeism, and accident rates (Mitchell 1977).

3.5.1 More is better? Linear intuitive thinking

Let me now turn to some of the wider issues concerning the behavioural approach to management. According to Staw (1986) the problem is not the theories but how they have been applied. Staw suggests that organizations have regarded single theories as panaceas. Many managerial interventions have changed only a small aspect of the organization while expecting major transformations. Staw suggests that a more holistic approach involving a battery of theories is required.

Perhaps, and yet Staw's reasoning is an example of 'first order thinking' (Watzlawick, Weakland and Frish 1974). That is, when one theory fails the response is to try 'more of the same'—in this case combining theoretical ideas to create a motivational Juggernaut. Sometimes there is more to be gained by stepping outside the immediate frame of reference (known as second order thinking) and examining the issues from a wider standpoint.

It was suggested in Chapter 1 that much of the organizational literature reflects linear intuitive thinking patterns which can obscure more complex possibilities. One such assumption implied by the behavioural approach to management is that 'more is better'. The presumption is that the more motivated and committed the workforce, the more effective the organization.

'More is better' logic overlooks the potential paradoxes of organizational life. For instance, evidence suggests that goal setting does motivate people (Locke and Latham 1990). That does not necessarily mean that the organization benefits, however. Evidence suggests that combining highly specific goals (the ones most likely to motivate) with bonus payments can damage social relations at work and undermine cooperation (Wright et al. 1993). We shall return to this point in Chapter 4 when we discuss 'total quality management' philosophy.

Goal setting also encourages persistence. We shall see in section 7.9.1 that persistence can severely undermine organizations if it is carried too far. Moreover, perceived efficacy can be counter-productive if it shades into an illusion of invulnerability. Likewise job satisfaction becomes an expensive luxury if it over-rides economic logic. For example, if engineers are more interested in designing technically sophisticated products than commercially viable ones.

'More is better' logic also underscores the organizational commitment literature. According to Randall (1987) too much commitment breeds conformity. Conformity may:

- stifle originality and innovation,
- encourage the presence of disruptive and/or poorly performing employees, and,
- discourage whistle blowing.

Highly committed employees, suggests Randall, are also a potential liability in difficult times because their whole identity is absorbed by the organization. Randall suggests that organizations should aim to procure moderate levels of commitment, thus allowing employees to retain their independence while still enabling pro-organizational behaviours.

3.5.2 Linear thinking and leadership theory

Linear intuitive assumptions also inform leadership theory. One basic assumption is that leaders lead and subordinates follow. This obscures the possibility that:

a leader's style may be partly determined by the attitude of employees (Blau and Scott 1963).

Zahn and Wolf (1981) suggest that the relationship between leaders and the led is reciprocal. They suggest that the notion of 'management style' is misleading as both leader and subordinates influence one another. Empirical evidence certainly suggests that leader behaviour is influenced by subordinate behaviour (Pfeffer 1977 citing Lowin and Craig). For example, supervisors react differently to poor performance depending upon how they see the problem. Supervisors tend to utilize motivational techniques, such as extra coaching and encouragement, where poor performance is attributed to ability rather than attitude. Where poor performance is attributed to attitude, supervisors typically resort to punishment and close control (Chow and Grusky 1980, Kipnis 1976, Podsakoff 1982, Sims 1980, Sims and Manz 1984, see also Podsakoff and Schriesheim 1985).

The leader's personal circumstances can also influence subordinate relations. Evidence suggests supervisors of large groups spend less time coaxing subordinates than supervisors of small groups. Moreover, less experienced and less confident supervisors rely more upon punitive measures (Podsakoff 1982). Tjosvold (1985 a,b) found that competitive supervisors were more intolerant of poor performers than cooperative ones. Both competitive and cooperative supervisors however, resorted to threats, and came to dislike subordinates whose performance was attributed to inadequate motivation.

In theory, transformational leaders are exempt from reciprocal influences as they seek to change subordinates' aspirations and outlook. This seems unlikely as it implies that transformational leaders succeed without listening to anyone for to listen is to engage in reciprocal influences. Indeed, just to encounter another person is to experience an exchange of influence. The impact may be very subtle but it is real nevertheless (Heider 1958). For example, you may have been very annoyed with someone. You intend to tell them exactly what you think of them. A glance at their demeanour, however, prompts you to think again.

Moreover, exemption from reciprocal influences, implies that transformational leaders are insensitive to subordinates' energizing influences. For instance, during the 1998 Proms season Sir Simon Rattle made musical history conducting Beethoven's Ninth Symphony. At one stage in the acclaimed performance Rattle stopped conducting in order to listen to the music. What does that suggest about the relationship between leaders and the led?

Transformational leaders may be fashionable but are they effective? Kets De Vries (1996) suggests that envisioning, empowering and energizing are insufficient. The leader must also be the architect of success, establishing the appropriate structures and systems. Yet charismatic leaders (charisma is an important dimension of transformational leadership) tend to emerge in times of crisis. The example of developing countries suggests that their achievements are qualified by the mess they leave behind through inattention to infrastructure and detail (Bryman 1992).

Transformational leadership theory also subscribes to 'more is better' logic. Yet charisma is potentially destabilizing and difficult to control (Trice and Beyer 1992). Moreover, just as there may be a fine line between genius and insanity, transformational leadership can become too much of a good thing:

When vision becomes unshakeable obsession, the potential for catastrophe may not be far away. (Bryman 1992, p. 173)

For example, unlike Churchill, Hitler came to believe that he knew better than his scientific advisors. Churchill not only mobilized the English language as a strategic weapon, he also succeeded in galvanizing lumbering Whitehall departments into action with his famous 'action this day' tabs and his willingness to probe the most minute detail (Reynolds 1993). Churchill also avoided the pitfalls of obsession, 'He is an unwise man who thinks there is any *certain* method of winning this war . . . The only plan is to persevere' (cited in Kegan 1993, p. 327).

> **Pause for reflection**
>
> A factory manager wishes to improve the motivation of process operatives. The work involves placing a cherry on top of iced buns as they pass along the production line.
>
> What measures would you recommend?

3.5.3 People are all?

The behavioural approach to management assumes that performance is controlled by the individual. Yet in many workplace situations, individuals exert only limited control over performance. In factories, for example, production is mainly determined by the speed of the line. Likewise, the pace of office work may depend upon market fluctu-ations, calendars of meetings, information flows, computer 'down-time' and so forth.

'If everyone minded their own business,' said the Duchess in Alice in Wonderland, 'the world would go round a great deal faster than it does.'

No doubt, yet people in organizations are not always content to mind their own business. Office politics can harm motivation and productivity. For example, an employee's work may be criticized unfairly by a jealous colleague or supervisor. Polit-ical behaviour in organizations is discussed in Chapter 6. Here it is sufficient to note that such influences are difficult to control.

3.5.4 The science of management?

The picture which emerges from the foregoing résumé of the literature may appear partly contradictory. If, after decades of research involving hundreds of studies, our theories are so doubtful why do we go on teaching them? Obviously, organizations have to make decisions about job design, payment structures and so forth. In a highly competitive world, arguably even a marginal improvement is significant (Meyer and Allen 1997).

According to critical theorists, however, the millions of pounds and dollars invested in behavioural studies serve a very different purpose. Critical theorists sug-gest that the real reason for scientifically rigorous research is not that it makes organizations any more effective, but,

that it legitimizes the idea of managers as impartial experts (Alvesson and Willmott (1996).

For instance, according to Carey (1967) the so-called Hawthorne Studies were scientifically worthless, yet that does not stop organization theorists referring to the so-called 'Hawthorne effect'.

Although the female operatives were initially encouraged to work as they pleased, they were quickly reprimanded for talking too much. Moreover, says Carey, output did not increase in the spirited manner suggested (Roethlisberger and Dickson, 1939). Two of the women were actually removed from the test room for insubordination and inadequate output and replaced by colleagues with the 'right' mental attitude. Even then, increased output was achieved mainly through intimidation. Carey concludes:

Supervision became more friendly and relaxed because output increased rather than vice versa. (Carey 1967, p. 415)

Not all behavioural research is biased in this way. Most academic studies are conducted with scrupulous care. That does not mean that it is value neutral, how-ever. Only that bias operates more subtly. Behavioural research derives its authority from notions of scientific rigour and clinical detachment. Yet who defines the research agenda? Who decides what questions are important and which variables are significant and how they are defined?

The organizational literature offers only the most limited insight into the emotional experience of work and organizational life. For example, Fineman (1996) describes job satisfaction as a crude emotional concept. Moreover, the interest in this chapter has been mainly upon harnessing emotion in service of rationality. (We shall see in Chapters 7 and 8 how stress and fear of failure are seen as undermining rationality). Evidence suggests expectancy theory can partly predict behaviour (Mitchell 1997). Yet does that mean that organizations can be made more effective by manipulating employees through an appeal to interests? Expectancy theory assumes that people are inherently rational. We saw in section 1.2.4 that our notions of rationality stem from deeply irrational forces.

Likewise, the treatment of gender in the managerialist literature is emotionally sterile. For instance, evidence suggests that affective commitment is not gender related (Aven, Parker and Mcevoy 1993). In other words, gender is 'scientifically' neutralized by treating it as an operational variable (Alvesson and Billing 1997).

3.5.5 Value-driven research

Critical theorists suggest that the alleged value neutrality of behavioural science does not make us more efficient but generates new ideas which:

- reproduce current values,
- legitimize existing forms of control, and,
- reproduce existing power relations (Knights and Willmott 1992).

Connotations of research as neutral, detached, objective and quantitative can be seen as another way of expressing masculine bias (Alvesson and Billing 1997, citing Jaggar). Indeed many academics who utilize qualitative methodologies have a hard time getting their work published, such is the control exerted by their 'number crunching' colleagues who sit on the editorial boards of leading journals and who control the allocation of research grants. Knowledge is a highly political entity. The conduct of research may be scientifically objective but the assumptions upon which theories and hypotheses rest are highly subjective. For example, trait theory (by no means dead and buried incidentally, see Northouse 1997) rests upon the 'born to rule' adage. Rigorous research into trait theory is not a neutral exercise but basically sustains class distinctions (Pfeffer 1977). Indeed, in 1998 the *Financial Times* reported that a typical board director of a FTSE 100 company is a 56 year-old man with a university education. One third of directors has a degree from Oxford, Cambridge or Harvard. Only 4 per cent are women (Oxbridge men dominate FTSE 100 companies).

> **Pause for reflection**
>
> Does the image of a 'Big Issue' seller resonate with your idea of leadership?
> If not, why not?

Recall that leadership research has been justified on the grounds that leaders crucially affect organizational performance. According to critical theorists, transformational leadership theory is not a scientific breakthrough so much as a celebration and reaffirmation of masculine values (Alvesson and Willmott 1996).

One dimension of masculine values is the implication that strong leadership conquers all. According to Pfeffer (1977) the organizational literature overstates the role of leadership. Leaders, says Pfeffer, can influence only a fraction of organizational exigencies. Moreover, they have no control over commodity prices, currency fluctuations, labour market conditions and so forth. Indeed, evidence suggests that transformational leaders are constrained by time and context (Bryman 1996). For example, the iconoclastic Anita Roddick has found it difficult to transcend supermarket chains who have copied 'Bodyshop' ideas.

Pfeffer suggests that the leader's main role is symbolic. Symbolism is the subject of Chapter 10. Here it is sufficient to note that, according to Pfeffer, leaders stand surrogate for action. For example, since it is impractical to sack everyone in a failing organization, the leader is usually removed as a *sign* to shareholders and other interested parties that the problems are acknowledged, and that something will be done. This raises a question, namely:

■ do leaders make an organization successful, or,
■ do successful organizations make a leader seem successful?

According to Pfeffer it is probably the latter:

Successful leaders, as perceived by the social system, are those who can separate themselves from organizational failures and associate themselves with organizational success. (Pfeffer 1977, p. 110)

Knights and Willmott (1992) suggest that the organizational literature obscures the unheroic aspects of leadership. Their own study shows that leaders seldom solve problems so much as use their power to deny their existence and to push responsibilities and pressures on to subordinates. Knights and Willmott further observe how leaders visit their own subjugation and insecurity upon followers.

It is important to remember that many organizational employees who qualify for the title 'leader' are only one stage removed from the people they supervise. I am thinking particularly of call centre supervisors and supervisors of large hotel dining rooms replete with television monitors and listening devices, in conversation with their hierarchical superiors:

I'm not very happy about Ann. She may need more training ... She's certainly lacking in confidence and speed. I don't know how she'll cope on Thursday with 300 seatings.

Ann's alleged inefficiency makes the supervisor appear competent and important. If the supervisor has their way, Ann will never cope.

3.5.6 Is the Organization Man dead?

Has anything really changed since the publication of Whyte's (1957) *Organization Man*? Whyte's thesis is that organizations value conformity above all else. Readers learn how to cheat personality tests so as to appear 'normal'. Diversity may now be fashionable (Thomas and Ely 1996) but within what limits?

Ideological bias exists not just in the framing of research questions, but also in the interpretation of results. For instance, evidence clearly and consistently suggests that job satisfaction and affective commitment increase with age (Meyer and Allen 1997). What does that mean, however?

A managerialist interpretation might suggest that employees who choose to remain, increasingly value the organization and their role within it. Note, however, that age rather than job level is the critical variable. A managerialist interpretation of the results would stress that employees experience satisfaction and give commitment regardless of reward, that money and career progression are not everything.

An alternative interpretation of the evidence is that the observed links between age and job satisfaction and commitment represent *post hoc* rationalization of events (Staw 1981). We will see in Chapter 7 how people shape their perceptions of reality (that is, whether they are happy to remain with a particular organization) to justify their situation. Suffice it here to say that life is surely more tolerable if 'needing to stay,' can be transposed into 'wanting to stay'.

Self-justification theory (see section 7.9.4) would of course imply that people adjust their behaviour to fit their rationale for staying. In other words, a kind of self-fulfilling prophesy is created whereby people behave as if they are satisfied and committed.

3.5.7 The motivation to do what?

Recall that motivation is central to the behavioural approach to management. Turning the issue on its head, why is it assumed that if people are productive they are *de facto* motivated (Alvesson and Willmott 1996)?

An important dimension of the behavioural management literature is:

'what is not'.

The literature takes production lines, call centres, and so forth as inevitable. Critical theorists argue that the behavioural literature offers nothing that is potentially emancipatory or conducive to deep reflection and questioning. At most, it offers the prospect of minor improvements to working conditions.

Besides, motivation to do what? It was suggested in the Introduction to this book that students of Organization Behaviour are entitled to look beyond productivity to the value of what is produced. For instance, in 1998, many UK hill farmers went bankrupt as prices collapsed. Lambs reared through months of hard work were sold for as little as £1 each. (Prices charged in supermarkets remained stable). By contrast, Alvesson and Willmott cite the moment Pepsi captured a 30.8 per cent market share as compared with rival company Coca-Cola's 29.2 per cent:

It was one of those moments for which you worked your entire career. We always believed, since the early seventies, when Pepsi was widely viewed as the perennial also-ran, that we could do it. All of us started out with that objective, and we never took our eyes off it. (Alvesson and Willmott 1996, p. 198, citing John Sculley with J. A Bryne, *Odyssey: Pepsi is Apple . . . A Journey of Adventure. Ideas and the Future*, New York: Harper & Row, 1988.)

Alvesson and Willmott ask:

What is the purpose of the Pepsi Corporation? Does it accomplish anything socially valuable? Work was self-evidently purposeful so long as more sweetened water was sold . . . A person working for the Red Cross, saving people from starving to death . . . a researcher tracking the mystery of cancer or AIDS could not have been more committed. (Alvesson and Willmott 1996, p. 199)

Summary

1 The behavioural approach to management basically assumes that happy employees are more productive than unhappy employees.

2 The role of the 'human factor' in production was first signalled by the so-called Hawthorne Studies.

3 Motivation is central to the behavioural approach to management.

4 Motivation theories centre upon the following variables:

   - need satisfaction,
   - pursuit of goals,
   - calculation of expectancies,
   - perceived self-efficacy,
   - perceived fairness of ratio of inputs, to outputs and social justice,
   - job design, and,
   - social influence.

5 Organization commitment concerns how individuals evaluate their position in an organization.

6 Committed employees:

   - possess a strong desire to remain with the organization,
   - are willing to exert high levels of effort on behalf of the organization, and,
   - believe in the values and goals of the organization.

7 Commitment is positively related to fulfilment of higher order needs.

8 Commitment can be undermined by stress, perceived injustice and disappointment with the organization.

9 Employees may experience multiple commitments. For example, an employee may owe a duty to their professional association as well as the organization.

10 The notion of multiple commitments can imply conflicting loyalties.

11 Leadership involves:

- securing organizational objectives, and,
- sustaining the people involved.

12 Leadership theory starts from the assumption that leaders are crucial to organizational effectiveness.

13 Leadership theory is concerned with identifying 'best' ways of leading.

14 The main approaches to leadership theory are:

- trait theory (assumes that leadership qualities are innate),
- style theory (links organizational effectiveness to the balance between the leader's concern for production and concern for people),
- contingency theory (links traits and style to the situation),
- path-goal theory (links subordinates' motivation and task demands to style),
- transformational theory (highlights the leader's role in empowering employees).

15 There is virtually *no* evidence to suggest that:

- job satisfaction affects productivity, or,
- that highly committed employees perform better, or,
- that leadership personality, style or behaviour influences organizational effectiveness.

16 There is, however, evidence linking satisfaction and commitment to other positive behaviours and vice versa.

17 On balance, behavioural theories of management are probably oversold.

18 Behavioural theories reflect linear intuitive thinking patterns which obscure other factors notably:

- the negative aspects of motivation, satisfaction, commitment and transformational leadership, and,
- reciprocal influences between leaders and the led.

19 Behavioural theories of management also assume that individuals control performance.

20 Critical theorists suggest that behavioural research serves mainly to legitimize the idea of managers as impartial experts.

21 Critical theorists argue that behavioural theories of management:

- reproduce current values,
- legitimize existing forms of control, and,
- reproduce existing power relations.

22 Critical theorists argue that leadership theory celebrates and reaffirms masculine values. The literature understates:

- environmental and organizational constraints,
- the symbolic significance of leadership, and,
- the leader's own subjugation.

23 Critical theorists argue that much productive effort is wasted in turning out goods and services of little worth.

Questions for Discussion

1 'No one could suspect that times were coming . . . when the man who did not gamble would lose all the time, even more surely than he who gambled.'

(C. W. Mills, *White Collar*, citing Peguy)

How does this quotation resonate with the subject matter of the present chapter?

2 Consider the following text of a job advertisement:

JOB ADVERTISEMENT

Lending Banker

City Centre Competitive Salary + Benefits

'Our distinctive flat management structure allows people to be innovative with autonomy and you will be genuinely encouraged to make your contribution to the further development of the bank.

'This is an ideal opportunity for you to build on your experience of dealing directly with clients, involving you in analysis of lending proposals . . . as well as liaising with external professionals including solicitors and valuers. You will also assume responsibility for the smooth running of the office in the absence of the Area Manager.'

Analyse the potential sources of job satisfaction implied by the advertisement.

3 'Clinical fascination lasts for about ten years. After that the vet's attitude becomes, "I want to make some money"'.

(Professor of veterinary medicine)

How far is this observation consistent with theories of motivation and job satisfaction?

4 Richard Branson is popularly regarded as an archetypal transformational leader. Yet Virgin Trains have yet to achieve a reputation for reliability.

How far is the performance of Virgin Trains consistent with the popular image of transformational leaders as the 'real movers and shakers of the world' (Bass 1990, p. 23)?

5 'Motivation is a "surrogate for meaning" in a world where experts dominate decisions about how organizations and jobs should be designed, and work frequently lacks any deeply valued meaning.' (Alvesson and Willmott 1996, p. 99)

Discuss.

6 'Do we know what doing work *feels* like?' (Fineman 1996, p. 547, italics in original)

Discuss.

7 'I meditate upon mankind's advancement
From flint sparks into million-volted glare
That shows us everything but the future—
And leaves us not much wiser than we were.'

      (Sassoon, 'Cleaning the Candelabrum')

How far is this also fair comment upon theories of motivation and leadership?

Further Reading

- Alvesson, M. and Billing, Y. D. (1997) *Understanding Gender and Organizations*, London, Sage.

- Alvesson, M. and Willmott, H. (1996) *Making Sense of Management*, London, Sage.

- Bryman, A. (1992) *Charisma and Leadership in Organisations*, London, Sage.

- Knights, D. and Willmott, H. (1992) 'Conceptualizing Leadership Processes: A Study of Senior Managers in a Financial Services Company', *Journal of Management Studies*, 29, 761–82.

- Meyer, J. P. and Allen, N. J. (1997) *Commitment in the Workplace: Theory Research and Application*, London, Sage.

- Northouse, P. (1997) *Leadership: Theory and Practice*, London, Sage.

- Randall, D. M. (1987) 'Commitment and the Organization Man Revisited', *Academy of Management Review*, 12, 460–71.

Chapter 4
Total Quality Management

The human being exhibits an instinctive drive for precision, beauty and perfection. When unrestrained by economics, this drive has created the art treasures of the ages.

(Juran 1974)

Defect means only a result lying outside a specified range. The product can still be rubbish, but it must be consistent rubbish. As someone put it in the Spice Girls' film *Spice World*, 'that was perfect, girls, without actually being any good'.

(Jackson 1998)

'The goods come back, but not the customer.'
(Deming 1986)

IMAGINE taking your place in an examination hall. Shortly after you begin writing your new pen drys up. You shake it. Ink sputters over your hands and smears the script. You write another line or two. The pen sputters more ink. The pen scratches out a few more words. Then it fails altogether. Five minutes have been lost. You raise your hand hoping that an invigilator will see you and provide an instant replacement. Another minute ticks by.

You have just become the victim of a quality failure. The issue is important because quality management techniques are increasingly used by organizations to achieve a competitive lead. Moreover 'total quality management' and lean production systems demand more from employees than the behavioural models of management described in Chapter 2. The purpose of this chapter is twofold. First, to describe recent changes in manufacturing techniques and philosophy. Second to consider the implications of those changes for Organization Behaviour. The issues discussed in this chapter include:

Key Issues

- What is 'total quality management'?
- Why is time now a competitive weapon?
- Why re-engineering?
- Modern times—but does the ghost of F. W. Taylor walk?
- Is 'the customer' always right?

4.1 What is 'Total Quality Management'?

TOTAL quality management is a business philosophy orientated towards achieving customer satisfaction (Cordon 1995, Deming 1986, Juran 1974, Ishikawa 1985). For example:

The business process starts with the customer. In fact if it is not started with the customer, it all too often ends with the customer. (Scherkenbach 1986, p. 1)

One of the most influential proponents of 'total quality management' was Edwards Deming (1900–1994). Deming was a statistician by training. He worked in the USA in the manufacturing industry. Deming's experience prompted him to challenge a basic assumption of USA manufacturing management. This assumption held that quality and productivity are incompatible. Deming tried to persuade industrialists to improve the quality of their products. It was the early 1950s, however, and American industry was prospering. There was no incentive to change and so Deming's ideas were largely ignored.

Japan's outlook was very different. The Japanese economy had been devastated by the Second World War and Japanese industrialists were receptive to Deming's ideas. In the 1950s the statement 'made in Japan' signified 'poor quality'. Now Japanese cars, washing machines, 'hi-fi' systems and the like are popularly regarded as the epitome of quality and reliability. The transformation of Japanese industry posed a serious competitive threat to other manufacturing nations. Significantly Deming's best-known work published in 1986 is called *Out of the Crisis*.

Deming begins by blaming senior American managers for allowing their manufacturing industry to fall into crisis. Top management, says Deming, failed to anticipate and meet customer requirements. Concern for short-term profits took priority over innovation and long-run viability. Moreover, according to Deming, employees are responsible for fewer than 15 per cent of production mistakes. The remainder are attributable to bad management.

Pause for reflection

Specify the attributes of a quality student notepad.

4.2 Deming's Fourteen Points of Management

DEMING'S prescriptions are summarized in his so-called 'Fourteen Points' of management listed in Figure 4.1.

Each of Deming's points is now explained in turn.

Figure 4.1 Deming's 'Fourteen points of management'

1. Create constancy of purpose for improvement of product and service.

2. Adopt the new philosophy.

3. Cease dependence upon mass inspection.

4. End the practice of awarding business on the basis of price tag alone.

5. Improve constantly and forever the system of production and service.

6. Institute training.

7. Adopt and institute leadership.

8. Drive out fear.

9. Break down barriers between staff areas.

10. Eliminate slogans, exhortations and targets for the work force.

11a. Eliminate numerical quotas for the work force.
11b. Eliminate numerical goals for people in management.

12. Remove barriers that rob people of pride of workmanship.

13. Encourage education and self-improvement for everyone.

14. Take action to accomplish the transformation.

4.2.1 'Create constancy of purpose for improvement of product and service'

Deming urges organizations to cultivate deep-rooted specialist competence. According to Deming, such competence is the foundation of excellence whereas opportunism is counterproductive. He cites the case of a furniture manufacturer who decided to diversify:

> Why not make pianos? [So] They bought a Steinway piano, took it apart, made or bought parts, and put a piano together exactly like the Steinway, only to discover they could only get thuds out of their product. So they put the Steinway piano back together with the intention to get their money back on it, only to discover that it too would now only make thuds. (Deming 1986, p. 129)

Deming exhorts organizations to identify a mission. Mere goal setting is insufficient, however. Managers must also plan how those aims will be achieved and identify the methods to be deployed. Such methods must optimize every part of the system. Anything less, says Deming, implies a loss to every component in the system. Moreover, planning must envisage five- and even ten-year timescales.

4.2.2 'Adopt the new philosophy'

In Deming's view defective products and poor service are:

- expensive, and,
- unnecessary.

Defects are expensive because they imply scrap, reworking, administrative costs and possibly legal suits and product recalls. Defects are unnecessary because they are almost invariably a product of the system, for example, inadequate knowledge, unsuitable materials, and communications failures.

Systems can be improved. Improvement, however, takes a long time. Deming argues that so-called 'fast tracking' career structures whereby managers expect to spend only two to three years in a job undermine organizations because they provide little incentive to initiate change. Indeed, they may actively discourage managers from addressing problems for fear of damaging their careers.

4.2.3 'Cease dependence upon mass inspection'

Quality, says Deming, cannot be inspected into goods and services. If defects can only be prevented by inspection then the process is incapable of meeting requirements.

Moreover, chains of inspectors can actually create defects because responsibility is diffused. For example, would you rather jump from a parachute which:

- has been passed by ten factory inspectors, or,
- has been inspected once, by the person who made it?

Inspection also costs money. (See the discussion on transaction costs in section 2.1.3). For instance, in 1925 the Hawthorne plant in the USA employed 46,000 people. Of these, no fewer than 11,500 (25 per cent) were inspectors (Deming 1993).

Pause for reflection

You have been entrusted with the task of selecting contract caterers for a club celebration.

1. On what criteria will you base your decision?
2. What employee relations policies and procedures will you look for among prospective contractors?

4.2.4 'End the practice of awarding business on the basis of price tag alone'

Deming sees suppliers as a vital part of the quality system. Deming urges organizations to cultivate long-term relationships with suppliers founded upon mutual trust and understanding. For example, Deming might have applauded the former Pullman Company's relationship with its catering suppliers:

There was loyalty to suppliers and accounts were paid promptly. In return no matter what happened the cars had to be supplied and a continuity of service was as important as the quality and price of the supplies. (Morel 1983, p. 164)

Pressurizing suppliers to cut prices merely tempts them to reduce their specifications, suggests Deming. Moreover, the price of supplies is only one factor in the equation. What counts is the overall cost. For example, supplies which are difficult to process increase expense.

Deming advocates single source suppliers. Fewer suppliers mean lower administrative costs. The risk of late deliveries and stockouts is reduced because single sourcing facilitates communication between supplier and purchaser and deeper knowledge of one another's needs and problems. Besides, says Deming, variation creates enough problems when only one supplier is involved. For instance, components may be technically excellent yet perform unpredictably in the production process or in the finished goods, 'Material from two suppliers would drive us out of our wits' (Deming 1986, p. 35).

Deming opposes using detailed criteria manuals to select suppliers. Far better, says Deming, to concentrate upon three essentials as follows:

1. The supplier's record for product development.
2. The supplier's commitment to research and development.
3. The supplier's general quality system.

4.2.5 'Improve constantly and forever the system of production and service'

The notion of continuous improvement is central to Deming's philosophy. Why not, argues Deming, why repeat mistakes? Every hotel built, for example, should be an improvement upon the previous one.

'Total quality management' comprises two strands namely:

1. quality of design, and,
2. quality of conformity to design.

Goods and services can only fulfil expectations if they are well designed to begin with. For example, poorly designed electrical systems in cars can trigger faults which are virtually impossible to rectify. Likewise, a hotel with poor sound proofing, slow 'check out' facilities and lacking office amenities in rooms is unlikely to satisfy business travellers even though the service is friendly and attentive. Deming suggests that the greatest potential for quality improvement usually rests in the product or service design. Forget the competition, says Deming. Instead of trying to emulate competitors, concentrate upon the customer and their needs.

The competitive advantage which accrues from a good design is lost if the design is badly produced. For instance, poor building quality will destroy the pleasure of the best designed house or sports car. Likewise, immaculate service in a restaurant cannot compensate for food poisoning.

Deming suggests that 'total quality management' is less to do with meeting specifications and more about reducing variability through improving the production processes to make them faster, cheaper and more reliable.

4.2.6 'Institute training'

Deming argues that organizations make too many assumptions about what people know and can do. Deming sees it as particularly important that employees thoroughly understand the context in which they work. Deming suggests dispensing with conventional organization charts which, he argues, only describe accountability. Organizations should replace these with system charts which show employees:

- what their jobs are, and,
- how their work interacts with other parts of the organization (Deming 1993).

For instance, it is one thing to instruct an employee to wash a table. If, however, the employee knows what the table is to be used for (a meeting, a meal, a surgical operation), they will be able to appreciate the standard of cleanliness required and respond accordingly (Deming 1993).

4.2.7 'Adopt and institute leadership'

'The job of management is not supervision, but leadership,' states Deming (1986 p. 54). According to Deming, organizations emphasize control at the expense of leadership. Deming calls for highly specific and highly challenging qualities of leadership. Deming (1993) prescribes managements' duties in 'fourteen points' of leadership (see Figure 4.2).

The points reflect three themes namely:

1. Knowledge as a basis for authority.
2. Developing interpersonal relations.
3. Cooperation not competition.

Deming urges managers to concentrate upon improving the system instead of blaming individuals for mistakes. For example, an organization which buys supplies of wood from abroad lost £50,000 because of currency fluctuations. Through discussion and analysis the purchasing director realized that the organization's treasury department could arrange to hedge the risk thus preventing future losses.

Furthermore, says Deming, focusing upon outcomes, ('management by objectives' for example), is counterproductive. Leaders, says Deming, should acquire in-depth knowledge about the work they supervise and foster cooperation and personal development. Above all, leaders should devote themselves to translating vision into action.

4.2.8 'Drive out fear'

According to Deming, many organizations are managed by fear. Fear of dismissal, for example. Fear, says Deming, is a substitute for planning and analysis. Moreover, reliance upon fear is counterproductive because it creates insecurity. Insecurity drives employees to concentrate upon obeying rules and to manipulate the system rather than making worthwhile and enduring improvements.

Deming opposes treating labour as a commodity. Redundancies, says Deming, generate short-term savings. The price, however, is longer term demoralization. The challenge to organizations, suggests Deming, is to find work for their employees.

Figure 4.2 Deming's 'Fourteen points of leadership'

1. To understand and promulgate the meaning of the system as a whole.

2. To facilitate understanding and cooperation among organization members.

3. To recognize individual differences and to create interest and challenge in work for everyone.

4. To engage in unceasing learning and to encourage learning in its broadest sense.

5. To coach and counsel but not to judge.

6. To understand system dynamics.

7. To develop knowledge and personal skills as a basis of power thus avoiding reliance upon authority.

8. To study results to improve performance as a manager of people.

9. To offer special help where needed.

10. To create trust and an environment which encourages freedom and innovation.

11. To resist insistence upon perfection.

12. To listen and learn without passing judgement.

13. To hold informal, spontaneous, non-judgemental meeting with employees at least once a year in order to develop an understanding of their concerns and aspirations.

14. To understand the benefits of cooperation and the costs of competition.

4.2.9 'Break down barriers between staff areas'

Deming argues that organizational departments must understand each other's needs and constraints. For example, the most minute difference in supplies can cause enormous variations in manufacture. Purchasing staff must therefore appreciate the importance of consulting production managers before making changes. Likewise designers need to communicate continuously with sales and production staff in order to ensure that their innovations meet customers' needs, and that they can be manufactured effectively.

Cross-functional teams provide the mechanism for communication and problem solving. Deming suggests that such teams should include both:

- staff with access to the requisite data, and,
- those who are critical in implementing the solutions developed.

The aim of such integration, suggests Deming, is not to suppress conflict but to enable it to be resolved in the organization's best interests. Cross-functional collaboration requires appropriate cultures and structures. Without these, says Deming, training programmes are worthless.

4.2.10 'Eliminate slogans, exhortations and targets for the work force'

Deming regards managerial slogans, exhortations and targets as evidence of leadership failure. Deming argues that if the systems are good and staff properly coached and trained, then entreaties to work harder and to make fewer mistakes are unnecessary.

4.2.11 'Eliminate numerical quotas for the work force'

Deming strongly opposes numerical performance targets and especially piecework. Piecework, says Deming, is an incentive to produce scrap and destroys pride of workmanship. Promoting pride in work automatically prompts operatives to improve the system. Creating such pride says Deming, is the most difficult part of improving quality.

Piecework is also costly to administer. According to Deming many factories employ more engineers on constructing work standards than in actual production. Moreover, says Deming, work study targets reflect the average worker. Yet statistically, half of the work force will perform above average and half below average. Peer pressure will restrict above-average performers from producing to their full potential, while below-average performers will struggle to meet standards.

Far from reducing ambiguity (see section 2.3.7), numerical targets actually create it, says Deming. For example, an airline employee is required to answer the telephone, make reservations and supply information. The stipulated target is to receive twenty-five calls per hour. The employee is also expected to exercise courtesy and not rush the customer:

She is continually plagued by obstacles: (a) the computer is slow in delivery of information that she asks for; (b) it sometimes reports no information, whereupon she is forced to use directories and guides. Christine, what is your job? Is it:

To make 25 calls per hour?

or,

To give callers courteous satisfaction; no brush off?

It can not be both. (Deming 1986, p. 73, italics in original)

Deming argues that statistical data is the only reliable basis for analysing and monitoring performance. Either a worker's performance is within statistical control or it is not, says Deming. Likewise cross-functional teams are encouraged to utilize such data to analyse problems objectively as distinct from merely seeking scapegoats.

Deming states that the only permissible numerical targets are those based upon fact, such as, 'Unless sales can be increased by 10 per cent, we shall be out of business next year,' and 'The law requires us to limit carbon dioxide emissions to 1 per cent.'

Pause for reflection

A factory assembles single fluorescent tubes.

1. How would you attempt to instil pride of workmanship?
2. Would your approach differ if the work involved assembling sophisticated electronic light systems for offices?

4.2.12 'Eliminate numerical goals for people in management'

Deming also opposes the practice of imposing performance targets upon managers. Deming argues that schemes such as merit rating and performance related pay are counterproductive because they:

- reward employees for manipulating the system rather than improving it,
- undermine team working by breeding competition and selfishness, and,
- are potentially unfair because performance can be affected by factors beyond an individual's control.

According to Deming, numerical targets are substitutes for management. A more productive alternative suggests Deming is for organizations to exercise meticulous care over selecting leaders and then to educate them in their obligations. Leaders' obligations include functioning as colleagues rather than judges. Leaders, moreover, should conduct annual three to four hour long interviews with staff aimed at providing support and encouragement. Organizations should also endeavour to accommodate employees who prefer to work alone rather than in teams.

Deming accepts that some extrinsic motivation is necessary in order to build esteem. His argument is that complete reliance upon performance related pay is destructive because it forces employees to manipulate the system to glean the reward as no other source of motivation exists (Deming 1993).

4.2.13 'Remove barriers that rob people of pride of workmanship'

Employees have a right to take pride in work and to do a good job, says Deming. Performance rating is the biggest obstacle to enabling pride of workmanship for salaried staff. Shop floor workers are even worse off, suggests Deming. They are treated like commodities and more exposed to managerial deficiencies than their salaried counterparts.

Such deficiencies include:

- confusion over what constitutes acceptable workmanship,
- supervisors with inadequate product knowledge, and,
- inadequate technical support.

For example, shop floor workers often work under pressure to meet quotas. They are instructed to 'run it' that is, turn out defective products. They may be hampered by cheap tools, poor machines, shortages of components and inadequate instructions and training. Moreover, says Deming, managers who insist that operatives are not paid to highlight such problems merely compound the sense of frustration. Likewise, many employee involvement programmes are substitutes for management because they avoid the real issues.

Professional and managerial staff experience similar problems, says Deming. For example, some companies allow their executives to arrive at their destination exhausted rather than pay full fares for more convenient flights. Deming regards such practices as 'penny wise, pound foolish'.

4.2.14 'Encourage education and self-improvement for everyone'

Deming argues that organizations require both good people and improving people. Deming encourages organizations to invest heavily in job-related training. Non-job related education, says Deming, is even more important, 'People require in their careers, more than money, ever-broadening opportunities to add something to society, materially or otherwise' (Deming 1986, p. 86).

4.2.15 'Take action to accomplish the transformation'

Deming's fourteenth point is a prescription for implementing the other thirteen. Deming urges organizations to proudly adopt the new philosophy, and, to communicate its implications to everyone in the organization. Deming sees improvement as a cyclical process. He urges organizations to begin reforming those activities with the greatest potential for improvement. Organizations are encouraged to adopt an experimental approach to change with careful pre-testing of developments and/or implementation upon a small scale. The results should then be studied. What was learned? What can be predicted? Informed by this new knowledge and understanding, the cycle of improvement is repeated in perpetuity. Deming emphasizes that patience is required. Real transformation can take five years or more to accomplish.

4.2.16 Inter-relations between the fourteen points

Deming stresses that his fourteen points are interdependent and complementary. For example, the award of single supplier status also reduces fear. Long-term security encourages suppliers to innovate, improve and develop their knowledge. Conversely a failure of one point may jeopardize the others. For instance, numerical targets not only generate fear, they can undermine an employee's performance. Communication, says Deming, is more effective than managing by fear. Employees need to understand what constitutes a mistake and its consequences. Although Deming advocates statistical process monitoring he emphasizes that information is not synonymous with knowledge. Deming urges organizations to cultivate what he calls 'profound knowledge' (Deming 1993).

> **Pause for reflection**
> Imagine a conversation between Edwards Deming and F. W. Taylor.
> What might they have said to one another?

4.3 New Wave Manufacturing

O**RGANIZATIONS** which have achieved a substantial lead in quality are increasingly seeking process refinements aimed at minimizing cost and enhancing flexibility. Let me now describe these developments.

4.3.1 Time-based competition

Time, it is said, is more than money. It has become a competitive weapon in its own right (Blackburn 1991, Stalk 1988, Stalk and Hout 1990). According to Stalk and Hout, quartering the time taken to produce goods and services doubles the yield of labour and working capital which can mean cost reductions as high as 20 per cent.

Time-based competition focuses upon eliminating waste. Waste is any operation which does not add value. For instance, searching for library books or queuing for access to a computer adds no value to study. Study would be more efficient if such operations could be eliminated. Likewise the time taken to position a drill or set up a machine represents only cost and never value. The same applies to holding stocks, transportation, storage and administration.

The aim of so called 'just-in-time' (JIT) production is to coordinate manufacturing so that supplies and partially processed assemblies arrive at the precise moment they are needed. 'Just-in-time' is sometimes known as 'making today, what is needed tomorrow' (Drummond 1992, Ohno and Mito 1988, Shingo 1988, Voss 1987). Whereas previously goods were made and stored in warehouses until sold, 'just-in-time' production aims to manufacture goods rapidly to order.

Time-based competition is also seen in product design. Today's airplanes, washing machines, and cars, contain less than half the number of components of older models. Screws and sub-assemblies have given way to 'clip on' modules. The underlying aim is to achieve simplicity. Simple designs are easier, and therefore quicker and cheaper to manufacture, and, more reliable in service (Schonberger 1982, 1986).

4.3.2 Flexible manufacturing

Taylor's principles of 'scientific management' assume long production runs of standardized products. Conventional manufacturing is predicated upon the assumption that product variety and cheapness are incomparable (Stalk 1988). By contrast, flexible manufacturing techniques aim to deliver a range of products quickly (Garud and Kotha 1994).

Conventional mass production utilizes large complex dedicated machines designed for speed and long production runs. Machines are manned by operatives in fixed positions, recruited and trained to fit specific jobs. By contrast 'just-in-time' and flexible manufacturing systems typically utilize small, inexpensive and relatively simple machines capable of producing a variety of items. Such machines are often mounted upon wheels so that they can be moved around and configured as required. The criteria for purchase has also changed. Return upon investment (ROI) calculations have given way to the question of whether a particular item of equipment is necessary to maintain competitive viability (Anderson, Manus, and Schroeder 1994).

4.3.3 Implications for employees

New manufacturing techniques imply different working practices. Whereas mass production brings the work to employees, new techniques typically involve employees moving to the work. Functional specialization has given way to contracts requiring employees to undertake a variety of tasks according to process demands, helping one another and going home when the day's orders are complete or staying behind to cope with demand. Whereas 'scientific management' involved 'de-skilling', new competitive strategies rely upon multi-skilling. Operatives may be required to undertake preventative maintenance and simple repairs to machinery in order to minimize stoppages and the cost of employing technicians and engineers (Drummond 1992, Shingo 1988, Ohno 1988). Likewise crafts' operatives may be trained to undertake a variety of tasks such as painting, joinery and plumbing.

4.3.4 Business process re-engineering

Business process re-engineering claims to go beyond the elimination of waste to redefining the purposes and principles upon which business is based. The so-called 're-engineering movement' was heralded by the publication in 1990 in the *Harvard Business Review* of an article by Michael Hammer entitled 'Re-engineering work: don't automate, obliterate'. It was followed in 1993 by Michael Hammer and John Champy's *Reengineering the Cooperation* which became one of the best-selling books of the 1990s. The authors made dramatic claims for re-engineering:

Reengineering is the *fundamental* rethinking and *radical* re-design of business *processes* to achieve *dramatic* improvements in critical, contemporary measures of performance, such as cost quality, service and speed. (p. 46, italics in original)

According to Hammer and Champy their message contained the most profound insights since Adam Smith's *Wealth of Nations* (see section 2.1.1). Whereas the first Industrial Revolution involved a transfer of power which brought people into factories, the so called re-engineering revolution promised to 'Profoundly rearrange the way people conceive of themselves, their work, their place in society' (Hammer and Stanton 1995, p. 321).

Re-engineering basically involves starting with a clean sheet. For example, instead of trying to improve product packaging, re-engineering involves questioning the need for packaging in the first place. More fundamentally, business process re-engineering dispenses with conventional bureaucracy. Instead the organization is designed around key business processes. Re-engineering basically involves:

- identification,
- analysis, and,
- simplification

of work processes. Whereas 'total quality management' emphasizes process enhancement, process re-engineering is more orientated to abandoning existing processes altogether and substituting new ones. (For more technical descriptions of the technique see Davenport 1993, and Johanasson et al. 1993).

Re-engineering is described as a search for new models of work, from industrialized simplicity to combining several jobs into one, that is, 'From simple tasks to multi-dimensional work' (Hammer and Champy 1993 p. 68) and from linear processing to simultaneous task accomplishment. Whereas both 'scientific management' and 'total quality management' stress 'one best way', re-engineering assumes that processes may have multiple versions, that part of the challenge of work is to determine what works best in a given situation.

Re-engineering implies hybrid centralized or decentralized organizations and a move away from functional departments to process teams. Re-engineering envisages organizations devoid of controllers and inspectors. Instead, workers make decisions working with minimal checks and controls. Case managers provide a single point of contact.

Re-engineering involves dispensing with organizational hierarchies by empowering employees to do more. The argument is that process re-engineering enhances worker satisfaction because it facilitates a sense of completion and accomplishment. Since workers perform a whole job, or a whole process or sub-process:

That by definition produces a result that somebody cares about. Process performers share many of the challenges of entrepreneurs. They are focused upon customers whose satisfaction is their aim. They're not just trying to keep the boss happy or to work through bureaucracy. (Hammer and Champy 1993, p. 69)

Re-engineering means eliminating layers of management. Those that remain are reduced to three functions as follows:

1. *Work engineer* (called process owner), dedicated to product design and compiling work orders.
2. *Coach*, dedicated to developing people.
3. *Leader*, dedicated to motivating staff and to creating an environment conducive to task accomplishment.

The suggestion is that this is radically different from the traditional view of management.

> **Pause for reflection**
> Would you rather work for F. W. Taylor or Edwards Deming?

4.3.5 The wider literature

You may have noticed that there is no shortage of books on the subject of 'quality'. I have chosen to focus upon Deming as his approach embraces both technical and humanistic elements. Other leading proponents of 'total quality management' (Shingo 1989, Juran 1988, Taguchi 1981, Crosby 1979, Peters and Waterman 1982) tend to emphasize one or the other.

That is not to suggest that the purely technical works are devoid of interest. For example, Shingo (1989) describes how Toyota designed their production systems to minimize the possibility of human error and to reduce the need for control. The so called Poka-Yoke system emphasizes production planning. Components for assembly can be designed, for instance, so that only the correct positioning will fit. Similarly, if ten items are to be assembled to form a product, the production system is designed to pass ten items to the operative (note the language of robotics incidentally). If the operative finds they have one item left over on completion of the task it is immediately obvious that a mistake has been made. The operative can then rectify the mistake before the error multiplies. Although much has been said in the present text about the limitations of mechanistic thinking, Poka-Yoke systems are an example of how effectiveness and indeed safety can be engineered into organizations. They may not eliminate human error but they can reduce the risk by a significant margin.

Taguchi's ideas on design are fascinating (Taguchi 1981, Taguchi and Wu 1985, Taguchi and Clausing 1990). (Do not worry about the mathematics, concentrate upon the ideas.) Whereas the 'total quality management' literature enjoins organizations to design for customer satisfaction, Taguchi's ideas are more specific. Taguchi suggests:

design quality is inversely proportional to loss.

Loss means the total cost of a product or service to the consumer. For example, a computer that has a higher power consumption imparts a greater loss than one with lower power consumption. A shirt that requires ironing imparts a greater loss than one which does not. The doctor or dentist who keeps a patient waiting imparts a greater loss than one with an accurate appointments system. A poorly indexed book imparts a greater loss to the reader than one which has been well produced.

> **Pause for reflection**
> How would you design a ruler to minimize loss?

Taguchi urges designers to design in order to minimize loss. For example, energy saving light bulbs which are increasingly being used in hotels and public buildings may have been inspired by Taguchi's philosophy. Interestingly, Taguchi argues that certain losses are scandalous, notably when manufacturers reduce specifications by a small amount in order to save money:

When a thief steals 10,000 yen the victim loses 10,000 yen so there is neither a gain nor loss to the whole society. But when the mid-value (of the tolerance level) is moved, the manufacturer imparts a larger loss, say a 20,000 yen loss—to consumers in order to make a 10,000 yen profit. (Taguchi, 1981, p.7)

Another important contribution to the 'total quality management' literature is Peters and Waterman's (1982) *In Search of Excellence*. The so-called excellence literature is discussed in more detail in section 9.3. Here it is sufficient to note that Peters and Waterman stress the importance of organizational culture and the inculcation of appropriate values among the workforce. According to Peters and Waterman sub-liminal performance is achieved through 'love of the product' which can in turn be created by charisma, inspiration and the promulgation of vision.

The pursuit of excellence is an attractive notion. Too attractive some would say. Unlike say Crosby (1979) who stresses control of variation but disguises it in a human-istic gloss, Peters and Waterman do not burden their readers with the more instru-mental aspects of product quality. Theirs is a dream culture of 'easy excellence' which stresses 'management by walking around' signifying appreciation, and kind-ling excitement. We shall see in section 9.3, however, that the excellence literature has a darker side.

4.4 Back to Scientific Management

'TOTAL quality management' and related techniques can be seen as a kind of 'second coming', almost as radical as Taylor's approach was in its day. The over-arching difference between Taylor and Deming's approach to management is that Taylor's is rooted in mechanistic thinking whereas Deming mixes metaphors. More specifically, Deming views organizational effectiveness as a combination of culture and control. In common with the 'excellence' literature (e.g. Peters and Waterman 1982), Deming stresses the role of transformational leadership in creating a 'quality' culture.

The combination of metaphorical perspectives may result in a more holistic view of organizational effectiveness than Taylor's. Yet it also poses a contradiction. What is unclear is how organizations are expected to deal with the tension implied by mixing metaphors. Transformational leadership rests heavily upon charisma (see section 3.4.5). Charisma is by definition an unstable force. Charismatic leaders are dis-tinguished by their ability to move people and organizations. Yet if 'total quality management' relies so heavily upon process control and careful adherence to procedure, what is there for transformational leaders to transform?

Charisma is also difficult to sustain. Organizations may discover that emblems such as 'obsession with quality,' and 'passion for quality' soon degenerate into empty slogans. The poster on the wall exhorting employees to better efforts may be all that is left of the impetus to reform.

Obviously it is partly a question of degree. Deming's vision of leadership centres upon coaching and personal development, not holding mass rallies in town squares. Even so, many organizations with a reputation for quality rely upon transactional approaches in order to sustain motivation and compliance. For example, a leading supermarket chain operates a structured programme of training and performance monitoring for its new staff. Staff receive instruction in a variety of roles, checkout operation, stocks, customer assistance and so forth. The achievement of specific levels of competency is matched with specific financial rewards. Tenure is also rewarded by a concessionary purchasing allowance of forty pounds a month. The latter stops many a restless employee seeking work elsewhere, 'It's a lot to lose,' said one woman. The Personnel Officer was less sanguine, however. 'You can't do anything off your own bat (initiative),' they said, 'you just get handed a package, "Go and do it."'

4.4.1 Deming and Taylor compared

Radical means 'going to the root'. Are Deming's ideas as radical as they seem? Deming uses different language from Taylor. Yet many of Deming's ideas resonate 'scientific management'. Figure 4.3 summarizes the points of correspondence:

Both Taylor and Deming purport to challenge fundamental assumptions of management. Taylor invokes the notion of 'mental revolution'. Deming uses the language of 'transformation'. Both Taylor and Deming are highly prescriptive and inflexible in their approach to management. Indeed, Deming's so called 'fourteen points' are expressed as imperatives (Anderson, Manus, and Schroeder 1994). Each begins with an instruction, for example, 'improve', 'remove' 'drive out'.

Taylor has been described as an obsessive and compulsive personality. The text of Deming's *Out of the Crisis* is punctuated with biblical references. What is their significance? Was Deming infused with a sense of self-righteousness? Was he trying to dignify work or using religious piety to mask economic exploitation?

Why 'fourteen' points of management and leadership respectively? Is it a coincidence that President Woodrow Wilson's suggestions for maintaining peace and harmony between nations following the devastation of the First World War were expressed in 'fourteen points'?

Both Deming and Taylor emphasize top managements' responsibility for initiating change. Although Deming pays more attention to the humanistic aspects of organiza-

---

Figure 4.3 'Scientific management' and 'Total quality management' compared

Emphasis upon transformation.

Emphasis upon top managements' responsibilities.

Emphasis upon controlling variation.

Emphasis upon systematically collected data as a basis for process control.

Emphasis upon best practice techniques.

Emphasis upon training and development.

tion than Taylor, he still assumes a division between managers and the managed. Deming like Taylor focuses upon managing other people's work.

Taylor regarded engineering as the key to organizational efficiency. Likewise Deming sees variability as a central problem of process management (Waldman 1994). Both emphasize the virtues of:

- a scientific approach to work and process improvement,
- systematically collected data as a basis for control, and,
- best practice techniques.

Taylor devoted himself to identifying optimal tools and techniques. Deming criticizes organizations for supplying cheap tools and other false economies. Taylor promulgated the 'one best way'. Deming likewise stresses process control. Taylor, for example, observed that, 'Neglecting to take the time and trouble to thoroughly standardize methods and details is one of the chief causes of setbacks and failure . . . It is uniformity that is required.' (Taylor 1947 p. 123).

The Mazda company has a good reputation for the quality of its products. Mazda's training manual states:

For all the work we perform in the workshop, a work procedure sheet has been provided . . . If the operator changes the work procedure . . . he may put the process . . . in jeopardy or increase the cost . . . Therefore, the operator should always observe the specified procedure faithfully. (Delbridge and Turnbull 1992, p. 62)

Taylor would surely have approved.

Both Taylor and Deming regard learning as important. Taylor, however, saw learning as confined to training employees for task execution. Deming emphasizes both process knowledge and wider education.

4.4.2 Taylor and Deming contrasted

Figure 4.4 shows how Taylor and Deming's ideas differ.

Figure 4.4 Taylor and Deming contrasted

Taylor	Deming
Instrumental leadership	Visionary leadership
Extrinsic motivation	Intrinsic motivation
Adversarial	Cooperation

Deming stresses transformational leadership with an emphasis upon charisma born of knowledge, consideration for people and intellectual stimulation. Taylor, by contrast, views the ideal leadership style as transactional (see section 3.5.5). Although both regard knowledge as the basis for authority, Taylor translates knowledge into monitoring and control. Deming, by contrast, views knowledge as the foundation of respect. Respect reduces the need for surveillance.

Taylor starts from the so-called 'Theory X' assumptions about motivation, whereas Deming proceeds from 'Theory Y' assumptions (see section 3.1). Deming argues that numerical control causes output restriction because it destroys motivation. Deming prefers to rely upon factors intrinsic to the work itself to motivate people, notably an assumed innate desire to produce good work. Furthermore, unlike Taylor, Deming acknowledges the limits of process engineering. He sees a link between organizational culture and pride in work.

Although Taylor recognized that efficiency requires interpersonal cooperation, arguably, his methods are calculated to engender conflict. For example, Taylor advocates individual performance rewards. Deming argues that such practices undermine customer service because they breed selfishness and friction. Deming regards competition as wasteful (Deming 1993).

4.5 Discussion

CLEARLY, 'total quality management' offers some new ideas. Whether those ideas have proved successful is unclear. Most of the evidence is anecdotal (Hackman and Wageman 1995). Without rigorous research controls it is uncertain whether improved organizational performance reflects 'total quality management' interventions or is due to other factors such as technology or currency fluctuations. Moreover, much depends upon how success is measured. Different measures can suggest very different conclusions.

4.5.1 'Total quality management' in practice

Another difficulty in assessing the effectiveness of 'total quality management' programmes is that organizations have implemented Deming's ideas selectively. The most commonly used 'total quality management' techniques in the USA are the formation of *ad hoc* problem-solving teams, training and competitive benchmarking (Hackman and Wageman 1995).

Benchmarking involves obtaining information about 'best practices' from other organizations in order to:

- assess customer requirements,
- learn about alternative work processes, and,
- guide the establishment of quality improvement goals.

Benchmarking has no place in Deming's ideas. Recall that Deming urges organizations to concentrate on the customer and ignore the competition.

Another prominent feature of 'total quality management' in the USA is employee involvement, whereby firms stage 'quality days' and celebrate quality related achievements. We shall see in Chapter 10 that symbols are important because they possess the power to move. Moreover, symbolic reward and recognition may stimulate involvement and motivation (see section 5.2.1). Recall, however, that Deming suggests involvement can become a substitute for rigorous attention to process management. Indeed evidence suggests that organizations rely more upon group processes and interpersonal skills to improve quality than process engineering (Hackman and Wageman 1995). This might mean that organizational references to 'objective' statistical control are largely rhetorical. Alternatively it could signify that Deming underestimates the importance of the human factor in achieving change.

4.5.2 Should organizations dispense with extrinsic motivators?

Many organizations claiming to practice 'total quality management' principles utilize quantitative performance measures. Such measures are usually linked to the achievement of specific quality goals. Although Deming opposes such practices, performance related rewards can enhance motivation, (see section 3.6.1). Indeed Iskikawa suggests that goal setting is potentially productive provided it:

- involves solving specific problems, and,
- those problems are defined in a manner consistent with cross-functional cooperation.

Significantly, Deming subsequently qualified his uncompromising stance on the issue. Deming (1993) suggests that some extrinsic motivation can build esteem. He argues that total reliance upon it is destructive because it means that the only source of motivation is to manipulate the system in order to obtain the reward.

Pause for reflection

A motor vehicle manufacturer sends a questionnaire to all customers who have bought new cars. The questionnaire requests feedback upon the standard of service provided by the dealer.

The results affect the dealer's bonus. The bonus constitutes a significant proportion of the dealer's profits.

The questionnaire is posted direct to the customer. The customer's name, address and purchase details are printed on the form. A pre-paid reply envelope is supplied.

Assume you are the dealer.

How would you try to maximize the bonus payment?

Deming would hardly have been surprised to learn that some dealers offer to help customers complete the questionnaire and offer a free tank of petrol in return for their cooperation. Likewise managers have been known to pay another organization to hold supplies, hide the cost in the accounts and then claim to have met their target of eliminating stocks (Zipkin 1991).

4.5.3 One best way?

Deming stresses pride in work and process control. The two factors are potentially incompatible. Pride in work implies job satisfaction. An important correlate of job satisfaction is autonomy (see section 3.3.8, and also Klein 1991). In theory, process control limits autonomy. A chef must always follow a recipe, for example. There is no room for a dash of spontaneous creativity. Likewise, a typical quality manual might contain over 3,000 procedures including document numbering systems, acceptance and rejection criteria for supplies, methods for checking and recording deliveries, rules for deleting obsolete documentation and so on.

In practice, there may be compensations. For instance, good tools, proper training and communication may reduce stress. A technician employed by a telecommunications company which implemented 'total quality management' said, 'Its great. You know exactly where everything is, and what you've got to do.'

Likewise, involving operatives in policy decisions concerning quality standards can imply another form of autonomy (Adler 1993).

Systematization can pose risks, however. It can lead to work being performed in a 'mindless' fashion (Langer 1989). The result can be costly mistakes or even dangerous if employees fail to notice subtle warnings. Moreover, when protocols fail, people typically apply them more vigorously rather than reflecting upon whether the protocols may have outlived their usefulness (Staw, Sandelands and Dutton, 1981).

4.5.4 Focus upon failure?

Improving existing products is cheaper and less risky than inventing new ones. Moreover, continued emphasis on improvement and problem solving can prevent a gradual deterioration in organizational performance and force managers to address problems before they become major crises.

It has been suggested, however, that 'total quality management' is reactive when a pro-active approach is required to stimulate innovation (Hackman and Wageman 1995). Improvement implies adaptive learning. It involves adjustment as distinct from experimenting with new possibilities. In rapidly developing industries such as electronics, product improvement can be like the canal owners of the eighteenth century trying to compete with the railways by raising speeds from four to ten miles per hour. Latterly Deming stressed the importance of design and innovation over the more technical aspects of quality. Organizations, says Deming (1993), depend upon their senior managers to design products and services which will attract customers and build a market. Moreover although it is important to listen to them, customers rarely anticipate requirements. It is for organizations to invent new possibilities. The guiding question says Deming, is, 'What product or service would help our customers more?' (1993, p. 10).

Achieving effective designs can pose issues of organizational culture and control. For example, evidence suggests that conventional bureaucratic organization hinders cross-functional integration (Lam 1996). Lam contrasts the rigid demarcation found in UK organizations (between designers and marketing, for instance), with examples from Japan where engineers are encouraged to become involved in general management including strategy formulation. Lam suggests that conventional hierarchical structures are ill-attuned to this purpose.

Bureaucracy may also limit the benefits which can be achieved from flexible manufacturing. Garud and Kotha (1994) have observed that many USA organizations misguidedly attempt to combine flexible production systems with Tayloristic principles of organization and control where self-organizing systems which emulate the human brain are required. (You may find it useful to turn back to Chapter 1 and in particular section 1.3.3 which explains how Garud and Kotha suggest invoking the human brain as a metaphor for production systems).

4.5.5 How much involvement?

'Total quality management' encourages employee involvement (Drummond 1992, Lawler 1994). In practice involvement is mainly confined to cross-functional teams operating at relatively senior levels. Participation in such teams may kindle excitement and motivation. Enhanced commitment can be counterproductive, however, if employees become overly attached their to innovations and subsequently seek to block change (see 3.6.1).

4.5.6 Leaner and meaner production?

The behavioural approach to management described in Chapter 2 was conceived in an era of mass production. The guiding premise was that 'scientific management' techniques failed to meet employees' social and psychological needs. Beneath the rhetoric new methods of production are potentially more demanding.

Few organizations claim to foster in-depth involvement at shop floor level. Shop floor employees are sometimes invited or required to suggest improvements. Wider reflection is rarely encouraged. It is doubtful whether such involvement enhances motivation. According to critical theorists it merely intensifies exploitation and subordination. Whereas Taylor was content to separate conception from execution, some applications of modern managerialism require shop floor operatives to contribute to activities associated with management and planning. In this view what appears as empowerment is actually subordination as it affords operatives little real decision making authority and may add to stress. The same applies to the increased responsibility and wider task demands implied by quick response manufacturing (see Cappelli and Rogovsky 1995, Dawson and Webb 1989, Drummond and Chell 1992, Graham 1993).

4.5.7 Supplier relations

'Total quality management' philosophy extends the traditional boundaries of Organization Behaviour. It requires organizations to integrate human resources management with strategic management, purchasing and process control.

It is unclear to what extent such integration is achieved in practice or is actually useful. Anecdotal evidence suggests that Deming's vision of organization/supplier relations is difficult to achieve in practice. Such are the dynamics of power relations that suppliers may experience purchasers' involvement as interference (see also section 5.5.4). Communication is sometimes seen as a smoke-screen for surveillance. Behind a veneer of cooperation coercion lurks (Drummond 1992).

Another feature of supplier relations concerns the replacement of traditional managerial control by simulated market control via cost centres and internal markets (Du Gay and Salaman 1992). For example, instead of referring patients to a consultant, general practitioners in the health service 'purchase' a consultant's services. Likewise, in local government, operational departments enter into service agreements for specialist services such as legal advice and personnel services. The existence of internal markets can undermine quality. For instance, Vesty (1998) has suggested that the number of mispronounced names on the BBC has risen because producers now have to pay for the service.

4.5.8 Business process re-engineering as inspired instrumentality?

Whatever the limitations of 'total quality management', business process re-engineering has yet to fulfil the claims made for it. Re-engineering's appeal seems to have been due more to rhetoric than substance. Jackson (1996) suggests that re-engineering appeals to masculine aggression. For example, men are invited to 'obliterate' and 'blast' their way through mighty obstacles.

In substance re-engineering places considerable faith in leaders to effect change (Willmott 1994). It assumes that managers can start from a 'clean sheet'. In practice, organizations are usually constrained to some extent by the past. Moreover, the notion of re-engineering management ignores the political reality of organizational life (see Chapter 6). Old approaches to management centred upon equity and performance obligations. 'A fair day's work for a fair day's pay', for example (Du Gay and Salaman 1992). New approaches stress added value. Employees are required to justify their employment by adding value to the product. Layers of management, by definition add cost rather than value. Yet evidence suggests managers have proved reluctant to engineer their own redundancy. As Willmott (1994) puts it, turkeys rarely vote for Christmas. Moreover, apparently few existing managers are able or willing to discharge their newly conceived functions (*The Wall Street Journal*, 1995, p. B1).

Far from being radical, the vision of leadership posed by advocates of re-engineering combines Taylor's emphasis upon process management and Deming's notions of charisma. Beneath the charisma re-engineering is basically 'scientific management' rescored in a different key.

For example, Adler's (1993) account of the revival of a failing USA car manu-facturing plant emphasizes the importance of strict standardization, combined with a limited 'no redundancies' policy intended to signify the organization's commitment to its staff. Whereas jobs were previously designed by engineers allegedly remote from the realities of the shop floor, these are now designed by workers themselves:

In radical contrast . . . team members themselves hold the stopwatch. They learn the techniques of work analysis, description and improvement. This change . . . has far-reaching implications for worker motivation and self-esteem. (Adler 1993, p. 103)

Critical theorists might be sceptical about Adler's claims to have created a 'learning orientated bureaucracy' (p. 108) where alienation has been supplanted by pride in work. They would argue that 'total quality management,' process re-engineering and related techniques perpetuate the assumption organizational effectiveness is a func-tion of engineering. Moreover, arguably modern manufacturing practices impose higher performance demands and require ever more intensive use of human resources. For example, in many organizations, work stations and equipment are ergonomically designed to facilitate maximum productive effort. Taylor enjoined workers to make every minute count (p. 132). Yet whereas Taylor's methods yielded forty-five seconds of motion per minute, modern plants extract fifty-seven seconds (see Adler 1993, Delridge and Turnbull 1992 p. 66).

How will market competition develop if engineers achieve sixty seconds of motion per minute?

4.5.9 'The customer is always right'?

It is probably fair to say that quality standards have improved over the last fifteen years or so. Cars are more reliable, railway companies are better at keeping passengers informed when delays occur, hotels are more punctilious about maintaining standards. Yet hardly a week goes by without a press announcement recalling a potentially dangerous product. There have been failures on a massive scale in cancer screening programmes. The insurance industry has spent years sorting out the effects of pensions mis-selling prompted by commission-hungry sales staff, and so it continues.

We shall see in section 6.4.7 that 'total quality management' initiatives may be symbolic rather than substantive. Here it is sufficient to note that Du Gay and Salaman (1992) suggest that customer responsiveness is actually a tool of control. Organizations use customer satisfaction questionnaires not so much to improve product or service quality but to monitor employees.

Yet the implication is that initiatives implemented in the name of the customer are *de facto* morally defensible (Du Gay and Salaman 1992, Grey and Mitev 1995). Arguably society benefits from quality goods and services. Yet there is a price to be paid. For example, some organizations are reported to receive 'just-in-time' deliveries every twenty minutes. We have yet to assess the environmental costs of lorries moving back and forth. Besides, what do we mean by quality? Does 'the customer' really require 250 varieties of personal stereos, twenty-four refrigerator colours to chose from (Stalk and Weber 1993)? What does society gain if manufacturing speed, scope and flexibility merely enhances our capacity to generate goods which cost more to sell than they do to produce (Morris 1934)?

Summary

1 'Total quality management' principles and philosophy are based upon the assumption that customer satisfaction is critical to sustained competitive viability.

2 An influential proponent of 'total quality management' was Edwards Deming. Deming urges organizations to take a long term view of profits.

3 The principal themes of Deming's philosophy are:

- transformational leadership,
- continuous improvement,
- process control,

- employee fulfilment and learning,
- internal and external cooperation.

4 Time-based competition and 'just-in-time' manufacturing techniques aim to eliminate waste and to increase flexibility.

5 Such developments imply a need for multi-skilled and semi-autonomous operatives.

6 Business process re-engineering involves dispensing with traditional bureaucratic structures and re-organizing around key business processes.

7 Some of Deming's ideas echo Taylor's approach to management. The main points of comparison are:
- the suggestion that fundamental change is required,
- the role of management,
- emphasis upon control of variation
- use of systematically collected data as a basis for control,
- use of best practice techniques, and,
- emphasis upon training.

8 The key points of contrast between Taylor and Deming's ideas are in their respective approaches to:
- leadership,
- motivation, and,
- cooperation.

9 The potential weaknesses of 'total quality management' include:
- loss of employee autonomy and consequent lowering of job satisfaction,
- misplaced reliance upon procedures,
- emphasis upon problem solving at the expense of innovation,
- over-commitment, and,
- intensified economic exploitation.

11 There are few reports of successful re-engineering initiatives.

12 Both 'total quality management' and process re-engineering assume that policies purporting to serve the customer are de facto morally defensible.

Questions for Discussion

1 Is it possible to distinguish between 'total quality management', new-wave manufacturing and 'scientific management'?

2 Does Deming demand the impossible when he urges managers to drive out fear from organizations? (You may find it helpful to consult Chapters 6, 9 and 10 before answering this question.)

3 Under privatization we are now responsible for the whole job including scheduling appointments, collecting the money and ordering parts. We are allowed thirty-eight minutes to do a job, not including travel time and people who are out when we call. I get nothing until the job's

done. That means, if I have to come back to fit a part—that all has to be done within the same thirty-eight minutes—ridiculous. . . . . The customers like it, they get a fantastic service. . . . . We get a productivity bonus of £3,000 a year if we meet our targets, but we can never meet them. You can't service a fire in less than an hour and a half—never mind thirty-eighty minutes including travel.

We have twelve staff in the central office now where there used to be nearly 100. They're all sitting there with long faces—nobody has a laugh any more.

They got rid of all their older staff to cut costs and then found they didn't have enough staff. Now they're training seventeen-year-olds to do in a year what it took me seven years to learn. It will be dangerous. A school leaver servicing a gas boiler, 'Oh I've never seen one of those (boilers) before.' (A gas heating technician)

Comment upon the technician's observations.

4 Should organizations dispense with performance related rewards?

5 In the UK some lorries carry a notice reading 'Well driven?' followed by a free telephone number.

What purposes do these notices serve?

6 In the UK dentists employed by the National Health Service (NHS) currently receive less than £5 for carrying out a clinical examination. Consider the following conversation between an harassed NHS practitioner and a dentist employed in private practice:

NHS Dentist: 'You charge £300 an hour! I'll bet you don't do many.'

Colleague: (Speaking thoughtfully), 'No, no I don't'.

What are the implications of existing NHS payment rates for quality of health care?

Further Reading

■ Deming, E. (1986) *Out of the Crisis*, Cambridge, Cambridge University Press.

■ Drummond, H. (1992) *The Quality Movement*, London, Kogan Page.

■ Du Gay, P. and Salaman, G. (1992) 'The (Cult)ure of the Customer', *Journal of Management Studies*, 29, 615–33.

■ Peters, T. and Waterman, R. H. (1982) *In Search of Excellence: Lessons from America's Best-run Companies*, New York, Harper & Row.

■ Stalk, G. (1988) 'Time: The Next Source of Competitive Advantage', *Harvard Business Review*, 66, 41–51.

■ Stalk, G. and Weber, A. M. (1993) 'Japan's Dark Side of Time', *Harvard Business Review*, July/August, 93–103.

■ Willmott, H. (1994) 'Business Process Re-engineering and Human Resource Management', *Personnel Review*, 23, 34–46.

Chapter 5
Power in Organizations

he said he didn't know when playfulness crossed over into harassment, and I said I have EXACTLY the same problem with horseplay and violence

A baronet discovered a tramp crossing his land. 'Trespasser!' said the baronet. 'Be gone with you!'

'What right have you got to order me off?' said the tramp.

'Why my ancestors fought for this land,' replied the baronet.

'Alright', said the tramp, 'I'll fight thee for it.'

(Anon)

POWER is a potentially sinister subject. The word 'power' resonates images of tyranny, murder and oppression. Power lurks behind the darker side of organizations; the disastrous explosion at Bhopal, the catastrophic fire on the Piper Alpha oil-rig, the sinking of the passenger ferry *Estonia*, the disappearance of the merchant ship *Derbyshire* and the continuing controversy surrounding the Hillsborough disaster. Yet imagine an organization without power.

'Power,' says Bierstedt, 'stands behind every association and sustains its structure. Without power there is no organization and without power there is no order' (1950, p. 735). Yet what is power? When a bonus payment is cut, when a redundancy notice is served, when a job application is rejected, we know at once the reality of power. Yet paradoxically, the most potent exercise of power may be invisible. Power relations can be subtly changing and ambiguous. In theory, managers command and employees obey. In practice, it is not always so. What may seem like absolute power matched by complete submission invariably masks a more complex relationship. Indeed, what appears as unquestioning obedience may actually be a covert form of resistance. It is useful, therefore, to understand something about the nature of power in organizations. The issues discussed in the chapter include:

1. What is power?
2. Where does power come from?
3. How is power exercised?
4. How can people in organizations gain or lose power?
5. How is resistance possible?
6. Where does ultimate power lie?

5.1 What is Power?

POWER is said to be like love, impossible to define but easy enough to recognize (Martin 1977). Everyone knows what power is until they come to define it (Bierstedt 1950). Indeed, Dahl (1957, p. 201) describes the task of defining power as akin to treading a 'bottomless swamp.' Even so, it is necessary to equip ourselves with a working definition in order to explore the concept of power and its ramifications for behaviour in organizations.

Power may be defined as:

1 'A has power over B to the extent that he can get B to do something B would not otherwise do' (Dahl 1957, p. 203).
2 'the production of intended effects' (Russell 1938, p. 19).

Note that Dahl conceptualizes power as:

power *over*,

someone, whereas Russell conceptualizes power as

power *to do*.

Dahl's definition suggests that power must overcome resistance in order to succeed whereas according to Russell, power need not imply resistance. The significance of this point is discussed in section 5.3.1 Suffice it here to note that all three definitions suggest that power involves compulsion. Power is sometimes easiest to perceive when it is absent. For example, in 1986 deregulation plunged the City of London into anarchy:

Once, it was dominated by the heads of powerful institutions—the Stock Exchange, Lloyd's, the Accepting Houses Committee—who possessed enough clout to get what they wanted.

Those days are gone. The old institutions have lost their influence. The newly important bodies in the City . . . see their roles in much more narrow terms.

(*Financial Times*, 23 March 1993, p. 21)

5.1.1 Differentiating power from authority and influence

First it is necessary to distinguish between power and two related terms, that is, authority and influence.

1. *Power*—the ability to compel regardless.
2. *Authority*—where A possesses a right to command, and B has an obligation to obey.
3. *Influence*—where A suspends their own judgement and accepts B's.

Authority exists where one person has a formal right to command and another has a formal obligation to obey (Wrong 1979, citing Gerth and Mills). Authority may be seen as institutionalized power. For example, a police officer has authority to 'stop' a motorist. The motorist is legally obliged to comply. Managers are said to possess a 'right to manage'. Employees are legally obliged to obey the employer's instructions provided these are lawful and within the scope of the employee's contract.

In authority relations it is the source of the command rather than its content that is crucial.

Obedience is owed to the office rather than a particular individual (Wrong 1979). One reason the fire on board Piper Alpha escalated to catastrophic proportions was that the duty manager had no authority to shut down the pipelines.

In contrast, power does not require authority. The baronet's ancestors (see page 122) were Norman invaders. They had no more authority to seize the land than the tramp. Nor did Hitler ask for permission to invade Poland. Yet both realized their intentions. Likewise, supermarkets have no authority to use information about buying habits obtained from customer loyalty cards. Yet no one stops them. In the case of Piper Alpha, a subordinate, seeing the seriousness of the fire, eventually took control and ordered a shut down. The order was obeyed despite there being no authority— though by then it was too late.

Whereas power and authority are potentially mandatory, influence, by contrast implies persuasion (Bierstedt 1950). Marx was highly influential but not powerful. In contrast Stalin was powerful but not influential (Bierstedt 1950). In the City of London the Bank of England has specific regulatory authority. It is also highly influential even in spheres where it has no formal powers—partly because of the power vacuum caused by deregulation. In organizations, employees may influence decisions through joint consultative committees and other mechanisms, yet the organization reserves the final say. Influence may have a decisive impact. For example, a person may be able to sway an appointments committee to choose their favoured candidate. An employee may withdraw a grievance or a salary claim as a result of a successful influence attempt. Crucially, however:

submission to influence is voluntary.

The influence target possesses the option of acting differently. For example, the aggrieved employee may change their mind and decide to pursue a formal complaint after all.

5.2 Where Does Power Come From?

WHAT gives A the capacity to produce intended effects? Bierstedt (1950) suggests power implies three things namely:

1. Numbers of people,
2. Social organization, and,
3. Resources.

According to Bierstedt, power depends upon all three coming together. Consider the following extract from an interview given by a thirty-six year old Sesotho farm labourer. The man was asked, 'Why did you leave the farm?':

The white man chased me off on account of sickness. I had TB. He evicted me while I was still getting treatment. But he didn't say that. He said that he couldn't manage any more to look after a lot of people. I found work but he spoiled it for me by phoning the white man and telling him not to do anything [with me] because I am scrap and so I failed to get that job. (Murray 1995, p. 70)

Note the imbalance of resources between the worker and the farmer. The worker owns nothing. He is physically driven off the land by a social organization which permits coercion. Loss of a job meant the loss of a home for the farm worker and his dependents. Moreover, the farmer exploits the social network to prevent the worker from finding a job at another farm. The farm worker is forced to take refuge in a shack settlement in a black township and pick up the threads of his disrupted life as best he can.

Conversely, the fusion of people, organization and resources, explains why small groups of well organized people can successfully defend themselves or pursue their objections against a much larger force. For example, in the 1980s a small voluntary organization known as CAMRA (Campaign for Real Ale) precipitated a fundamental change in consumer demand contrary to the wishes of the large brewing firms. More recently, relatives of the *Derbyshire*'s crew who were killed when the ship sank in a typhoon, won their eighteen-year campaign to compel a government enquiry into the disaster.

In organizations power derives from where each person stands in the division of labour and organizational communication system (Wrong 1979). The structure of power and authority relations is reflected in job descriptions, organization charts and the like.

Different types of organizations utilize different types of power, however. Let me now turn to those differences.

5.2.1 The bases of power

Note that power requires resources. According to Etzioni (1959, 1965b, 1975) there are three types of organization which can be differentiated according to which resource they mainly use to control the lower echelons, referred to by Etzioni as lower participants. Etzioni identifies three basic resources, as follows:

1. Coercion
2. Remunerative power
3. Normative power.

Coercion means the ability to manipulate physical sanctions including physical chastisement, forcible detention, to deprive a person of food, sleep and other physiological needs. Coercive organizations are those in which inmates would not voluntarily remain. Force is therefore required in order to obtain compliance. Examples of such organizations include jails, detention centres, concentration camps and some psychiatric hospitals.

Remunerative power refers to the ability to manipulate material rewards and sanctions including salaries, wages, promotions and training. Utilitarian organizations engage in producing goods and services for sale in the market place. Such organizations cannot compel employees. Nor are they able to inspire people to work voluntarily. Material inducement is therefore required to procure compliance. Such organizations include factories, hotels and commercial enterprises.

Normative power rests upon human need for approval and recognition. It refers to the ability to manipulate symbols including medals, badges and certificates. Normative organizations are those whose mission is primarily idealistic or value-based. Such organizations include the church, political groups and voluntary organizations. According to Etzioni, schools, universities and hospitals also count as normative organizations. Since members are already highly committed, material rewards are wasted. Moreover, coercion would destroy commitment. Such organizations utilize symbolic reward to heighten commitment. Such organizations rarely require resort to sanctions. Where sanctions are used they too are predominantly symbolic. For example, the ultimate sanction of the church is excommunication. The silencing of the bell, the closure of the holy book and the extinguishing of the candle to signify the miscreant's exclusion from the order. In the Territorial Army the only sanction is to be sent home.

> **Pause for reflection**
>
> Why might a group of labourers work overtime to help build an exhibition stand in return for a promotional T-shirt and yet refuse to do the same task in return for an overtime payment?

5.2.2 Power and involvement in organizations

According to Etzioni, particular types of power generate particular types of response. Figure 5.1 summarizes the power and involvement combinations suggested by Etzioni's theory.

Figure 5.1 Etzioni's typology of power and involvement

Power	Involvement
Coercion	Hostile/Alienative
Remunerative	Calculative
Normative	High Moral

Coercion typically produces alienative involvement. Alienative involvement is characterized by hostile attitudes towards the organization. Extreme coercion, however, can lead to apathy. For instance, Bruno Bettleheim (1943) who was incarcerated in a concentration camp noted that inmates lost the will and the energy to express hostility. Remunerative power is associated with so-called calculative involvement. Calculative involvement falls between hostility and wholehearted commitment. Normative power is associated with moral involvement. Moral involvement is characterized by high identification with the organization. (See also the discussion on organization commitment in section 3.4).

All three bases of power are capable of producing intended effects. Coercion is direct and requires minimal communication with the power target. However, coercion requires constant vigilance making it expensive to maintain—hence the high cost of keeping people in jail. Moreover, once coercion has been applied persuasion seldom works. Remunerative power requires resources and is capable of generating only conditional commitment. Normative power, by contrast, rests upon the power target's internalized acceptance of the power-holder's goals. It is capable of generating high involvement at relatively little cost because of the power target's identification with the power holder. Symbols can be highly compelling. The labourers referred to in section 5.2.1 were happy to work for a commemorative T-shirt printed with the exhibition logo, to feel part of events rather than mere hired hands.

5.2.3 Congruent and incongruent organizations

Etzioni suggests that organizational effectiveness depends upon utilizing whichever form of power is most appropriate to the particular type of organization. Organizations where predominant power and involvement combinations match are said to be congruent. (This does not preclude some reliance upon a secondary form of power. For instance, some utilitarian organizations manipulate symbolic rewards to stimulate commitment, ceremonial dinners and 'employee of the year' awards, for example.) Indeed, after you have read Chapter 10 you may conclude that Etzioni perhaps underestimates the role of symbols in organizations and not least, the power of symbols to sanction as well as reward.

According to Etzioni, organizations strive towards congruence while seeking to avoid incongruence.

Exceptionally, incongruent power and involvement combinations can work. For instance, a former prison inmate known as Jimmy Boyle became involved in a rebellion against the prison authorities. Boyle continued to defy the authorities even when ultimately incarcerated in an iron cage. The vicious spiral was broken when Boyle was transferred to a special unit. When Boyle arrived a warder made him a cup of coffee and handed him a knife to cut his luggage (Boyle 1973). Such gestures of trust and cooperation pre-empted hostility because there was nothing to defy.

Dual organizations are an exception to the rule of congruency. Such organizations rely upon two forms of power simultaneously (Etzioni 1975). The military is a good example of a dual organization as it relies upon both normative power and coercion. Military personnel are rewarded with decorations but they are also controlled by force which may include the death penalty.

5.2.4 A compliance continuum

Etzioni suggests that organizations can be seen as existing along a compliance continuum according to whether an organization is an extreme or mild example of its type. For example, according to Etzioni a factory is a more extreme example of a utilitarian organization than say an architects firm because of the latter's professional orientation. Similarly a hospital porter will be more normatively controlled and exhibit a higher level of commitment than say, a hotel porter.

Etzioni further suggests that the dominant form of power affects other organizational variables including leadership styles. Etzioni suggests that normative organizations emphasize expressive or transformational leadership whereas utilitarian organizations are more instrumental or transactional in their approach (Etzioni 1975). (See section 3.5.5.)

> **Pause for reflection**
> Why might an open prison be just as alienating as a high security jail?

5.2.5 Is Etzioni's theory a tautology?

Etzioni's theory may seem to state the obvious. Surely it is tautological to say that coercive organizations rely upon coercion as the predominant method of control?

To some extent, this is true of all theories. Theories basically take common sense and organize it. Part of the value of Etzioni's theory is that it prompts us to consider the exceptions to linear and intuitive thinking. For example, whereas Etzioni predicts that high security prisons are more alienating than low security jails, evidence suggests that people confined in open prisons may be just as alienated as those incarcerated in maximum security establishments. In open prisons inmates are confronted with the paradox of freedom and confinement (Smith and Hepburn 1977). Likewise Etzioni's theory suggests that physicians working in public service hospitals experience greater satisfaction than their private sector counterparts. Yet the reverse may be true. Physicians working in private hospitals may be less exposed to bureaucratic strictures than their public sector counterparts. Greater autonomy enhances satisfaction (Burns, Andersen and Shortell 1990).

Etzioni's theory also has implications for understanding organizational change. An important example in recent years has been the shift to privatization and compulsory competitive tendering in former public service organizations. Etzioni's theory suggests that such change can create tension because it involves a shift in organizational compliance structures. Such organizations are forced to become more utilitarian. Financial considerations compete for precedence with value-based objectives. For example, in the UK some general practitioners are unhappy about working to targets, 'We don't have time to talk to patients any more,' said one doctor.

Likewise, some museum curators have felt their motivation and job satisfaction have suffered following demands to forgo scholarship in favour of giving collections greater public appeal. Yet such transitions can be productive. Some managers have welcomed the new autonomy and responsibility afforded by cost centre management. Indeed, the Church of England's 10,500 clergy are currently campaigning for utilitarian employment contracts to protect themselves from arbitrary treatment by bishops (Overell 1998).

5.2.6 French and Raven's typology of power

Etzioni's theory deals with the bases of power. It identifies, in very general terms, *what* people in organizations control that enables them to obtain compliance. Another influential typology is French and Raven's five and latterly six bases of power (French and Raven 1968, Raven and Kruglanski 1970, Raven 1974 and also Podsakoff and Schriesheim 1985). French and Raven's typology of power is summarized in Figure 5.2.

Figure 5.2 French and Raven's typology of power

Coercion	The ability to deprive, that is, to decrease another's outcomes.
Reward	The ability to control that which another party values, that is, to increase another's outcomes.
Expertise	Possession of specialized knowledge.
Information	Possession of or control of access to important data concerning the organization and its environment.
Legitimacy	Synonymous with authority, that is, the power which emanates from a person's position in the organization.
Referent	Ability to exert charisma, to procure commitment.

French and Raven's typology is potentially confusing because it mixes the bases and forms of power. Its value is that it enables us to see power from a different intellectual standpoint to that of Etzioni. Legitimacy, that is, authority, is the basis of formal power in organizations, but it can be used to punish, to reward, or to obtain access to information. For instance, a prisoner may receive a reward for good behaviour but the reward remains rooted in coercion because the value of the cigarette stems from the prisoner's incarceration.

5.2.7 Knowledge as power

An important difference between Etzioni's typology and French and Raven's schema is that Etzioni excludes knowledge as a base of power. It was Francis Bacon (1561–1626) who observed 'knowledge is itself power'.

The medieval monks, for example, derived much of their power from their monopoly of handwriting skills (Kieser 1987). Likewise, in the popular cartoon strip known as *Andy Capp*, a technician arrives to repair the television. He taps it with a screwdriver. The television starts working again.

'You won't be charging much just for thumping it with a screwdriver,' says Andy.

'Just ten pence,' replies the technician. Andy pays up happily.

The technician then adds, 'And a pound for knowing where to thump it.'

Although knowledge can be seen as a material resource, it merits special discussion, particularly as we move away from the so-called 'smokestack' economy with its emphasis upon financial capital to a growing emphasis upon intellectual capital (Toffler 1992). Such transformation not only places a premium upon the organization's ability to recruit and retain knowledgeable staff, but it means that employees possess a significant degree of control over the means of production. The physical assets of organizations such as advertising agencies and law firms, are negligible compared with the intellectual capital employed. Moreover, some employees know more about the technical aspects of their work than the general managers who supervise them. For example, very few managers in the financial services industry claim to understand derivatives and the other exotic financial instruments in which they trade. Such knowledge is the property of a small cadre of specialist mathematicians known as 'rocket scientists'.

5.3 How is Power Exercised?

ONE afternoon in Liverpool I heard a disturbance in the street. I walked to the window to investigate. On the street below, a taxi had stopped at a strange angle. The door was hanging open. A man was pointing a machine gun inside. Horrified, I moved to telephone the police. Then I realized that it was probably too late, and that I might be more use as a witness. By now the street seemed to swarm with gun-men. Four youths were lying face down in the road, guns pointed at their heads. The gun-men were screaming instructions at the youths. 'Look at me! Look at me!' yelled one.

Then I realized the gun-men were police officers. It was a brutal, frightening scene. One misplaced gesture and someone could have been shot dead. Such is the reality of power.

The exercise of power requires both:

capability and intention.

Yet power can succeed without either capability or intention, provided the power target believes in the reality of both (Bacharach and Lawler 1980). For instance, the guns used in the police raid may not have been loaded. Yet judging by the youths' submissive behaviour the threat seemed credible. Interestingly, threats can succeed where the actual deployment of force might fail (Bierstedt 1950). For example, threatening to go to court can achieve successful settlement, whereas suing to judgement can end in disaster—as not a few prosecutors for libel have discovered to their cost, including Oscar Wilde and Jonathan Aitken. Likewise, the threat of sanctions may prompt an employee to comply with the employer's directives, whereas actual disciplinary action might founder upon a technicality, or result in the manager being censured for being 'heavy-handed'. Managers sometimes have to use their formal powers very carefully.

Coercion is not the only form of power which requires neither capability nor intention. Some managers are highly adroit at manipulating their employees with vague promises of rewards which seem plausible but which are actually illusory. In one case a manager secured the unquestioning compliance of a subordinate for nearly five years on the basis of a tacit promise that when the manager was promoted, the subordinate would occupy the manager's old job. When the manager was promoted his first act was to commission a restructuring exercise which resulted in his old job being abolished (Drummond 1991).

Expertise can also be more apparent than real. Articles of apprenticeship still refer to the 'mysteries of' the trade or profession in order to make the work seem more difficult than it actually is. The elaborate use of jargon and technical and 'management speak' serves a similar function. For example:

'The negotiations were very difficult.'
('We had a cup of coffee and a nice chat together.')

'We will have to re-engineer the whole system.'
('There are a couple of paragraphs in the manual which need updating.')

Expert power rests in the recipient's belief that the expert is serving their interests and not their own (Wrong 1979). We discuss in detail in Chapter 6 how people in organizations may pursue their own agendas. Suffice it here to note that the expert's professed concern for their client may cloak self-interest. 'See if you can spin it out, Mr Rumpole,' says the clerk as he hands the barrister a lucrative case.

Doctors sometimes claim that unless they receive additional resources such as a new computer, a more convenient office, better secretarial facilities, 'patients will die'. Health service managers call this tactic 'shroud waving'. Likewise customers who ask 'expert' advice about which stereo or computer to buy usually end up purchasing what the store wants to sell.

Some professional monopolies are under threat. The media has enabled the medical profession to be challenged in a manner which would have been considered unthinkable thirty years ago (Toffler 1992). The rise of 'alternative' approaches to healing such as aromatherapy and acupuncture have called into question conventional, expensive treatments. Accountants are increasingly trespassing upon the lawyer's traditional provenance without being prosecuted. Actuaries are venturing into business management consultancy.

Such developments have far reaching implications for managing change in organizations and investment in training and education. They also imply shifts in the balance of power in organizations. For instance, twenty years ago the staff in the computer 'mainframe' department held the power to bring the organization to a standstill. We never hear of them now.

5.3.1 Invisible power

Coercion is sometimes seen as the ultimate form of power because of its associations with brute force and terror. Yet the most subtle exercise of power may be that which is invisible known as unobtrusive power (Bacharach and Baratz 1970, Lukes 1974). Unobtrusive power is defined as:

the ability to prevent conflict and unwelcome issues from arising.

Unobtrusive power rests in unchallenged assumptions about what is appropriate. For example, the idea that we are impotent in the face of bureaucracy (Roberts 1984). Unobtrusive power is seen in the 'taken for granted' aspects of organization. For instance, on 14 March, 1998, a Vietnamese worker employed on an oil rig in the South China Sea was washed overboard. The employee was never seen again. Although such accidents occur frequently, we seldom hear of them. The company which owns the rig did not care to publicize the news. The workforce regard such incidents as inevitable—the price to be paid for employment.

5.3.2 'Non-decisions' as power

Another term for unobtrusive power is 'non-decision' (Bacharach and Baratz 1963, 1970).

Non-decisions require the ability to define reality for others.

The notion of 'non-decision' is vividly portrayed in Wilfred Owen's poem 'Disabled'. The poem concerns a soldier who has been seriously wounded:

Now, he will spend a few sick years in institutes,
And do what the rules consider wise,
And take whatever pity they may dole.

Evening falls and it grows cold. The soldier is left sitting outside in a wheel chair shivering:

. . . in his ghastly suit of grey,
Legless, sewn short at the elbow.

The staff have obviously forgotten him. The poem ends with a indictment of institutes which still resonates true:

How cold and late it is! Why don't they come
And put him to bed? Why don't they come?

One form of 'non-decision' is known as the mobilization of bias whereby organizations embody a set of values which work against certain people (Bacharach and Baratz 1970). For instance, in 1998 an appeal to the European Court of Justice against the decision of a railway company to refuse a concessionary travel pass to an employee's lesbian partner failed. The court said that since the company rules stipulated that travel passes were only granted to the partners of married employees, the employee had not been unfairly discriminated against. Indeed, until relatively recently sexual harassment in the workplace was regarded as inevitable.

> **Pause for reflection**
>
> A group of hospital physiotherapists are concerned that their abilities are not fully utilized. Consultants are depriving patients of the best possible health care prescriptions because they are unaware of the full range of treatments available.
>
> What might explain this problem?

Likewise, certain forms of technology work against women. Drummond and Kingstone-Hodgson (1996) have suggested that many traditionally heavy industries including fishing and construction might not necessarily require strenuous physical effort. They suggest that the technology has changed very little over the years because it acts as an institutional barrier to women's employment.

5.3.3 Who defines reality in organizations?

The power to define reality in organizations is not evenly distributed (Hardy 1985). A fundamental 'non-decision' in organizations is the so-called 'right to manage'. Roberts (1984) suggests managers are conceived of and conceive themselves as 'morally neutral characters' (p. 287). Yet, argues Roberts, self-interest often lurks behind the appearance of organizational commitment. For instance, Katz (1982), suggests that the murderous behaviour of Nazi officials was often motivated by the prospects of career advancement. Similarly:

I see everything that goes out of here. Yesterday, Alan (a new assistant) showed me a letter he had written to a client. I ripped it up. . . . tore it to bits . . . I said: 'That is not how we address a client.' (Partner in an HRM consultancy firm)

The manager's behaviour amounts to a bid for dominance. He has used his knowledge of the firm's house style to bully the newcomer and undermine his confidence.

5.3.4 Seduction as power

The supreme exercise of power exists where the power holder controls the power holder's wants (Lukes 1974). Education, advertizing, socialization and other forms of communication subtly shape our desires. Such unobtrusive power is seen in 'what is not'. For example:

All I ever wanted to do was to be a hairdresser. Sometimes, when it's dark I think, 'do I really have to get up,' but once I'm here, I enjoy it. I just love being a hairdresser. (Female hairdresser aged forty-nine)

I began work as a hospital almoner. That was considered a 'nice' thing for a young lady to do. (Social worker aged sixty)

On Saturday you might go up to London and eat spaghetti bolognese. That was considered very daring. (Female graduate describing Cambridge life in 1958)

Note that the actor in each of the foregoing vignettes is female. Moreover, even those born into relatively privileged backgrounds are constrained by forces which are invisible but compelling nevertheless. Even when they break free, it is hardly as if they go far—up to London to eat spaghetti bolognese. In organizations unobtrusive power is seen in employees' ambitions to obtain overtime in order to help pay for a holiday or some other luxury, in graduate training programmes which encourage ambition to a point—and so on.

5.4 The Dynamics of Power

5.4.1 Informal power

So far, power has been discussed as structural phenomenon. In theory an employee is allotted sufficient power to enable them to do their job, no more and no less. In practice people in organizations can acquire power beyond what their formal role might suggest. Power without authority is sometimes known as illegitimate or informal power (Drummond 1991, Mintzberg 1983, Pettigrew 1973). Informal power arises because organizations cannot legislate for every contingency. Figure 5.3 depicts the problem.

Organizational rules specify what employees can or cannot do in particular circumstances. For example, financial regulations may stipulate which organizational office holders have authority to sign cheques or issue contracts.

Yet in every organization there is inevitably room to exercise discretion. Indeed without it the organization would soon run into difficulties—hence the industrial relations tactic known as 'work to rule'. Discretion means that a person has the option of acting differently. For instance, a manager might make an informal job offer rather than wait a fortnight for the Personnel Office to issue a formal letter. Strictly speaking, the manager has no authority to bind the organization. Yet unless the manager acts, the candidate might seek employment elsewhere to the ultimate detriment of the organization.

5.4.2 Sources of informal power

The possibilities for acquiring informal power in organizations are virtually infinite. Mechanic (1962) suggests that informal or discretionary power arises in three ways, that is, through access to:

Figure 5.3 Zones of control in organizations

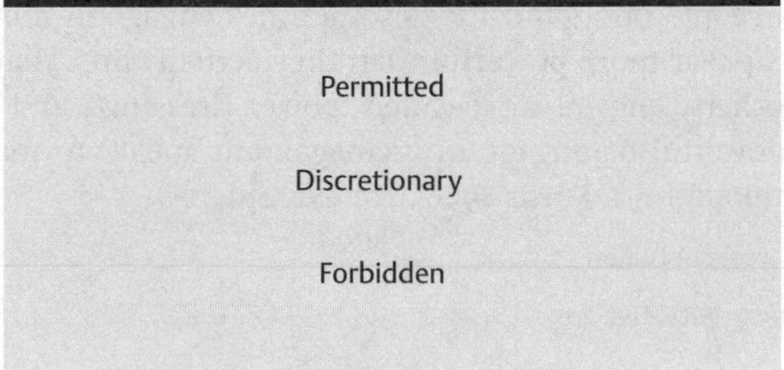

Permitted

Discretionary

Forbidden

1. People,
2. Information, and,
3. Instrumentalities (resources).

Junior employees are often entrusted with photocopying or filing confidential documents. They may be the only people who know how to operate software or other specialized equipment. In moments of stress senior staff may unburden themselves to juniors. Employees meet socially and exchange information and news. Staff working in open plan offices often hear about matters which do not concern them officially but interest them greatly nevertheless.

Some organizations attempt to curb lower participant power by confining entry to certain parts of buildings to senior staff, installing confidential fax machines, marking documents for restricted circulation and so forth.

Even so, informal power leaks from the formal structure. Junior staff still meet seniors in the lift. Offices still have to cleaned. Visitors still have to walk through the door.

> **Pause for reflection**
> Why might job freedom be experienced as a worse tyranny than working to strict rules and instructions?

Even the most junior employee has some discretion over their work. In practice, such discretion may be very wide and can be used to increase power. Employees may inveigle their way on to important committees or insert themselves as intermediaries in negotiations. Managers may delegate work in order to concentrate upon those tasks which hold the potential to increase their power. Such tasks may involve acquiring specialist knowledge which is needed for decision making or leading an important project. Informal power can even be exercised simply by doing one's own job with special efficiency. Another reason open prisons may be more alienating than high security jails is that the comparative absence of rules and formal structure may allow staff considerable informal power.

Such power can be alienating if it is used arbitrarily because inmates see sanctions as unrelated to their behaviour and hence beyond their control (Alpert 1978). Likewise in organizations, fewer rules and regulations can actually mean that supervisors enjoy more power—not least because they can make the rules up as they go along to the discomfit of employees.

Informal power can also succeed without capability or intention provided it appears credible. People in organizations sometimes engage in impression management in order to appear more powerful than they actually are. They may pretend to know powerful others, engage in so-called 'power dressing', and ingratiate themselves with the powerful or engage in 'management speak' to make them appear important (Drummond 1991, Korda 1976). For example:

'Clearly the *decision* rests between . . .'

'The risks I must *choose* between are . . .'

'I *will* sign it'

5.4.3 Power and the impact of time

Power relations are inherently dynamic and thus apt to change over time. For instance, if rewards are administered regularly they may come to be experienced as coercion because of the threat of withdrawal (Wrong 1979). Charisma is difficult to sustain and so tends to become routinized (Bacharach and Lawler 1980). The inmates of concentration camps may come to identify with their captors (Bloch 1947).

Informal power is usually legitimated in time (Martin 1977). Any source or person who is regularly consulted becomes an authority (Wrong 1979). Coercion is converted to legitimate authority in order to enable the powerholder to assert a moral right over that which has been taken by force. For example, Shakespeare's deposed King Richard II is forced to sign a document acknowledging his alleged misgovernment and 'voluntarily' relinquishing his rights to the throne. Within organizations job descriptions, organization charts, standing orders and committee structures are redrawn to reflect new roles, new responsibilities, new rules and new powers (Drummond 1991).

> **Pause for reflection**
>
> A factory operates a 'just-in-time' system of production. (See section 4.3.1). In what ways is the organization vulnerable to industrial action?

5.5 From Power to Resistance

Politics, suggests Wrong (1979), includes not only power but also a struggle to escape from power. In organizations, informal power can be used either to further organizational objectives or to mount resistance, that is, to attempt to escape from power. The concept of resistance is important to organizations because insurgency is potentially destabilizing and may frustrate important objectives including the realization of productive potential. Conversely, from an employee's perspective resistance is potentially liberating. It is the means by which the apparently powerless can avoid impositions which threaten something of value.

5.5.1 The scope for resistance

The potential for resistance arises because:

no form of power is absolute.

This is because all power relations are reciprocal:

Power relations are always two-way; that is to say however subordinate an actor may be in a social relationship, the very fact of involvement in that relationship gives him or her a certain amount of power over the other. (Giddens 1979, p. 60)

In other words, no matter how asymmetrical the balance of power, the power target always retains the option of acting differently. For example, in medieval monasteries the abbot's rule was definitive. Yet monks occasionally murdered their abbot in desperation to escape from power (Assad 1987). 'Publish and be damned,' the Duke of Wellington told his blackmailer. Likewise, the Nazis were subtly undermined by their apparently cooperative local agents:

A directive ... may have to be transferred and translated (reformulated, elaborated, operationalized) several times before it reaches its destination and becomes implemented. Such processes ... provide some scope for detaining, deflecting, or diluting. (Lammers 1988, p. 439)

5.5.2 Resistance in organizations

Recall that the potential for resistance rests in involvement in a relationship. An important form of involvement in organizations is agency. Agency arises because organizations purchase labour power which must then be converted into productive work. The space between purchase and conversion provides a margin of discretion for employees to exercise resistance (Clegg 1989, 1994). In other words, 'The very structure of the capital–labour relationship presents the opportunity for exploiting capital's dependence on labour' (Knights and Willmott 1990, p. 6).

More colloquially the key to resistance is:

dependency.

Organizations depend upon employees to execute directives.

The impetus to resistance in organizations stems from the potential for tension between organizational and individual interests (Knights and Willmott 1990, Gouldner 1954, Weber 1947). What is good for the organization may be detrimental to its employees and vice versa. Although most of the literature has focused upon shop floor workers, managers are also capable of offering resistance (Drummond 1998, La Nuez and Jermier 1994).

Capitalist organizations typically rely upon bureaucratic controls to prevent insurgency (Braverman 1974, Clegg and Dunkerly 1980, Ouchi 1980). Such mechanisms are rarely perfect, however, We saw in section 2.2, for example, how employees can thwart work study controls and engage in quota restriction. Here is another example of how an employee may exploit the space between purchase and conversion. The case concerns an exasperated owner of a hairdressing salon talking about a recalcitrant employee:

Say she had an appointment at midday and somebody walked in the door at quarter to [twelve] and said, 'Could I have my hair cut?', she'd say, 'We-ll I have got someone coming in shortly.' Then the [midday appointment] would come in at ten past [twelve], so she'd spent the last 25 minutes doing nothing. (Drummond 1997, p. 104)

In this case the employee is exploiting the appointments system to engage in quota restriction. In fact, the possibilities for resistance in organizations are virtually infinite. For example, the Chinese Civil Service was once controlled by low ranking clerks who used delay, pedantry, selective amnesia and local knowledge to thwart management (Sterba 1978). Likewise, idealistic social policies have been frustrated by staff implementing these in an instrumental fashion or distracting leaders with arguments over details (Mulford 1978, Fourcher 1975).

5.5.3 Strategies of resistance

Collinson (1994) has identified two generic strategies, that is:

- 'resistance by distance,' and,
- 'resistance by persistence'.

'Resistance by distance' occurs where employees try to escape managerial domination by 'distancing' themselves physically or symbolically from those in control. Examples include doing the bare minimum, maintaining 'them' and 'us' attitudes, and avoiding social contact wherever possible. For example, an interesting case study by Knights and Roberts (1982) shows how staff countered spiralling managerial pressure by withdrawing psychologically. 'Feeling unable to control or influence what is demanded of them for the sake of the company, they attempt to control all that's left—their own actions and attitudes' (p. 61).

In contrast, 'resistance by persistence' involves holding management to account, demanding greater involvement in the organization and challenging decisions. For example, in the following vignette the owner of the hairdressing salon referred to in section 6.6.2 is attempting to galvanize the recalcitrant employee into action:

I was thinking, I know what I will do. I will get this sign outside of the door and make it as plain as day that we are a barber shop. I said [to the employee], 'Right, we are going for it . . . When you come into work in the morning, the first job is out with the board, up and ready with tools in hand, get the first victim [customer] in, and crack on from there.' (Drummond 1997, p. 105)

The employee had other ideas, however. The employer again:

She [the employee] said, 'It's a bit of a naff [poor] sign,' and wouldn't put it out. Every morning I'd say, 'Put the board out.' She'd say, 'It catches me [sic] fingers.' (Drummond 1997, p. 105)

The salon owner ended up carrying the board out.

Drummond (1998) has invoked the metaphor of ju jitsu to conceptualize the dynamics of resistance. Ju jitsu rests upon the notion of a weaker person overcoming a stronger one through the scientific application of movement. Drummond recounts how a junior manager was instructed to implement a decision by a local government directorate to close a swimming pool. The decision to close the pool was based upon income and expenditure calculations which showed the pool was operating at a substantial loss. A member of the senior management team secretly supplied the junior manager with the details. The junior manager then realized that the figures excluded 50 per cent of the pool's income. The junior manager subsequently confronted senior management with this information at a public meeting—to management's extreme embarrassment as they were forced to rescind the decision. What occurred at that juncture was metaphorically speaking an exercise of 'atemi jitsu', that is, striking the opponent's weak spots.

Alternatively, in the language of Mechanic's (1962) schema, lower participant power was a function of access to information (the figures), persons (a sympathetic senior colleague), and instrumentalities (admission to the meeting).

5.54 The ambiguity of agency

Since such overt disobedience runs the risk of incurring sanctions, resistance can be extremely subtle. Drummond (1998) further recounts how the junior manager also engaged in a form of kendo, that is, harmonizing with one's opponent's movements in order to dissipate their energy.

In this case, the manager exploited his brief to foster community relations to thwart management's decision:

They (the pensioners' swimming club) were discussing how they could help (the pool) and we came up with the idea of a jumble sale. They made £200—it went nowhere with running costs but it was symbolic, it showed commitment. I could see it would make a good story . . . They asked me what I thought they should do with the money and I said the best thing would be if you could actually go down there (to the town hall) and give it to him, (the leader of the council) which they did.

The leader of the council was impressed by the gesture and began to have second thoughts about the decision.

Although the manager was harnessing the community to mount resistance, he could legitimately claim that he was only doing his job. Such may be the ambiguity of human agency.

> **Pause for reflection**
>
> Consider the following statements:
>
> - *The Times* is read by those who rule the world.
> - The *Daily Telegraph* is read by those who think they rule the world.
> - The *Guardian* is read by those who think they ought to rule the world.
> - The *Financial Times* is read by those who own the world.
>
> In the light of this information, which newspaper would you opt to read?

5.6 Discussion

THIS chapter began with a concern to understand what prevents organizations from degenerating into anarchy. According to Hobbes without power there is:

No arts; no letters; no society; and which is worst of all, continual fear and danger of violent death; and the life of man, solitary, poor, nasty, brutish, and short. (*Leviathan* (1651) Pt 1, ch. 13)

On the one hand, power holds organizations and society together. Power enables accomplishment, hence the power of music, the power of science, the power of love, the power of silence and so on. Power prevents the tramp from exploiting brute strength to seize another person's property. Yet what of the victims of the Nazi holocaust whose lands were seized by force and for whom life became, 'poor, nasty, brutish and short'. Did they experience the breakdown of power or the reality of power?

Similarly, it might be wise to opt for readership of the *Daily Telegraph*. Readers of the *Guardian* are doomed to perpetual frustration. Those who own the world may be in a highly influential or even powerful position—but ownership exists only in law. War, natural disasters, market failure, political upheaval can sweep all away. Rulers can be displaced. Yet those who think they rule the world, however, are sustained by their delusions. Delusions can be better than reality.

In theory a discussion of power has no place in an Organization Behaviour textbook. In theory, it should be sufficient to focus upon authority. If this chapter has succeeded then it should be obvious why authority is partial. Power is part of the fabric of organization. To appreciate the reality of organizations it is necessary to know something about the nature of power.

This point becomes easier to understand if we see power and authority not as literal entities, but as metaphors. They are linguistic devices which enable us to comprehend compliance, organization and accomplishment. Recall all metaphors are incomplete. Authority may explain why, for example, people generally report to work on time and behave in a reasonable manner. Yet unauthorized acts occur day in, day out, in organizations. Indeed, organizations can only function if people are sometimes prepared to act without authority.

The most difficult aspect of power is to explain what the metaphor represents. The present chapter has tried to address this challenge by presenting conceptualizations in order to enable the reader gain some feel for the existence of power as distinct from authority and influence. Even so, you might well ask, what is the point of mastering the various schema presented in this chapter? Are we any wiser for knowing the difference say between Etzioni's and French and Raven's typology?

Bacharach and Lawler (1980) suggest that in order to understand power it is necessary to look behind power and to see what the concept sensitizes us to. For example, when we drive past a field of peas or potatoes or some other crop bearing a sign 'Grown for Tesco' or Asda or some other large supermarket chain, we encounter a metaphor of power. When we hear reports of police in South Africa beating suspects, we see the metaphor of coercive authority that produces such abuses of power. The physical and mental harming of children and elderly people in institutions suggests that the dividing line between Etzioni's moral or normative organizations and coercive types may not be absolute. Organizations may slip from one to the other. Military failures in Kosovo remind us that power does not always succeed. Vietnam, an earlier imbroglio, exemplifies how the weak can successfully resist the strong and how the strong can become involved in a war that is unwinnable.

The notion of power enables us to see how the experience of organizational life can be very different from the authority relations suggested by formal documentation. Indeed, organization charts, job descriptions and the like are basically metaphors. More precisely, they are highly abstract icons which depict the organization in a particular way. They are rooted in mechanistic thinking which assumes that organizations are stable entities. Again it is not what a particular metaphor reveals that matters so much as what it conceals. The metaphor of power enables us to see that structure does not exist upon sheets of paper. Nor does it hold rigid like royal icing. Structure is forever being formed and reformed as roles are negotiated and renegotiated, as control is gained or lost, as authority exerts itself or abdicates, as charisma moves people to action or loses the power to move.

The metaphor of power illuminates the subtle undertones of organizational life, the oblique changes in relationships and patterns of dependency that may occur. Such developments may be barely perceptible yet possess transformative potential.

The next chapter explores the tactics which people in organizations may use in order to increase their power and further their interests. Here it is sufficient to note that the metaphor of power with its connotations of fear, greed, and destructiveness sensitises us to the irrational and sometimes cruel face of organizations. We shall see in Chapter 10 that people in organizations are not above imputing misfortune to witchcraft. Such are the mysterious workings of power, there may be no other explanation.

5.6.1 Power and the reality of organizations

On a more practical level the study of power sensitizes us to the dynamics of organization. It allows us to see beyond the notion of organizations as rule bound, machine-like entities. Instead we see organizations as inherently ambiguous and subtly shifting.

We shall see in Chapter 8 that occupational stress imparts a high cost to people, organizations and society. One potential cause of stress is role ambiguity—where the individual is uncertain where their duties and responsibilities lie (see section 8.3.2). The study of power enables us to see how role ambiguity can arise. It enables us to see how people become more or less powerful than their formal role prescriptions suggest, and how reporting lines can become blurred and job descriptions rendered irrelevant as power relations change—often almost imperceptibly.

One word which has hardly been mentioned in this chapter is responsibility. The organizational literature assumes that power and responsibility match (Barnard 1938). The study of informal power enables us to see how the balance between power and responsibility can become highly asymmetrical thus adding to stress.

We shall also see in Chapter 8 that dual careers are another source of stress (see section 8.4.4). Much of the stress literature focuses upon alienating the symptoms of stress. The study of power enables us to see stress as emanating from 'taken for granted' assumptions about what is appropriate, notably the demarcation that organizations impose between work and family life. The study of power also sensitizes us to the tension between organizations which tacitly espouse conformity and family life while making demands which undermine social stability (Whyte 1957).

Personal and sexual harassment are also stressors (see section 8.3.4). The study of power in organizations allows us to see such incidents as part of a much larger picture, of power differentials and 'taken for granted' assumptions which permit psychic violence and selfish behaviour: 'I ripped it up.'

Likewise, are the hospital consultants referred to in section 5.3.2, a case of none so blind as those who see their authority threatened by another body of knowledge?

The study of power also reveals how organizations are vulnerable to resistance. Critical theorists may be correct in suggesting that resistance does little to alter the fundamental imbalance of power which exists in capitalist organizations. They may even be correct in suggesting that resistance often serves only to reinforce existing systems of power (Clegg 1979).

Yet there is ample evidence to suggest that the balance is not as asymmetrical as organizations might prefer. Moreover, there is also the potential for resistance to consider. For example, 'just-in-time' production systems (see section 5.5.4) assume minimal stocks, making them highly vulnerable to stoppages and other forms of industrial action.

Just how pervasive is resistance in organizations?

Acts of overt resistance may be the mere tip of the iceberg. Drummond (1991) suggests that at least 80 per cent of requests and instructions issued in organizations are never implemented. Some are even reversed without the organization knowing. For example, Drummond (1991) recounts how a manager selfishly attempted to extend his share of space in an open plan office by moving his filing cabinets outwards. The staff surreptitiously moved them back a centimetre or so every day until the manager actually occupied less space than was his in the first place without ever realizing what had happened! How many similar instances occur day in day out with no one any wiser?

5.6.2 The power of organizations

So far the discussion has mainly focused upon power within organizations. Let us briefly turn to the power of organizations. Toffler (1992) suggests that power, that is, *real* power, is not psychological but material. According to Galbraith (1984), Western society has moved through three distinct phases. In medieval times society rested upon coercion. Then the apparatus of power comprised stocks, ducking stools, branding irons and the omnipresent shadow of the gallows. Society has since passed to reliance upon remunerative power. In Walter Greenwood's novel *Love on the Dole* first published in 1933, the fictional character Harry experiences the reality of such control:

Was this what was meant by growing older? . . . A shilling a week . . . Cigarettes, pictures and threepence for a bet and—broke until next pay day. Gosh! (1975, p. 77)

According to Galbraith reliance upon material control is giving way to normative power. Seduction, Lukes (1974) reminds us is much cheaper than getting people to do what they would not otherwise have done. For 'cigarettes, pictures and threepence for a bet', read, 'a pizza on a Tuesday, a curry on a Friday and a trip out on a Sunday and—broke until next pay day.' The difference is, we think we are well off. Gosh!

It is one thing to question the status quo. It is another to envision alternatives. George Orwell's *Animal Farm* provides a graphic if symbolic account of what can happen when the existing order is supplanted by another. Organizations which dispense with conventional authority structures experience problems of another kind (Baker 1982). Utopia means 'nowhere' (Watzlawick, Weakland and Frisch 1974). But then, perhaps that is what we are meant to think.

Let us end on a light-hearted and optimistic note. When the Marx Brothers were making a film called *A Night in Casablanca*, Warner Brothers who had earlier made a film entitled *Casablanca* threatened legal action. Here is an extract from Groucho's reply to Warner Brothers:

Apparently there is more than one way of conquering a city and holding it as your own. For example, up to the time that we contemplated making this picture, I had no idea that the city of Casablanca belonged exclusively to Warner Brothers. . . . I just don't understand your attitude. . . . I am sure that the average movie fan could learn in time to distinguish between Ingrid Bergman and Harpo. I don't know whether I could, but I would certainly like to try . . . . You claim you own Casablanca and that no one else can use that name without your permission. What about 'Warner Brothers'? Do you own that, too? You probably have the right to use the name Warner, but what about Brothers? Professionally, we were brothers long before you were. . . . even before us there had been other brothers [including] 'Brother Can You Spare a Dime?'. (This was originally 'Brothers Can You Spare a Dime?' but this was spreading a dime pretty thin, so they threw out one brother and gave all the money to the other one and whittled it down to 'Brother Can You Spare a Dime?') (Marx 1995, p. 15)

Eventually the Marx Brothers heard no more from Warner Brothers legal department. The moral of the story is that even the most powerful monolith may be defeated by the pin prick of ridicule.

Summary

1 Power is difficult to define but easy to recognize.

2 Power can be seen as the ability to achieve intentions regardless of resistance.

3 Authority exists where A possesses an acknowledged right to command and B an acknowledged obligation to obey.

4 Power rests upon compulsion whereas influence is voluntary.

5 Power can be exercised without authority.

6 Power requires a combination of people, social organization and resources.

7 In organizations power derives from structure, that is, the division of labour and communication system.

8 Etzioni suggests there are three basic power resources. These are:

- physical coercion,
- remunerative power, and,
- normative (symbolic) power.

9 According to Etzioni each form of power is associated with a particular form of involvement.

- Coercion is associated with alienation and hostility.
- Remunerative power is associated with calculative involvement.
- Normative power is associated with moral involvement.

10 Another influential contribution to the literature on power in organizations concerns French and Raven's typology. French and Raven identify six forms of power as follows:

- coercion,
- reward,
- expertise,
- information,
- legitimate,
- referent.

Note, though, that French and Raven confuse bases and sources of power.

11 Knowledge is an important source of power in organizations.

12 Power can succeed without either capability or intention provided that the power target believes both are real.

13 The most subtle exercise of power may be that which is invisible known as 'non-decision'.

14 'Non-decisions' depend upon the ability to define reality for others.

15 Defining reality is a key task of management.

16 People in organizations can acquire power informally.

17 Informal power arises because organizations cannot legislate for everything.

18 The possibilities for acquiring power informally are very wide. Broadly speaking they may be seen as arising from access to:

- persons,
- information, and,
- instrumentalities.

19 Power relations may change over time. In particular, informal power tends to be legitimated.

20 Informal power can be used to mount resistance.

21 Resistance arises because no form of power is absolute. Organizations utilize bureaucratic controls to prevent resistance. Such controls are rarely perfect however.

22 The impetus to resistance in organizations stems from the potential for tension between organizational and employee objectives.

23 In organizations the scope for resistance resides in agency.

24 Two possible strategies are:

- 'resistance by distance', and,
- 'resistance by persistence'.

25 Resistance can be extremely subtle. It may appear as compliance.

Questions for Discussion

1 'A kind word and a gun are better than a kind word alone.' (Attributed to Al Capone)

Discuss with reference to power in organizations.

2 'Ignorance is bliss.'

Discuss with reference to power in organizations.

3 Distinguish between power, influence and authority.

Which of the three would you prefer to possess and why?

4 'Nothing will come of nothing.'

(*King Lear* Act 1, Sc.1 l[92])

Discuss with reference to the acquisition of informal power in organizations.

5 How can people in organizations effect resistance?

6 In organizations, where does compliance end and resistance begin?

Further Reading

- Drummond, H. (1991) *Power: Creating It, Using It*, London, Kogan Page.

- Drummond, H. (1998) 'Go and Say "We're Shutting:" ju-jutsu as a metaphor for analysing resistance,' *Human Relations*, 51, 1–19.

- Etzioni, A. (1975) *A Comparative Analysis of Complex Organizations*, London, Collier MacMillan.

- Hardy, C. (1985) 'The Nature of Unobtrusive Power', *Journal of Management Studies*, 22, 384–99.

- Mechanic, D. (1962) 'Sources of Power of Lower Participants in Complex Organizations', *Administrative Science Quarterly*, 7, 349–64.

- Roberts, J. (1984) 'The Moral Character of Management Practice', *Journal of Management Studies*, 21, 287–302.

- Wrong, D. H. (1979) *Power, Its Forms, Bases and Uses*, Oxford, Basil Blackwell.

Chapter 6
Politics and Political Behaviour in Organizations

now come on Mr Johnson, we have this EVERY year — the contents of the store-cupboard do not BELONG to you, they are for you to ALLOCATE

Worry and responsibility are part of the price of power. Real power does not lie in documents and memos outlining your terms of reference and area of jurisdiction: it lies in what you can achieve in practice.

(Jay 1993, *Management and Machiavelli*)

THE announcement, 'There will now be a party political broadcast . . .' prompts most people to switch the television off. Politics are frequently seen as the ultimate in boredom; self-important people arguing endlessly about remote and unimportant issues. While this perspective is not completely unfounded, it hardly does justice to the significance of politics and political behaviour in organizations. Politics is not just about international affairs, parliaments and domestic issues. Organizations are themselves systems of political activity. Economics may influence organizational decisions but politics is the ultimate arbiter. It is not enough for managers to be planners, analysts and to direct strategy. They must also be politicians. The issues addressed by this chapter include:

- Why are organizations political?
- How to play politics.
- How to recognize political tactics.
- Political correctness.
- Organizational politics: good or bad?

6.1 Why are Organizations Political?

IN theory, politics have no place in organizations. Organizations are supposedly rational entities engaged in the pursuit of particular goals. Moreover, decisions are based upon the principle of maximizing utility. This perspective assumes, however, that the decision makers:

- share a clear and common goal, and,
- are psychic,

that is, able to predict future consequences, and the organization's future preferences.

In reality such assumptions rarely apply. Organizations are typically composed of different sub-units (hereafter called departments) espousing different cultures each with different outlooks and priorities. Decisions are often surrounded by considerable uncertainty. Decision makers may disagree about what should be done. For instance, in 1998 Citrop merged with Travellers' organization. The merger is apparently part of a ten-year expansion plan. Citrop's goal is to acquire ten billion customers. The issues almost defy imagination. Will the merger work? What should

Citrop do next? One option is to continue merging with other organizations. Mergers are risky, however. Another possibility is to poach customers from other banks. That takes time and invites retaliation. Is the ultimate goal too ambitious anyway?

6.1.1 The essence of politics

Such questions highlight the essence of politics namely:

■ disagreement,
■ diversity,
■ scarcity, and,
■ interest.

If everyone in organizations agreed all the time, there would be no politics. In other words, the potential for political activity arises wherever *disagreement* exists. One factor which can prompt disagreement is *diversity*. Complex organizations comprise sub-units. Some units are more powerful than others and each may have different goals (Hickson, Hinings, Lee, Schneck, and Pennings 1971). Diverse goals can create conflict. For example, software engineers may want to provide the organization with a highly sophisticated and technologically advanced IT system. Line managers may simply want a design which enables them to communicate with one another.

Scarcity can prompt political activity if there are competing claims upon resources. If department A requires ten additional items and department B the same number, and if the budget is sufficient for only ten between them, then clearly scope for conflict exists.

A central feature of politics is the notion of *interest*. Interests are defined as positions which people wish to protect or goals they seek to achieve (Miller 1962). If no one cares whether company A is awarded a contract for supplies in preference to company B, then there is no disagreement about the matter and potentially, no politics. In other words, virtually any decision, be it a matter of grand strategy or fixing the date, time and place of the office Christmas celebration is potentially political.

Organizations are shot with interests. For convenience, interests may be classified into three categories, that is:

1. task,
2. external, and,
3. career (Morgan 1996).

Task interests concern an individual's work in the organization. For instance, it is in hospital managers' interests for patients to be discharged as quickly as possible. It is in general practitioners' interests for patients to remain in hospital. Likewise, it may be in a manager's interests to retain spare vehicles to cover for breakdowns. If, however, the cost of those vehicles is charged to the manager's profit and loss account, it may be in their interests to dispose of them.

External interests include domestic pressures, obligations to professional associations and trade unions, and relationships with subcontractors, suppliers and customers. For instance, the motor trade comprises a web of relationships with buyers and sellers occasionally making concessions to facilitate a colleague's sale. Business functions on the tacit understanding that favours are returned. Management may not like the 'wheeling and dealing' which takes place, (not least because of the potential for fraud), but will recognize that some flexibility is required for the market to function.

Career interests can prompt people to resist change or to support decisions which are against an organization's best interests. For instance, managers may appoint mediocre candidates to subordinate positions in order to protect themselves from challenge. They may oppose policies which would involve them in more work, diminish their power base or disrupt their comforts. Conversely, career interests may prompt employees to suppress reservations about decisions which may not be in the organization's best interest but which suit the individual's purpose.

6.1.2 Politics as means of resolving conflicting interests

Organizations can be seen as political cauldrons where argument, compromise and negotiation occur constantly (Allison 1971, Mintzberg 1985, Morgan 1996, Pfeffer 1982). The existence of disagreement, scarcity, diversity and interests mean that conflict in organizations is inevitable. Conflict requires resolution.

Politics can be seen as the means whereby conflict is resolved.

Politics, according to Aristotle, involves recognizing the interplay of competing interests. Politics is a non-coercive means of producing order out of diversity (Crick 1976). In the words of Lasswell (1963), politics, not economics, determines who gets what, when and how in organizations. There is no political activity in a dictatorship because disagreement is not permitted. Strictly speaking the so-called 'right to manage' suggests that the same applies in organizations. Yet as we saw in section 5.6.1, no power is absolute. Employees invariably possess some discretion. It is in the exercise of discretion that political activity is seen.

Pause for reflection

A theatre manager has a problem. The company of actors want to break away from performing popular plays and wish to stage more esoteric works. The manager has reservations about this idea because many of the proposed works are expensive to produce as they involve large casts. Moreover, they rarely attract capacity audiences. Yet the manager feels it is important to maintain morale.

Advise the theatre manager.

6.2 How to Play Politics

POWER and politics are closely linked. The distinction lies in mobilization. Whereas power rests in the *ability* to achieve intended purposes (see section 5.1)

politics centres upon *how* capability is mobilized in order to achieve desired results.

(Pfeffer 1982)

We saw in section 5.5.2 how access to persons, instrumentalities and resources can give rise to informal power. Access is only the potential to realize outcomes, however. Political activity involves turning potential into power. Let us now examine how this can be accomplished.

6.2.1 Political tactics

Political tactics include:

1. Obtaining control of financial resources.
2. Creating resource dependence.
3. Influencing the decision process.
4. Unobtrusive measures.
5. Coalition building.

Each of these is now discussed in turn.

6.2.2 Paying the piper: obtaining control of financial resources

We saw in section 5.2.1 how control of material assets is a fundamental source of power. In theory, organizational funds and budgets are allocated objectively according to each department's needs. In practice, managers can do better or worse than objective conditions suggest according to their willingness to play politics and their skill in doing so.

The most sought after resources are known as slack resources. Slack resources are those which are not allocated to a specific purpose. Control over such resources implies an increase in power because they provide the manager with a margin of discretion, so called 'slush' funds, for example (Pfeffer 1982).

6.2.3 Becoming indispensable

In 1916 Winston Churchill was suddenly dismissed from office. Churchill recognized that his only hope of restoration was if colleagues came to require his support. 'Need is all,' he wrote (Gilbert 1971).

In other words, Churchill recognized that power rests upon dependence. People in organizations may try to create dependency in order to increase their power or protect their interests. There are basically three forms of dependence as follows:

1. Resource dependence,
2. Psychological dependence, and,
3. The ability to manage uncertainty.

Resource dependence exists where an individual or department controls something vital to the organization. For instance, railway signals staff and air traffic controllers are organizationally powerful because their knowledge is both unique and essential. In 1997 an employee of the Cooperative Retail Society known as Andrew Regan utilized confidential information obtained during the course of his employment to engineer a near-successful takeover bid for the Society.

Another dimension of dependence concerns the resources which employees remove from the organization if they leave. For instance, university lecturers sometimes create research centres as future bargaining counters. In 1998 a planned takeover of the City law firm known as Wilde Sapte by accountants Arthur Andersen was cancelled because of high profile departures from the firm following the merger announcement which meant that as far as Andersen's were concerned, 'The business it wanted had changed.'

The collapse of negotiations was said to be a 'huge blow' to Andersen and the start of an 'extraordinarily tough time', for Wilde Sapte (Rice and Kelly 1998).

In order to work effectively, managers must delegate. Delegation is a double-edged entity because it creates both freedom and dependence. Management involves a balancing act between creating freedom of action while maintaining a reserve of power. The relationship can be like the medieval kings and barons:

The kings used to go out periodically and knock down the baron's castles: withheld information and unreferred decisions are the bricks that corporation barons build their castles with.

(Jay 1993, p. 51)

One option for dealing with recalcitrants, suggests Jay, is for managers to take control of the departments (castles) of their least efficient subordinates. It is a risky tactic, but, if the manager succeeds in transforming the department, other subordinate managers will move in fear of suffering the same fate. The aim, says Jay, is to achieve a position where barons can be moved without question. This does not mean that the 'king' will move them, 'So long as they know that he can, they are likely to take pains to ensure that he does not have to' (p. 53).

Subordinates can create *psychological dependency* by making themselves indispensable to powerful others. A famous historical example is Martin Borman's relationship with Hitler. Borman made sure he was always on hand whenever Hitler required assistance even though it meant working highly unsociable hours. Borman ostentatiously supported Hitler in all matters, even Hitler's most questionable judgements, while quietly taking every opportunity to discredit rivals. Borman's desk was outside Hitler's office. Anyone wishing to see Hitler was obliged to apply through Borman (Trevor-Roper 1972).

Organizations dislike uncertainty because it makes planning difficult and implies risk and instability. Consequently the *ability to manage uncertainty* is a political weapon. Organizational departments which reduce uncertainty command particular power (Hickson et al. 1971). When an IRA bomb blew Manchester city centre apart in 1995, worried shop owners were not interested in forensic details or buildings' safety. They looked to who would restore the city centre to order and enable them to resume business. The chief executive's department of the local council grasped the initiative and thus swept to ascendancy.

The ability to deal with uncertainty is closely linked to expert power (French and Raven 1968, Wrong 1979; see also section 5.2.6), that is:

- a monopoly of specific information, and,
- the ability to ensure such knowledge is critical to the organization.

The more difficult that knowledge is to substitute and the more central that knowledge is to the organization, the greater the power. This explains why hospital consultants remain powerful despite the creation of professional management functions. Indeed, one way of advancing your interests is to deliberately create a crisis, (or the appearance of a crisis) and solve it (Korda 1976). An IT system can always be programmed to break down at a vital moment, a horrendous budget deficit can always be created, critical negotiations can always appear to be close to collapse.

6.2.4 Influencing the decision process

Organizations can be seen as decision making systems (Morgan 1996). The decision making process is the epicentre of political activity because it is at the point of decision that interests:

- stand to gain, or,
- to lose (Drummond 1996a).

Consequently people frequently try to influence the decision making process. Pfeffer (1982) suggests three possibilities as follows:

1. Control over the decision premises.
2. Control over the alternatives considered.
3. Control of information about the alternatives.

Each of these is now discussed in turn.

We shall see in section 7.2 how, in theory, organizational decision problems define themselves. In practice people often argue about what the issues are. This is partly because of the sheer perplexities of decision making, but also because the manner in which a problem is defined has a profound influence over the outcome (Drummond 1996a, Schon 1993). In more formal language, obtaining *control over the decision premises* means being able to specify the goals or constraints which must be satisfied (Pfeffer 1982). Developing countries, for example, have a long history of being sold technological solutions by vested interests:

Every country in Africa can show examples of modern facilities which ... are now rotting unused. We have schools, irrigation works, expensive markets and so on by which someone came and tried to 'bring development to the people'. If real development is to take place, the people have to be involved ... for development means the development of the *people*. Roads, buildings, the increase of crop output are not development; they are only the tools of development. A new road extends a man's freedom only if he travels upon it.

(Nyerere, 1973 p. 59)

As with nations, so with organizations. Interests may compete for ownership of a problem if it seems advantageous to do so. Alternatively they may be careful to distance themselves from matters which seem likely to turn out unfavourably.

> **Pause for reflection**
>
> A food processing plant has a problem. The plant prepares meals for a leading supermarket chain. A condition of the contract is that strict food hygiene procedures are observed. Any ingredients which touch the ground *must* be discarded. Management is concerned about the high proportion of mushroom cartons reported as accidentally dropped.
>
> What is the problem?

If you are the company lawyer you might suggest the mushroom cartons are a legal problem and make work for yourself renegotiating the contract. The supplies department might say that the crates have too many holes in them, and given additional staff, they could work with the supplier to redesign the crates. The personnel department might argue that operatives require training in correct handling techniques. The security department might worry that the crates are being dropped deliberately and subsequently sold. They might support one of the other departments' claims in order to protect themselves from scrutiny.

Another way in which interests can further their objectives is by obtaining *control over alternatives considered*. In theory, decision makers generate all conceivable options before deciding upon a course of action (see section 7.1). In practice, decision makers typically consider only a few possibilities. Interests try to ensure that undesirable alternatives are screened out. Screening frequently occurs under the guise of making the decision process manageable. For instance, operational managers may have examined sixteen software packages. The evaluation committee, however, may choose from a short list of two or three alternatives. Likewise, appointments panels may see only three or four of the 200 candidates who have applied for a vacancy.

Another common political ploy involves writing policy papers and position statements containing statements such as, 'There are three options . . . ', or, 'we are faced with two alternatives . . . '

In my experience such documents can play a decisive role in shaping events especially if introduced early in the process (Drummond 1991). It is surprising how floundering committees will seize upon even the most casual and ill-thought ideas if they are committed to paper.

Another political tactic is *control information about the alternatives*. In theory, decision makers gather all the relevant data about a particular option and analyse it extensively (see section 7.1). In practice, the information which decision makers receive may be highly processed and carefully presented. More specifically, interests try to ensure that their preferred option appears in a good light. For instance, Andrew Pettigrew (1972) became a participant observer of a process involving a decision to purchase a computer. Pettigrew noted how an employee known as Kenny used his position in the communication network to draw management's attention to his favoured option, for example, by mentioning it more frequently than alternative machines. Interests may also take the opportunity to denigrate alternatives. Denigration can be subtle, damning with faint praise, for example.

Once interests have achieved control of an aspect of the decision process, it is rarely challenged (Drummond 1991, Pfeffer 1982). It is unclear why this should be so. Time constraints may be one factor. Another possibility is that people may be unwilling to exhibit mistrust. This may partly explain why organizations can become involved in escalation fiascoes (see section 7.9).

Interests sometimes behave in an underhand manner. People 'forget' to put a paper before a committee. Prospective candidates are fed misleading information about the organization to discourage them from pursuing their application. Favoured contractors are supplied with inside knowledge and so on.

6.3 How to Recognize Political Tactics

R**ECALL** that the essence of politics is disagreement. How do people in organizations attempt to win arguments? We saw in section 5.3.1 that the most effective exercise of power is that which is unobtrusive. Politically adroit managers prefer to pursue their interests in a subtle fashion. Political tactics may be grouped as follows:

- establishing objective criteria,
- involving outside experts,
- manipulation of the organizational agenda,

■ creating coalitions, and,
■ cooptation.

Each of these is now discussed in turn.

6.3.1 Establishing objective criteria

Making demands supported by threats is a crude and risky way of exercising power. Force generally stirs resentment. Moreover, if the other party is powerful a conflict of wills may ensue. Such conflict creates losers. To lose is to suffer humiliation. To win is to humiliate the other party and fuel a desire for revenge.

Demands are more likely to be met if they appear legitimate. For example, it is easier to defend a salary claim which is based upon the rate of inflation or comparisons with other companies or professions than it is to justify an arbitrary figure. This is known as negotiating on the basis of objective criteria (Fisher and Ury 1983).

Objective criteria are those which all parties agree are a legitimate basis for negotiations. To take another example, 'last in first out' may be seen as a legitimate criteria for deciding redundancies. The difficulty and hence the scope for political activity, is, what constitutes objective?

> **Pause for reflection**
>
> Your organization has two hundred employees who travel to work by car. All are currently allocated car parking spaces. The organization is due to move to a new building where there are only fifty car parking spaces.
>
> How would you allocate the fifty spaces?

There are many criteria which could be adopted any one of which might be regarded as legitimate. For example, disabled employees could receive first priority. Staff who need to travel to and from the building frequently might receive next priority, especially those whose work involves transporting heavy equipment. Alternatively, the organization might charge for the spaces in order to reduce demand. Management might argue that seniority is the traditional criterion. The trade unions might suggest it is fairer to draw lots.

The point is, people in organizations try to use the criteria which best suits them and try get these accepted as objective (Salancik and Pfeffer 1974). In a redundancy situation management may argue that selection for redundancy should reflect projected operational requirements regardless of tenure. Disagreement can arise because objective criteria do not exist as absolutes but only to the extent that they are accepted as legitimate. Recall that equity theory (see section 3.3.4) suggests that it is not whether something is fair that is crucial, so much as whether it is seen to be fair. Part of the art of politics is choosing criteria which others will regard as legitimate. Returning to the criteria for redundancy, for example, management suggest that operational requirements must come first, followed by tenure. The merging of interests in this way is the essence of constructive negotiations. Yet sometimes people use objective criteria to cloak their own interests. In the popular television programme known as *Yes Minister* two senior civil servants decide that their favoured candidate for Prime Minister is the vacuous Jim Hacker. It is in their interests to see Hacker appointed as he is the most manipulable of ministers. The choice, however, is presented as, 'For Britain'.

Similarly, people in organizations sometimes say, 'Option A is best for the company,' when what they really mean is, 'Option A is best for me.'

6.3.2 Involving outside experts

John Harvey-Jones once described the consultant as someone who borrows your watch in order to tell you the time. Although that may be an exaggeration, organizations sometimes do employ expensive consultants to endorse decisions which are already made. Consultants derive their authority by appearing to be both expert and impartial.

In other words, it is not what is said that matters so much as who is saying it, that is, preferably a household name.

Consultants are often employed to lend support to policies or viewpoints where an internal party is insufficiently powerful to obtain support for its viewpoint. For example, the government may place a team of inspectors into a school to show that the school management has failed.

In practice consultants may not be as objective as they seem. Consultants are typically highly adroit at interpreting their brief and alive to the subtle signals directing their conclusions and recommendations. Consultants are also aware that future work depends upon pleasing the person who has commissioned their services (Pfeffer 1982). For instance, a manager may employ a consultant to undertake staff development when the real purpose is to prompt the consultant to write a report suggesting that staff relations have broken down due to a particular individual's mismanagement. All the manager has to say to the consultant is, 'You may not get much cooperation from the staff. There are some tensions in there which may need to be aired . . .'

6.3.3 Controlling the agenda

Politics also determines what gets discussed in the organization, when, where and by whom. Another political tactic for the pursuit or protection of interest is to obtain control of the agenda. The possibilities include:

- non-decisions,
- agenda fixing, and,
- invoking the hidden agenda.

In section 5.3.1 and 5.3.2 we saw how power is reflected not only in what is, but also in 'what is not' known as '*non-decisions*' (Bacharach and Baratz 1963). Defending interests requires resources and the skilful deployment of resources. Moreover, there is always the risk of a challenge succeeding. It is much safer to prevent a challenge from ever arising. The 'non-decision' tactic involves calculated inactivity aimed at preserving the status quo. Inactivity can take the form of allowing proverbial sleeping dogs to lie. It can also involve deliberately delaying matters in order to weaken the other party by depleting their resources and destroying morale. Another form of 'non-decision' involves invoking rules. Organizational rules sometimes fall into abeyance. Informal practices spring up. One way of exerting power without appearing to is to point out such infringements (Bacharach and Baratz 1970).

The *agenda fixing* tactic aims to prevent others from pursuing their interests by denying them an audience. The agenda may not be a literal one. The reluctance of some organizations to recognize trade unions is a form of agenda fixing. Likewise, 'in-house' magazines rarely publish material critical of the company. As regards the actual agenda of meetings, a common ploy for preventing or at least limiting discussion of an issue is to ensure that it appears at the bottom of the list. For instance, a schoolteacher raised a grievance about a salary award. The head teacher deliberately retained the item for 'any other business' on the governors' agenda. It was eight o'clock at night when 'other business' was called. It was winter and the school heating had been switched off hours ago. The governors, cold, tired and hungry were eager to get home. Earlier that evening the governors had spent fifty minutes discussing the state of the gymnasium floor. The salary claim was dismissed in thirty seconds as the governors packed their brief cases.

A *hidden agenda* exists where interests utilize one issue as a smoke-screen for pursuing another. For example, lovelorn individuals sometimes invent an excuse to see or to telephone the person of their desires. In organizations, a manager might invite staff of department A to participate in interviews for staff appointments in department B. What appears as a thoughtful and courteous gesture is actually the prelude to a subsequent merger. Mergers and takeovers often provide a smoke-screen for rewarding people, for the paying-off of old scores and for the removal of incompetents. They may provide a manager with an excuse to restructure a department or implement some other change which might otherwise have been impossible. I know of a case where a departmental manager hid behind a merger to remove an inefficient secretary. Those who live by the sword usually die by the sword. Shortly afterwards a more senior executive also used the merger as an excuse to force early retirement upon the manager. The displaced secretary's comments can be guessed.

Another form of hidden agenda is to deliberately understate the importance of a decision (Drummond 1991, Pfeffer 1982). One tactic is to pretend the change is purely cosmetic. In public service organizations, for example, profound shifts in power structures are sometimes represented as the mere tidying up of administrative details. Other tactics include burying an important issue amid trivia in order to down play its significance, and asking a decision maker to authorize a course of action when they are rushed or otherwise preoccupied. For example, 'Just sign this before you go please: it's nothing, purely routine.'

'Nothing' can turn out to be quite important (Drummond 1991).

A further variant of the hidden agenda ploy is to introduce change gradually. For example, loading employees with new duties one at a time, or depriving someone of power little by little. This tactic sometimes works because it seems petty to object to minor changes, even though the other party senses the longer term implications of events. Eventually the changes become so institutionalized that they are difficult to reverse. The supreme effect is where the other party does not even realize what has happened, that is, they lose sight of the absolute magnitude of change (see section 7.5.3). Another manipulative tactic which is sometimes used to move ineffective employees is to suggest that they are now wasted in their current jobs, and, that their talents are required elsewhere. Elsewhere usually means a backwater appointment though it may be dressed up as important. Such a ploy can minimize conflict because even if the employee realizes what has happened, they have at least been allowed to retain their dignity. It is not what you do that matters so much as how you do it.

6.3.4 Coalitions: building alliances

Safety exists in numbers. Organizations may be seen as systems of interdependent activity. Alliances known as coalitions, be they internal or external, are founded upon the shared interests of participants (Bacharach and Lawler 1980). Coalitions may be formal or informal. The organizational management team is potentially the dominant coalition. Managers can also seek to build coalitions through judicious use of promotion opportunities to advance loyal supporters. Politics can prompt some strange alliances. Employees may combine forces with people with whom they have little in common or even detest if it is in their interests to do so.

6.3.5 Cooptation

Cooptation involves drawing people into the decision process who might otherwise stand outside it. The purpose of cooptation is to make others feel powerful by involving them, or appearing to involve them, in decision processes. Setting up committees is the most common form of cooptation. Committees are sometimes supplied with detailed reports, charts, graphs, to symbolize their importance while the real decisions are actually made elsewhere. 'We will love them to death,' as one insightful manager put it.

6.3.6 Politics and symbolic activity

In 1998 the car company Chrysler and the car company Daimler-Benz secretly began talking about a possible merger. Both companies knew that their long term prospects were bleak. Daimler believed that its highly profitable luxury cars business would suffer as the quality of volume cars improved. Chrysler realized that it lacked the organizational presence and competence required to secure global status. After four months the negotiations were almost complete. All that remained was a 'wrap up' meeting to finalize legal details:

'Everything was going fine, and then the name came up,' says one participant. The Germans were adamant that the title should reflect Daimler-Benz's history, and the fact that their company was the bigger part of the merger. (Chrysler) . . . was equally determined (to be) . . . at the front. . . . Neither side would budge.

(Simonian 1998, p. 37)

The merger was too important for it to be ruined by an argument over the name of the new company. Eventually a compromise was reached. It shows the importance of symbols, however.

Symbols play an important role in politics because they are a subtle means of exercising power (Pfeffer 1981, 1982). The symbolic life of organizations is the subject of Chapter 10. Here it is sufficient to note that the most common symbols of power in organizations are office space, office furnishings, so called 'power dressing', access to the executive car park, premium expense accounts and the like. Even the positioning of a mail tray can be symbolically significant.

Even language is politically significant because it is part of the symbol system and the means whereby people construct reality.

Pause for reflection

What is this a photograph of?

You may say, 'A house of course'. It is obvious is it not? Yet would it interest you to know that planning permission is for a stable? Would it further interest you to know that the person building the 'stable' was twice refused planning permission to build a house on the site? So far the authorities are powerless to intervene because the building under construction conforms exactly to the plans approved by the local council. For instance, there is running water and electricity to the site. To the rear of the property (not visible from the photograph) there is a verandah for the horse to seek shelter in bad weather. Surely a lucky horse, say local residents.

Language also serves to conceal doubt (Starbuck, Greve and Hedberg 1978). The disastrous Somme campaign of the First World War owes much to staff officers telling senior commanders what they wanted to hear at the planning stage. When the attack failed, senior commanders were careful to blame the troops and junior officers. Likewise, managers use language to present their own performance in a good light (Drummond 1991, Stephenson 1985). Men tend to use the pronoun 'I' in order to claim the credit for success whereas women are more likely to say 'we'. Men are also less willing to ask questions and more likely to minimize their doubts than women (Tannen 1995).

Language also plays an important role in ingratiation behaviours (Appelbaum and Hughes 1998, DuBrin 1978, Wortman and Linsenmeiier 1977). Every organization has its share of Uriah Heeps pursuing their interests via sycophancy, flattery, and self-effacing behaviours, known more colloquially as 'boot licking' and 'yes man' (or woman) tactics. For instance, an irritated subordinate overhearing an ambitious colleague studiously agreeing with the Chief Executive's every word during a discussion about operational matters said, 'I see Her Grace is talking with Her Grease.'

Organizational business is often conducted via coded messages. Coded language can substitute for the use of raw power. For example, a manager may say to a subordinate, 'I think the Board would want to respond to that,' or, 'I am not sure what view the Board would take of that,' when what they really mean is, 'Have a care!'.

6.3.7 Political correctness and organizational legitimacy

Symbols can be more important than substance, hence for example, the notion of political correctness. Organizational survival is not just about manufacturing quality goods and services. Survival is ultimately political, dependent upon an organization's standing in the community (Meyer and Rowan 1978). For instance, organizations which rely heavily upon sponsorship generally avoid becoming identified with controversial figures for fear of undermining their perceived legitimacy. Likewise, the ancient University of St Andrews restored defunct Latin titles and offices in order to distance itself from more recent foundations. Conversely when Granada's takeover bid for the Forte organization was announced, Forte's chairman, Roco Forte, happened to be away shooting. It was a damaging coincidence because it signified complacency; one reason why Granada's bid succeeded.

Organizations establish planning departments and strategy groups to signify control and purposiveness. Customer relations departments and 'help lines' symbolize commitment to quality. An interesting example of the importance of symbols was seen when the Bank of Japan's credibility was threatened by corruption scandals and the suicide of one its directors. Although dress code in Japanese organizations requires men to be clean shaven, the bank deliberately employed a bearded outsider to help create a new image (Tett 1998).

6.3.8 Symbolic action and conflict resolution

Recall that politics centres upon disagreement. A symbolic response may be sufficient to resolve conflict if it reaffirms the other party's sense of power (Pfeffer 1982). For example, the trade union of a public service organization complained about the poor state of staff facilities. The director offered to visit the depots and duly undertook a programme of tours. Although the visits changed nothing, the trade union was impressed by the display of commitment. Indeed, the visits probably achieved more than material change. Upgrading depots is an expensive business. Any such programme would have been slow, probably partial and therefore a continuing source of friction.

At the individual level, conflict can sometimes be defused just by saying to the other person, 'I understand' (Drummond 1991, Fisher and Ury 1983). The words commit the negotiator to nothing, not even agreement with the other person's viewpoint. Their power lies in signifying recognition of the other person's problem or differing viewpoint. Similarly an apology alone often succeeds because it restores the other person's self-esteem (Kim and Smith 1993).

> **Pause for reflection**
>
> The tenant of a property has been killed by fumes escaping from a gas heater. The gas heater was fitted by the operatives employed by the public works department. The case is headline news in the local press and television.
>
> As departmental director what action would you take to protect yourself?

In a crisis such as this a politically adroit director would make themselves highly visible even though there is little they can actually do. Yet their absence would be disastrous as it would signify an uncaring attitude. Making one's self available to answer media enquiries and issuing unreserved apologies is not only symbolically significant, it is also a means of retaining the initiative. For those reasons, the director might also be well advised to announce an immediate investigation and to suspend from duty key figures in the chain of command (including the next most senior) pending the outcome.

Symbolic rewards and punishments can be highly potent. The gain or loss of a title such as 'director' or 'chief executive' may be more important than a gain or loss in remuneration. Nursing staff in psychiatric hospitals have fought to retain uniforms because they serve as a distancing mechanism. It is sometimes possible to deprive someone of real power provided the symbols of power are left in place. Likewise, in negotiations politically adroit managers always allow the defeated party to maintain face, leaving them with their bus fare home as the saying goes (Drummond 1991).

Even success and failure can be political. John Kennedy took great care to ensure that actions which showed him in a good light during the Cuban missile crisis were placed on record for posterity (Allison 1971). Likewise, managers may find it convenient to preserve documents vindicating their decisions and to destroy those containing evidence which could be seen as disconfirming their judgements. Recall the suggestion made earlier that organizations are supposedly rational entities. Symbols, including language, enable us to see that they are not so much rational as rationalizing (Morgan 1996).

It was Bertold Brecht who suggested that what matters is not the play but the performance. To a considerable extent, organizational success is about stage management (Drummond 1991, 1992). The politically competent manager is careful to cultivate the appearance of success, and, to avoid being identified with failure. For instance, a chief executive of a local council presented a slide show depicting the Council's achievements. There were pictures of new houses being built in the borough, of factories opening up and of children working in well-equipped and generously staffed schools. There were no images of graffiti, of boarded up shops, of crumbling buildings and other signs of urban decay.

6.4 Discussion

6.4.1 Politics and political behaviour: good or bad?

Evidence suggests that most managers are aware of the existence of political behaviour in organizations, and, of the importance of playing politics. Yet few claim to like it (Gents and Maare 1980, Stephenson 1985). Hardly surprising if this chapter is taken to imply that organizations are sinister places where only the ruthless and the unscrupulous survive and prosper.

Politics can have disturbing connotations, the 'rat race', for example. As Jay (1993) reminds us, political success does not always mean moral acclaim. We saw in section 3.5.5 how transformational leadership theory enjoins managers to empower subordinates, to create cohesion and a team spirit. However, the politically adroit manager may prefer Machiavelli's axioms, of divide and rule, of being feared rather than loved. When the wife of Shakespeare's deposed Richard II asks if she might be allowed to accompany her husband into exile Richard remarks, 'That were some love, but little policy'.

The deposed Richard's insightful remark is relevant to organizations today. Hospital patients are left on trolleys in corridors for hours to enable a consultant to make a point about bed shortages. Making special arrangements to move the patients into wards is some love but little policy as it may enable hospital managers to deny that a problem exists. Likewise Tom Bower's (1996) account of Robert Maxwell's mysterious death is not only an indictment of Maxwell but also of the lawyers, accountants and bankers who put their interests before those of the swindled Mirror Group pensioners.

Political activity can undermine organizations. For example, if incompetents obtain preferment, or if interests succeed in blocking necessary change. It has even been suggested that 'whistle blowers' in organizations are more likely to be heeded if they are high status individuals (Near and Miceli 1995). The argument against organization politics is that compromise and negotiation absorb time and energy and take precedence over technical rationality. For example:

There were at least thirty committees connected with Taurus. Most of them nothing to do with the Exchange but they all seemed to have a bearing on it. They were springing up all over the City spawned by . . . twelve years of debate. The committee of London clearing bankers had a committee on Taurus, so did the registrars, so did Snoops, and Jones. You add them up and everybody was giving input to Taurus.

(Drummond 1996b, p. 70)

No wonder Taurus failed in the end. There were just too many conflicting interests surrounding the project.

Political activity is by no means automatically counterproductive, however. According to Peters and Waterman (1982) excellent firms are characterized by a conspicuous absence of political activity. Significantly such firms did not remain excellent for very long (Pfeffer 1992).

The argument that politics undermines technical rationality reflects a mechanistic mind set as it assumes the correct (optimal) course of action, 'one best way' (see section 2.2.1), for example, is known at all times. Yet how can organizations know what is needed for survival and growth? For example, over the years, the UK clearing banks have ventured into estate agency, international custody, company registration, investment banking, and other activities often only to exit from these again even though such moves were once promulgated as strategic imperatives. Indeed, will the mergers between Citrop and Travellers and between Chrysler and Daimler-Benz succeed? What should Wilde Sapt do to recover its position?

The idea that politics undermines technical rationality presupposes an overarching rationale. In reality organizations are shot with rationales and counter-rationales. What constitutes an optimal course of action for one department may have disastrous ramifications for another.

Politics can also create the impression of 'muddling through' (Lindblom 1959). Instead of following a coherent strategy, decisions seem perpetually 'fudged', and sometimes compromised out of recognition. The organization seems to drift along. Problems which should be dealt with are ignored until they become crises (Mintzberg, Raisingham, and Thoeret 1976). On the other hand, once elected to office, most politicians discover that the problems of government are far more difficult than they seemed in opposition. The axiom, politics is the art of the possible is as relevant to managers as it is to governments.

Besides, political activity is by no means invariably selfishly motivated. Politics can promote good decisions and/or prevent bad ones. It is only because other managers are willing to play politics that necessary change results (Bacharach and Lawler 1980, Hayes 1984, Pfeffer 1982, 1992). Playing politics can involve risking one's own credibility. For instance, managers often perform a delicate balancing act when seeking support for a venture. If expectations are pitched too modestly, the project may fail to excite enthusiasm. Conversely, if too many promises are made, the venture may ultimately be seen as a failure. If ten staff are needed, how many does the manager actually bid for?

Downs (1967) suggests that managers inevitably accumulate 'skeletons in cupboards' just to get the job done. For example, job vacancies are sometimes engineered to promote good candidates. Specifications are sometimes tailored to ensure that the best supplier is awarded a contract. Such practices may leave the manager vulnerable to accusations of impropriety.

Let me approach the issue from another angle. What if managers and employees were apathetic? If no one cares enough to argue, then what? Langer (1989) suggests that more damage is done in organizations by mindless acts of vandalism than by political activity. Arguably managers who avoid politics do their organizations a disservice. Political competence, that is, the ability to negotiate, tolerate ambiguity, procure resources, exercise sensitivity, flexibility and restraint, may be every bit as important as analytical and technical skills (Hayes 1984, Jay 1993, see also Stephenson 1985).

In my experience it is the managers who are indifferent to politics or who are politically inept that subordinates find frustrating. Without someone to champion their cause, they see other departments getting the best of everything. When salary reviews and other opportunities for advancement are in prospect, they know there is no one to fight for them. Moreover, it may be precisely those managers who engender hostility and suspicion. Lacking political adroitness they are apt to rely upon their formal authority when dealing with staff. Authority can translate into crude threats and innuendo. Much more skilled is the manager who, for example, effectively dismisses an employee while making it appear that they are doing the person a favour by allowing them to take early retirement.

6.4.2 Is political behaviour inevitable?

This chapter began by suggesting that power and politics are fundamental to understanding behaviour in organizations. Critical theorists might suggest that the importance of politics is overstated. According to critical theorists political activity has little impact upon the deep structure of power in organizations (Clegg and Dunkerly 1980, see also Burrell and Morgan 1979). In this view, joint consultation committees, grievance procedures and the like function more to contain and manage conflict than to actually deal with it, known as repressive tolerance (Lammers 1988). When all is said and done, managers retain the power to manage and employees are still left with a basic obligation to obey.

It is difficult to escape from politics. Music is sometimes seen as a non-political exemplar. Yet evidence suggests that music is by no means apolitical. String quartets, for example, are riven with conflict. The quartet's survival depends less upon members' musical talents than their ability to deal with the tensions that surround them (Murigham and Conlon 1991).

While all organizations are potentially political arenas, political activity may vary in intensity from organization to organization and from situation to situation. According to Pfeffer (1982) political activity is least pronounced in organizations where power is highly centralized. Presumably this is because such organizations minimize the amount of discretion available to employees. Political activity may also be less pronounced where the environment is fairly stable. Conversely, insecurity can increase the propensity to managerial politicking. Poor performance is a prime source of insecurity (Eisenhardt and Bourgeois 1988).

In my experience political activity is often more pronounced in what Etzioni calls normative organizations, that is, education, health, and social services than in the more utilitarian organizations such as construction, cleaning and cleansing companies (see section 5.2.1). This is not to suggest that the latter are apolitical. On the contrary I have seen some lively 'turf wars' between cost centre managers. Even so, they seem on the whole to be less riven with politics, perhaps because the core knowledge base of such organizations is technical and therefore highly specific. That may suggest there is less scope for disagreement, that is, there is more emphasis upon 'doing' than discussing what should be done.

Morgan (1996) suggests that too much emphasis upon politics can lead to people becoming paranoid, convinced that conspiracy and intrigue are everywhere. Paranoia, suggests Morgan, can prompt people to search for hidden meaning in the most innocent acts such as making the coffee.

Perhaps Morgan was thinking of Metternich's reaction upon learning of a statesman's sudden death. Metternich is alleged to have said, 'I wonder what he meant by that.'

Yet even a simple gesture such as making coffee *can* have political connotations. Some male executives make a point of brewing their own coffee to symbolize their professed non-sexist orientation. Conversely, some women in organizations deliberately avoid pouring the coffee for fear of reaffirming the 'mother' stereotype. Certain organizations make great play of single status facilities and the like. The absence of uniforms and segregated canteens does not mean, however, that such organizations are devoid of status differences. Instead power and status are expressed in different ways.

It is also important to remember that political manoeuvres and machinations can fail. Disraeli referred to party politics as a 'greasy pole'. The analogy also applies to political activity in organizations. Politics can enable managers to rise but can also prompt their downfall as skills become obsolete and attitudes and outlooks unfashionable, and as others vie for position (Pfeffer 1992). Beneath the surface, things are not always what they seem. Many a manager has discovered to their cost that their apparently loyal supporters are secret and determined enemies. No one is absolutely essential. As the proverb goes, grave yards are full of people that were indispensable.

Influence is a pervasive entity and an unpredictable force (Bacharach and Lawler 1980). The divided can rise above their differences and unite in order to achieve a purpose. Cooptation inevitably involves a surrender of power. Interests sometimes allow themselves to be coopted because they believe that they can achieve more by influencing from within rather than from the outside. Decisions do not necessarily mean an end to the pursuit of interest. As the sagacious Sir Humphrey in the popular television programme *Yes Minister* put it, 'A decision is only a decision if it's the decision you want. Otherwise its a set-back.'

Interests have many options for dealing with set-backs. Decisions are sometimes ignored, diluted, delayed, referred for further investigation and so on (Drummond 1996a).

Timing is important in politics and difficult to get right. Pfeffer (1992) recounts how a brilliantly argued report which might have changed the course of the Vietnam War made no impact simply because it was published at the wrong time. Likewise Drummond (1991) suggests that many promising organizational initiatives have failed at the embryonic stages because they were hailed as solutions before decision makers were ready to recognize the existence of a problem.

Chance is another factor that even the most politically competent manager cannot control. It is surely no accident that the board game 'Monopoly' is played with dice. The dice symbolizes the role of uncertainty in human affairs. Decisions can be over-taken by events. A week is a long time in organizational politics also. As we shall see in the next chapter, and as Wilde Sapt and Arthur Andersen discovered to their cost, the best laid and almost successful schemes can go awry. Politics may go a long way in deciding who gets what, when, where and how. Luck may have the last word.

Summary

1 Politics play a crucial role in organization behaviour.

2 The essence of politics lies in:

- disagreement,
- diversity,
- scarcity, and,
- interest.

If resources were plentiful and if everyone agreed all the time, there would be no political activity in organizations.

3 Interest plays a pivotal role in politics.

4 Organizational interests can be classified as follows:

- task,
- external, and,
- career.

5 Politics provides a non-coercive means of resolving conflicting interests, of producing order out of diversity.

6 Power and politics are closely linked.

7 Power rests in the *ability* to achieve intended purposes. Politics concerns *how* capability is mobilised in order to achieve results.

8 Political tactics used by people in organizations include:

- obtaining control of financial resources,
- creating resource dependence,
- influencing the decision process,
- unobtrusive measures, and,
- coalition building.

9 Organizational decision processes can be the focus of intense political activity because the point of decision is where interests stand to gain or to lose.

10 Interests may attempt to influence the decision process by obtaining control over:

- the decision premises, or,
- the alternatives considered, or,
- information about the alternatives.

11 Politics involve argument. The tactics which may be deployed to win arguments include:

- establishing objective criteria,
- involving outside experts,
- manipulation of the organizational agenda,
- creating coalitions, and,
- cooptation.

12 Symbols play an important role in politics because they are a subtle means of exercising power.

13 Examples of symbols of power in organizations include office space, office furnishings, so called 'power dressing', access to the executive car park, and premium expense accounts.

14 Symbolic action can be more important than substance.

15 Political behaviour is not invariably selfish or counterproductive. Politics can promote good decisions and restrain bad ones.

16 Political competence may be as important in executives as technical skill.

17 According to critical theorists, political activity seldom disturbs the deep power structure of organizations.

18 Too much emphasis upon politics can produce paranoia. Conversely, even the most mundane activity *can* be politically significant.

Questions for Discussion

1 'If everybody minded their own business, . . . the world would go round a great deal faster than it does.' (*Alice's Adventures in Wonderland, The Complete Illustrated Works*, p. 60)

   Discuss with reference to the relationship between politics and technical rationality.

2 What skills does the politically competent executive require?

3 'How do you control a group? You formalize it, bureaucratize it and give it lunch.' (Executive of UK commercial organization)

   Discuss with reference to politics and political behaviour in organizations.

4 Politics is sometimes described as 'the art of the possible'.

   Discuss with reference to the notions of technical rationality and utility maximization.

5 'He who builds on the people builds on mud.' (Machiavelli, *The Prince* (1513) Ch. 18 (trs. A. Gilbert))

   Discuss.

Further Reading

- Drummond, H. (1991) *Power: Creating It, Using It,* London, Kogan Page.
- Drummond, H. (1992) 'Triumph or disaster: What is Reality?' *Management Decision*, 30, 29–33.
- Hayes, J. (1984) 'The Politically Competent Manager', *Journal of General Management*, 10, 24–33.
- Jay, A. (1993) *Management and Machiavelli,* London, Century.
- Meyer, J. W. and Rowan, B. (1978) 'Institutionalized Organizations: Formal Structure as Myth and Ceremony', *American Journal of Sociology*, 83, 340–363.
- Pfeffer, J. (1982) *Power in Organizations*, Boston, Pitman.

Chapter 7
Decision Making in Organizations

> It is not given to human beings ... to foresee or predict to any large extent the unfolding of events. In one phase men seem to have been right, in another they seem to have been wrong. There again, a few years later ... all stands in a different setting.
>
> (R. J. Robert, *Winston S. Churchill: His Complete Speeches 1897–1963*, Vol. VI)

O**N** Thursday 23 February 1995, Barings' Bank stood as one of the oldest and most respected organizations in the City of London. Yet barely three days later, on Monday 27 February, Barings' declared itself insolvent. The bank's sudden and dramatic collapse was traced to the unauthorized activities of a single trader known as Nick Leeson. In their lucid and engaging account of Barings' fall, journalists John Gapper and Nicholas Denton describe the tension as Leeson's activities began to be uncovered shortly after four o'clock that afternoon:

> It made no sense because ... Every single contract they could identify was losing money. ... Using Barings' precious capital, Leeson had taken the largest losing bet in history. It [Barings'] could have lost more than £200 million already, but the frightening thing was that Leeson had pushed it into a bottomless hole. Barings' ... did not have much capital. The Nikkei was falling and Barings' bill was growing even bigger. The Baring Foundation's shares had a balance sheet value of £308 million and it had a further £101 million in loan capital. If Leeson's losses ate through this Barings was finished.
>
> (Gapper and Denton 1996, p. 23)

Leeson's final losses exceeded £800 million, that is, twice Barings' capital. The cause of the collapse was traced to Barings' decision to place Leeson in charge of both trading and settlement activities (known as front and back office) in Singapore. Normally the back office acts as a check upon fraud and misconduct as it processes the paperwork associated with trading. Leeson's control over both functions enabled him to conceal his unauthorized trading until the losses became catastrophic (Gapper and Denton 1996).

Business history is rich in instances of ill-judged decisions, 'what if's', and 'if only's'. The decision sciences literature offers many sophisticated tools of analysis and computation. Decisions are ultimately made by people, however. The purpose of the present chapter is to highlight some of the realities of decision making.

Decision making involves grappling with risk and ambiguity. Sometimes organizations become committed to fateful ventures without anyone apparently having made a 'decision'. How do we explain that? Why do organizations sometimes pursue failing projects yet abandon potentially successful ones? Why is intuition sometimes uncannily accurate? The issues addressed in this chapter include:

Key Issues

- How should decisions be made?
- When is a problem 'a problem'?
- Reality or illusion? Decision making and information.
- When is a decision not a decision?
- Are people irrational?
- Sensible shortcuts? Decision heuristics.
- Control or the illusion of control?
- Are groups dangerous?
- Try try again? Escalation in decision making.
- The limits of rationality.

7.1 How Should Decisions be Made?

THE word decision is derived from Latin meaning 'to cut'. A decision can be defined as a clear and volitional commitment to action. Economic decision theory assumes that decision makers are motivated to maximize profits or other potential benefits, sometimes known as optimizing utility. In order to maximize utility the decision maker should proceed as follows:

1 Define the problem.
2 Clarify and prioritize the goals.
3 Generate all conceivable options for goal attainment.
4 Evaluate every option.
5 Compare the consequences of each option with the goals.
6 Select the option with consequences most closely matching the goals.

In practice, decision makers seldom adhere to this prescription. The model assumes that the decision maker possesses perfect information and unlimited time, which is seldom the case. Instead, decision makers are said to opt for 'bounded rationality', that is, limiting themselves to a few options and choosing one which 'will do'—known as satisficing (March and Simon 1958, Simon 1960).

Note, however, the notion of 'bounded rationality' still presumes that decision makers adhere to economic logic and observe the basic sequence of intelligence gathering, evaluation and choice. Both models depict the decision maker as an analytical machine following a set of programmed steps rather like a computer. The reality may be very different. Let me now explain why.

7.2 When is a Problem 'A Problem'?

Both the economic and bounded rationality models of decision making (hereafter referred to as sequential models of decision making) imply that problems arrive neatly packaged and clearly labelled for decision makers' attention. The model further assumes that all problems are duly attended to.

In practice, decision issues do not define themselves automatically. Is the bottle half full or half empty, for example? Mobile telephones are said to emit radiation. Is it dangerous? Who defines danger? Problem definition is important because it determines how issues are seen, shaped and accorded priority (Drummond 1996a).

Organizations are shot with problems competing for attention. Evidence suggests that some problems may be neglected for upwards of twenty-five years. Even then they may only be addressed if they become crises (Mintzberg, Raisingham and Thoeret 1976). We saw in sections 5.3.1 and 6.3.3 how people may suppress issues or frame them in a manner which suits their purposes. Besides, serious issues are not always immediately obvious while the most pressing problems are not always the most important in the longer term. Yet as Janis (1989) notes only the squeaky wheels are oiled.

Pause for reflection

An estate agent and chartered surveyor decided to open a branch office in Smalltown about eight miles from the main office in Largetown. The decision maker subsequently decided to leave Largetown altogether and transfer the whole operation to Smalltown. The decision maker said that it was necessary in any case to move from the existing premises in Largetown because of constant attacks by vandals.

Within six months, however, it is becoming clear that the business has declined.

What is the problem?

7.2.1 Organizations as garbage cans

It was suggested in Chapter 1 that metaphors play an important role in understanding organizations. An interesting metaphor concerning decision making is the notion of organizations as garbage cans. We also saw how organizational theorizing tends to reflect linear intuitive thinking assumptions (see section 1.4.2). An important assumption is that:

problems precede solutions.

The garbage can metaphor highlights a very different possibility. In reality:

'solutions' often chase 'problems'.

In this view organizations are metaphorical dustbins into which problems and solutions are tipped at random and where the 'solution' sometimes defines the 'problem' (Cohen, March and Olsen 1972). For example, organizations sometimes purchase software (solutions) and then seek applications (problems) for it. Organizations may invent projects in order to keep their research and development staff busy. The personnel department may rewrite rules and policies in order to justify their existence.

Logically, evaluation precedes choice. Yet evidence suggests that in practice evaluation and choice occur simultaneously (Mintzberg, Raisingham and Thoeret 1976). They may even occur in reverse, that is, decision makers first decide and then construct the rationale for choice—rather like Alice in Wonderland, sentence first, verdict later. In the case of the estate agent, locating a new office is a solution which prompts the decision maker to redefine the problem. Note too how the decision maker conceptualizes the problem as merely one of transferring offices. In fact, the decision maker failed to realize that relocation actually meant starting again. That is what is meant by the suggestion that decision issues are not self-defining.

The sequential model further assumes that options are evaluated against goals. The 'garbage can' metaphor implies that the means are often made to fit the ends. For example, in 1915 the British Government considered mounting a full scale military expedition in order to capture Constantinople and thus precipitate an end to the First World War. The only available resources, however, comprised twelve old battleships. The government then decided that a naval bombardment of the forts guarding the route to Constantinople (known as the Dardanelles) would suffice to frighten the Turks into surrendering (Gilbert 1994).

Sequential models further suggest that 'solutions' resolve 'problems'. The garbage can metaphor highlights a very different possibility, namely that 'solutions' can create 'problems' (Hatch and Ehrlich 1993). This is sometimes known as the 'operation successful, patient dead' syndrome (Watzlawick 1988) whereby the solution proves more dangerous than the problem.

7.2.2 'The tragedy of the commons': the unexpected and inevitable

All decisions have unintended consequences. Sometimes, however:

the consequences are the very opposite of what was intended.

A useful metaphor for understanding how policies can contain the seeds of destruction is known as the 'tragedy of the commons' (Hardin 1968). The commons were stretches of land offering free grazing rights. Economic logic dictates that each peasant graze one more beast. The cumulative impact of everyone behaving logically is that the land is over-grazed and thus ruined for everyone.

A modern parallel concerns a £500 million IT venture commissioned by the London

Stock Exchange known as Taurus. Project Taurus collapsed because the design was too complex. It became complex because the banks, brokers, custodians and company registrars all had different needs. Since no one was prepared to compromise, the Stock Exchange made the mistake of trying to satisfy everyone. Taurus eventually comprised no fewer than seventeen different designs welded together (Drummond 1996b). Thus did the pursuit of rationality at one level create collective chaos.

7.3 Reality or Illusion? Decision Making and Information

RECALL that the sequential model of decision making assumes perfect information. Yet all information is 'false' because it is an abstraction (Brown 1989, see also section 1.4.4). An abstraction may be accurate as far as it goes but we can never grasp the whole. For example, the Gallipoli commanders were dismayed to discover that their maps conveyed little impression of the steepness of the cliffs and the exposed nature of the landing beaches.

We also saw in section 6.3.2 that information may be withheld or intentionally biased. The Warren Report was the received account of the assassination of President Kennedy until various journalists exposed important omissions and inaccuracies.

7.3.1 The symbolic significance of information

The sequential model assumes that information guides decision making. There is another perspective, however, which suggests that:

information serves more to legitimize the decision making process by conveying the appearance of rationality.

(Drummond 1996b, Meyer and Rowan 1978, Quaid 1993)

No responsible banker, for example, will lend money to a commercial venture without first seeing a business plan. The purpose of compiling a business plan is to analyze the prospects including projected costs and revenues. Although those figures may be based upon the most careful research and analysis they are ultimately guesswork because the assumptions upon which they are based cannot be known. For instance, while a prospective hotelier can assume an occupancy rate of say 80 per cent, no guarantee exists that the target will be achieved. (For a further discussion of the symbolic significance of information see section 10.3.3).

7.3.2 Can risk be controlled and managed?

There are only two certainties in this life, that is, death and taxes. Most organizational decisions involve risk.

Risk is associated with mathematics and statistical probability. For example, Pauchant and Mitroff state, 'Risk management involves evaluating the cost of a risk after multiplying the probability of occurrence' (1992, p. 93). Likewise textbooks on financial engineering often contain instructions like 'assume 60 per cent risk'.

While quantification helps managers to gain a sense of perspective:

mathematical models imply that risk is something which *can* be predicted and controlled.

Yet probabilities cannot be known for certain. What is the likelihood of a clearing bank failing? The danger is that quantification can lull decision makers into a false sense of security.

Moreover, the fact that the probability of an event is low does not mean it cannot happen. For example, the operators of the Channel Tunnel maintained that there was little likelihood of a serious fire occurring underground, and besides, the evacuation arrangements were more than adequate. Yet in 1995 the tunnel was severely damaged by fire and fatalities narrowly avoided. Even seemingly obvious statistical laws are by no means absolute. For example, although there is an equal probability of achieving 'heads' or 'tails' when a coin is tossed (assuming an unweighted coin), statisticians dispute the number of times a coin needs to be tossed for the laws of probability to operate.

7.3.3 Reality as received images

How do we know what we know? We saw in section 1.1.2 that metaphors are inherently partial. We 'know' what the First World War was like through photographs of men and horses floundering in mud. We glimpse the hell where youth and laughter go through poetry. Yet what we 'know' are basically received images of the war (Dyer 1993). It is not what those received images reflect that is significant so much as what they obscure. The death of Diana Princess of Wales is associated with 100,000 people queuing to sign books of condolence and laying flowers. What of the 100,000,000 others who did not participate in those activities?

7.3.4 The hall of mirrors

The point is that decision makers can easily forget that they are dealing with abstraction, bias and guesswork. Assumptions can seem like solid fact. Statistics, probabilities and risk management departments can create an illusion of control (Drummond 1996c).

Moreover, although our capacity to generate and transmit data has grown exponentially, that does not necessarily make us better decision makers. Too much information can be as harmful as too little. Evidence suggests overload can create over-confidence in one's data (Caldwell and O'Reilly 1982).

7.4 When is a Decision Not a Decision?

7.4.1 'Decisionless-decisions'

Recall that the word 'decision' implies a clear volitional choice between alternatives. The sequential model implies that 'outcomes' flow from 'decisions'. Yet individuals and organizations can find themselves engaged in a course of action or confronted with an outcome which is not readily traceable to any specific decision. How can that happen?

The notion of decision is basically a metaphor. It is a device which enables us to explain outcomes (Brown 1977, 1989; Morgan 1980, 1983). It is not what the metaphor illuminates that is significant in this context so much as what it obscures. One important factor which is obscured by the notion of decision is the impact of the passage of time. For example, the very act of remaining with a particular firm for a long time can create pension entitlements, seniority rights and so forth. Although these issues may have had no influence on the decision to join the firm, their cumulative impact may make it too expensive to leave. The individual thus finds themselves bound by so called 'decisionless-decisions' that is through mixing extraneous interests with another decision. This is sometimes known as making 'side-bets' (Becker 1960).

Recall that the sequential model assumes perfect information. Yet people cannot always foresee the long-term consequences of their actions—America's involvement in Vietnam, for example. Likewise, the British government assumed the First World War would end before Christmas 1914.

In the so-called 'dollar auction' experiment participants are invited to bid for a dollar coin. There is no reserve price. In theory, therefore, the coin can be obtained for as little as one cent. A special rule of the auction, however, is that the second highest bidder must pay the bid price.

> **Pause for reflection**
>
> Would you participate in a 'dollar auction'?

Teger (1980) reports that people typically enter the auction for fun. They soon desist, however, as the price of the coin rises. Eventually two bidders become locked into an escalatory spiral without ever intending to. The 'dollar auction' syndrome is a prime example of a 'decision-less decision' and may partly explain why some airlines, petrol companies and newspapers become involved in near-suicidal price wars.

The sequential model also obscures the subtle twists and turns which decisions can take. For example, no one decided that project Taurus should become large and complicated. What happened was that the various constituents, banks, brokers and so forth insisted upon a succession of amendments to the design. The amendments were minor in themselves, but their cumulative impact increased the complexity exponentially, and, in ways that were not immediately obvious.

Likewise, in the case of Gallipoli, no sooner had the War Council opted for a naval bombardment than ministers began to suggest that troops should be found to support the navy after all. Gradually a venture which involved minimal risk and commitment evolved into a full-scale and ultimately disastrous expedition.

7.4.2 Decisions as myths

Another potentially useful metaphor is the notion of 'decisions' as myths. Myths are defined as partial representations of reality which gain and lose credence over time. Myths represent the dominant viewpoint about the nature of reality and what should be done (Hedberg and Jonsonn 1977). For example:

- 'What business are we in?'
- 'Who are our customers?'
- 'How can quality be improved?'

The notion of myth helps us to see that issues such as core competencies, strategic threats and opportunities and other organizational imperatives do not exist as absolutes but only as people define them. They are myths, partially true and therefore partially untrue.

Organizations can be seen as shot with myths and counter myths competing for dominance. Myths gain and lose credence over time. For instance, the explosion at Chernobyl destroyed the myth that safety systems designed into nuclear power plants are infallible.

7.5 Are People Irrational?

7.5.1 Prospect theory

Decisions which involve uncertainty inevitably entail risk. The sequential model assumes that decision makers will only choose a risky option if the prospective gains are high enough to compensate for the risks involved. According to behavioural scientists, however, certain situations prompt risk seeking. Risk seeking means:

an outcome that is certain is rejected in favour of a gamble with an equal or lesser outcome.

Prospect theory predicts that people tend to become risk seeking when decisions are defined as:

a choice between a certain loss or the distinct probability of an even larger loss.

For example, a person faced with a loss of £2,000 is offered a choice between a sure gain of £1,000 or a 50 per cent chance of winning £2,000 or nothing at all. Evidence suggests that most people (approximately 70 per cent of the population) would opt for the riskier alternative. Only when the decision maker has adjusted to the initial loss are they likely to chose the more rational option which offers a certain £1,000 (Kahneman and Tversky 1979, 1982; Tversky and Kahneman 1981). Prospect theory may explain why, for example, most racecourse betting on 'long shots' occurs during the last race (Bazerman 1994).

Prospect theory further suggests that in certain situations people become risk averse. Risk averse means:

an outcome that is certain is preferable to a gamble involving an equal or higher outcome.

People typically become risk averse when faced with a choice between gains. Prospect theory holds that most people prefer a certain gain to the prospect of gambling upon a potentially larger one. For example, prospect theory predicts that a sure gain of £10,000 is preferable to a 50 per cent chance of gaining £20,000. Risk aversion is potentially irrational because it may prompt decision makers to forgo the option promising the highest objective utility (Kahneman and Tversky 1979, 1982; Tversky and Kahneman 1981).

Pause for reflection

You have spent £30 on a theatre ticket. Ten minutes into the performance you feel bored and restless. You wish you had never bought the ticket.

What is the correct course of action?

7.5.2 The implications of prospect theory

Prospect theory suggests that the manner in which a problem is formulated (framed) determines decision makers' behaviour. Although prospect theory was developed to explain monetary decisions it may be relevant to a variety of scenarios. For instance, if decision makers see themselves as in a situation of attempting to preserve jobs they may be ultra cautious in their approach to risk, whereas if they define the situation as one of avoiding additional redundancies they be attracted to high risk strategies (Bazerman 1994).

Prospect theory may also explain escalation (Whyte 1986, see also section 7.9). The disastrous decision to launch the spaceship Challenger may have been prompted by risk seeking behaviour prompted by decision makers' unwillingness to accept the losses which would result from postponement (Janis 1989, Whyte 1989).

Prospect theory also implies that people can be manipulated. Imagine an investor has lost £30,000, that is, half of their retirement monies of £60,000 following an unsuccessful speculation in the commodities market. Imagine a commission hungry advisor who then says, 'You have lost that money unless you invest the other £30,000.' Emphasizing the previous loss may tempt the investor into taking a reckless gamble with their remaining funds instead of seeing the situation for what it has become, that is, £30,000 to invest.

From an economic standpoint past investments (sometimes known as sunk costs) are irrelevant to decisions about the future. The correct criterion for subsequent decisions is the best return upon investment (Northcraft and Wolfe 1984). This means that the correct course of action in the case of the play is to leave the theatre. Remaining only compounds the loss. Yet many people would elect to stay feeling that it is the only way they can obtain their money's worth.

7.5.3 Evaluating risk

Behavioural scientists suggest that people are also systematically biased in how they evaluate risk:

■ More attention is paid to outcomes which are considered certain than those which are considered as merely probable, and,
■ improbable events are usually ignored (Bazerman 1994).

This may explain why many people in the UK continue to consume beef despite the possibility of contracting a fatal disease. Although the risk is apparently remote that does not mean beef is safe to eat. As the political scientist Graham Allison (1971) reminds us there is, 'an awesome crack' between the impossible and the improbable. For example, the McDonald corporation probably assumed that the likelihood of two unemployed people even defending (far less partly winning) a long and complex libel suit against leading lawyers was so remote that they could discount it. McDonald's subsequently became involved in one of the longest and costliest court cases in legal history and one which did far greater damage to the company than the original allegations (Vidal 1997).

Prospect theory further predicts that:

losses are more keenly felt than gains.

Behavioural scientists suggest that the pain of losing say, £100 is more acute than the pleasure of gaining £100. This implies that decision makers may take undue risks or engage in disproportionate efforts in order to recoup losses. For example, a solicitor once undertook considerable personal injuries work upon behalf of a major trades union. The trades union then changed its policy and decided to retain several firms. The solicitor subsequently spent the next five years in a fruitless and debilitating attempt to regain the work. In this case it was not the loss itself which damaged the solicitor's practise so much as the reaction to the loss.

Decision makers tend to be more sensitive to relative magnitudes of change rather than absolutes.

In other words, the latest increase or decrease in value has more impact that the overall gain or loss. For instance, people tend to be more conscious of the latest 5 per cent increase in petrol prices than the cumulative sum of successive rises over a period of time. This may explain why governments usually raise taxes gradually.

Psychologically, the difference in value between a gain from £100 to £200 seems greater than the difference in value between £1,000 and £1,100 even though objectively the two outcomes are identical (Kahneman and Tversky 1982). The same applies to perceptions of loss. Negotiators are thus well advised to seek concessions piecemeal and to avoid making dramatic demands.

7.6 Sensible Shortcuts? Decision Heuristics

RECALL that the sequential model requires the decision maker to analyse their options in great detail. Behavioural scientists suggest that in practice decision makers utilize mental shortcuts known as heuristics. Heuristics can help decision makers to simplify their task. However, they can also induce error. Such heuristics include:

- the 'vividness effect',
- the 'representativeness effect', and,
- the 'anchoring and adjustment' effect (Tversky and Kahneman 1973, Bazerman 1994).

Each of these is now explained in turn.

7.6.1 The 'vividness effect'

The 'vividness effect' can undermine the decision-maker's judgement in that:

1. Dramatic events seem more probable than mundane events.
2. Vivid images have more impact upon decision making than factual and statistical data.

Evidence suggests that, for most people, the prospect of being involved in an air crash looms larger than the likelihood of being involved in a car crash even though statistically, driving a car is more risky than flying in a plane. This is because air accidents make headline news whereas car accidents are seldom publicized. This is known as the 'vividness effect'. The 'vividness effect' arises because instances which are more easily recalled *appear* more numerous than an event of greater or equal frequency which is less easily recalled.

The 'vividness effect' can undermine decision making because choices are based upon limited data, that is, that which is more easily recalled. For instance, John De Lorean persuaded the American government to invest millions of dollars in a sports car manufacturing venture which subsequently failed. De Lorean succeeded by projecting a glorious vision of the future which detracted policy makers' attention from their dry but prescient statistical analyses (Schwenk 1986).

7.6.2 Representativeness heuristic

The representativeness heuristic refers to instances where a decision maker categorizes an individual, item or event according to its resemblance to a past individual, item or event. For example, a manager may predict a new product's performance according to its similarity to past successful or unsuccessful products.

Although this strategy can provide useful initial estimates, it can result in managers taking decisions based upon inadequate information or ignoring more reliable sources of information. Another risk is that decision makers see only the similarities between past and present and not the differences. For example, decision makers may miss subtle changes in the environment or in someone's behaviour. Such biasing can also lead to ethically questionable behaviour including discrimination and injustice.

7.6.3 The 'anchoring and adjustment' effect

Imagine you are asked to estimate whether the price of a certain share will rise or fall. A broker's report indicates that the company is strong, well managed and has consistently achieved above average returns. The broker forecasts a 15 per cent increase in the share price over the next year. What is your own estimate of the prospects?

Evidence suggests that your answer will be influenced by the initial estimate of 15 per cent. This is known as the 'anchoring and adjustment' effect whereby decision makers arrive at their own estimates by adjusting upwards or downwards from whatever reference point is provided (in this case 15 per cent). For example, prospective employers typically base their offers upon a candidate's existing salary rather than considering their absolute worth.

Such biasing can undermine decision making because the effect has been observed even where the information supplied is completely arbitrary or otherwise misleading. One reason why first impressions are important is that people do not always adjust from their initial psychological reference point.

> **Pause for reflection**
> Which would you prefer:
> - to accept a lottery ticket from a shopkeeper or,
> - choose the ticket yourself?
>
> You can assume that the shop-keeper is honest.

7.7 Control or Illusion of Control?

MOST people would prefer to choose their own ticket, even though rationally it makes no difference to the prospects of winning. Psychologically it is important, because choice imparts a sense of control, albeit an illusory one. More formally, such behaviour is irrational because it reflects:

a greater expectation of success than objective probability warrants (Langer 1975).

Behavioural scientists suggest that most people possess an innate desire to control chance events and to 'beat the odds' (Langer 1975, p. 323). For example, gamblers have been observed to throw hard when they require a high number on a dice and softly when they require a low number. This phenomenon is known as the illusion of control.

The illusion of control is the opposite of learned helplessness (Langer 1975). It is the erroneous belief that outcomes can be influenced. For example, fruit machines incorporate 'nudge' and 'hold' buttons to heighten players' sense of control (Fisher 1993). Inducing a sense of control can reduce the depression which flows from feeling helpless. For example, hospital patients are sometimes offered a limited choice over how their treatment is administered in order to reduce perceived dependency. Self-efficacy is a double edged entity, however, as it can lead decision makers to overestimate their capability.

7.8 Are Groups Dangerous?

DECISIONS are often made by groups. Groups can enhance decision making by bringing together a range of skills, experience and outlooks. Conversely, group decision making can pose particular dangers. Although the empirical evidence for what follows is by no means absolute, an appreciation of group dynamics can help managers to anticipate and manage risk. The principal risks derive from:

- status differentials,
- group norms,
- risky and cautious shifts,
- polarization, and,
- 'groupthink'.

Each of these is now discussed in turn.

7.8.1 Status differentials

Groups exist for a purpose. The fulfilment of purpose requires group members to interact with one another. Interaction implies exchange of emotions and stimuli. Through such exchange people become conscious of the psychological impact of other members of the group.

Such interaction creates an awareness of formal and informal status differentials within the group. Such differentials can impair decision making because high status members tend to dominate the group. They typically initiate and receive more communications which enhances their influence. Since high status individuals are treated with greater deference than low status members, their views are more likely to be accepted even when they are wrong (Zander 1982). Consequently pronounced status differentials act to suppress full and open discussion.

7.8.2 Group norms

A norm is a standard against which the appropriateness of a behaviour is assessed. Group norms reflect a shared understanding of what is or is not acceptable. Norms apply to issues which matter to a particular group. For example, some groups impose dress codes, while others express criticism in coded language.

Norms play an important role in enabling groups to function. The existence of norms can prevent embarrassment or conflict by suppressing mention of taboo subjects. Norms can be economically efficient in that they may enable the group to expedite business by rendering some decisions automatic, such as excluding certain categories of people from membership. Norms can also impart a sense of identity and shared values which can provide a focal point to energize and revitalize the group.

Crucially, however:

norms dictate the behaviour of group members, not individuals' thoughts or feelings.

The price of group membership is conformity. Group norms may prompt individuals to support decisions which they privately disagree with and which are detrimental to the organization (Hackman 1976, Shaw 1981). Pronounced status differentials may compound the risk as high status members typically adhere strongly to group norms (Zander 1982).

7.8.3 Risky shifts, cautious shifts and polarization

Risky shift occurs where a group makes a decision which is *more risky* than an individual operating alone would make (Stoner 1961). Cautious shift occurs where a group makes a decision which is *less risky* than an individual operating alone would make (Cartwright 1973). Both phenomena are important because risky shift can lead groups to accept probabilities which are rationally indefensible, whereas excessive caution can lead to missed opportunity.

It is unclear what prompts either risky or cautious shift. It has been suggested that groups are not prone to either risk or caution so much as polarization. Polarization means that:

groups tend to magnify the dominant viewpoint.

For example, if group members are doubtful about a particular issue to begin with, group discussion will stress the doubts and vice versa (Doise 1969).

Although there is evidence to support the polarization explanation, again it is unclear why it should occur. One explanation is that sharing of opinions creates a sense of commitment to the initial viewpoint. Another suggestion is that group members are swayed by one another's advocacy. Another possibility is that the security of group membership induces members to support a decision which is more drastic or more cautious than they would accept as individuals. This is known as diffusion of responsibility (Shaw 1981).

Polarization has also been linked to prospect theory. Recall that prospect theory predicts that individuals are risk-averse in positively framed situations, and risk-seeking in negatively framed situations. Conceivably, group discussion encourages articulation of the issues in multiple frames thus moderating the impact of any one specific frame of reference (Bazerman 1984). Moreover, evidence suggests that group discussion creates the reverse effect to that observed for individuals, that is:

- a risky shift on positively framed issues, and,
- a cautious shift on negatively framed issues (Neale et al. 1986).

7.8.4 'Groupthink'

'Groupthink' is another source of pressure for conformity. 'Groupthink', however, is potentially more dangerous than the pressures emanating from status differentials or the existence of group norms. Whereas the latter result in deliberate suppression of judgement, 'groupthink' occurs subconsciously. It involves the involuntary suppression of members' critical faculties.

'Groupthink' results in diminished mental rigour because fear of upsetting the cosy atmosphere discourages members from engaging in analysis and debate. The symptoms and consequences of 'groupthink' are as follows (Janis 1972, Janis and Mann 1977):

1. *An illusion of invulnerability*: the absence of conflict creates a air of cohesiveness which then leads to an illusory sense of invulnerability. As there is no dissent, group members come to believe that their judgement is infallible.

2. *Rationalization or discounting of negative information*: since negative feedback is potentially disconcerting, group members tend to 'explain away' or underemphasize such information. Potential warnings are thus ignored and members' perceptions of reality become distorted. For example, NASA officials are said to have downplayed the risks involved in launching the space shuttle Challenger (Janis 1989, Whyte 1989).

3. *An uncritical belief in the group's inherent morality*: since the group seems united, members are apt to assume that the group's decisions are ethically defensible. As such, the group may direct aggression outwards and to other groups.

4. *Stereotyping*: the group's desire to maintain consensus makes it difficult to accept change. The group's perceptions of reality thus become stereotyped. Stereotyping impedes the recognition of subtle changes in others' capabilities or behaviour. For example, the Americans regarded the Vietnamese as primitive, inferior and incapable of engaging in effective opposition. This image blinded the government to their opponent's growing military strength and diplomatic adroitness (Janis 1972).

5. *Self-censorship*: 'groupthink' leads individuals to suppress their doubts and disagreements for fear of upsetting the cosy atmosphere.

6. *Pressuring of deviants*: any group member who does contradict the consensus or tries to expose the group's illusions is made to feel their behaviour amounts to disloyalty.

7. *An illusion of unanimity*: 'groupthink' results in silence being interpreted as assent. That factor plus self-censorship leads to a false sense of unity. This becomes a

self-reinforcing dynamic, that is, the greater the perception of unity, the more reluctant group members are to unsettle it.

8. *The emergence of 'mind-guards'*: so-called 'mind-guards' are self-appointed individuals who act as filters to prevent group leaders and other influential members from hearing dis-confirming information. A famous example of a mindguard in action is Robert Kennedy's censorship of policy makers who began to express doubts about the decision to invade Cuba which subsequently culminated in the Bay of Pigs fiasco. Kennedy allegedly told dissenters not to press their doubts since the president had made up his mind. Instead, Kennedy urged them to lend the president their full support (Janis 1972).

'Groupthink' can be managed to some extent. Involving outsiders and/or experts in discussions may highlight risk and expose other inadequacies. Utilizing sub-groups to consider different aspects of a problem can enable the full group to comment more objectively upon each sub-group's recommendations than they otherwise might. This technique also improves the probability of a compressive analysis being brought to bear upon issues.

Another possibility is to utilize parallel groups whereby the group is divided up and each group addresses the problem independently. Parallel groups can facilitate divergent thinking and thus lead to multiple perspectives upon an issue and a broadening of the options. Leaders can also try to force group members to consider the potential consequences of their decisions and insist upon treating all decisions as tentative, thus allowing time for reflection and re-appraisal. If these tactics fail or are impractical it may be wise to dissolve the group (Janis 1972).

Pause for reflection

'I don't understand it. Clients sell their good shares and hang on to the rubbish.'
(A stockbroker)

Can you explain clients' behaviour?

7.9 Try, Try Again? Escalation in Decision Making

BY now it should be clear that there is plenty that can go wrong in decision making. When plans fail to turn out as expected, decision makers may be faced with a dilemma. Do they persist in the hope of turning matters around, or, do they quit and cut their losses? Persistence involves the risk of compounding the difficulties whereas quitting means forgoing possible eventual success. Here, for example, is a solicitor's experience of her first day having taken two colleagues into partnership. At

3 p.m. the solicitor (Christine) telephoned her partners' office to discover that they had taken the staff for a champagne lunch:

It was my practice. These people were out at my expense . . . time that they should have been in the office . . . I felt really sick. . . . I thought to myself it was probably just a one off, lets see how it goes. (Drummond 1995, p. 270)

The issue is important because behavioural scientists suggest that such dilemmas often prompt decision makers to persist even when the situation is obviously hopeless. Such unwarranted persistence is known as escalation. Escalation is defined as:

persistence with an investment decision beyond an objectively defensible point.

(Bowen 1987, Drummond 1996, Staw 1981, 1996)

The concept of escalation is relevant to a variety of scenarios ranging from large-scale ventures such as the Paris Euro-Disney project and the Channel Tunnel debt crisis, to decisions over whether to remain on hold on the telephone, wait for a bus, remain in a marriage or repair an old car.

7.9.1 Why do people persist?

The precise reasons for unwarranted persistence are unclear. The following variables may be relevant:

1. Project economics.
2. Information poverty.
3. Social and psychological pressures.
4. Organizational and contextual factors.

Each of these is now discussed in turn.

7.9.2 Project economics and escalation

Persistence in the face of difficulties can be logical especially where a project involves heavy investment and returns are dependent upon completion (Northcraft and Wolfe 1984). Project economics can bind decision makers to a sub-optimal course of action, however (Staw and Ross 1987). For example, Sheffield's tramline system has yet to achieve forecasted passenger receipts. Persistence is partly dictated by the sheer cost of removing the tram lines. Another restraining factor concerns the salvage value of the project. There is little demand for second-hand tram cars.

Organizations may also find themselves bound by penalty payments to subcontractors and suppliers and other exit costs. Likewise, the expense of purchasing new equipment may force an organization to persist with obsolete technology.

Pause for reflection

1. Envisage tomorrow
2. Tomorrow night, compare your vision with actual events.

How accurate was your vision?

If your vision was less than 100 per cent accurate, explain why.

7.9.3 Information poverty and escalation

Persistence may also be dictated by uncertainty. It can be difficult to know whether a venture will succeed. For example, the potentially dangerous characteristics of the Mercedes 'A' Class vehicle only emerged just as the product was about to be launched.

Although negative feedback ultimately destroys the decision maker's commitment to the venture, it may be some time before failure becomes well and truly apparent (Bowen 1987). For example, as the weeks, passed, Christine the solicitor referred to in Section 7.9.1 wondered what to do for the best:

As days went by, my bookkeeper . . . never seemed to find any of them there. People used to phone up and say I can't get a reply from your office in ——. This is at three-thirty in the afternoon.

(Drummond 1995, p. 271)

Yet whenever Christine telephoned her partners, 'It was "Oh we got back at . . . [sic]." It would usually be three minutes after I tried to contact them,' (Drummond, 1995, p. 271). Even when it becomes obvious that expectations are not being met it may be sensible to persist in order to give a venture a chance to work. For example, in the case of a poorly selling product, it may be prudent to reconsider the marketing campaign and advertising budget. In this view persistence can only be deemed irrational (and therefore reprehensible) if decision makers ignore clear information that expectations are futile.

7.9.4 Behavioural theories of escalation

Behavioural scientists argue that people seldom respond as rationally to negative feedback as information poverty theorists maintain. Behavioural scientists suggest that escalation usually begins with bright prospects which subsequently prove illusory. Whereas information poverty theorists suggest that failure prompts an *objective* review of future prospects, behavioural scientists suggest that:

decision makers typically re-invest in order to conceal their mistakes known as the self-justification motive.

In this view the prime cause of escalation is ego-defensiveness. Decision makers, it is suggested, persist in the hope of turning matters around in order to prove to themselves and to other people that they were right all along. Ego-defensiveness may be particularly pronounced where the decision maker knows that they will be held personally responsible for the failure, and especially if the decision maker knows that their job is at stake (Brockner 1992, Fox and Staw 1979, Staw 1996, Staw and Ross 1987). For example, managers responsible for recruiting staff have been observed to bias their subsequent rating of recruits' performance favourably (Schoorman 1988).

Whereas information poverty theorists suggest that escalation is sustained by lack of information, behavioural scientists point to the manner in which people process their data. Decision makers, it is suggested:

- actively seek out information which justifies persistence, and/or
- discount or even ignore dis-confirming data (Staw and Ross 1987).

Such biased information processing may enable decision makers to erroneously convince themselves that the problems are temporary or trivial, that success is imminent and so forth. For example, in 1993 an £80 million IT venture known as Taurus was cancelled before completion because of extreme technical difficulties. Those difficulties were more obvious to relatively detached outsiders than those working on the project:

I think they (the technical team) were just optimistic and couldn't believe that it wouldn't work. They believed they knew how to make it work but it would just take longer and would cost a bit more. And you would have to put in phenomenal effort to prove that wasn't true.

(Drummond 1996, p. 141)

Even when failure becomes obvious to the individual, social pressures may drive decision makers to persist. For example, Margaret Thatcher's personal identification with so called 'Thatcherite' policies precluded a change of direction even when it was obvious that persistence was undermining her premiership. Likewise, destructive price wars between petrol companies, newspapers, airlines and supermarkets may be fuelled by unwillingness to lose face, and even desire for revenge (Teger 1980).

7.9.5 Organizational and contextual escalatory pressures

Complex organizational projects may ultimately acquire a momentum of their own which is difficult to halt. An administrative infrastructure may have been created to support a project. External constituencies may have invested money in connection with it. For example, the Canadian government's persistence with a loss-making trade fair known as 'Expo 86' was partly prompted by pressure from hotel companies who had invested in anticipation of a huge influx of visitors (Ross and Staw 1986).

One reason project Taurus survived as long as it did was that completion became an end in itself when it was only a means to an end. Consequently the decision makers concentrated upon solving the problems at the expense of considering the existence of many problems or whether the project was still worth completing. A member of the technical team describes the vicious circle, 'It was like one of those toys you bash with a hammer. You bash one peg down, another one flies up at you. Bash that peg down again, another one flies up,' (Drummond 1996, p. 102).

7.9.6 Means/ends reversal

This form of unwarranted persistence is known as

'means-ends' reversal (Watson 1994, 1995)

whereby decision makers lose sight of what they are actually trying to achieve. De Bono (1977, 1990) depicts the problem brilliantly by alluding to a hen that is trying to demolish a section of wire in order to reach a dish containing food. The hen becomes so preoccupied with breaching the wire that it fails to realize that the objective is to reach the food so it never looks for alternative ways of solving the problem like going round the wire.

The same happens in organizations. People pursue business plan targets, rush to meet timescales, solve problems, launch initiatives and so forth without ever stepping back and asking, 'why, what am I trying to achieve?'

7.9.7 De-escalation

Unwarranted withdrawal from a potentially successful project is also possible. Returning to the case of Gallipoli, the naval attack came within an 'ace of success', (Gilbert 1994, p. 57), when it was abandoned in favour of a disastrous military expedition:

If only the naval attack had been tried for a second time, if necessary a third time, then the terrible slaughter on the beaches and in the trenches of the peninsula could have been avoided.

(Gilbert 1994, p. 59)

The sinking of three ships by mines in an area supposedly swept clear of mines were what is known as *informative losses* in that they clearly suggested that expectations were unrealistic. In such circumstances de-escalation is defensible even though in retrospect it may have been a mistake.

De-escalation is irrational if it occurs in response to *non-informative losses*. 'Mental budgeting' theory suggests that:

- decision makers compartmentalize resource allocations by setting so called 'mental budgets' for different ventures, and,
- are apt to withdraw once the budget is exhausted (Heath 1995).

Budget depletion represents an uninformative loss because, by itself, it tells the decision maker nothing. 'Mental budgeting' can thus result in unwarranted withdrawal if investment ceases simply because the budget is exhausted.

'Mental budgeting' theory contradicts escalation theory because it implies that irrational withdrawal is a more probable response to failure than irrational persistence. Research is at a very early stage, however. Conceivably certain circumstances may prompt irrational persistence while other circumstances commonly result in irrational withdrawal.

Although 'mental budgeting' theory was developed to explain individual decisions, the concept is also relevant to organizations. How many potentially promising ventures are curtailed because 'there is no money in the budget'? Escalation scenarios capture attention because they are visible and sometimes dramatic. Yet the losses accruing from missed opportunity may be much greater.

7.10 **Discussion**

B^Y now you might be asking yourself, if people are such bad decision makers, how do we survive? Not all behavioural scientists agree that people are inherently irrational. For example, Ebbesen and Konecni (1980, p. 23) argue that the literature portrays human beings as, 'Intellectual cripples, limited in their capacity to think, and biased by cognitive processes that interfere with rational decision making.'

At the very least, it is important to remember that much of the evidence upon which our theories are based is experimental. Experimental findings only highlight tendencies. For example, Kahneman and Tversky's (1979) so-called framing effects were observed in approximately 70 per cent of the population studied. What of the remaining 30 per cent? Experiments are confined to a very narrow range of variables. Early studies of escalation suggested that decision makers were indeed influenced by misplaced attachment to sunk costs. However, when the level of project completion was added to the experimental framework, the sunk cost effect disappeared (Conlon and Garland 1993).

Experiments are also divorced from the pressures of reality. Experimental simulations present decision makers with clearly defined problems and clear information. Moreover, it is surely easier to tick a box marked 'withdraw' in a laboratory simulation than it is to close down a complex venture.

The psychological literature is concerned with deviations from rationality known as decision error. To study decision error presupposes that we know what the correct course of action is (Funder 1987, Lopes 1981).

Pause for reflection

A decision maker plans to use their redundancy payment to enter business. The plan is to sell expensive baby clothes such as velvet suits and party dresses costing approximately £100 per item. The 'mark up' is 33 per cent.

The shop will be located in a small tourist town with a proportion of affluent residents. The town already supports several speciality shops though two similar ventures have failed in the past.

Estimate the prospects of success.

As this case shows, the correct course of action cannot be known. Likewise, organizational decisions usually involve a host of uncertainties. Critics of the strategic planning literature argue that it is arrogant to assume that decision makers can foresee events five or ten years ahead (Etzioni 1989, Mintzberg 1994). Committing organizations to grand plans can be dangerous.

Behavioural scientists assume that information itself is unproblematic. The behavioural literature suggests that it is our tendency towards biased processing which undermines decision making. We have seen, however, that this perspective is partial. Information may be accurate as far as it goes and yet misleading. The collapse of financial markets in the Far East in 1997 now seems to have been inevitable and yet it surprised analysts:

Scientific certainties have taken a beating. . . . Several international banks that had appeared to be at the forefront of risk had to eat humble pie after the summer's financial turmoil threw up losses unpredicted by their internal risk models.

(Graham 1999, p. 3)

7.10.1 The 'irrationality of rationality'?

This chapter began by describing the so-called sequential model of decision making. The assumption has been that the model itself is sound. Attention has focused upon the human and organizational constraints which prevent decision makers from maximizing utility.

Yet is the model unassailable? The model's basic premise is that computation and analysis hold the key to maximizing utility. This implies that emotion and intuition are dysfunctional when it comes to decision making—note the gender bias of this perspective (Langley et al. 1995, Mumby and Putnam 1992). For instance, escalation theory is partly concerned with potential links between emotion and deviations from economic rationality.

It is not what this perspective reveals which is important but what it conceals. Most of us have made decisions which later seem foolish or pointless. Yet we may also have made sensible (rational) decisions which have left us feeling frustrated or unhappy. For instance, I know of a colleague who appointed a secretary. The recruitment process was impeccable. Analysis clearly indicated that the appointee was undoubtedly the best person for a job. Yet the appointment was a disaster because the two parties did not like one another.

Pause for reflection

The shop project referred to in section 7.10 has started badly. The shop opened in November. It is now February and hardly an item has sold. The owner must now decide whether to purchase spring and summer stock costing approximately £7,000. As funds are exhausted, credit facilities would be required committing the decision maker to repaying £500 per fortnight.

What is the correct course of action now?

In fact, the decision maker bought the goods on credit. The result was to compound the difficulties. Months later hardly an item had sold and bankruptcy loomed. In an outburst of anger the decision maker said:

Why should I stay open, getting deeper into debt just to see the agents get their money. They shouldn't have sent me so much stock in the first place. Its their fault I'm in this mess.

Blaming the agents was irrational but it shifted the responsibility on to another party thus enabling the decision maker to justify closing down the shop. In other words, irrational emotions including anger can enable people to take rational decisions.

The sequential model assumes that decision makers can maximize utility by comparing their options against predetermined goals. Yet De Bono (1995) suggests that:

analysis will only take us so far.

Maximizing utility implies creativity, innovation and the ability to see opportunities. De Bono suggests that decision makers need to:

design ways forward.

7.10.2 Where do goals come from?

The sequential model further assumes that decision makers' goals are fixed and immutable. If this were true, a good many sales staff would be redundant. The purpose of employing sales staff is to change peoples' preferences to match the goods on offer. For example, a dog breeder sold a male pup. The pup died before the customer could collect it. The breeder decided to try and foist an unsold female pup on to the customer, 'I convinced him (the customer) that he would be best with a dog. Now I've got to persuade him that he would rather have a bitch.'

Far from pursuing fixed goals, decision makers may:

discover their preferences through action.

We know that people sometimes enter car showrooms without the least intention of buying a car and leave clutching a signed order form. What is unclear is how decision makers structure and restructure their perceptions of decision problems, risk and opportunity. We know relatively little about the cognitive and social processes and the twists and turns whereby people arrive at something called a 'decision'.

7.10.3 Mixing metaphorical perspectives

Part of the purpose of the present chapter has been to show why decision makers' best laid plans frequently go awry. To express this more formally, the aim has been to highlight the limits of control based theories of organization which suggest that good management can eliminate risk and danger.

We can best appreciate the point by envisaging metaphors of power, politics and decision making in conjunction with one another. For example, among other things, the metaphor of power allows us to see that control is never total. The metaphor of politics suggests why feedback and information are never perfect. The metaphor of decision allows us to see that often, what we call 'decision making' is not about making the plans for the future so much as making sense of what has already happened.

Combining metaphorical perspectives allows us to see that time never stands still. The organizational context shifts. The hidden pursuit of interest never ceases. Enemies unite for a purpose. Resistance probes for weaknesses. The balance of power moves. Projections become detached from reality. Decision makers substitute optimism for facts. Power becomes detached from responsibility. Ambiguity always lurks.

We shall return to the limits of control based theories of organization later in this discussion. Here it is sufficient to note that when power, politics and decision making metaphors are combined, it becomes easier to see why apparently successful leadership may be an illusion. Successful leaders may be better at managing appearances than reality (see section 3.5.5). Successful leaders may be those who capitalize upon doubt, confusion and ambiguity to present themselves in a favourable light. It also becomes easier to see why 'good' leaders can fail. One of the paradoxes of organization is that leaders who fight for their staff and their departments, who try to do a good job, often become casualties.

Mixing metaphors also sheds light upon motivation theory (see Chapter 3). For example, we can see how easily perceived inequity can arise as a result of the changing fortunes of time. It is not easy for organizations to give due credit to people when success or failure can depend upon so many factors, and when people may be willing to claim credit while seeking to avoid blame. We can also understand why perceived inequity may not just centre around pay and other forms of compensation. For example, we see how power and authority relations can change, and how an employee can experience increased or diminished status as a result. More importantly, combining metaphorical perspectives enables us to see that such shifts may be beyond the control of management. There may be nothing for it but for the employee to take matters into their own hands to restore equity.

Appearances can be deceptive. The managerialist literature depicts managers as 'leading' and 'motivating', that is, as in control. Combining notions of power, politics and decision making basically amounts to a metaphoric reconstruction of an activity which we call 'management'. When we utilize a different metaphorical lens we see managers much more at the mercy of events and reciprocal forces than control-based theories of organization might suggest.

Control-based theories of organization depict managers as formulating and implementing plans. Mixing metaphors of power, politics and decision making enables us to see why organizational policies, practices and procedures tend to lag behind events. They are responses to sense-making activities. As such, part of what we call 'management' involves constructing imaginary Maginot lines, that is, responding to that which has gone before. This is one reason why large organizations can be much more vulnerable than appearances suggest. Another reason is that sense making is itself a political activity, as decision makers attempt to define reality in a manner that suits their purpose. We are apt to see large organizations as impregnable forces. Combining metaphorical lens's helps us to understand why their 'guns' may be pointed in the wrong direction.

Control-based theories of organization assume an ontological reality. In this view a particular behaviour is either one thing or another. For example, behavioural theories of organization allow us to see either compliance or resistance. It cannot be both. Mixing metaphors of power, politics and decision making enables us to penetrate the surface and to see 'more of what is there'. Subservience masks rebellion. Obedience contains elements of recalcitrance. We also see that people are quite capable of displaying one set of attitudes while privately holding another—just as the fawning beggar secretly despises those who dispense charity.

7.10.4 What is efficiency?

Above all, mixing metaphorical perspectives prompts us to question, what is efficiency? The machine metaphor depicts efficiency as a scientific phenonemon. In this view an IT system, for example, is efficient if it minimizes cost. Mixing metaphors of power, politics and decision making casts a different perspective. It enables us to see that efficiency is also social. In this view, an IT system is efficient if it commands social support.

If this seems a bizarre suggestion, (and I can well imagine the engineer or project manager reading this groaning with despair) remember that efficiency is also a metaphor. For example, a famous Punch cartoon depicts a group of Daleks at the foot of a flight of stairs. The caption reads, 'This certainly buggers our plans to conquer the universe.' The cartoon gains its humour from the juxtaposition of opposites, that is, the supreme masters of the universe defeated by something as mundane as a flight of stairs.

We saw in section 1.1.1 how all knowledge is basically metaphorical. The Daleks are basically metaphors of power. Like the sequential model of decision making, power is depicted as cold, rational and analytical. The Daleks take the allusion a stage further by depicting supreme power as encased in metal machines operating (in theory) at 100 per cent efficiency. This image of power excludes any suggestion of the power of art, music, literature and mysticism to move and to inspire. We shall see in Chapter 10 that non-rational forces play an important role in sustaining organizations. Perhaps our dehumanized view of efficiency explains why the Daleks finished up at the foot of the stairs (Drummond and Kingstone-Hodgson nd).

Summary

1 Economic theory assumes decision makers engage in utility maximization.

2 In practice, decision makers may limit their options and seek satisficing solutions, known as bounded rationality.

3 The problems facing decision makers include:

- information poverty and ambiguity,
- multiple problems competing for attention,
- solutions which become problems.

4 In theory, information informs decision making. In practice, information may serve more to legitimize decisions.

5 Computation implies risk is something which can be managed and controlled. This assumption may create a false sense of security.

6 Our perceptions of reality often reflect received myths and images.

7 In theory outcomes are the product of decisions. In practice, 'decisionless-decisions' are also possible.

8 Prospect theory predicts people typically become risk seeking when choosing between losses, and risk averse when choosing between gains.

9 Decision makers are apt to discount small risks.

10 Losses have greater psychological impact than gains.

11 People are more sensitive to relative than absolute magnitudes of change.

12 Potential error inducing decision heuristics (shortcuts) include:

- the 'vividness effect',
- the 'representativeness effect', and,
- the 'anchoring and adjustment' effect.

13 Group decisions may be influenced by:

- status differentials,
- group norms,
- risky and cautious shifts,
- polarization, and,
- 'groupthink'.

14 Group dynamics may result in:

- suppression of dissent,
- diminished mental rigour, and,
- unwarranted risk taking.

15 Escalation refers to persistence with an investment decision beyond an economically defensible point.

16 The primary factors associated with escalation are:

- project economics,
- information poverty,
- social and psychological pressures including personal responsibility for failure,
- organizational and contextual factors.

17 Unwarranted de-escalation is also a possibility. Unwarranted de-escalation may be prompted by:

- information poverty,
- 'mental budgeting'.

18 Prescriptive models of decision making imply that:

- detached analysis and computation are synonymous with efficiency, whereas,
- emotion and intuition are dysfunctional.

This may not be always be true.

Questions for Discussion

1 'The urgent drives out the important'.

Discuss with reference to organizational decision making.

2 According to former Prime Minister Lloyd George, Britain won the First World War because she made fewer mistakes than the enemy.

Discuss with reference to organizational decision making.

3 The UK clearing banks have been described as 'too large to fail'.

Discuss with reference to organizational decision making.

4 Discuss the view that when it comes to decision making, ultimately players have little option but to 'play their cards and take their chances' (Bowen 1987).

5 'The best laid schemes o' mice an men
Gang aft a-gley.'

       (Robert Burns, 'To a Mouse')

Discuss with reference to organizational decision making.

6 Alvin Toffler (1992) has suggested that competitive viability is not about having the most information but knowing the limits of the data.

Discuss this suggestion with reference to organizational decision making. (You may find it helpful to refer back to Chapter 1, section 1.2.3 especially).

7 'Nothing is certain.'

(Samuel Beckett, *Waiting for Godot*)

Discuss with reference to organizational decision making.

Further Reading

- Bazerman, M. H. (1998) *Judgement in Managerial Decision Making*, New York, John Wiley.

- Drummond, H. (1996) *Effective Decision Making,* London, Kogan Page.

- Drummond, H. (1996) *Escalation in Decision Making: The Tragedy of Taurus,* Oxford, Oxford University Press.

- Etzioni, A. (1989) 'Humble Decision Making', *Harvard Business Review*, July/August, 122–6.

- Kahneman, D., and Tversky, A. (1982) 'The psychology of preferences,' *Scientific American*, 246, 162–70.

- Mintzberg, H. A., Raisingham, D., and Thoeret, A. (1976) 'The structure of unstructured decision processes', *Administrative Science Quarterly*, 21, 146–75.

- Mumby, D. K. and Putnam, L. L. (1992) 'The politics of emotion: a feminist reading of bounded rationality,' *Academy of Management Review*, 17, 465–486.

- Schwenk, C. R. (1986) 'Information cognitive biases and commitment to a course of action,' *Academy of Management Review*, 11, 290–310.

- Staw, B. M. (1996) 'Escalation research: An update and appraisal.' In Z. Shapira (ed.) *Organizational Decision Making*, Cambridge, Cambridge University Press.

Chapter 8
Workplace Stress

'I usually get in just in time to see the nine o'clock news. Sometimes its the ten o'clock news.'

(Corporate lawyer)

'Will this surgery *never* empty?'

(General practitioner)

'I sit at this computer all day. Then I have two children to pick up from the nursery every night, feed them, see to the husband, see to me. I have maybe an hour to myself, then its bedtime. Life *is* boring.'

(Secretary)

'Will work for Prozac.'

(Notice on an office door)

'Do you realize you have contributed nothing to bringing up our child?'

(Wife of a company executive speaking to her husband)

IT is 8.30 p.m. at London's Waterloo Station—the evening rush hour. Swarms of people in suits and rain coats scurry towards the commuter platforms. At 8.57 the train to the dormitory town of Egham in Surrey draws to a halt. Doors slam: figures in suits and light coloured raincoats exchange the warmth and bright lights of the railway carriage for darkness and freezing drizzle. Collars are pulled up as people steel themselves to walk the rest of the journey home. Next day, the same train transports the same people back to Waterloo. The brakes hiss and squeal as the carriages reach the buffers. The suits and raincoats hurry to the station exit. A long row of carriage doors stand gaping open. It is not yet 8 o'clock.

Stress is sometimes called the 'black plague' of modern times. It is said to cost industry and the health services billions of pounds annually. Although it may seem trite to refer to the pressures of modern living, the cliché is relevant. When President Kennedy was assassinated in 1963 there were only two television channels in Britain. When Diana Princess of Wales was killed in 1997, there were over forty. In 1963 British consumers could choose between two types of crisps, 'plain' and 'cheese and onion'. Now there are countless varieties of potato snacks. In 1963 parking restrictions were a rarity, as were burglar alarms and security gates. Working patterns were also very different. Relatively few people commuted long distances, working wives were comparatively rare. Moreover, employees might well remain in the same organization and even the same job throughout their working lives. Organizations were much smaller. The notion of global competition belonged to science fiction. Many of the professions were forbidden to advertise and also protected by fixed fees. Sunday was indeed a day of rest as virtually all shops and places of entertainment closed.

Modern life is potentially stressful because human ability to adapt to change is limited, yet adaptive demands have risen and show no signs of abating. Fax machines, electronic mail and mobile phones may make communication swifter and easier, but they also create work, and imply greater intrusion of work into personal life, and rapid obsolescence. For instance, today's 'state of the art' hand-held computer is, almost literally, tomorrow's museum exhibit. Likewise, today's exemplary customer care facilities are outdone by competitors tomorrow. Many of today's professionals can expect to need to retrain at least once. Then there is the omnipresent sceptre of redundancy. No occupation can be considered safe any more. The world may be a global village but it means that some people are obliged to spend months of the year working thousands of miles from home leaving families to cope for themselves. This chapter examines the cost of it all in human stress. The issues addressed by this chapter include:

Key Issues

- What is stress?
- Why is stress harmful?
- What causes stress?
- Is stress a middle-class syndrome?
- Are you burned out?
- Is stress a necessity or a luxury?

8.1 What is Stress?

THE word stress derives from the Latin word *stringer*, meaning to draw tight. The concept of stress emanates from physics and engineering whereby pressure is seen as resulting in strain and ultimately fracture—hence, for example, 'nervous breakdown', or, 'the straw that *broke* the camel's back'. Modern behavioural scientists regard stress as:

a person's *adaptive* response to any form of stimulus which places *excessive* psychological or physical *demands* upon them.

A *stressor* is any psychological or physical factor which places excessive demand upon the individual. Stress results from:

the difference between the demands placed upon the individual and the individual's ability to cope with these.

(Ivancevich and Matteson 1980).

Note that the individual must experience the demand as excessive for stress to result. This explains why different people find different things stressful. For example, some people find it difficult to concentrate in noisy environments such as open plan offices, whereas others appear unaffected.

8.1.1 Stress patterns

Evidence suggests that people respond to excessive demands in three phases as follows:

1. Alarm,
2. Resistance,
3. Exhaustion.

This is known as the 'general adaptation syndrome' (GAS) (Selye 1974).

Stage one occurs when an individual encounters a stressor. Metaphorically speaking an *alarm* bell rings such as, 'I'll never finish this job on time,' or, 'will this surgery never empty?'

The stressor then presents the individual with a choice between coping with the situation or avoiding it known as 'fight' or 'flight'.

The second stage, *resistance*, occurs when the person decides to try and cope with the situation. For example, they may brew a strong cup of coffee in an attempt to revive their energies. They may forgo their lunch break or decide to work late. Sometimes the individual succeeds in meeting the demands placed upon them. Prolonged exposure to stress can lead to *exhaustion*, however, as the individual's ability to cope crumbles (Selye 1974).

8.1.2 Stress as a struggle to stay afloat

More recently stress has been conceptualized as a mismatch between the individual and their particular environment (Cumings and Cooper 1979). Individuals, it is suggested, attempt to maintain a stable relationship between their thoughts and emotions and their environment.

In this view, a person may be seen as possessing a 'range of stability' wherein they can cope fairly comfortably with the physical and emotional demands of their environment. A stressor is any factor which drives the individual beyond their 'range of stability', forcing them to respond in order to restore stability. This is known as the adjustment process or coping strategy.

8.2 Why is Stress Harmful?

PROLONGED exposure to stress is associated with a long list of illnesses. There may be two reasons for this. First, stress can damage the body's immune system—rather like the AIDS virus, thus leaving the person vulnerable to life-threatening illnesses including coronary thrombosis (heart attack) and strokes. Stress is also linked to numerous less threatening but nevertheless debilitating conditions such as headaches, ulcers, and insomnia.

Second, people experiencing stress may resort to excessive smoking or excessive alcohol consumption—the executive who pours a large whisky as soon as they arrive home, for example. Likewise they may find it difficult to find time for exercise or a proper meal—resorting to a 'Mars Bar' for lunch, for example (Cooper, Cooper and Eaker 1988).

Stress can cause psychological as well as physical damage. In particular, depression is linked to stress. Evidence suggests that depression damages the ability of the body's immune system to protect itself against pathogenic processes which cause illness and disease. It is unclear whether altered immune function is caused by depression as such, or behavioural changes which typically accompany depression such as disrupted sleep patterns, poor appetite and increased alcohol consumption. One theory suggests that depression results from exposure to uncontrollable stressors. Another possibility is that depression is itself a stressor. What is clear, however, is that depressed people are susceptible to illness (Weisse 1992).

Organizations also pay a price for stress in absenteeism, turnover, poor quality, accidents and conflict. One estimate suggests that work related stress accounts for 10 per cent of British Gross National Productivity (Cooper, Cooper and Eaker 1988). For instance, the government has expressed concern at the growing number of teachers seeking early retirement on grounds of ill health, straining pension funds as a consequence. Stress is also becoming a factor in choosing a career. For instance a young doctor said:

I was the only applicant for the job. Once there would have been forty or more. General practice isn't what it was. People who once would have been in hospital are discharged into the community. Complaints are more frequent . . .

Organizations may also face expensive lawsuits from employees alleging damage to their physical or mental health as a result of exposure to stress in the work place (Ivancevich and Matteson 1980). For example, former miners are currently suing the government for hundreds of millions of pounds in compensation for damage to their health allegedly resulting from poor safety standards. Insurance companies have paid billions of pounds in claims from individuals who have developed fatal cancers resulting from exposure to asbestos (Adams 1998). Likewise, a former employee of Northumberland County Council accepted an out-of-court settlement of £175,000 in compensation for stress. The employee known as John Walker returned to work and suffered a relapse of a previous nervous breakdown. Management were held legally liable for failing to improve Walker's working conditions. The court ruled that an employer owes its employees a duty not to cause them psychiatric damage by the amount or character of work they are required to perform (Burrell 1997).

Pause for reflection

Why is it that composers and writers working by candlelight and quill pen, in cold damp dwellings produced works of music, art and literature which are without parallel in modern times?

8.3 What Causes Stress?

ALTHOUGH people find different things stressful, evidence suggests that certain factors are associated with stress. The main workplace stressors are shown in Figure 8.1.

Each of these is now discussed in turn.

8.3.1 Working conditions and stress

Inappropriate working conditions are a source of stress. Potential stressors include working fast, engaging in work which involves high levels of physical effort and/or long hours, work that is repetitive or otherwise monotonous, or work involving risk and danger. The same applies to noise, fumes, too much or too little light, and environments that are too hot or too cold (Cooper 1984, Cooper and Smith 1985,

Figure 8.1 Work-related sources of stress

Working conditions

Role in the organization

Relationships at work

Career development

Organization structure and climate

Ivancevich and Matteson 1980). Such stressors are potentially invidious not least because people may not experience these as unpleasant or be conscious of their effects.

Shift working is potentially stressful because it causes:

- severe disturbance of circadian rhythms,
- physical and psychological ill-health, and,
- social and domestic disruption (Tetterdell et al. 1995).

Shift working disrupts the body by affecting blood temperature, blood sugar levels, metabolic rate and general mental efficiency. In certain occupations such as nursing and air traffic control, shift working has been identified as a central source of stress. Rail staff objected to the introduction of flexible rostering because it entailed more intense and irregular working patterns even though it actually meant fewer working hours (Totterdel et al. 1995, citing Starkey 1988).

Night shift working imposes greater adaptive costs than day time shift working because of the increased recovery time. For example, there have been many reports of airline pilots falling asleep at the controls especially upon night flights. (Cabin staff say they know from a plane's handling whether the crew are asleep.) Some employees welcome shift work, however. For instance a yawning dining car attendant who had served breakfast on the 05.05 hours Leeds to Kings Cross, and dinner on the 17.05 from Kings Cross to Leeds trains said, 'We do two fifteen hour days followed by a short day (ten hours). Its not bad because it gives me a three day week.'

Such employees may be less stress prone. For example, nurses who choose to work at night exhibit greater tolerance than those for whom no choice exists (Barton 1994).

Too much work (quantitative overload) is potentially stressful. Examples of overload include; time pressures, deadlines, arduous travel, noise, frequent interruptions (open plan offices for example); all of which can increase the sense of strain (Cooper and Payne 1988). Work that is perceived as too difficult (qualitative overload) is also stressful (French and Caplan 1972). For example, staff in call centres are required to cope with both forms of overload. Computers enable supervisors to monitor the speed at which staff answer calls, their actual performance on the telephone and even the amount of time spent in the toilet. Anecdotal evidence suggests that many people find the work and the insecurity of being monitored against continually rising sales targets intolerable.

Long hours are another form of overload which can lead to ill health through:

- people becoming over-tired, physically and mentally,
- prolonged exposure to workplace stressors, and,
- inappropriate life style habits including heavy smoking, inadequate exercise and poor diet.

Evidence suggests that Britain has the highest working hours in Europe, that is, 44.7 per week as compared with around 37 elsewhere. Long hours seem to affect women more than men. Husbands whose wives work long hours, however, are more prone to depression and anxiety.

Evidence suggests that tiredness, (and depression and anxiety) increase risk-taking propensity. For example, tired doctors in casualty are less likely to conduct a long series of time consuming tests for a potentially life threatening variant of an illness. Moreover, anxious individuals are more responsive to negative information and may spontaneously generate more negative thoughts and associations making negative outcomes seem even worse, thus undermining the capacity for judgement and decision making.

Evidence further suggests that:

- relatively small changes in mood can have dramatic effects upon risk taking, and,
- people are generally unaware of changes in risk taking propensity (Maule et al. 1998).

How long is too long? Work which regularly involves more than forty-eight to fifty-six hours per week is potentially harmful. The impact of long hours may be greater, however, in jobs requiring close attention such as driving or involving repetitive work. (Coach drivers are allowed to drive for up to fifteen hours at a stretch punctuated only by short rest breaks). Long hours in jobs involving heavy physical labour are less harmful though only to a point. For instance, in rural areas during the haymaking season it is not unusual to see farmers falling asleep over their beer in the local pub.

Age can mediate the impact of long hours. People aged over forty find it hardest to cope. For instance, one consultant said of his days as a junior doctor:

It's not so bad when you're young and you know that its only going to be for a couple of years or so. Besides, you have to get the experience, and the only way you can do that is to . . . see lots of cases. Once or twice, after being on my feet all weekend, I fell asleep at the wheel . . . I couldn't do it now.

Working long hours may not damage health directly but can prompt people to engage in maladaptive behaviours which subsequently undermine physical and mental well being. For example, long distance coach drivers report drinking excessive quantities of tea and coffee with consequent sleep disturbance (Sparks et al. 1997).

Work underload is another potential source of stress as it correlates negatively with job satisfaction and positively with sickness absence (Cox 1980, Melamed et al. 1995). Underload is defined as where people are employed in jobs which are beneath their capacities. Underload includes:

- tasks which are too narrow or which lack stimulus, that is, are devoid of creativity, problem solving or social interaction, and,
- tasks involving close attention but which provide little stimulation in return.

Examples of potential underload include monitoring patients in intensive care, office jobs devoted to filing or record keeping. Employees who are over-qualified for their jobs may also experience stress resulting from underload, graduates working as supermarket cashiers and warehouse attendants, for example. The effects of underload are exacerbated where long periods of tedium are punctated by sudden arousal, notably police work (Cox 1980).

8.3.2 Role in the organization and stress

Three role-related factors have been identified as potentially stressful. These are:

1. Role ambiguity,
2. Role conflict,
3. Responsibility for others.

Each of these is explained below.

Role ambiguity arises when role requirements are unclear. For example, where standards are vague, where an employee is unsure about for what and for whom they are responsible. Ambiguity may be heightened by change. For instance, taking on a new job, working for a new supervisor, moving to a new firm or shifts in company policy (Ivancevich and Matteson 1980). Some students find open ended essays stressful precisely because the brief is open to interpretation.

Role conflict arises when an individual is faced with:

- conflicting job requirements, or,
- averse role requirements, or,
- illegitimate role requirements.

Conflicting role requirements occur where specific elements of a particular job are inconsistent with one another.

Dentists are said to suffer from role conflict. Trained to relieve pain, they see themselves as inflicting it. Non-clinical tasks such as administrative work and building and managing a practice are another source of role conflict (Cooper, Mallinger and Kahn 1988). Likewise supermarket cashiers find themselves torn between the rules of management and customer demands (Rafaeli 1989).

People prone to anxiety tend to suffer more from role conflict than more sanguine individuals. They also react to it with more pronounced tension (Warr and Wall 1975).

Averse role requirements concern tasks which employees find unpleasant. For instance, staff in social services offices often have to deal with clients with low personal hygiene. Police work is ranked as among the five most stressful occupations in the world with a high rate of burnout (see below) and drop-out. The most averse role requirements in police work are facing unpredictable situations, confronting people with weapons, and dealing with domestic disputes. Even the more congenial occupations are not devoid of averse role requirements as a parish council clerk discovered:

We got to ten o'clock at night and the chairman said, 'Any other business?'

Councillor So-and-So got up and said, 'A plastic bag has blown into the hedge near the abattoir. I want that minuting.'

The clerk, who is paid £360 per annum for attending at least twelve meetings a year plus dealing with all correspondence and follow-up work continued, 'The last clerk lost her marbles (went mad). I can see why.'

Illegitimate role requirements are demands perceived as outside the scope of an employee's contract or otherwise unfair, inappropriate or demeaning (Ivancevich and Matteson 1980). For example, the driver of an articulated lorry chalked on the back of the vehicle, '£3.75 AN HOUR TO DRIVE THIS'.

Likewise, a sales assistant employed by a major high street electrical retailer gave this as a reason for wanting to leave:

We get instructions to push certain makes of video because the margins are high. They (the videos) are always breaking down and people have to wait weeks for parts. I hate having to sell something which I know is rubbish.

Responsibility for people, and to a lesser extent, for material assets, are potential stressors. Stress may arise from the need to make hard or unpopular decisions, or engaging in interpersonal conflict. Moreover, people with significant responsibilities usually have to contend with role overload, conflict and ambiguity (Ivancevich and Matteson 1980).

8.3.3 Relationships at work and stress

Relationships at work includes both superior/subordinate relations and relationships with colleagues. Broadly speaking, evidence suggests that managers who score low upon consideration (that is, the more negative, exploitative and authoritarian types) tend to create job pressure which may engender stress (Beck 1972). Evidence strongly suggests, however, that social support from colleagues reduces stress as it has a beneficial effect upon health (Cartwright and Cooper 1997, French and Caplan 1972, Uchino, Cacioppo and Kiecolt-Glaser 1996).

8.3.4 Sexual harassment

Another potentially stressful dimension of workplace relations which is gaining increasing recognition is sexual harassment (Schneider, Swan and Fitzgerald 1997). USA regulatory guidelines define sexual harassment as including:

- unwelcome sexual advances,
- requests for sexual favours, and,
- other verbal or physical conduct of a sexual nature.

Sexual harassment occurs where submission to sexual requests is:

- an explicit or implicit condition of employment, or,
- influences an employment decision, or,
- where behaviour is such that it interferes with work performance or creates a hostile or offensive work environment.

Evidence suggests that sexual harassment is widespread (Stockdale 1991). Estimates suggest that in the USA, one in every two women will suffer harassment during their working lives. Many acts of harassment are minor in themselves. It is their cumulative impact which leads to stress. This may partly explain why few incidents of sexual harassment are reported. Victims are more likely to try and placate the person who is harassing them (short of submission, seek support from friends or family, try and ignore the harasser, or blame themselves).

Sexual harassment poses a serious issue for organizations. Not only can it lead to expensive litigation and adverse publicity, but, even at low levels, it can undermine morale including job satisfaction and organization commitment. It is also associated with increased absenteeism and turnover. Sexual harassment can also harm an employee's relationships with coworkers and supervisors (Schneider, Swan and Fitzgerald 1997). For instance, avoidance strategies can create tension where the victim's work requires frequent interaction with the person who is harassing them.

Women are by no means the only potential victims of sexual harassment. In 1998 a UK Industrial Tribunal found that Britain's youngest woman bank manager had hounded a young trainee to dismissal because he was a man. Among other unfair treatments she made him mop the floor and issued formal warnings for relatively minor offences for which female employees received mild, informal reprimands. The Tribunal also had a sharp word for the bank saying that pious statements about treating people equally are not enough. However sincere and well intentioned these may be, organizations must take active and practical steps to ensure they are implemented (Jenkins 1998).

8.3.5 Career development and stress

Career stress refers to job insecurity, perceived obsolescence, performance appraisal, impending retirement, and blocked promotion. Although career stress can affect employees at all levels, those in middle age are the most vulnerable. Middle age is the time when promotion opportunities generally decrease and the individual faces competition from younger people (Ivancevich and Matheson 1980). Middle age may also be a time where the cumulative impact of other stressors begins to take its toll.

8.3.6 Organization structure, climate and stress

Work devoid of opportunities for participation can lead to strain and escapist behaviour as compensation for the sense of helplessness. Professor Michael Marmot, Director of the International Centre for Health and Society at University College London was recently reported as saying:

It is not the busy jobs that are the most stressful but rather the jobs where a worker has the least control over conditions, the least variety of tasks and the least opportunity to develop new skills.

(Houlder 1998)

The reverse is also true. Participation can mitigate stress because it creates a sense of control, of involvement, and improves communication (Sauter, Hurrel and Cooper 1989).

> **Pause for reflection**
> Redundancy is often followed by marital breakdown.
> Can you explain why this is so?

8.4 Stress: The Home/Work Interface

THE old adage of employees being required to leave their troubles at the factory gate is unrealistic. Events in an employee's private life can also lead to stress which spills into the workplace. Managers need to be sensitive to the possibilities therefore. Besides, as we shall see, the division between work stress and non-work stress is seldom distinct; each can influence the other.

The sources of non-work stress are potentially infinite. For convenience they may be grouped as follows:

- life transitions,
- 'daily hassles',
- the impact of personality,
- the home/work interface, and,
- socio-economic status.

Each of these is now discussed in turn.

8.4.1 Life transitions

Life transitions refers to major events in a person's life. Change in one's personal life can produce stress and ultimately lead to illness. Holmes and Rathe (1967) identified a list of potentially stressful events ranging from death and divorce to preparing for Christmas, in order of potential stressfulness.

Stressfulness is defined as the magnitude of adjustment required. For instance, change implies disruption of attachment bonds which can prompt depression. Depression is associated with illness (Weiss 1992, see also section 8.4.4). Death of a spouse heads the list with a point score of 100 followed by divorce which scores 73 units.

According to Holmes and Rathe most people can cope with up to 150 life change units in one year. Scores of 150 to 300 entail a 50 per cent chance of illness. Above 300 units the chance increases to 70 per cent. It is easy to see how people can accumulate high scores. For instance, divorce (73 units) may entail a change of residence (20 units), a hefty mortgage commitment (31 units), a change in eating and sleeping habits (16 + 15 units), and subsequent remarriage (50 units). Add in Christmas and vacations (12 + 13 units) and the score reaches 230 units.

The evidence for Holmes and Rathe's predictions is tenuous, however. Much may depend upon an individual's resilience. Moreover, some people actually thrive upon change seeing it as an opportunity for advancement and growth. Such individuals may be less susceptible to illness (Kobasa 1979, Kobasa Maddi and Kahn 1982). Moreover, life transitions perceived by the individual as positive carry less susceptibility to illness. Conversely, events that are uncontrollable, such as death of a spouse or enforced redundancy are more strongly associated with illness and depression than events that are controllable such as marriage or voluntary redundancy (Ashford and Black 1996).

> **Pause for reflection**
>
> Jot down a list of everything that has irritated you today.

8.4.2 Stress and 'daily hassles'

Daily hassles are defined as, 'irritating, frustrating, distressing demands that to some degree characterize everyday transitions with the environment' (Kanner et al. 1981, p. 3).

In more colloquial langauge 'daily hassles' refers to disruptions suffered by people day in, day out, including traffic jams, late-running trains and buses, the noise of a neighbour's television, running out of milk, an incorrect bill, and so on. Although 'daily hassles' are counter-balanced to some extent by uplifting events, they are potentially more stressful than major life transitions (Kanner et al. 1981).

8.4.3 Stress and personality

Certain types of people may be more stress prone than others. Two cardiologists known as Friedman and Roseman have identified two personality profiles known respectively as Type A and Type B. Type A personalities are defined as competitive types who do everything rapidly. They are the sort of people who have at least two telephones on their desk, and cram their diaries full of appointments. For example:

I asked for an appointment with the Chief Executive. His secretary rang back and said 3rd of July at two o'clock. (This was in April!) I said, 'But it is urgent.'

The secretary had another look at the diary. 'Alright then, ten o'clock.'

Type A people are highly competitive. They typically work long hours and regularly take work home. Type A personalities feel under constant pressure to perform. They set themselves high standards which almost invariably elude them. They are impatient with people and can be abrasive. By contrast, Type B personalities are usually unhurried. They are apt to be reflective and unassuming. Type B's are rarely overtly competitive. That does not necessarily mean that Type B's make bad managers. Type A's can be more froth than substance, starting twenty projects and finishing none. They are also more prone to escalation in decision making (Schaubroeck and Williams 1993, see also section 7.9). Type B personalities can appear dilatory and lightweight but may actually be highly effective especially at the higher echelons where reflection and restraint are important.

Returning to the issue of stress, Type A people may be more prone to heart disease than Type B's because of the underlying anger and hostility felt by Type A personalities. The relationship between personality and health is not clear cut, however. For instance, Type A's may be less prone to illness than Type B's as they are more likely to seek medical attention and to heed doctors' recommendations than their more sanguine counterparts. Indeed, more recent evidence suggests that people who are insecure, negative and distressed (known as Type D) are four times more likely to suffer a second heart attack than others (Adams 1998, see also Cartwright and Cooper 1997).

8.4.4 Stress and the home/work interface

The interface between home and work is another potential source of stress (Cartwright and Cooper 1997). More specifically, job and family conflict can be conceptualized as a lack of fit at the interface of work and family roles. Lack of it can occur in two ways as follows:

1. Where work interferes with family life.
2. Where family life interferes with work.

Work/family conflicts are associated with heavy alcohol consumption—that is, five drinks or more a night (Frone, Russell and Cooper 1997). Although it is unclear whether workplace stress is transmitted from one person to another, there is definite evidence that partners communicate their moods to one another to such an extent that the well being of a cohabiting partner can be undermined (Jones and Fletcher 1996).

Family/work conflict appears to have the most damaging effect upon individuals' health. The precise links are unclear, however. One suggestion is that employees who are distracted by family demands (such as caring for a sick child) suffer a loss of self-image because they feel inadequate to the job. Loss of self-image may trigger depression which then harms the body's immune system thus rendering the individual susceptible to illness (Frone, Russell and Cooper 1997).

Potentially debilitating conflict can arise in other ways. In many middle-class families the wife bears most of the responsibility for managing the home. In such households husbands are often abroad for long periods. Relocations are frequent and mandatory. The wife may be required to entertain business colleagues, attend social functions in connection with work and the like. Dual careers where both husband and wife work can be so exhausting that partners become ineffective in both roles (Cartwright and Cooper 1997).

8.4.5 Socio-economic status

Although stress is often depicted as a middle-class syndrome, evidence suggests that those lowest on the occupational ladder may be most vulnerable. Moreover, the relationship between socio-economic status and health may be concomitant. For example, a study of British Civil Servants over a ten-year period noted that the risks of mortality increased as grade decreased. Significantly, all staff had access to National Health Service provision and all worked in an office environment.

One explanation for the findings is that staff in the lowest grades smoked more than their senior counterparts—though the latter consumed more alcohol. Another possibility is that people lowest on the socio-economic scale lead more stressful lives because they have fewest coping resources such as education, quality of environment, and income (Adler et al. 1994, citing Marmot et al.).

8.5 Are You Burned Out?

How do people respond to prolonged stress? Burnout occurs where the individual's emotional and physical resources are depleted to such an extent that they are no longer able to cope with the demands of the job. It applies to jobs involving high levels of interpersonal contact. Burnout is characterized by:

- emotional exhaustion,
- feeling distanced from others, known as depersonalization, and,
- diminished personal accomplishment (Cordes and Dougherty 1993, Lee and Ashforth 1996).

Research upon the topic of burnout started from the assumption that work involving high levels of emotional arousal (health care professionals, for example), could be damaging. *Emotional exhaustion* is sometimes known as 'compassion fatigue'. It is characterized by inadequate energy and a feeling that one's emotional resources are consumed. Emotional exhaustion may be accompanied by feelings of frustration or tension as employees feel unable to respond to clients' needs, feeling unable to give any more and dread at the thought of returning to work for another day.

Depersonalization is characterized by unfeeling attitudes towards clients, coworkers and the organization. Clients cease to be people and instead become objects. Visible symptoms of depersonalization include:

- the use of derogatory or abstract language or jargon,
- imposing a rigid division between professional and personal life, and,
- withdrawal behaviours.

For instance, doctors referring to their patients as 'punters'; solicitors withholding their home telephone number from clients, and social workers becoming absorbed in petty administrative tasks in order to minimize client contact. Employees have even been known to lock themselves in their offices, refusing to answer the door for hours on end. They may become moody and exhibit impatience with clients.

Diminished personal accomplishment refers to a tendency to engage in negative self-evaluation. The individual feels that they are becoming progressively less competent and are achieving less and less.

8.5.1 The causes of burnout

The most critical determinant of job burnout is the nature of the employee–client relationship (Cordes and Dougherty 1993). The risks of burnout are increased where client contact is direct, frequent, of long duration, and involves dealing with chronic as distinct from acute problems. The likelihood of emotional strain may be greatest in the helping professions as these typically involve almost constant personal contact with people, often in emotionally charged situations. Feedback from clients is generally unrewarding, that is, either non-existent or negative. For example, a Legal Aid criminal lawyer exhibiting symptoms of burnout said, 'They (clients) don't want experience. They want someone who'll call them by their first name and bring them cigarettes.'

The risks are compounded if the job entails responsibility for the client's welfare and future well-being. Overload and role ambiguity also increase strain.

Employees who are over-achievers or who have unrealistic expectations and high ideals are among those most prone to burnout. Such individuals not only expect a lot from themselves but also the organization. For example:

They teach you all these fancy treatments in dental school but you never get a chance to practise them because they aren't available on the health service.

(A young dentist)

You leave college with all sorts of ideas but as soon as you get into a school you come against THE SYSTEM . . . 'We don't do that here.' You soon lose heart.

(A young teacher)

Burnout is also more probable among employees for whom work is central to their lives. Such employees are prone to emotional exhaustion because they see work and its consequences as extremely important.

Older employees, especially those who are married and/or have children appear to be less prone to burnout. It is unclear why this should be so. One explanation is that older employees lower their expectations. They do not expect gratitude from clients or adequate resources from the organization. Another possibility is that promotion may alter an individual's perceptions of the organization leading them to perceive that resources are adequate. Promotion may also mean reduced client contact (Cordes and Dougherty 1993).

> **Pause for reflection**
>
> Do you know whether you are happy or not?

8.5.2 How widespread is burnout?

Researchers are beginning to doubt whether burnout is confined to the helping professions. Conceivably, any job involving high levels of interpersonal contact may lead to burnout. Sales representatives, public relations executives, waiters, hotel reception staff, indeed, general managers occupy much of their time engaging in interpersonal contact acting as negotiators, disturbance handlers, figureheads and so forth.

Cordes and Dougherty (1993) suggest that burnout may be most probable in occupations involving high frequencies of interpersonal contact of high intensity. Social workers, counsellors and doctors, for example, may be the most prone to burn-out. Occupations involving moderate levels of interaction or interactions of moderate intensity are less vulnerable to burnout, hotel receptionist, shop assistant, train guards, for example. Least vulnerable to burnout may be those whose work involves little interpersonal contact and where such contact is of low intensity; railway signals staff, software engineers, laboratory technicians, for example.

Job burnout depends not only upon the demands made of the employee but also the resources available to help meet those demands. The risk of burnout may be reduced if organizations provide strong social support and constructive appraisal, thus increasing an employee's sense of competence. Other potentially helpful resources include control, participation in decision making and autonomy. Evidence suggests, however, that demands have greater impact upon people than resources (Lee and Ashforth 1996).

8.6 Stress and Unemployment

IT is not only work that is stressful. The experience of being unemployed can damage an individual's happiness, self-esteem and psychological well-being (Warr 1987). It is unclear precisely how unemployment affects people. One explanation is that loss of a job means not only less money, but also deprives the individual of status, identity, structured time, forced activity, and contact with the outside world. Potentially, the better the job, the greater the sense of loss (Warr 1983).

Another possibility is that stress results less from missing the past and more from being unable to secure an attractive future. Initially the individual may view the prospect of unemployment with optimism, a chance to catch up on jobs around the house, for example. Optimism may be sustained for a while by redundancy payments, tax rebates, and by the belief that finding another job will be easy. Optimism turns to pessimism and a growing sense of helplessness, however, as funds are depleted and rejection letters arrive. Ultimately helplessness may set in. If that happens, the individual may give up searching for work altogether (Hayes and Nutman 1981).

8.7 Can Stress be Managed?

HIGH levels of stress in the workplace may not be inevitable. Organizations can take action to reduce the causes and symptoms of stress. The possibilities include:

1. The creation of an appropriate working climate.
2. Work design.
3. Ergonomics.
4. Employee assistance programmes.
5. Individual self-help.

Each of these is now discussed in turn.

8.7.1 Creating an appropriate working climate

Organizations may reduce stress by creating a climate which is conducive to trust and openness (Cartwright and Cooper 1994). For example, graduate recruitment brochures sometimes advise prospective employees to gauge the atmosphere of the organization—do people seem to be enjoying their work, is there much laughter or joking? In some organizations it is unthinkable for employees to use their full leave entitlement, or to leave before eight o'clock at night even though there is nothing to do. In the City of London, for example, employees can be seen working at their computer screens late into the evening. Often they are playing games to occupy the time.

8.7.2 Work design

Organizations can also review how work is designed. For example, clarifying reporting relationships and responsibilities may help to reduce ambiguity. Excessive loads may be reduced. Job enrichment programmes may be initiated to obviate underload and increase autonomy (see section 3.3.6). Flexitime arrangements may reduce the stressful impact of family/work conflicts (Frone, Russell and Cooper 1997). Organizations may also create opportunities for employee participation (Schuler and Jackson 1986). Employees can be encouraged to reframe their perceptions of ambiguity, that is, to see it as an opportunity for autonomy, creativity and originality (Lee and Ashforth 1996).

8.7.3 Ergonomics

The ergonomic aspects of the workplace environment may repay attention. For instance, it would be illegal to keep animals in the conditions pertaining in many open plan offices, noisy, overcrowded, badly lit, with no opportunities for privacy.

8.7.4 Employee assistance programmes

While such initiatives have the advantage of addressing the causes of stress, they may be costly or otherwise difficult to implement. For example, we will see in Chapter 9 that it is not easy to change an organization's culture if indeed it can be changed. Another approach is to treat stress directly. Organizations can promote employee health and well-being by offering coaching in stress management and time management. Some organizations offer employee counselling and health promotion facilities, sometimes known as 'employee assistance programmes' (EAP), (Cartwright and Cooper 1994, Quick and Quick 1984). Occupational health units and child care facilities are fairly common in large organizations. Canteen facilities are another means of reducing stress. Many organizations provide access to sports facilities for use before and after work and at lunch times. Some organizations also offer assistance to employees suffering from drug or alcohol dependency. For example, Ford makes confidential counselling and support available to any of its 33,000 employees who have a drink problem (Breach 1998).

8.7.5 Individual self-help

Individuals can also help themselves. Regular exercise is associated with lower levels of stress and depression (Folkins 1976). Mood is the most transient dimension of psychological well-being and therefore potentially the most responsive to exercise. For example, evidence suggests that employees who are regular participants in work-site exercise programmes experience better mood states and physical well-being than non-participants.

Relaxation is another potential coping mechanism, taking frequent breaks from work, setting time aside for yoga or meditation, even selecting restaurants with slow service (Cooper, Cooper and Eaker, 1988).

Employees can also attempt to exert more control over their working environment. Recall that in section 5.5.1 it was suggested that employees frequently possess a considerable margin of discretion at work. Such discretion can be used to reduce stress and tension, by managing hierarchical superiors, for example, (Cooper, Makin and Cox 1993), or cultivating one's own support group informally (Ganster, Fusilier and Mayes 1986).

Another possibility is to report sick occasionally. Although stress-related absences are costly to organizations, evidence suggests that measures aimed at reducing employee absence may be counter-productive. In a study of nurses Hackett and Bycio (1996) concluded that occasional absence may function as a coping mechanism by enabling employees to regain control of excessive levels of mental and/or physical fatigue.

Evidence suggests, however, that such measures may convey only short-term benefits by reducing strain, improving absence levels and mental health. They have little impact upon job satisfaction, organization commitment and physical health, however (Baglioi and Cooper 1988, Cooper and Sadri 1991, Reynolds, Taylor and Shapiro 1993). Likewise, the benefits of health promotion programmes are often transitory. In 70 per cent of cases employees abandon their intentions to take more exercise (Ivancevich and Matteson 1988). Perhaps setting time aside to take exercise becomes too stressful!

> **Pause for reflection**
>
> If stress is such a problem, why does life expectancy in the Western world continue to rise?

8.8 Discussion

RECALL that stress has been linked to the pace and complexity of modern life. Indeed, you could even say that stress has become a metaphor for modern life. Why should this be so?

Recall also that metaphor enables us to explain one thing via the medium of another. We saw in section 2.1 that work once occupied a very different place in people's lives. The advent of capitalism involved a transition from self-employment to selling one's labour. Although the number of people in self-employment has risen over the past decade or so, life for the majority of people remains dependent upon employment in large-scale organizations in order to gain the means of subsistence.

Dependency implies subservience in a power relationship which is highly asymmetrical. For example, the employment relationship demands a strict separation between work and family life. Although the provision of work place nursery facilities may alleviate stress, the nursery represents the boundary between work and home life.

Likewise, although organizations may pay lip service to equal opportunities, they basically espouse so-called family values. Gender, race and sexual orientation remain formidable barriers to employment, promotion, and quality of working life.

Subservience becomes most apparent when there is a need to escape from it. For example, the process worker may be unable to make a personal telephone call from work without obtaining special permission. Holidays are rationed. Moreover, they cannot be taken spontaneously but must be booked in advance or can only be taken at certain times. The bereaved or separated gay or lesbian person must hide their grief, their anger, their debilitating depression leaving others wondering why they appear to have 'lost it'.

Subservience is also seen in the 'taken for granted' aspects of organization. What does it mean to have no control over the pace of work, or how work is performed? What is it like to work subject to constant surveillance, or in open plan offices which afford no privacy? We know that people's mood and energy levels fluctuate, yet organizations demand the same level of performance, day in day out.

Furthermore, for a great many people, the pay is barely above subsistence levels. Slavery may have been abolished. Yet for many people 'freedom' is a choice between long hours of low paid work, or losing state benefit.

Is it just too easy to tell firms to manage people at work differently and treat them better as Cartwright and Cooper (1994) suggest? Or is part of the solution to stress every bit as obvious as that? Workplace politics, power struggles, sexual harassment and bullying are real enough and engender damage. Surely management could prevent the worst excesses. Is there any need to look for deep causes, or, is putting a stop to antisocial behaviours merely scratching the surface?

Critical theorists might suggest that most of the literature merely addresses the symptoms of stress and not the causes. Critical theorists might react scathingly to the suggestion that employees take more control over their working lives. Critical theorists might say that it overlooks the realities of power in and around organizations. Indeed, some organizational initiatives barely address the symptoms. NatWest, for example, publishes a staff pamphlet on excessive drinking and drug abuse (Breach 1998). It may be better than nothing but it is difficult to see a pamphlet making huge inroads on the problem.

In the USA women now comprise 48 per cent of the workforce, 40 per cent of all workers are dual-earner couples and 20 per cent are single parents. Moreover, in today's downsized organizations, nine- or ten-hour working days are the norm for professionals (Friedman, Christensen and Degroot 1995). Almost thirty years have passed since the publication of Alvin Toffler's *Future Shock* (1970), which pointed to the breakup of bureaucratic monoliths. Yet the fact remains that most organizations operate as if employees still have the support of a full-time partner at home (Friedman, Christensen and Deroot 1995).

It was suggested earlier that people in lower socio-economic groups suffer most from the effects of stress because they possess fewest coping resources. Potentially, the stressors are correspondingly greater too. On many inner city estates in Britain, people live and move knowing that violence constantly lurks beneath the surface. For instance, Manchester City Council found it difficult to let properties where the upper floors are constructed of timber as prospective tenants are fearful of arson attacks. Conversely, one of the Council's most successful innovations was its patented security door.

8.8.1 Stress: much ado about nothing?

If stress is as damaging as has been claimed, why does life expectancy in the Western world continue to rise? Is it simply that, but for exposure to stress, we would live even longer? Or do the benefits of modern day technology and changes in social patterns ultimately outweigh the attendant stressors? Dual careers may be burdensome, particularly for women, but is financial dependency upon a partner and being confined to home with young children any less stressful?

Modern transport facilities and household appliances deprive us of exercise and release of tension. I imagine few readers have ever beaten a carpet, for example. Conversely, our bodies are saved from the damage caused by unremitting physical labour. The range of entertainment and shopping facilities now available twenty-four hours a day, seven days a week in many areas may pose problems of choice. Yet is this state of affairs preferable to the sheer boredom (and accompanying tension) of the British Sunday of the 1950s graphically portrayed in John Osborne's play *Look Back in Anger*?

According to Toffler (1992) society is becoming less homogenous. For example, in Britain gone are the days when whole communities went to church on a Sunday morning. Yet rhythm and regularity of cohesive social patterns can be oppressive. In former mining communities in Britain, for example, women were often left to supervise the children while the men engaged in Saturday night drinking sprees. On Sunday the man might stay in bed until midday when the public houses re-opened. Lunch was at two (that is, after closing time), followed by a further spell asleep until the public houses re-opened at seven. Thus passed the weekend. Personal freedom does not necessarily equate to happiness, however. Suicide levels are highest in countries where the Roman Catholic church is least influential (Scandinavia, for example) and vice versa.

In Victorian times the average duration of a marriage was fifteen years. It is still fifteen years. The difference is that in Victorian times, death separated couples whereas now it is divorce—a less stressful event than bereavement according to Holmes and Rahe (1967).

Today, social security benefits, superannuation schemes and other forms of insurance cushion us from the very worst effects of death, retirement, unemployment and chance misfortunes. It was not always so. We may feel driven to distraction by 'daily hassles' yet surely our problems are trivial compared with those of our forebears for whom flood, pestilence, crop failures and other cataclysmic events were real possibilities, and the only defence was to place a device known as a witchpost in the chimneys. Witchposts were once as popular as today's DIY kits. (For a discussion on the uses of witchcraft in organizations see section 10.5.)

From the standpoint of the developing world stress is very much a Western problem. Indeed, when one considers the resurgency of disease, the scourge of AIDS and the evolution of antibiotic-resistant strains of viruses, stress is at best a self-inflicted injury which does not justify the current expenditure of resources. Some might say that stress is a luxury.

8.8.2 Stress as symbolic

Finally, let me briefly pursue the theme that the prevalence of stress is exaggerated from another angle. The text of the present chapter has been compiled from a distillation of hundreds of medical, physiological and psychological studies, each dealing with a fragment of something for which, for convenience, we invoke the metaphor 'stress'.

An important assumption made by the psychological and medical literature is that stress is a medical or psychological abnormality. Moreover, the literature assumes that control and order are all-important. In this view, stress and burnout are pathological—something to be got rid of. Likewise, ambiguity is viewed as counterproductive.

There is a small corpus of literature, however, which offers a very different explanation, namely that:

stress is symbolic.

The symbolic life of organizations is discussed in Chapter 10. Here it is sufficient to note that evidence suggests that members of relatively low status occupational groups (teachers, social workers, and nurses, for example), are more likely to *claim* to experience stress than members of more powerful occupational groups. For example, the medical profession, claiming stress may be interpreted as a sign of weakness, whereas in some occupations not burning out means not working hard enough (Barley and Knight 1992).

Likewise, role ambiguity can assume different meanings in different social settings—even in the same profession. For example, a study of hospital social workers revealed that in some settings ambiguity is construed as restrictive, yet in other settings it is construed as liberating (Meyerson 1994).

This is not to suggest that the psychological/medical literature is wrong, only that it is partial. Moreover, some of the more specialist medical evidence is particularly open to interpretation. We can see stress as a medical issue, a compound of physiological and psychological interactions. Alternatively we can see the literature as basically a picture of society taken from another angle.

Summary

1 A *stressor* is any psychological or physical factor which places excessive demand upon the individual.

2 Stress results from the difference between the demands placed upon the individual and the individual's perceived ability to cope with these.

3 Stress can undermine organizations because it is associated with illness, increased risk of accident and other counter-productive behaviours.

4 The principal sources of work related stress are:

   - working conditions,
   - role in the organization,
   - relationships at work,
   - career development, and,
   - organization structure and climate.

5 Potentially stressful working conditions include:

   - environmental factors such as dirt, noise, inadequate lighting and exposure to physical danger,
   - shift working, especially at night,
   - work overload, qualitative or quantitative and excessive hours,
   - work underload.

6 Potentially stressful role related factors include:

   - role ambiguity,
   - role conflict including conflicting, adverse, and illegitimate role requirements, and,
   - responsibility for others.

7 Potentially stressful workplace relationships include those characterized by:

- inconsiderate management, and,
- sexual harassment.

8 Career development stressors centre upon job insecurity. Employees in middle age are most vulnerable.

9 Organization structure and climate refers to opportunities for participation.

10 People also experience stress in their private lives which can affect the organization. The principal sources of non-work stress are:

- life transitions
- 'daily hassles'
- the impact of personality,
- the home/work interface, and,
- socio-economic status.

11 Burnout occurs where the individual's emotional and physical resources are depleted to such an extent that they are no longer able to cope with the demands of the job.

12 Burnout is characterized by:

- emotional exhaustion,
- depersonalization, and,
- diminished personal accomplishment.

13 Burnout is associated with the so-called 'helping professions' such as social work, but may affect anyone whose job involves interpersonal demands.

14 Unemployment is also potentially stressful.

15 Organizations can take action to reduce the causes and symptoms of stress. The possibilities include:

- creation of an appropriate working climate,
- work design,
- ergonomics, and,
- employee assistance programmes.

16 Employees can protect themselves against the effects of stress to some extent by engaging in appropriate life style behaviours including regular exercise.

17. Stress may, however, be more symbolic than clinical.

Questions for Discussion

1 Consider the following case study:

The organization is an estate agent's office in a small town. Estate agents act as intermediaries in property transactions on a commission basis. The agency deals with domestic property only. Commissions range from 1 per cent to 1.5 per cent of selling price. Property prices typically range from £40,000 to £250,000. Most transactions are in the £40,000 to £100,000 range.

The staff undertake a variety of tasks including:

(a) Making appointments for prospective purchasers to view properties. It is not unusual for purchasers to ask to see ten or more different properties.
(b) Receiving telephone and personal enquiries from prospective purchasers.
(c) Despatching sales literature.
(d) Accompanying prospective purchasers upon property viewings.
(e) Carrying out 'follow-up' enquiries to obtain feedback from prospective purchasers who have viewed properties.
(f) Carrying out periodic 'stay in touch' calls to sellers.
(g) Acting as intermediaries in negotiations between buyers and sellers. Staff have authority to accept offers and to facilitate subsequent negotiations.
(h) Participating in sales review meetings.

The office manager has sole responsibility for valuing properties and producing sales literature.

The state of the market is ambiguous. Some properties, moderately priced ones especially, sell quickly.

Approximately 60 per cent of listings have been on the market for about six months, 20 per cent for over a year.

Staff have to cope with frustrated clients, 'Why is my property not selling; what are you doing about it?'

Staff work to sales targets.

Your task is to:

(a) Analyze the potential sources of workplace stress.
(b) Comment upon potential compensatory factors.
(c) Set out and justify your recommendations.

2 Consider the following case study:

The case concerns a postal sorting office in Tanzania. Employees are required to unload mail bags from ships as they arrive. Each shipment brings in about 500 bags each weighing 30 kilos. The mechanical loaders are often broken. However, employees are forbidden by quality standards regulations to drag the bags so they must carry them. Such regulations further require the task to be undertaken at speed. The temperature in the sorting office ranges from 25 to 30 degrees centigrade. The mail bags are dusty. They often contain spices which cause choking coughs and eyes to water. The roof of the sorting office is lined with asbestos. There is no ceiling.

Many of the employees are suffering from TB. There is no health insurance or sick pay. Unemployment within the region is high.

The vans used to transport the mail bags frequently break down. Supervisors are forbidden to hire alternative transport, however. Supervisors' instructions are to meet targets and keep costs down.

Illegal drug trafficking is an increasing problem. Supervisors are required to call the police to any suspicious package. Not only does that take time, but, it can result in conflict with the senders. Supervisors often receive angry enquiries,

'Why did you report my parcel?' Supervisors also have to deal with complaints about other delays.

Your task is to compare and contrast potential employee and supervisor stressors.

3 Consider the following case study:

The case concerns a specialist call centre which exists to enable deaf and dumb people to conduct business through a specialist interpreter. Many of the clients are males who use the service to make appointments with prostitutes. Staff are required to translate clients' communications word for word, including offensive and sexually explicit language. One employee said:

'We have to ask (the prostitutes) what they charge and what services they provide. You have to relay it back word for word. One caller used to see a prostitute who called herself "Big Tits". I had to ring up and say, "Is Big Tits there?" '

Your task is to:

(a) Identify and explain the potential sources of workplace stress.
(b) Suggest measures which employees might take to reduce the impact of stress.

4 Consider the following case study.

The organization is a charitable foundation known as a hospice which cares for terminally ill people in the last stages of their illness. An important part of the nurses' role involves talking with patients and in particular, helping them come to terms with their approaching death. Nurses are also required to offer intensive support to families who are often highly distressed.

Your task is to:

(a) Advise the hospice managers upon the phenomenon of burnout among nurses.
(b) Identify the particular behaviours which managers should remain vigilant for.
(c) Suggest how the risks of burnout can be reduced.

5 'Misfortune loves company.'

Discuss with reference to workplace stress.

Further Reading

■ Cartwright, S. and Cooper, C. (1997) *Managing Workplace Stress*, London, Sage.

■ Cooper, C. L., Makin, P. and Cox, C. (1993) 'Managing the boss,' *Leadership and Organization Development Journal, 19*, 28–32.

■ Cordes, C. L., and Dougherty, T. W. (1993) 'A review and integration of research on job burnout,' *Academy of Management Review, 18*, 621–656.

■ Ivancevich, J. M. Matteson, M. T. and Richards, E. P. (1985) 'Who's liable for stress on the job?' *Harvard Business Review*, March/April 60–75.

■ Schneider, K. T., Swan, S. and Fitzgerald, L. F. (1997) 'Job-related and psychological effects of sexual harassment in the workplace: empirical evidence from two organizations,' *Journal of Applied Psychology, 82*, 401–415.

■ Watts, M. and Cooper, C. L. (1992) *Relax: Dealing with Stress*, London, BBC Books.

Chapter 9
Organizational Culture

'To wives and sweethearts: may they never meet.'   (Old navy toast)

'No money no soap.'   (Engraving on a former pit-head baths serving counter)

'Please go away.'   (Notice on an office door)

A merchant banker once received over 200 applications for one vacancy for a graduate trainee. Determined to lighten the task of shortlisting, the banker threw half of the forms into the bin without even looking at them. When a colleague protested at the waste of human potential, the banker replied, 'You wouldn't want to work with someone who was unlucky would you?'

This cruel story suggests a clue to merchant banking culture. Most people would agree that cultural differences exist between organizations and within organizations. In a hospital, one ward seems brisk and cheerful whereas another is nicknamed 'the morgue'. On the factory floor there may be pronounced differences between one group 'us', and another, 'that lot over there'.

The topic of organizational culture is important for two reasons. First because part of the organizational literature suggests that creating an appropriate organizational culture is the key to organizational effectiveness. For instance:

The merchant bank founded by Siegmund Warburg had been innovative, prizing an employee's achievement rather than his or her background. But the intensity was diluted as it grew and merged with the Public School ethos of Rowe and Pitman.

(Cohen et al. 1995)

Warburgs lost its independence in 1995. Analysts now predict that the impending stock market flotation of Goldman Sachs will destroy the bank's distinctive partnership culture which has enabled it to recruit people of outstanding talent ('Goldman team steps closer to windfall', unattributed newspaper article, 1998). Allegedly, the investigation into the murder of the black teenager Steven Lawrence was neglected because of a racist police culture. Indeed, Manchester's Chief Constable David Willmott told the subsequent public inquiry that racist attitudes were institutionalized in the Manchester police.

Second, many managers say that their hardest task is changing culture. Indeed, part of the organizational literature suggests that culture is beyond managerial control. The issues addressed by this chapter include:

Key Issues

- What is culture?
- Why is culture important?
- The rise of corporate culturism
- Sub-cultures and the organizational underworld
- Organizations *as* cultures
- The dynamics of culture
- Culture's sinister side

9.1 What is Culture?

ALMOST everyone knows what organization culture is, until they try to define it, that is. Culture is both an important concept, and an elusive one. The word culture is derived from the Latin, meaning to till the soil (Hofstede 1994). The concept is borrowed from anthropology though anthropologists disagree about what culture means (Smircich 1983). Within the organizational literature culture has been defined as:

'The way we do things round here,' (Deal and Kennedy 1982), and,

'Why the organization is what it is,' (Riley 1983, p. 437).

While these definitions impart a flavour of the concept, they are extremely vague. More formal definitions of culture focus upon the ideologies, norms, customs, shared values and beliefs which characterize an organization. At this level culture has been described as the social or normative glue which holds an organization together. Jaques (1952), for example, defines culture as the

customary and traditional way of thinking and doing things, which is shared to a greater or lesser degree by all members, and which new members must learn and at least partially accept in order to be accepted (p. 251).

A more modern definition depicts culture as the '*software of the mind*' that is, '*the collective programming of the mind which distinguishes the members of one group or category of people from another*,' (Hofstede 1994, p. 5, italics in original).

According to Hofstede, culture is learned rather than inherited—unlike personality which is part inherited and part learned, and human nature which is entirely inherited. Perhaps, yet how is this 'software' written, and who writes it?

'Culture' is distinct from 'climate'. Climate concerns the relatively tangible aspects of organization such as decision-making procedures and official channels of communication. By contrast, culture concerns the relatively intangible deep structure of organization. As we shall see, culture centres upon shared meaning, the negotiation of meaning, and the symbolic world that results from interaction (Denison 1996).

9.2 Why is Culture Important?

Pause for reflection

The UK boarding school sector has declined sharply over recent years due to social and political changes. One survival strategy has been for schools to merge. One proposed merger involved a Nonconformist school and a Church of England school, both located in the same town. The Nonconformist school stresses self-discipline. For example, the school uniform is based upon 'smart-casual' attire. The Church of England school is a much more formal rule-governed organization. The school uniform requires traditional attire. For instance, hats must be worn in public at all times.

Imagine that you are leading the negotiations:

1. What problems would you anticipate?
2. What would be your strategy for concluding the merger?

One question is whether the proposal makes sense upon paper. For example, does it enable better utilization of staff, buildings and other resources? If so, attention might then focus upon the issues involved in redrawing organization charts, harmonizing job descriptions, drawing up procedures for assimilation, and so on.

In fact, the merger collapsed. The parents of the Church of England school were fearful of their children being exposed to what they regarded as an inappropriate cultural environment. The merger was a rationally defensible idea which failed because it involved too high a cultural price.

Historically, organizational effectiveness has been seen as a technical problem beginning with F. W. Taylor (see Chapter 1) and latterly in the 'total quality management' a re-engineering literature with its emphasis upon eliminating variation (Chapter 2). The upsurge of interest in organizational culture is relatively recent, dating from the early 1980s (Guest 1990, Meek 1988). Figure 9.1 lists the main factors which lie behind the sudden and dramatic upsurge in interest.

Each of these is now discussed briefly in turn.

9.2.1 Trade competition

We saw in section 4.1 how trade competition from Japan has prompted particular interest in 'total quality management' and process re-engineering. Although much of

Figure 9.1 Factors driving an upsurge of interest in organizational culture

Why the sudden interest in culture?

1. The advent of trade competition from Japan.

2. Mergers and acquisitions activity.

3. The growing emphasis upon intellectual capital.

4. Equal opportunities legislation.

5. Growing awareness of the cultural price of employing misfits.

the literature focuses upon the instrumental aspects of production and service delivery, as we shall see, it also implies cultural change (Guest 1990, Meek 1988).

9.2.2 Mergers and acquisitions

Changing economic forces have resulted in organizations becoming larger. Many organizations have grown through mergers and acquisitions (Denison 1996). Business history is rich in examples of disappointing corporate marriages. Moreover mergers and acquisitions increasingly involve cross-border transactions. The failure rate of cross-border transaction is particularly high, between 50 and 80 per cent according to one study (Cartwright and Cooper 1995).

9.2.3 Intellectual capital

During the 1980s mergers and acquisitions were primarily aimed at buying hard assets. In recent years, however, mergers and acquisitions have been prompted more by the prospect of acquiring intellectual capital. Many prospective mergers and acquisitions have failed through key staff leaving—sometimes reducing the target firm to near worthlessness. For example, in 1995 Warburgs decided that it needed to merge with another investment bank if it was to survive. The prospect prompted leading staff to seek jobs elsewhere (Cohen et al. 1996).

Likewise, when a pharmaceutical company bought another pharmaceutical enterprise because of its research strengths, many of the research and development staff discreetly suspended work on their best innovations in case they decided to leave and needed to take the projects with them (Murray 1988).

9.2.4 Equal opportunities

Equal opportunities legislation has forced many organizations to recruit workforces which reflect the racial and gender balance of the population. This development too has been seen as implying cultural change. For instance the engineering industry has been urged to foster a family friendly culture in order to attract and retain women (Wood 1995). In the late 1990s numerous complaints of sexual harassment by women police officers were upheld by industrial tribunals suggesting the need for cultural change.

9.2.5 Cultural price of employing misfits

Employers are increasingly considering cultural fit as well as technical competence when recruiting employees (Howard 1988). For instance, when Whitbread wanted to achieve new standards in their Country Club hotels they dispensed with employees whose style no longer fitted in with the quality culture they were trying to achieve.

9.3 The Rise of Corporate Culturism

IN a nutshell then, organizations are increasingly embracing the notion of corporate culturism. Corporate culturism assumes that:

organizational effectiveness depends upon creating cultures which are consistent with the organization's mission. (Deal and Kennedy 1988, Pascale and Athos 1982, Peters and Waterman 1982, Wilkins and Ouchi, 1983)

Popular enthusiasm was kindled by the publication in 1982 of Peters and Waterman's *In Search of Excellence* and subsequent derivatives (Peters 1988, Waterman 1987). The excellence literature (as it became known) basically:

- highlighted the limitations of mechanistic thinking and bureaucracy, and,
- emphasized the role of values, charisma and symbolism in sustaining an organization and in promoting excellence.

Transformational leadership (see section 3.5.5), say Peters and Waterman, is the key to building excellent organizations. Peters and Waterman suggest that the leader's primary role should be to:

- promote shared values and beliefs,
- create meaning in work,

- make work satisfying and emotionally rewarding,
- empower employees to give of their best.

In essence, say Peters and Waterman, the leader's role is to create a strong and unified culture with an emphasis upon innovation and customer care. Managers should manage by 'walking around'. Organizations should be teeming with purposeful activity, people hammering out problems—not becoming embroiled in political strife (see also Waterman 1987).

A defining feature of excellent companies, say Peters and Waterman, is a palpable 'love of the product and the customer', (p. 16):

Poorer-performing companies often have strong cultures, too, but dysfunctional ones. They are usually focused on internal politics rather than on the customer, or they focus on 'the numbers' rather than on the product and the people who make and sell it. (p. 76)

Peters and Waterman may have had in mind this young research engineer employed by Hewlett-Packard:

I always wanted to work there, ever since I bought a Hewlett-Packard calculator . . . I was so impressed with it. . . .

People say that if you stay with HP (Hewlett Packard) for four years, you stay forever, because no other company is good enough. . . . They get the best out of people—you feel valued. . . . Its the satisfaction of knowing that you are making good products and not just making money. . . .

The culture is very informal. I know that if I contradict the marketing man and say 'That's rubbish,' I won't be punished for it. . . .

There are role models, people who have done incredibly well in the time they have been there.

Peters and Waterman go further, however. They state that '*every* man seeks meaning' (p. 76).

According to Peters and Waterman, even the lowliest, most routine jobs in organizations can be made meaningful. Creating meaning in work, they suggest, is an essential role of leadership. In their chapter entitled, 'Hands On, Value-Driven', executives are told:

Figure out your value system. Decide what your company *stands for*. What does your enterprise do that gives everyone the most pride? Put yourself out ten or twenty years in the future: what would you look back on with greatest satisfaction? (Peters and Waterman 1982, p. 278)

Moreover, fun and meaning in work go hand in hand with profits:

Excellent companies are among the most fiscally sound of all. But their value set *integrates* the notions of economic health, serving customers, and making meanings down the line. As one executive said to us, 'Profit is like health. You need it, and the more the better. But it's not why you exist.

(Peters and Waterman, p. 102)

Pause for reflection

Before we became a bank the attitude was always, 'We are the biggest.' In many ways, that is still the attitude among a lot of staff and management.' (Employee of the Halifax Bank, formerly the Halifax Building Society).

The Halifax Bank has been described as having a complacency culture (see section 3.5). How would you attempt to change it?

What difficulties would you anticipate?

9.3.1 Excellence: an iron fist in a velvet glove?

It is hard to resist the transcendental language and soaring optimism of the excellence literature even though many of Peters and Waterman's 'excellent' organizations no longer qualify for this appellation (see also section 6.5). Yet if we look beneath the surface, the dream culture may not be what it seems.

In a penetrating exposé of the excellence literature, Willmott (1993) suggests that Peters and Waterman's notions of excitement, of a sense of belonging in work, of being part of the best and so forth, amount to an Orwellian trick of 'doublethink'. 'Doublethink' means that employees are encouraged to believe that by devoting themselves to the organization they not only achieve autonomy, but are transformed into 'winners'.

It is more than that, however. With its emphasis upon values, corporate culturism basically seeks to control the hearts and minds of employees. Far from empowering employees, corporate culturism actually implies an extension of control. Hitherto, organizations exercised control by rule. Corporate culturism attempts to dictate how employees *should* think and feel about what they produce (see also Ray 1986, Thompson and McHugh 1995, Willmott 1993).

For example, Willmott (1993) cites as evidence the following quotation from the excellence literature:

These devices—vision, symbolic action, recognition—are a control system, in the truest sense of the term. The manager's task is to conceive of them as such, and to consciously use them.

(Peters 1988, p. 486; Willmott p. 530, Willmott's italics)

According to Willmott, the emotional manipulation implied by the so called 'human relations' school described in Chapter 3 is insignificant compared with corporate culturism's invidious twist whereby:

the employee's sense of self-worth is linked to their attitude to work.

Willmott notes, 'Employees are encouraged to *devote* themselves to its [the organization's] values and products, and to assess their own worth in those terms' (p. 522, italics in original).

In other words, if you do not love the organization and its products, there is something wrong with you.

9.3.2 Should we take corporate culturism seriously?

The prospect of living out corporate values is a chilling one. Should we take the excellence literature seriously? Deal and Kennedy (1988) maintain that successful manipulation of culture can yield an additional two hours of productive work per day. The claim is vague, and as Thompson and McHugh (1995) point out, unsubstantiated.

In section 3.6.1 we discussed how linear intuitive patterns of thinking have influenced the organizational literature. Corporate culturism rests upon 'more is better' logic as it assumes a linear relationship between social cohesion and productivity. Thompson and McHugh (1995) suggest, however, 'more' cohesion can actually mean conformist thinking (see also Randall 1987 and also section 3.6.1), or just conformist behaviour (Ogbonna 1992). Another potential irony of corporate culturism is that a strong culture may be difficult to change. Schien's (1992) model which suggests that managers can dissolve ('unfreeze') and reconstitute (refreeze) cultures at will may be more difficult in practice than it appears on paper.

Moreover, there is plenty of anecdotal evidence to suggest that people are well able to resist corporate brainwashing. For example, when McDonald's despatched Ronald McDonald to the London Borough of Haringey in a public relations exercise, parents were not amused when he addressed their children as 'my little fries' and asked a six-year old if she had a boyfriend:

The Deputy Mayor . . . calls in. He is wearing his chain of office and calls for respect for different cultures. But Suna is still furious.

'The only culture on offer to our children here is the opportunity to purchase a burger. It's degrading.'

(Vidal 1997)

Likewise, Michael Lewis (1990) recounts Salomon Brothers' failed attempt to indoctrinate him. Lewis was advised by a friend who had been through the interview process that the subject of money was taboo:

When they ask you why you want to be an investment banker, you're supposed to talk about the challenges, and the thrill of the deal. . . . That money wasn't the binding force was, of course, complete and utter bullshit.

(Lewis 1990, p. 121)

Lewis conformed outwardly in order to secure the job. Inwardly, it was a different matter. Lewis said, 'Learning a new lie was easy. Believing it was another matter.' (Lewis 1990, p. 121).

Willmott (1993) argues that corporate culturism should be taken seriously because, even though it fails to inspire, it can restrain. We saw in section 5.3.1 how the most subtle exercise of power rests in unquestioned assumptions about what is appropriate. Corporate culturism does not encourage critical reflection, quite the opposite. More specifically, corporate culturism attempts to:

- subtly dictate wants, and,
- the criteria for showing how these are achieved (Willmott 1993)

The advertisements in the glossy weekend newspaper supplements are an attempt to dictate wants. For instance, do fitted kitchens, bathrooms and studies constitute the 'ideal home?' Why does the notion of 'fun' play such a prominent role in society? 'Fun' can act as a restraint, because it detracts from spiritual, emotional or intellectual development. For example, the 'fun puzzles' fed to school children—what constraints upon learning and self-development do they subtly impose? The cult of fun that sets the criteria suggests that to experience transitory enjoyment is tantamount to fulfilment. Self-actualization is a restaurant lollipop?

9.4 Sub-Cultures: Exploring the Organizational Underworld

CORPORATE culturism centres upon the notion of unity. The idea is that management sets the tone and others follow. In section 1.2 we saw how organizations are potentially many things simultaneously. Metaphoric thinking implies there is no one 'organization', so much as a myriad of sub-cultures.

For instance, medical staff may espouse very different norms and values to those of the hospital managers and administrators. The orientation of research and development staff is likely to differ from that of accountants. Arts and social sciences departments in universities often seem culturally different from their science and engineering counterparts. Meek (1988) suggests that sub-cultures are most obvious in professional organizations such as large teaching hospitals and colleges of further education. According to Meek, sub-cultures become manifest as they compete for resources and prestige.

Yet sub-cultures do not necessarily follow neat departmental lines. Nor can we depict employees as belonging to one particular sub-culture.

- Employees may consciously or unconsciously subscribe to many cultural enclaves.
- Employees may even 'belong' to opposing cults simultaneously.

To suggest that sub-cultures are everywhere, however, is as good as saying they are nowhere. Figure 9.2 identifies three types of sub-culture (Martin and Siehel 1983).

9.4.1 Enhancing sub-cultures

Enhancing sub-cultures basically amplify the dominant culture. Examples include elite university departments, specialist units in hospitals, and the organizational enclave associated with a flagship venture.

Figure 9.2 A typology of sub-cultures based on Martin and Siehel, 1983

	Forms of sub-culture
Enhancing	An organizational enclave where the core values of members are more fervent than those held by the dominant culture.
Orthogonal	An enclave which basically accepts the dominant values of the organization while simultaneously espousing its own occupational values.
Counter	An enclave which espouses values which directly challenge those of the dominant culture.

Pause for reflection

'The law has become a business. Careers are made on long hours and big bills, not serving the client.   (Corporate lawyer)

How might the employee cope with the new culture?

9.4.2 Orthogonal sub-cultures

Orthogonal sub-cultures commonly exist in professional departments of large firms. For example, lawyers, architects and surveyors employed in local government may subscribe to the values of the organization while retaining allegiance to their occupational identities. (See also the reference to professional commitment in section 3.4.7.)

9.4.3 Counter-cultures

Counter-cultures are a threat to the dominant culture. Organizations which grow by merger and acquisition sometimes discover that they have created counter-cultures strong enough to undermine the organization. According to Martin and Siehel, counter-cultures are often led informally by charismatic personalities, De Lorean at General Motors, for example.

Martin and Siehel further suggest that organizations may try to control counter-cultures by allowing them limited autonomy. For instance, Barings was originally a merchant bank. In the early 1980s Barings acquired a small stockbroking firm as an experiment. The stockbroking firm was led by the charismatic Christopher Heath. Heath insisted upon near total autonomy as a condition of the merger. A cultural clash soon developed between the two divisions. Merchant bankers value caution and long-term relationships with clients. By contrast, stockbrokers typically live for the day, earning (sometimes losing) spectacular sums of money by exploiting short-term market opportunities. Tensions mounted as the stockbroking division resisted the imposition of risk management disciplines and financial controls. The stockbrokers too were resentful as they were generating most of Barings' profits (Gapper and Denton 1996).

Organizations seldom tolerate leaders of counter-cultures indefinitely (Martin and Siehel 1983). De Lorean was eventually ejected from General Motors. Barings sacked Heath in 1992 after the stockbroking division began losing money. Significantly, Barings was still trying to bring its stockbroking division under control when the bank collapsed. Heath's legacy of informality had lived on. Controls were inadequate, enabling Nick Leeson to conceal losses resulting from unauthorized trading with disastrous consequences for Barings (Gapper and Denton 1996).

9.4.4 Cultural diversity and national culture

Culture can divide among many other lines. Organizations are employing increasingly diverse labour forces partly because of mergers and acquisitions activity, partly because of the impact of equal opportunities legislation, and partly because of labour market migration patterns. In California, for example, the mixture of ethnic groups exceeds 50 per cent of the population (Goffee 1997). Cultural diversity can mean different attitudes towards a variety of factors including time, authority, acceptance of power inequalities, desire for orderliness, and the need for wider social belonging (Goffee 1997).

Evidence suggests that systematic differences exist between national cultures (Hofstede 1980, 1994). For example, Dutch job applicants are apt to undersell themselves in the eyes of Americans. In France, where status is valued, the emotional distance (known as power distance) between managers and employees is much greater than in Sweden, a less hierarchical society. Dutch applicants use modest CVs and avoid extravagant promises. In more feminine societies (Sweden, Norway, the Netherlands and Denmark) failing in school is a minor mishap whereas in more masculine societies (Japan, Austria, Italy, Switzerland and West Germany) it is seen as total disaster. More feminine societies place more emphasis upon working to live rather than the opposite. In more feminine societies, conflict resolution is characterized by negotiation and compromise, whereas in more masculine societies fighting it out is the norm (Hofstede 1994). Incidentally, the UK scores midway on the scale of masculinity.

The evidence is conflicting, however, as part of the organizational literature suggests that the needs of capitalist appropriation over-ride cultural diversity. For instance, Pascale and Athos (1982) observed numerous similarities in the volume and form of communications between American and Japanese organizations. Contrary to popular perceptions, Japanese managers are not notably more consultative in their approach to decision making than their American counterparts. Moreover, American workers may actually be more committed to their organizations (see section 3.4) than their Japanese counterparts (Lincoln 1989, Luthans, McCaul and Dodd 1985, Marsh and Mannari, 1973, Near 1989). The Japanese tradition of lifetime employment only ever applied to a minority of employees. Moreover, it has come under increasing strain as economic conditions change. For example, in 1998 Toshiba embarked upon a radical programme of restructuring, shedding jobs and businesses in a manner said to have left analysts 'gasping' (Abrahams 1998, p. 25). (Note though, that literature mixes culture and climate).

Pause for reflection

Hospital porters and cleaners are among the lowest paid of health service staff. In recent years they have faced significant job insecurity as a result of government policies aimed at extracting 'value for money' from hospital trusts.

Describe the cultural ethos which you would expect to find among portering and cleaning staff.

9.5 Organizations *as* Cultures

So far it has been mainly assumed that:

culture is something an organization *has*.

In other words, culture has been seen as an operational variable, that is, something which can be measured and manipulated like job satisfaction, motivation or organization commitment (Jelinek, Smiricich and Hirsch 1983).

There is another intellectual standpoint, however. In section 1.2 we saw how the notion of organization is basically a metaphor, a linguistic device which enables us to understand one thing through the medium of another. For 'organization' we can substitute 'culture'. When we substitute 'culture' as a root metaphor, we no longer see rules, structures, technology and so forth, but, norms, language, and shared meaning. In other words, we can also conceptualize culture as:

something an organization *is* (Smircich 1983).

This view implies:

organizations *are* cultures.

Let us now examine culture from a different perspective.

9.5.1 Culture is what an organization *is*?

What can a different conceptualization reveal about the nature and dynamics of culture that another intellectual standpoint hides? In an influential analysis of the concept of culture, Jelinek, Smircich and Hirsh (1983) suggest that corporate culturism reflects monochromatic thinking which oversimplifies culture. Monochromatic thinking assumes that culture can be managed. Indeed, according to Schein (1992) the issue is simple. Either the leader manages the culture, says Schein, or the culture manages the leader. Moreover, says Schein, the *raison d'être* of general management lies in getting sub-cultures to work together. In other words, one of the key themes of the corporate culturist literature is that:

leaders define the organizational culture.

Schein then argues, somewhat contradictorily, that managers can only discover what an organization's culture is by trying to change it. Schein may have been thinking of Gouldner's (1954) study of a gypsum mine. For many years the mine operated under the indulgent management of 'Old Doug'. Recruitment observed family and community ties. Starting and finishing times and lunch breaks were regarded as approximate. Operatives enjoyed free use of company materials. Dismissals were unknown. For instance:

If a worker wants to take home any glass, tin, nails or wood, all he has to do is to get a slip foreman and the gateman or big boss won't say a word. They (top management) know that foreman will have enough brains not to give too much, but just enough to help a fellow out.

(Gouldner 1954, p. 51)

Likewise:

If you ever go over to the lunch room at 9 o'clock, you will find the whole gang from the warehouse eating. . . . Yet the fellows don't take advantage, they're reasonable.

(Gouldner 1954, p. 52)

Old Doug died. His successor, known as Mr Peele, was determined to enforce discipline. The surface workers grudgingly acquiesced. In the mine itself, however, management by rule proved incompatible with the culture of responsible autonomy that had developed in response to difficult and potentially dangerous working conditions. The miners were accustomed to organizing the work themselves, to making their own decisions about safety. They were also used to engaging in periodic drinking sprees in order to relieve stress at the expense of appearing for work next day. Peele's efforts to achieve a cultural change failed.

It was suggested in section 1.4.2 that researchers tended to dismiss the existence of paradox, contradiction, and ambiguity in organizations as distractions rather than legitimate and important issues for enquiry (Quinn and Cameron 1988, Jelinek, Smircich and Hirsch 1983). In other words, organizational researchers traditionally start with a colour television and try to reduce the picture to black and white.

By contrast, conceptualizing organizations *as* cultures assumes the colour in the picture is part of organizational reality and experience and should be studied as such. Gouldner's study of the gypsum mine does just that. It allows us to see that what may appear as tardiness and recalcitrance is ambiguous, for it simultaneously points to the existence of self-organization and responsible autonomy.

Gouldner's study allows us to glimpse two other important elements of culture namely:

1. The underlying structures of meaning in the organization, and,
2. How people's perceptions, interpretation and behaviour continually shape the structure of meaning. (Jelinek, Smircich, and Hirsch 1983)

We saw in section 1.2.1 how the notion of 'organization' implies that organizations exist as instruments for accomplishment. Once we begin to see organizations as cultures, we no longer see 'organization' a noun, but, subtly different, 'organizing' a verb (Perrow 1979, Smircich 1983). In the context of the gypsum mine, for example, we see 'organizing' and shared meaning in the timing of tea breaks and helping fellows out. There is no need for managers to specify what employees may or may not take from the mine. The limits to tolerance are tacitly understood and observed.

Dress codes are an interesting example of how actions and behaviour are shaped by structures of meaning and vice versa. For instance, in 1998 the collapse of the Russian economy signalled a period of ominous uncertainty in the stock market. Simultaneously stockbrokers' traditional sombre suits and conservative shirts gave way to flashy turnback cuffs, lime green and salmon pink linings, and turquoise pinstripes (Curphey 1998).

Precisely how and why 'acceptable dandyism' (Curphey 1998, p. 44) became the new dress code is unclear. Certainly, no organization rule book imposed it. Yet such strictures are real enough to those experiencing them. In the next chapter we examine the symbolic aspects of organization, that is, language, ceremony and ritual in more detail. The present chapter will focus mainly upon the notion of shared meaning and its implications for management.

9.5.2 Culture and cultural identities

Once we see organizations as cultures it becomes easier to understand why culture may not be managements' exclusive property. Employees create culture for themselves. For example, David Collinson's (1988) study of shop floor masculinity suggests that nicknames can serve an important sociological purpose as they enable cultural identities to be expressed:

Electric lips was unable to keep secrets. Pot Harry was so nicknamed because, as a teaboy thirty years before, he had dropped and broken all the drinking pots. 'Tom Pepper' was reputed to have never spoken the truth in his life.

(Collinson 1988, p. 185)

Incidentally, note the longevity of one nickname—thirty years.

Corporate culturism assumes the norms, values and beliefs of organizational members are the factors which create unity and predict behaviour. Meek (1988) suggests, however, that these are highly unpredictable entities. Managerial manipulation can backfire and/or:

overlook the factors that do generate stability.

Meek suggests that values, norms and beliefs have as much potential for conflict as they do for cohesion. For instance, in the case of the engineering shop referred to earlier, the company decided to produce an 'in-house' magazine. The aim, in true 'excellence' style, was to create a new organizational climate of trust and openness. Staff, however, promptly nicknamed the magazine 'Goebbel's Gazette' and said to one another, 'Thank-you for bringing it to my Achtung' (Collinson 1988, p. 187).

9.6 The Dynamics of Culture

Recall that Martin and Siehel (1983) regard counter-cultures as a threat to the dominant culture. This is an example of linear intuitive thinking whereby employees are either 'for' the organization, or 'against' it. In section 1.2.1 we saw how metaphoric thinking can reveal the existence of paradox, contradiction and ambiguity in organizations.

Seeing organizations as cultures reveals a more subtle and paradoxical possibility namely:

counter-cultures can simultaneously oppose the dominant culture *and* promote stability.

Culture sensitises us to the sometimes ambiguous and contradictory nature of organizations. Counter-cultures may facilitate production *not* because of managerial motivation strategies, but, paradoxically, in opposition to management.

Pause for reflection

A multi-national company decided to apply Deming's ideas on building constructive relations with its suppliers (see section 4.4.2). The programme of planned cultural change has involved substituting cooperation for coercion. The Director of Purchasing is concerned because although staff are observing the new policy, as soon as a crisis occurs they revert to threats and intimidation, the older staff especially.

Advise the director of purchasing.

The director of purchasing may simply be underscoring the difficulties of achieving real cultural change. Yet there may be another explanation. It was Al Capone, I think, who said that a kind word and a gun are better than a kind word alone (see section 5.9). Conceivably, the older staff understand the realities of power. The counter-culture seen during times of stress may explain why vital reserves of aluminium, copper and plastic are maintained. If staff listened to the director of purchasing they might have good relations with their suppliers, but alas, no supplies.

Gouldner's (1954) account of the miners is another case in point. Latterly, the miner's virtually ran the mine in defiance of management. Likewise, Ackroyd and Crowdy's (1990) highly engaging ethnography of a slaughterhouse shows how the appearance of managerial control can be an illusion. Day-to-day production management was decided by the slaughtering teams themselves. Managers rarely dealt directly with the teams and never attempted to direct their work. Like Gouldner's gypsum mine, the nature of the work precludes detailed intervention. Although slaughter houses operate like production lines, the work cycle and pace of work vary considerably according to the kind of animal being slaughtered and dressed. In this case, animals tended to arrive unpredictably in batches of 200—pigs, cows, sheep, lambs. The gang would then decide how tasks should be distributed to work stations, which member of the gang would work where, and the pace of the line. Although gangs were formally led by chargehands, in practice:

Each gang had a strong informal hierarchy, dominated by the fastest and most accomplished workers ... The task of sticking (severing the arteries of) the stunned animals carried the highest status and was invariably included in the work cycle of the senior man.... Sticking is the single act that is most easily identified with killing. Symbolically it marks the boundary between life and death.

(Ackroyd and Crowdy 1990, p. 6)

9.6.1 The sinister side of culture

Recall that Willmott suggests that corporate culturism is totalitarian. That is not to suggest, however, that counter cultures are benign and cosy enclaves:

Pancake Tuesday was celebrated by 'greasing the bollocks' of the apprentices with emulsion and then locking them in the shithouse, bollock naked. The lads had to 'take it' in order to survive on the shop floor. Having graduated through the degradation ceremonies, they would be recognized as mature men worthy of participating in the shop floor banter and culture.

(Collinson 1988, p. 189)

Any manager who behaved in this way would be sued for assault.

Paradoxically, counter-cultures can fill gaps in management control. Collinson (1988) notes that in the organization he studied, one apprentice was constantly attacked because he was lazy. One worker said to Collinson, 'Has he (the apprentice) told you about his dreams, 'cos that's all he does here.' (Collinson 1988, p. 194).

Likewise, Ackroyd and Crowdy (1990) report that workers perceived as not pulling their weight were continually harassed by their colleagues. Boots would be filled with fresh blood:

A carcass would be pushed hard along an unpowered overhead 'sliding' into the path of a worker . . . entrails would fly across the workspace aimed at a particular person.

(Ackroyd and Crowdy 1990, p. 6)

Significantly, gang leaders were rarely subjected to harassments or practical jokes.

9.6.2 Culture and the limits of control

By now it may seem that:

the counter-culture is the organization.

Recall that organization is a metaphor which enables us to conceptualize 'something else'. Rules, operational procedures and so forth may suggest how the organization *should* operate (Brown 1960). Culture is one factor which dictates what happens in practice.

For instance, a gang of criminals known as the Krays operated for many years in full knowledge of the police. Although the police rule book tells them to arrest all law breakers, in practice, the police apply their powers selectively. Initially, the Krays were not perceived as a threat to social boundaries, 'They didn't mug old ladies or hurt kids; they only hurt their own. The "old bill" didn't want the "ag"; then they went too far,' (Hobbs 1988, p. 60).

Likewise, Van Maanen (1973) notes that police recruits absorb the real skills needed for the job, not in training school, but working with a partner on the beat. The new recruit, 'Becomes aware that nobody's perfect and, as if to reify his police academy experiences, he learns that to be protected from his own mistakes, he must protect others' (Van Maanen 1973, p. 413).

9.6.3 Ambiguity and multiple meanings in organizations

We saw in section 7.2.1 how traditional mechanistic thinking presumes that 'problems' have 'solutions'. Corporate culturism sees 'unity' as a solution. Rather less emphasis is placed upon the problems which unity can cause, or, whether unity is all that it seems.

Smith and Simmons (1983) have observed that:

action which unifies at one level can be divisive at another.

Recall the words of the Hewlett-Packard employee in section 9.3. The employee continued:

I could earn a lot of money working for ——. But they aren't *us*. —— are just out to make money. They don't give a damn about the product. They are *Satan*.

This is the other side of unity. That is, the unified group 'us' has a strong belief in its inherent morality while projecting its hostility on to a rival company 'Satan'. The employee is exhibiting signs of 'group-think' mentality which, as we saw in section 7.8 is dangerous because it can blind people to their own weaknesses and other group's strengths. Likewise, Smith and Simmons (1983) note how a charismatic leader unified a group of medical staff, but at the expense of making them contemptuous of the work of other medical professionals, thus undermining staff's ability to evaluate treatment programmes. It is a small step from unity to arrogance.

Unity and division are by no means invariably clear cut, however. We saw in section 1.2 how organizations can be many things simultaneously. Organizational events, that is, what we see, hear, and experience in organizations can also be ambiguous. Ambiguity means:

capable of more than one meaning.

So far culture has been presented as *either* total unity or inevitable division. Yet:

unity *and* division can exist in organizations simultaneously.

Ed Young's (1989) study of a small clothing factory is a good example of how organizational events can be vested with different levels of meaning, and how unity and division can exist in tandem. Ostensibly the factory embodied a distinctive and unified culture. For example, staff united in common celebration by wearing a rose to celebrate St George's day. Yet management saw the shop floor as a world of its own. Indeed, that same event was also the focal point for the expression of deep-seated divisions, tension and hostility.

The factory comprised two groups of machinists. One group made working clothing. This group enjoyed a steady stream of orders. The staff were mainly long-standing employees working to support a family. By contrast, the second group, employed in making bags, experienced a much more precarious existence. Work was sporadic, 'lay offs' frequent, and turnover high. The staff tended to be younger than in the workwear group. Few had family responsibilities.

The workwear group regarded themselves as superior to mere 'bag' machinists. The status division between the groups was reflected in arrangements for the collection of money, and the subsequent distribution of the roses. That is, each division organized its own collection and distribution. Moreover, although work groups socialized after hours, they did so only within the confines of their separate divisions.

We saw in section 7.8 how status divisions emerge in groups. In fact, informal status divisions are to be found everywhere—for those sensitive enough to observe them. For example, Robert Roberts's (1973) ethnography of Salford slum life in the early years of the twentieth century highlights status divisions between the poorest of the poor. For instance, net curtains denoted respectable poor whereas newspaper coverings on windows signified approaching destitution. Likewise, Hobbs describes the system of social stratification in a Hackney pub:

[The section at the front of the bar] is reserved for hard-men, full-time villains, and CID officers. . . . Drinkers . . . . enter and walk through . . . acknowledging friends and acquaintances, but ignoring the corner men and car dealers. . . . The further from the entrance an individual manages to establish himself, the higher his status. Section 3 is no man's land . . . Only itinerants and strangers drink in this area.

(Hobbs 1988, p. 143)

The same applies to organizational life. In schools, teachers of more academically orientated subjects such as mathematics and English are accorded more status than teachers of more practically orientated subjects, though both groups are paid the same. In factories, piece workers often rank higher than their hourly paid counterparts even though their basic conditions of service are identical.

Such differences may seem whimsical. Yet status differences can have far-reaching effects upon organizational life. In hospitals, patients perceived as socially valuable command more attention than their less socially valuable counterparts. Certain crafts' unions have preferred to see membership dwindle rather than merge with manual unions because of the implied diminution in status. Young (1989) notes status claims effectively restricted managements' freedom to transfer surplus labour from one work group to another. Likewise, Whyte's (1949) study of the social structure of a restaurant noted that tensions were most likely to erupt when lower status individuals (waiters) gave direct orders to higher status individuals (cooks).

9.7 Discussion

Recall that in section 1.2.1 we saw how our perceptions of organization have been dominated by mechanical imagery which sees organizations as instruments of accomplishment. Much of the organizational literature is concerned with issues of causality and control. For example, what motivates people, what factors promote job satisfaction, and so forth. The literature on organization culture discussed in this chapter alerts us to deeper issues of meaning and the subtle processes of organizational life.

Durkeim (1934) has suggested that as family ties loosen in modern society, the only substitute for the traditions and values that are essential to any form of integrated society is the occupational group. The corporate culturist literature attempts to substitute the organization and 'love of the product' for religion. For example, McDonald's founder Ray Kroc refers to 'the *gospel* of Quality, Service, Cleanliness and Value' (Peters and Waterman 1982, p. 268, italics added).

Willmott (1993) suggests that the notion of cultural control also represents a shift in basic assumptions. Recall that the Human Relations School and its derivatives (see section 3.1) assumed a basic consensus between managers and the managed which tended to be upset by insensitive managers. According to Willmott corporate culturism does not assume this consensus but actively seeks to create it.

9.7.1 **Rules are rules?**

The organizational literature depicts managers as controlling and directing operations. Culture highlights how organizational life is negotiated rather than rule governed. For example, the eventual arrest and conviction of the Krays owed little to police powers of detection and almost everything to the lead officer's skill as a negotiator. 'Nipper' Reed, as he was known, went to considerable lengths with the Home Office to negotiate immunity from prosecution for key witnesses in return for highly damaging evidence against the Krays (Hobbs 1988).

The jazz metaphor referred to in section 1.5.2 suggests that employees are not so much rule bound as forever testing boundaries to see how far they can go (Hatch, nd).

The notion of culture allows us to see that in organizations, roles, boundaries and standards are not given so much as tacitly negotiated and renegotiated over time. In other words, the notion of culture enables us to see that organizations are not static machines but forever changing. Moreover, we saw in section 7.4 that action does not flow from clear cut decisions. The notion of culture enables us to see further. That is, intuitive linear thinking assumes that great events flow from solemn decisions of great magnitude. The idea of negotiation, however, implies that the most profound changes may be extremely subtle.

A cultural perspective helps us to see that organizational effectiveness is more than a matter of technical efficiency. In schools, children are instructed to 'stop talking'. The assumption that talking is dysfunctional is often carried over into working life. Many workstations are designed to prevent it. Yet the talker is not necessarily idling the time away. A cultural perspective allows us to see that talking is a way of oiling the social wheels. The web of relationships created through talking, mutual help and exchange of information can play a critical role in facilitating production especially in times of crisis.

Managers may not be able to control the emergence of status divisions but they can take care to minimize their impact and avoid upsetting the natural order of things. For instance, in the case of the restaurant, the existence of physical barriers between cooks and waiters helped lower the tension (Whyte 1949). Paradoxically, managers can only manage or avoid cultural clashes by recognizing the limits of their power. For example, when two different organizations occupy the same office facilities, it may be more effective to separate groups (two kettles, two enquiry desks, two filing clerks and so forth) than to insist that they share and share alike.

You may feel that many of the cases referred to in this chapter centre upon trivial things, the wearing of a rose, for example. Perhaps, and yet why do we see these as trivial? Is it because so much of the management literature focuses upon issues such as technology and structure that we are in danger of missing a whole dimension of organizational life? Workplace squabbles over small and sometimes seemingly ridiculous things are often status claims. People will fight for control of the stock cupboard if the stock cupboard is organizationally significant.

The issues themselves may be mundane. It is what lies beneath them that matters.

When the 'teaching' and 'non-teaching' sections of the personnel departments argue over the precise location of the Christmas tree in an open plan office what is actually being played out is the tension between the two groups. 'Non-teaching' sees itself as the poor relation of 'teaching', it occupies least space, has the lowest ratio of staff to case load. The Christmas tree was the one thing over which 'non-teaching' felt it could exert control, 'At least *we* are having our share of the Christmas tree,' said an employee.

This is not to suggest that culture pertains only to managing organizations. Sensitivity to culture is an essential prerequisite of surviving in organizations. Survival is as much about knowing what is and is not done, where the status claims lie and tensions exist as it is about professional skill and technical knowledge. We may not be able to measure culture but we can observe its subtle nuances and obliquely shifting dynamics (Schein 1996).

We saw in section 9.6.1 that counter-cultures may be no less sinister than the claims of the corporate culturist literature. Counter-cultures can be cruel, especially to older workers, women and ethnic and sexual minorities (Mills 1988, and Alvesson and Billing 1997, Ch. 5). For example, one employee told Collinson, 'They think it's soft to stir tea with a spoon. You've got to use your ruler, so you don't look effeminate' (Collinson 1988, p. 193).

Likewise, 'no money, no soap', and the navy toast that celebrates marital infidelity.

Managers are sometimes accused of condoning such cultures or of creating the organizational climate which produces sexist or racist attitudes. This perspective may well be valid in many cases. The notion of counter-culture, however, suggests other forces may be at work. If organizations *are* cultures, logically culture may the one factor over which employees can exert influence—because they become part of the culture which is continually created and recreated.

Yet how deep is this influence? Recall that culture too is a metaphor, a linguistic device which enables us to understand something else. When we examine an organization's culture what are we seeing? For example, Collinson suggests that the expression of masculinity which was a defining feature of the organization he studied, actually serves as a bolster for perceived feelings of inferiority. Colleagues on the shop floor see themselves as 'genuine' that is, as distinct from 'nancy boys in th'offices' (Collinson 1988, p. 186).

This perception and acting out of themselves as 'genuine', suggests Collinson, is a way of countering the knowledge that they are actually the least skilled and most dispensable members of the workforce. This may also explain why junior staff are often seen 'lording it' over school leavers. Utterly subordinate themselves, they compensate by controlling what they can.

In other words, what we call culture is simultaneously a manifestation of the deep structure of power in society. As we saw in section 5.3.1, the supreme exercise of power exists in received assumptions about what is appropriate. By compensating for gaps in managerial control, the miners, the slaughtermen and doubtless countless others are actually contributing to their own economic oppression.

Culture may reflect economic oppression yet the managerialist literature starting with Taylor (see Chapter 2) and latterly espoused in 'total quality management' and 'process re-engineering' (Chapter 4) and 'excellence' (see section 9.3), has either tried to eliminate the so-called 'non-rational' forces of organization or bring them under control.

This chapter has shed some light upon how organizations may be influenced by forces which are beyond management. We begin to understand, for example, why the police are apt to 'close ranks' when allegations of misconduct are being investigated. We can see why the spread of BSE has been difficult to check given the culture of the slaughterhouse and the concomitant expressions of masculinity whereby showers are scorned (see also section 12.3.4). Interestingly Hobbs (1988) suggests that London's East End police force have become part of the culture they police. The question is:

- how far managers manage culture, and,
- how far do managers become part of the culture they manage?

9.7.2 Culture and rationality

The culture theme is often exploited in the old Ealing comedies. The plot is similar to Goulner's (1954) study of the gypsum mine whereby the avuncular manager maintains organizational peace and stability through an intimate knowledge of the cultural dynamics of the workplace born of sensitivity and long experience. Along comes the brash dynamic young executive with pronounced ideas upon improving efficiency. The result is a strike. We saw in section 1.2.4 how our ideas about what constitutes rational are basically sexual. Culture brings us back to this point, that is,

what is rational?

Recall the suggestion in section 9.4.4 that economic imperatives may over-ride cultural differences. Does this imply that the former building societies will achieve the necessary cultural change to enable them to function as banks? Was it rational to attempt to merge a Church of England school with a Nonconformist foundation, however strong the economic case for doing so? Judging by the number of mergers and acquisitions which have not lived up to expectations, the answer seems to be that economic rationality will take us only so far. This raises an intriguing question:

can something which defies economic logic succeed by dint of cultural synergy?

Summary

1 Culture is rooted in the beliefs, values, and assumptions held by members.

2 Culture is concerned with the negotiation of meaning, the symbolic world that results from interaction.

3 Culture is important because organizational effectiveness is more than a technical problem.

4 Corporate culturism assumes that organizational effectiveness requires consistency between the organization's culture and its mission.

5 Corporate culturism rests upon promoting shared values and beliefs, seeking to capture the hearts and minds of employees.

6 Corporate culturism is potentially totalitarian in that it links employees' sense of self worth with their attitude to work, and restrains self-development.

7 Proponents of corporate culturism have been slow to highlight the limitations and ironies of its underlying assumptions namely:

- unpredictable consequences of attempting to manipulate sentiment,
- 'group-think' syndrome,
- reluctance to accept change.

8 Corporate culturism charges management with creating a unitary set of values. In reality, organizations are not one culture but many.

9 Sub-cultures can be classified as:

- enhancing,
- orthogonal,
- counter.

10 Evidence suggests that systematic differences exist between national cultures.

11 It is unclear how far national differences impact upon organizations, or how the imperatives of industrialization override cultural differences.

12 Corporate culturism assumes that culture is something an organization *has*.

13 Culture can also be conceptualized as something an organization *is*.

14 Reconceptualizing organizations *as* cultures highlights 'organizing' as distinct from 'organization'.

15 Perceiving organizations as cultures highlights the limits of managerial control and enables us to understand why culture may not be the property of management.

16 Cultural identity is often expressed in the seemingly mundane aspects of organization: nicknames, for example.

17 Counter-cultures can simultaneously oppose the dominant culture *and* promote stability, self-organization and responsible autonomy.

18 Counter-cultures are not always cosy enclaves, however.

19 The counter-culture may define organizational priorities, for good and/or for bad.

20 The concept of culture highlights the potentially ambiguous nature of organizational life. Unity and division can exist simultaneously.

21 The concept of culture also illuminates how organizational life is negotiated rather than rule bound.

22 The concept of culture brings us back to the question, what is rational?

Questions for Discussion

1 Imagine that you are about to open a small factory assembling vending machines.

   What type of culture would you aim to create and why?

   How would you set about trying to achieve your aims?

   What difficulties do you anticipate, and, how would you attempt to overcome these?

   How might your approach differ if the organization was a research and development department in an electronics company?

2 Organizations often install new IT systems in order to achieve a cultural change.

   Comment upon this policy.

3 Do managers manage culture, or, does culture manage managers?

4 Schein (1996) has suggested that organizational culture cannot be measured with questionnaires but can only be observed.

   Discuss.

5 Why is it important for managers and employees to understand their organization's culture?

6 'The mundanity of everyday is an illusion.' (Young 1989, p. 201)

   Discuss this statement with reference to organization culture.

7 Imagine that you are Tom Peters.

   How would you defend yourself against accusations of totalitarianism.

8 How does the concept of culture highlight the limitations of mechanistic approaches to management?

9 Long hours are the norm in professional jobs in the City of London. Yet anecdotal evidence suggests that many employees remain in offices even though there is no actual work to do. Alternatively, employees apparently working at their computer screens at eight o'clock in the evening are actually playing computer games.

   What does this information suggest about the culture of those organizations?

Further Reading

■ Ackroyd, S., and Crowdy, P. A. (1990) 'Can culture be managed? Working with raw material: the case of English slaughtermen,' *Personnel Review*, 19, 3–13.

■ Collinson, D. (1988) 'Engineering humour: masculinity, joking and conflict in shopfloor relations,' *Organization Studies*, 9, 181–199.

- Jelinek, M., Smircich, L., and Hirsch, P. (1983) 'Introduction: a code of many colours,' *Administrative Science Quarterly, 28,* 331–338.

- Mills, A. J. (1988) 'Organization, gender and culture,' *Organization Studies, 9,* 351–369.

- Ray, C. A. (1986) 'Corporate culture: the last frontier of control,' *Journal of Management Studies, 23,* 287–299.

- Smircich, L. (1983) 'Concepts of culture and organizational analysis,' *Administrative Science Quarterly, 28,* 339–358.

- Thompson, P. and McHugh, D. (1995) *Work Organizations: A Critical Introduction* London, Macmillan.

- Willmott, H. (1993) 'Strength is ignorance; slavery is freedom: managing culture in modern organization,' *Journal of Management Studies, 30,* 515–552.

Chapter 10
The Symbolic Life of Organizations

> Say, from whence
> You owe this strange intelligence? or why
> Upon this blasted heath you stop our way
> With such prophetic greeting?
> *(Macbeth* Act 1, Sc. 3, 1.72)

'I am just going outside and may be some time.'
(Captain Oates last words in *Scott's Last Expedition* (1913))

I⟨T⟩ is a hot day in London's Finsbury Park. The time is just a little after two in the afternoon. Outside on the grass, among the crowds of people, two women are sharing a bottle of wine. Inside the pavilion a group of men in business suits, jackets slung over the chairs, are drinking beer and talking about someone 'very clever'. Basement offices exude a languid air. Magazines are piled near computer work stations. Here and there young men drift across the office floor. Some wear red braces, others yellow. On one desk a Mont Blanc 149 Meiserstuck fountain pen has been left on a pad of paper as carelessly as if it were a Bic ballpoint.

What are we seeing here? Until recently, our images of organizations centred upon work tasks, rules, and decision making. This chapter transports us to the sensual and emotional realm of organizations. The cloak of organizational rationality is lifted to reveal sorcery, superstition, and the suspicion of witchcraft.

In this chapter organizations are not managed by executives, finance officers, and administrative assistants and the like, but by a panoply of licensed fools, honest brokers, kingmakers, and weird sisters acting out mysterious rites and ceremonies. It is a world of fortune tellers and witch-finders, of dread portents and evil spirits. It is a world which eludes scientific proof. Yet it is both real and important. The issues discussed in this chapter include:

Key Issues

- What is symbolism?
- Symbols as energy controlling
- Secrecy as symbol
- Witchcraft and organizations

10.1 What is Symbolism?

BEFORE we enter the mystical realm of organizational symbolism, first let me define the terminology. Organizational symbolism concerns:

Those aspects of an organization that its members use to reveal or make comprehendible the unconscious feelings, images and values that are inherent in the organization. Symbolism expresses the underlying character, ideology or value system of an organization. (Dandridge, Mitroff and Joyce, 1980)

For example, in 1999 Hanson dispensed with its twenty-year-old logo of knotted US and British flags in favour of a design comprising building blocks and also with an 'H' in it. This decision was intended to distance Hanson from its history as a conglomerate, and to emphasize the company's involvement in building materials. The group also changed the name of its US companies, and, coincidentally announced a new centralized decision-making structure (Pretzlik, 1999).

10.1.1 Symbols and signs

The word *symbol* centres upon the idea of *sign*:

A symbol is a sign which denotes something much greater than itself, and which calls for the association of certain conscious or unconscious ideas in order for it to be endowed with its full meaning and significance. (Morgan, Frost and Pondy, 1983, p. 5)

For example, the wearing of a white coat may signify 'doctor', crown may signify 'king' or 'queen', '£' may signify money. Note, however, that an important qualification applies. A sign becomes a symbol only when it is vested with a deeper level of meaning than surface appearances suggest. For example, a traffic sign may indicate 'no right turn'. That does not make it a symbol, however, because it possesses no deeper significance than what surface appearances suggest. Conversely the lighting of a candle may be symbolically significant if it denotes bringing of light, that is, relief from suffering or enlightenment. In other words:

- all symbols are signs, but,
- not all signs are symbols (Morgan, Frost and Pondy 1983).

Pause for reflection

You have inherited enough money for life provided you invest wisely. You have a choice of two firms of advisors. One comprises mainly young staff. The office is brightly furnished, the decor flamboyant. The atmosphere is informal. Staff are casually attired, there is much laughing and joking in the office. Clients are addressed by their first names. The second is an old fashioned firm. The staff are long serving. The office is furnished with leather Chesterfields and solid mahogany desks. The atmosphere is very formal. The staff wear business suits. Prefixes are invariably used to address clients.

Which firm would you appoint to manage your investments, and why?

Precisely how something becomes symbolically significant is a mystery. What is certain, however, is that symbols can be highly potent. For example, hospital waiting lists have come to signify a crisis in public health care provision. Likewise, I would not be surprised if you chose the old fashioned firm to handle your investments because appearances symbolize stability and continuity.

Since symbols imply shared meaning, logic suggests that they can be manipulated to produce effects. For example, the £300 Mont Blanc pen left on the desk—*as if it were a Bic ballpoint*. What does that signify? We will return to the manipulation of symbols later in this chapter. Suffice it here to note that Mont Blanc pens are available in two colours, black and maroon. Maroon is slightly cheaper, but black far outsells maroon—why?

10.2 Types of Symbol

W^E saw in section 5.1 that power means the production of intended effects. Symbols are a source of power because of their capacity to produce 'intended effects'. There are three types of symbol as follows:

1. Verbal.
2. Actions and events.
3. Material.

Each of these is explained in turn.

10.2.1 Verbal symbols

Verbal symbols include myths, legends, stories, jokes, names and rumour, the use of coded language. Stories do more than enliven coffee breaks and entertain newcomers, 'Stories function to communicate presumptions or values which, in subtle ways, limit and enrich what participants see and believe and feel,' (Wilkins 1983, p. 89).

For example, Bill Hewlett and Dave Packard are depicted as legends in the firm which they founded. New employees quickly learn how 'Bill and Dave' started the company in Bill's garage and made some of their first products in the Hewlett oven. Repetition of the story both communicates and reaffirms the corporate culture.

We saw in Chapter 1 that language is not merely descriptive, but ontological. Language can be seen as a symbol system which structures our perceptions and beliefs. Words are not mere labels but deeply concerned with the nature of being (Morgan 1980, 1983; see also section 1.6.2). For example, where men are described as 'forceful' or 'masterful', women are described as 'aggressive', 'strident' or 'hectoring'. Men are 'ambitious', women 'pushy'. In the financial services industry sexual imagery is deployed to convey success—clients and colleagues in other firms are 'raped' (Lewis 1990) or have their faces 'ripped off' (Partnoy 1977). Profitable traders are accorded the title 'big swinging dicks' to equate success with sexual potency. Conversely, the Church utilizes a system of language based upon euphemism:

- visitation = quality inspection
- guidance = performance appraisal
- vocation = ambition.

Another important element of organizational storytelling is the promulgation of myth. Myth has a particular meaning in the context of organizational symbolism, that is, 'A narrative of events . . . [that] has a sacred quality; the sacred communication is made in symbolic form (Meek 1988, citing Cohen p. 468).

Management ideologies and myths aim to provide meaning and purpose for organizational activity. The promulgation of myth is seen in stories about managers who saved the organization and accounts of other heroic exploits (Turner 1986).

10.2.2 Actions and events as symbols

Symbolically significant actions and events include meal breaks, the shaking of hands to signify commitment to a contract or reconciliation after a quarrel, signing ceremonies, meetings, and team briefings.

We will discuss the function of rites and ritual in more detail later. Here it is important to note that symbolic action plays an important role in sustaining organizational life. Emissaries are despatched to test reactions. Hints are issued to signal concessions, or to subtly impose control. For example, in the popular television programme known as *Yes Minister* junior civil servants are not rebuked openly but taken for a disciplinary drink by their hierarchical superiors. Likewise, when the fictional retiring cabinet secretary mentions his impending retirement to the aspiring Sir Humphrey, he emphasizes that his successor would need to be a person of 'discretion'.

'Naturally,' replies Sir Humphrey, thus tacitly conceding the demand not to reveal his predecessor's mistakes.

Sir Humphrey then asks the cabinet secretary how he plans to spend his time in retirement. The question really means, 'What price my promotion?' The cabinet secretary replies that he hopes to devote time to the arts—a veiled demand for a board appointment. The appointment is negotiated over a cup of coffee. A decision has been made without any direct mention.

10.2.3 Material symbols

Material symbols include uniforms, status symbols, awards, logos and other company insignia (Dandridge, Mitroff and Joyce 1980, Morgan, Frost and Pondy 1983). Corporate architecture can serve to express corporate strategy (Berg and Kreiner 1990). For instance, a low flat building design may symbolize a flat management structure. As late as the 1980s, government brokers in the City of London wore top hats in order to distance themselves from ordinary brokers (Durham 1992). The absence of material symbols can also be significant. For instance, some executives decline to carry personal organizers in order to avoid appearing as mere scribes. Instead, if they need to write something down they produce a slip of paper from a pocket.

10.3 How Symbols Function

W^E have already seen that symbols are a source of power through their ability to produce effects. Let me now try and systematize that knowledge.

Symbols serve three potentially overlapping functions as follows:

1. Descriptive
2. Energy controlling
3. System maintenance (Dandridge, Mitroff and Joyce 1980).

Each of these functions is now explained in turn.

10.3.1 Symbols as descriptive

We saw in sections 6.4.6 and 6.4.7 that actions have both technical consequences and expressive ones:

- Actions which are instrumentally effective can have disastrous expressive consequences.
- Conversely, actions which are instrumentally useless can serve a vital expressive purpose.

Symbols can shape reality. For example, dealing with death is a relatively uncommon experience in the Western world. Morticians manipulate symbols to prevent their work being disrupted by emotional outbursts from distressed onlookers. Morticians basically aim to impart an appearance of life and normality. The corpse is got up to look as if asleep. The eyes are closed thus averting the death stare. If someone dies at home the bedroom is tidied and left to look as if nothing untoward has happened. Funeral parlours are made to look like ordinary lounges (Barley 1983).

Pause for reflection

Imagine you are the captain of a ship in war time. The ship has just returned to port after an extremely difficult mission. The crew are looking forward to a much needed period of rest and recuperation.

   Suddenly, you receive an order to prepare the ship for immediate action. This is the 'last straw' which could well prompt the exhausted crew to mutiny.

How would you handle the situation?

Symbols are the means whereby the experience of organization is expressed, sometimes known as the management of meaning (Smircich and Morgan 1982, Pfeffer 1977). The management of meaning goes beyond Mintzberg's (1973) notions of managers as figureheads to the 'deep structure' of how reality is shaped and defined and the significance attached to particular events.

The management of meaning can achieve more than reliance upon formal authority. For example, Quaid (1993) recounts how the management of an organization commissioned a job evaluation project in order to reassert control without appearing to. The writing, analyzing and scoring of job descriptions imparted an air of scientific objectivity to the exercise which served as a smokescreen for manipulation.

As regards the ship's crew, the captain and first lieutenant took the unusual step of going down on to the decks and starting the work themselves. Seeing this, the crew joined in voluntarily because the leaders' actions signified the importance of the task.

Another example of the power of symbols to convey meaning is the so-called Freudian slip. That is:

The unintended words and actions which destroy surface appearance and reveal some underlying and hidden intention or meaning. (Morgan, Frost, and Pondy 1983, p. 8)

For instance, when Prince Charles visited the hospital where Princess Diana was treated before she died, he is alleged to have said 'congratulations' to the staff (Sancton and MacLeod 1998). Likewise, an employee is encouraged by their manager to apply for internal promotion. The employee then mentions that another company is recruiting. 'There may be real possibilities there,' says the manager, thus unintentionally revealing that they have no intention of promoting the employee.

10.3.2 **Symbols as energy controlling**

Symbols have the power to move or to constrain. Symbols can increase or decrease tension, inspire, attract, repel, terrify, and even enable people to relive a previous existence. For instance, in a riot the police officer's helmet often ends up being kicked along the pavement because it is the symbol of power. A man who exhibited voodoo dolls in order to terrify a woman into having sexual relations with him was convicted of rape. In war, the most determined conflicts are often fought over targets which are strategically worthless but symbolically significant—Verdun, for example, (Drummond 1991). The image of financially ruined Lloyds' names begging outside headquarters may have prompted Lloyds to negotiate settlements with debtors formally liable down to their last set of cuff links (Raphael 1995).

We saw in section 5.2.1 how organizations may manipulate symbols in order to stimulate effort and build commitment—'employee of the year' awards, for example. Organizations can also manipulate symbols in order to generate fear. For instance, just as the severed heads of rebels and traitors were once publicly exhibited, executives sometimes refer to 'scalps on belts' to signify their determination to brook no obstacles.

10.3.3 **Symbols as maintaining social order**

Symbols can help to maintain social order by concealing the naked use of power. One form of concealment is to convey information in a manner which depersonalizes potentially contentious issues. For example, 'there is no money in the budget,' or, 'our customers will not like it'.

Sugar-coating of statements and actions is another possibility. Here is a brilliant example of how to insult someone with impunity without offending them:

We have read your manuscript with boundless delight. If we were to publish your paper it would be impossible for us to publish any work of a lower standard. And as it is unthinkable that, in the next thousand years we shall see its equal, we are to our regret, compelled to return your divine composition. (Izraeli and Jick 1986, citing Sociologists for Women in Society Network, 1982).

Refusals such as this provide codified responses to potentially difficult situations. They provide a series of rationalizations which enable the rejected party to cope with the tension and anxiety generated by the act of refusal. It is more than that, however. Symbols can convey more than one level of meaning. The foregoing communication simultaneously reaffirms editorial power and authority to decide what is acceptable and who will have their work published. Likewise, the foregoing managerial refusals reaffirm who decides what is an acceptable course of action and who is entitled to funds.

Likewise Rosen's (1985) study of a business breakfast shows how praise can conceal an invidious twist:

Walter started talking about the 'things the agency does for all of us'. He mentioned that expenses rose by '18 per cent during the past year, but the pension is fully funded. It's very expensive, but all of you have worked for it.' (Rosen 1985, p. 38)

As Rosen notes, the agency is presented as a benevolent but suffering provider. The words 'very expensive' imply that employees do not actually work for all they get, the agency has to bear the unfair financial strain. Pension rights are presented paternalistically as a 'gift'. Workers are 'good' so they will get it. Employees are obliquely reminded of the organization's power to give and therefore, by implication, to take away if employees misbehave.

10.3.4 The ambiguity of symbolic action

Symbolic action can be subtle and ambiguous. We send Christmas cards to remember people in order that we can forget them for the rest of the year. We make donations to charity in order to justify our own excesses. We write job references which are more significant for what is left unsaid.

In organizations, policy meetings are called to reduce tensions by creating a sense of involvement while simultaneously signifying the importance of cooperation (Gagliardi 1986). Ceremonies can infuse people with optimism and energy, facilitate the incorporation of new members, and enhance a sense of personal worth. They are also a means of signalling power shifts in the organization (Turner 1986).

Likewise, sharing information can be a subtle way of showing employees what small cogs they are in the proverbial wheel. Dress can serve to camouflage or define identity or accomplish both (Rosen 1985). The gold watch awarded for long service can also symbolize exploitation. Christmas parties are ostensibly an invitation for social distances to be lowered. Yet by walking round tables talking to staff, senior managers are effectively reaffirming the division between managers and the managed. They are enacting a ceremony of authority (Rosen 1988).

10.4 Secrecy as Symbol

EVERY organization is populated with secrets. Secrecy serves as a boundary mechanism separating high and low status personnel (Murphy 1980). Often the content of the secret is trivial compared to the social organization created by the existence of secrecy:

The secret offers . . . the possibility of a second world alongside the manifest world; and the latter is decisively influenced by the former. (Simmel 1950, p. 330)

A fascinating study of tribal secrecy by Murphy (1980) describes how the Kpelle people of Guinea were controlled by societies of elders each purporting to possess unique, important and secret knowledge. The 'horn society' alone knew how to control the evil activities of witchcraft. The 'spirit society' alone knew how to rid the community of departed spirits of dead people known to be causing trouble.

The reality, notes Murphy, was rather different. The elders manipulated secrecy to inculcate fear and respect, and to legitimize the separation and exclusion of members of social categories or groups from decision making.

Secrecy was maintained by coercion. Punishment or even death would surely befall anyone attempting to penetrate the sacred veil. Such were the mysterious powers of the secret society.

Pause for reflection

The text of this pause should not appear in bold type. However, due to a fault with the software, bold can appear in unwanted places and is difficult to eradicate.

Your task is to write a comedy sketch focusing upon driving away evil spirits **which are corrupting my machine.**

Your equipment comprises:

- a piece of old carpet,
- a cheese grater,
- a soda syphon, and,
- an ironing board.

In organizations, secrecy can serve a similar purpose. Details of mergers and organizational restructuring are often kept secret in order to inculcate fear and respect for elders (senior managers) and to provide a 'sacred "veil"' (Murphy 1980, p. 203) behind which elders can manipulate decisions. The existence of 'private and confidential' generates inequality of knowledge which in turn conveys rights and privileges.

10.5 Witchcraft and Organizations

ONE day, in Chiawa, Zambia, a tractor carrying farm workers overturned and nine people were killed. Although the driver of the tractor was subsequently found to have been extremely drunk, there was no question that the accident was caused by witchcraft. This incident coming on top of a series of other mishaps convinced the chief that there was too much evil in the village. A witchfinder was duly hired to carry out cleansing duties.

Organizations too are riven with primitive fear and superstition. All that separates the modern corporation from tribal behaviour is a veneer of rationality. When managers perceive that there is 'too much evil' in the organization they too hire witchfinders in the shape of auditors and external consultants to carry out cleansing duties. In the modern corporation investigations name evil doers. (Significantly, employees often refer to investigations as witchhunts.) Restructuring exercises which result in dismissal, demotion or transfer can be seen as a way of driving out evil influences.

Yamba (1997) noted an upsurge in the activities of the local witchfinder in Chiawa, following a spate of deaths from AIDS-related illnesses. Likewise, recourse to witch-finders in organizations increases during times of turbulence, stress and uncertainty (Clark and Salaman 1996).

Witchcraft serves to make sense of destabilizing events:

The concept of accident or chance . . . is not present in Chiawa discourse. Any occurrence becomes an accident only when a witchfinder . . . declares it as such. (Yamba 1997)

Since witchfinders stand to extort huge sums from those identified as witches, very few occurrences are deemed accidents. Much the same goes for the fees paid to professional experts.

By the same token, organizations resort to sorcery to explain mischance. For 'angry gods' read 'economic trends'. For 'fortune telling' read 'analysts predict'. For 'storms and thunder' read 'adverse trading conditions'.

Life can be very cruel for suspected witches. (Incidentally, the *Concise Oxford Dictionary* defines witches as persons with unorthodox views.) In Chiawa sixteen people died from being compelled to drink the witchfinder's 'tea' (poison) in order to prove their innocence. In organizations highlighting the activities of evil spirits and declaiming witches:

- enables people to make sense of events, and,
- enables managers to deflect attention from their performance.

> **Pause for reflection**
>
> Why did the fictional Oliver Twist's request for 'more' prompt outrage among the governors of the workhouse?

10.6 Rites and Ritual in Organizations

R**ITES** and ritual are important dimensions of the symbolic life of organizations. According to the *Concise Oxford Dictionary*:

- *rite* means 'form of procedure, action required', and
- *ritual* means 'involving religious or other rites, prescribed order of performing . . . rites'.

Rites and ritual are usually associated with religion, last rites, for example. Yet many organizations resemble monasteries—replete with hallowed corridors, meetings held punctually, repetitively and continuously like monastic prayers, 'Meetings are the sacred hallmarks of the work day and the work week,' (Larsen and Shultz, p. 296). Likewise, quality manuals, standing orders and the like function as sacred texts. Indeed they are sometimes referred to by employees as 'bibles'. (See Bowles 1989 for an interesting discussion on the role of the modern corporation in supplanting the Church in dictating social meaning).

We observe rites and participate in ritual every day though usually unconsciously. A good example is the dinner time conversation between partners:

A   'Did you have a nice day darling?'
B   'Not too bad. How about you?'
A   'Not too bad . . .'
B   'Kids been good?'
A   'Yes.'
B   'Good.'

The questions are predictable and so are the answers. It is as if both parties slot in a prerecorded tape and play it, for no one is actually listening.

Similarly in organizations the form of procedure required in answering the telephone is, 'how are you?'

Moreover, the required response is equally ritualistic. The caller is not meant to launch into a diatribe about their state of health or present preoccupations.

Another example is the ritualistic question asked at the end of job interviews, 'Have you any questions?'. The required form of procedure is to ask one or two—not to keep the panel there all day!

10.6.1 The function of ritual

Ritual represents the dramatization of a myth and can be used to reinforce values and goals. As such:

rituals are more important for what they signify than what they actually do (Pettigrew 1979).

For example, the process of consultation is more important than the outcome (Pfeffer 1981, Ury 1991). Consultation signifies that the other party is important. Failing to consult even on trivial matters can provoke rebellion against a change which would otherwise have been accepted. So-called rituals of rebellion enable people to act out hostilities which cannot be expressed in normal day-to-day relations (Meek 1988). Standing jokes about management are basically a ritual of rebellion. Joking relationships represent 'a mutually permitted form of disrespect' in an otherwise potentially conflictual situation (Collinson 1988, p. 182). Joking rituals help to maintain stability by lowering tensions.

The appointment of a new leader can be highly ritualistic. A great fuss is made. Recruitment consultants (known, not insignificantly as 'head-hunters') are engaged.

Suites of draft documentation are submitted to committees for approval. Elaborate programmes of interviews, presentations and dinners (trial by knife and fork) are arranged.

The ritual is expensive and time consuming but emphasizes the special skills involved in leadership and the objectivity of the recruitment process (Pfeffer 1977). In reality, the appointment may already have been made. The point is, everything is made to appear fair and above suspicion. 'Book prices' serve a similar purpose in the used car trade.

> **Pause for reflection**
>
> Organizations are sometimes criticized for the amount of money they spend upon logos and other insignia.
>
> Imagine that you have just presided over a merger between two companies. How would you defend expenditure upon new uniforms, repainting vans, new designs for notepaper and so forth?

As Smircich (1983) points out, a sense of commonality, that is shared meaning, or taken-for-granted assumptions is essential for organizational activity in order to avoid constant interpretation or reinterpretation of meanings. Ritual implies shared meaning. Shared meaning serves as a form of code. Codes promote efficiency because they facilitate shortcuts (Smircich 1983b). For example, when the auctioneer hammers the gavel ('going, going, GONE'), a binding contract exists immediately. Such rituals enable people to conduct business via tacit understandings. There is no need to renegotiate the relationship every time they meet.

10.6.2 The function of rites

Rites are organizational procedures which possess both:

- a practical and an expressive content, and,
- a manifest and a latent purpose (Beyer and Trice 1987, see also Trice and Beyer 1984).

Rites express culture. Culture is expressed through the use of language, the choice of setting and ritualized behaviours, all of which heighten shared understanding.

Rites are also a subtle means of controlling people. For example, the ostensible purpose of induction programmes is to familiarize new employees with the organization. Yet they also subtly direct the employee in the performance of their duties. For instance, coworkers often use the induction meeting to assert their rights and to define the new recruit's responsibilities under the guise of helpfulness.

Similarly, a latent function of retirement dinners and leaving presentations is to neutralize potential hostility.

10.6.3 Types of rites

The more common organizational rites include:

- rites of passage,
- rites of degradation,
- rites of enhancement,
- rites of renewal,
- rites of conflict reduction,
- rites of integration, and,
- rites of creation (Beyer and Trice 1987).

Each of these is described in turn.

Rites of passage denote an individual's transition from one existence to another. Rites of passage include weddings, funerals, and graduation ceremonies. The purpose of such rites is to separate people from a previous existence.

For example, in the military, separation of new recruits from civilian life involves a drastic haircut and donning of a uniform. The recruit's mind and body are then rebuilt through vigorous training and humiliations. Recruits then undergo rites of incorporation via a passing out parade.

Rites of degradation involve dismissing or disempowering people. Degradation typically follows the pattern used for tribal leaders (see also Garfunkel 1956, Gephart 1978). There are three stages, namely:

1. Scapegoating—the individual becomes publicly identified with the organization's problems and failures.
2. Discrediting—the individual is criticized by an ostensibly objective report.
3. Public removal from power.

The impeachment of President Clinton resembles the rites of degradation. In organizations, investigations are commissioned to catalogue an individual's failures and misdemeanours. Governments despatch teams of inspectors into allegedly failing schools and education authorities to procure the requisite evidence. Disciplinary hearings then follow. Likewise, failing professionals are 'struck off' in order to restore public confidence in the profession as a whole.

In contrast to rites of degradation, *rites of enhancement* convey good news. Rites of enhancement involve ceremonial activities aimed at enhancing the status and social identities of particular organizational members. For example, outstanding apprentices are presented with tools as prizes, thus symbolizing the organization's commitment to training and the pursuit of excellence.

Rites of renewal refer to 'away days', residential conferences, and the like. Such activities enable employees to express their frustration with the organization before participation in exercises aimed at designing ways forward. For example, participants may explore new ways of working as a team.

Organizations generally prefer to channel conflict rather confront it. *Rites of conflict reduction* enable organizations to do precisely that. Such rites are practised in joint consultative committees, grievance procedures, procedures for disputes resolution and the like. Rites of conflict reduction are also seen in false fights, posturing, and taking up of rhetorical positions. Such behaviour can be alarming to anyone unfamiliar with the ritual. For example:

This is an outrage! This case should never have been brought to a disciplinary hearing!! I have never seen such complete incompetence!!! If anyone should be sacked, it is the manager!!!!

The management keep quiet. They have heard it all before. They know that it is a token exhibition intended to impress the employee.

Rites of integration refer to activities aimed at fostering organizational unity. Meetings are perhaps the most common example. Schwartzman (1986) suggests that meetings are symbolically significant because they bring different groups and interests together and define them as 'the organization'. Meetings create a sense of identity. Meetings constitute and reconstitute the organization over time.

The organization is 'known' through meetings

just as a monastic foundation is known through the cycle of prayers.

Other rites of integration include office parties, the works' outing, and coffee breaks. Such events also give rise to the expression of organizational sub-cultures (see section 9.4). For example, cultural enclaves may be seen huddled around a table eating their lunchtime sandwiches, swapping information, plotting a 'deed without a name'.

Rites of creation facilitate the accomplishment of major organizational change. Rites of creation involve establishing new scripts for behaviour and integrating these into ongoing social arrangements. Rites of creation include changing letterheads, renaming buildings and departments, instituting new rules and ceremonies. For example, the newly privatized UK railway companies were quick to repaint their rolling stock.

Such expenditure may seem extravagant but rites of creation are the means whereby a new organizational identity is created and publicized. Morgan (1993) suggests that establishing an appropriate identity can be more important than strategy, for example 'New Labour'.

10.7 Discussion

THE purpose of this chapter has been to highlight a dimension of organizational life which is obscured by the more instrumental texts. The aim has been to show that organizations are not just people making decisions, interacting, performing different tasks and working to a collective purpose. Sensitivity to symbolism allows us to see that production processes are not just about technical rationality but are also determined by rites, symbols and ideas which reflect a world view (Gagliardi 1996, Turner 1986, 1990).

10.7.1 Linking symbols and metaphoric thinking

The notion of organizational symbolism brings us back to the theme of Chapter 1, that is, organizations can be understood at many different levels according to the metaphorical lens invoked. The present chapter is informed by the metaphor of text which suggests that social scientists should read social life as if it were a living document (Morgan, Frost and Pondy 1983). In this view production processes are themselves symbol systems (Gagliardi 1996), including, for example, the opening scene of this chapter. The activities in the park, the magazines by the computer, the Mont Blanc pen, the pad upon which it rests and even the desk itself emit messages. If this seems exaggerated, consider 'chairman', 'manager', 'manpower', 'manning levels', 'man management'. What worldview does this terminology symbolize (Smircich 1983b)?

It was suggested in the Introduction to this book that the organizational literature is preoccupied with measurement and prediction. For example, we measure levels of stress, job satisfaction, and organizational commitment in different organizations and among different occupational groupings. We attempt to predict the factors most likely to motivate people in a particular situation. We saw in Chapter 1 that the purpose of invoking unconventional metaphors is to see 'more of what is there'. The study of organizational symbolism centres more upon interpretation than measurement and prediction. Studying symbolism can enable us to probe surface appearances. Like political sensitivity it is a way of knowing 'what is really going on', and of alerting us to the existence of ambiguity and multiple meanings in organizations.

10.7.2 Mixing rationality, sorcery and superstition

Sensitivity to the symbolic life of organizations enables us to see the trappings of rationality, (business forecasts, organizational restructuring, team briefings, and so forth), in a different light. We see through the clinical language of psychology to more primitive elements of human behaviour. For example, it was suggested in section 1.2.5 that the term 'stress' provides a rationalization for antisocial behaviour in organizations. Likewise, is the phenomenon known as 'group think' (see section 7.8.4) a euphemism for witch hunting?

Notions of sorcery and superstition enable us to reconceptualize organizations in a playful manner. Play is important because it is a means of provoking new thought patterns (De Bono 1997). For example, in place of company cars, imagine broomsticks. Instead of 'timescales for completion', imagine 'before the next full moon'. We can also reverse images. A delightful Punch cartoon depicts three witches in conference around a cauldron. Each is holding a 'Filo-fax' style organizer open at the diary page. The caption reads, 'When shall we three meet again?'

It is more than that, however. We saw in section 5.5.1 how people in organizations can become more or less powerful than their formal role prescriptions might suggest. Sensitivity to the symbolic life of organizations allows us to see that the discharging of formal roles is not enough. Not only do organizations need technicians, administrators, budget controllers and so forth, they need employees to play other roles simultaneously. For example, organizations need 'honest brokers' to mediate between conflicting factions, licensed fools to challenge received ideas and so on (Deal and Kennedy 1988). Meredith Belbin's (1981) pioneering work on group effectiveness made a similar point using different language. According to Belbin, effective groups require people to enact fairly specific roles, including planter of ideas, shaper, and completer-finisher. Such roles may be as important, or even more important, than a person's formal job.

Pause for reflection

Your organization has recently won a contract. It is normal practice to arrange a signing ceremony. However, in this instance, the negotiations were protracted and difficult. Your organization achieved substantial price concessions but at the expense of provoking acrimony.

It has been suggested that, in the circumstances, it might be advisable to dispense with the signing ceremony.

Comment upon this proposal.

10.7.3 Driving evil spirits away

Earlier allusions to witchcraft may seem far fetched. Yet such action is potentially logical. In ancient mythology calling a evil spirit by its name was a way of ridding oneself of its malignant influence. It was suggested in section 5.3.1 that the most potent exercise of power is that which is invisible. Warding off an evil spirit means defining reality, naming the manipulation, thus robbing it of its power (Ury 1991).

We also saw in section 5.5.4 that power relations are inherently dynamic and shifting. A signing ceremony accompanied by generous compliments is potentially all the more important if negotiations have been bitter, as it enables people to reconstruct reality. Reconstruction paves the way to amicable and mutually beneficial future relations (Ury 1991). Such is the transformative potential of symbolic action.

10.7.4 Symbols as double edged

While symbolic activity can promote organizational effectiveness, symbolism is a double edged entity.

Symbols intended to express one pattern of meaning can be reconstituted to yield a different interpretation (Morgan, Pondy and Frost 1983). For example, for some people, symbols reinforcing the pursuit of excellence can signify their own inability to reach the standard required (Morgan, Pondy and Frost 1983). Likewise, myths and stories do not invariably unify. They can be sources of conflict especially in times of rapid social change (Meek 1988).

Indeed, the symbolic character of organization can be in opposition to management (Morgan, Pondy, and Frost 1983). For example, an organization which prided itself upon its equal opportunities policy engaged a disabled person. The newcomer subsequently said:

I wouldn't say they (colleagues) discriminated against me. Only my desk was tucked away in a corner—underneath the first aid box—next to the emergency exit.

People in organizations can *enact* an organizational climate which can severely undermine other peoples' ability to work. For example, some managers recruited from the manufacturing industry to the health service have proved disastrous appointments.

10.7.5 Symbols as a substitute for substance

Politicians are sometimes accused of paying more attention to presentation (spin) than substance. Organizations are similarly vulnerable as:

ritual can become a substitute for management.

For example, many firms operate elaborate security arrangements which look good but are actually useless. Visitors are required to complete long questionnaires before being issued with an identity card. Yet once in the building, no one ever inspects the card or even asks for it back when the visitor leaves.

Even operationally useful procedures can descend into empty ritual. Accounts are 'signed off' with scarcely a glance. Meetings become perfunctory. Due form is observed but the essential dynamism has died. Instead, people engage in rites of conflict reduction, taking up predictable positions upon issues. No one is listening or has any need to listen because, like a Sunday church service, it is always the same. For example, Smircich (1983b) recounts how a particular executive manipulated language in order to create the impression of harmony. Notably, the word 'challenge' was used as a euphemism to gloss over the existence of serious problems. Likewise, performance appraisal interviews can become empty rituals with no real communication between the parties. The same can happen to apparently spontaneous conversations with colleagues. Significantly the role of marriage guidance counsellors is not to advise so much as to restore communication between couples.

Pause for reflection

Private banks see their central role as providing a high level of personal service to wealthy individuals. A market research survey suggests, however, that most clients actually prefer to transact business via the internet. Moreover, the preference for internet dealing includes relatively sophisticated transactions such as obtaining stockmarket advice and portfolio evaluations.

While some private banks are experimenting with internet facilities, others refuse to accept the survey findings insisting that internet services will be an extra and not a replacement for personal attention (Mackintosh 1998).

What might explain dissenting banks' judgement?

We saw in Chapter 6 how people in organizations can interpret reality in a manner that suits them. Decision makers may refuse to accept that core competencies which were once the pride of the organization have become obsolete. For example, Dandridge (1986) suggests that employees who have become accustomed to serving only elite clientele may ignore changing market conditions which require a shift to a downmarket identity. This may be precisely the problem which some private bankers are experiencing. Such is the prestige of associating with wealthy clients that they cannot and will not accept clear evidence of impending redundancy.

10.7.6 Management and magic

Symbolism takes us into a hall of mirrors where nothing is quite what it seems. On the one hand, as we saw earlier, symbolic action can counter manipulation. On the other hand, symbolic action is itself manipulation. As Jelinek, Smircich, and Hirsch (1983) note, symbolism has the power to convert something as traumatic, unambiguous and final as death into life and normality.

Symbolism brings us to the boundary of superstition. Superstition refers to decisions made for no scientifically supportable reason. Just how superstitious are we? The language of rationality provides a socially acceptable gloss for superstition. Few managers would dare admit to consulting fortune tellers, but see no contradiction in basing decisions upon economic forecasts which are basically guesswork. Most managers would scorn the idea of consulting a witch-doctor yet happily absorb the prognostications of management gurus—witch-doctors in pinstripes according to Clark and Salaman (1996).

Some cultures are much more openly superstitious. For instance, despite a formidable reputation for quality and marketability, Japanese car manufacturers reputedly time the launch of new models to coincide with 'lucky' days. Hong Kong is one of the most vibrant free markets in the world, yet no building can be constructed without engaging the services of a feng shui consultant to ensure that the design facilitates maximum access for good luck dragons (Bevan 1995). Big banks regularly have new offices screened for potential bad feng shui which may disrupt commerce. Marks and Spencer were obliged to obtain the approval of the local feng shui expert before opening their Hong Kong branch—a process equivalent to obtaining local authority planning permission (Russell 1995).

Clark and Salaman (1996) suggest that although we live in a rationalist, high-tech society, magic and superstition are important. Magic, they say, is a technology which can be expressed in rules and formulae:

The fundamental function of magic is to control the critical uncertainties of the natural world —to make rain, bring victory, ripen the harvest—through the manipulation of supernatural agencies—magic prescribes the way in which people (organizations?) can overcome the dangers and threats that face them. (Clark and Salaman 1996, p. 97)

For example, when an invention is adopted as industry standard that does not necessarily mean it is a good invention. It means that the process of testing and calibration is seen as providing defence against the critical uncertainties of the world. The same goes for breeding from pedigree stock. As any breeder knows, the possession of a pedigree is no guarantee of success, yet certification is an essential prerequisite for marketing stock.

Clark and Salaman (1996) argue that many managerial interventions including 'total quality management' and 're-engineering' are attempts to bring about the desired condition by prompting the behaviour associated with it. For example, by increasing customer satisfaction by making shop assistants smile:

They are today's version of the rain making ritual: focusing upon *ideal* connections between events, not real ones—trying to produce causes by producing the results. It's like trying to make it rain by putting up umbrellas. (Clark and Salaman 1996, p. 101)

10.7.7 From symbols to aesthetics

Superstition can be a smokescreen for economic exploitation, and a nonsense. For example, Russell (1995) reports that the recommendations of feng shui consultants to reduce stress are basically commonsense, such as oiling creaky doors. Like the secret Kpelle societies, commonsense is disguised by mystical nonsense. For example, extracting a solemn promise from a company to avoid alcohol and sexual relations until a particular contract is signed (Russell 1995).

Yet the odd thing is, sometimes, when we put up our umbrellas, it does rain. Perhaps it would have rained anyway. Or is it that logic and reason will only take us so far? Exposed as we are to uncertainty, and the peril of evils that uncertainty involves, are we justified in using all our senses and intuition to boost our perceived efficacy?

The study of symbolism brings us to another dimension of organizational life and one which the literature has barely begun to address. That is, the aesthetic side of organizations. Aesthetics concerns sensory perception and the interplay between the physical, social and symbolic aspects of organization.

There is evidence to suggest that such interplay can influence organizational outcomes. For example, some corporate boardrooms can induce a two dimensional vision of reality with all that implies (Gagliardi 1996, citing Rosen). Gagliardi also describes organizational failures which are traceable to aesthetics. For example, a bank launched a large-scale programme to create a new ethos of customer care. According to Gagliardi, however, the physical setting:

The thickness of the walls, the monumental character of the entrance . . . luxurious carpets and tapestry in the management offices . . . solicited feelings of solidity, comfort, safety . . . and superiority over the world . . . rendering barely credible the ambition to invert the image of dominance that the artifacts embodied. (Gagliardi 1996, p. 575)

It was suggested in section 1.6.3 that science may not have all the answers when it comes to understanding organizational life and predicting behaviour. Either that, or we change our view of science:

'the resources of science are far from being exhausted. I think that an evening in that study would help me much.'

'An evening alone!'

'I propose to go up there presently . . . I shall sit in that room and see if its atmosphere brings me inspiration. I am a believer in the *genius loci*. You smile, friend Watson. Well, we shall see.' (Cited in Gagliardi 1996, p. 576)

Summary

1 The study of organizational symbolism enables us to penetrate surface appearances.

2 Symbols express organizational culture values and identity.

3 A symbol is a sign possessing deeper significance than surface appearances suggest.

4 Symbols are a source of power because they can produce 'intended effects'.

5 There are three types of symbol, namely:

  ■ verbal,
  ■ actions and events, and,
  ■ material.

6 Symbols serve three functions, namely:

  ■ descriptive,
  ■ energy controlling, and,
  ■ system maintenance.

7 Symbolic action can be subtle and ambiguous. For example, organizational events which lower social barriers, may simultaneously reaffirm authority relations.

8 Secrecy is a form of symbol, capable of producing intended effects.

9 Rationality may disguise primitive fear and superstition in organizations.

10 Allusions to witchcraft and naming witches:

- enables people to make sense of events, and,
- enables managers to deflect attention from their performance.

11 Rites and ritual are important dimensions of the symbolic life of organizations.

12 Rituals are more important for what they signify than what they actually do.

13 Rites are organizational procedures which express culture and act as a subtle means of controlling people.

14 Examples of organizational rites include:

- Rites of passage,
- rites of degradation,
- rites of enhancement,
- rites of renewal,
- rites of conflict reduction,
- rites of integration, and,
- rites of creation.

15 The metaphor of 'text' suggests that organizations should be read as if they were a living document.

16 Production processes can be seen as symbol systems, determined as much by rites and ritual as by technical rationality.

17 Although symbols can be manipulated, the effects of symbolic action are not always predictable.

18 Although symbolic action sustains organizations, organizational procedures can descend into empty ritual.

19 Superstition means irrational belief.

20 Magic is a code for the control of uncertainty.

21 Many managerial interventions are tantamount to trying to make rain by putting up umbrellas.

22 And yet . . .

Questions for Discussion

1 'Symbols are the very stuff of management behaviour. Executives after all do not synthesize chemicals or operate trucks; they deal in symbols,' (Peters, 1978, p. 10).

Discuss.

2 Design an organizational logo for;

- an oil company,
- a hospital trust, and,
- an animal welfare charity.

Explain your rationale in each case.

3 'Life is not *like* theatre but *is* theatre,' (Clark and Salaman 1996, p. 92)

Discuss.

4 Imagine you have taken control of a poorly performing chain of sandwich bars.

What forms of symbolic action would you consider important, and why?

5 Imagine you are the chief executive of an insurance company. A recent audit has highlighted the corporate hospitality budget which includes lavish entertainment of clients and employees at racecourses, concerts and other events.

Defend your policy.

6 Why are symbols sometimes more important than substance?

Discuss. (You may find material from section 6.4.6 helpful.)

Further Reading

■ Beyer, J., and Trice, H. (1987) 'How an organization's rites reveal its culture,' *Organizational Dynamics, 15*, 5–23.

■ Dandridge, T. C., Mitroff, I., Joyce, W. F. (1980) 'Organizational symbolism: a topic to expand organizational analysis,' *Academy of Management Review, 5*, 77–82.

■ Deal, T. and Kennedy, A. (1988) *Corporate Cultures: the Rites and Rituals of Corporate Life*, Harmondsworth, Penguin.

■ Morgan, G., Frost, P. J., and Pondy, L. R. (1983) 'Organizational symbolism.' In Pondy, L. R., Frost, P. J., Morgan, G., Dandridge, T. C. (eds.) *Organizational Symbolism*, London, JAI, 3–35.

■ Peters, T. J. (1978) ' Symbols patterns and settings: an optimistic case for getting things done,' *Organizational Dynamics, 9*, 3–23.

■ Pfeffer, J. (1977) 'The ambiguity of leadership,' *Academy of Management Review, 2*, 104–112.

■ Rosen, M. (1988) 'You asked for it: Christmas at the bosses' expense,' *Journal of Management Studies, 25*, 463–480.

Chapter 11
A Guide to Studying Organization Behaviour

'Is this the library?'

> (First year undergraduate—in May)

'I wasted time. Now doth time waste me.'

> (Shakespeare's deposed King Richard II)

Sir Antony: 'Your worship, I need not say—'
The Bench: 'Then do not say it'.

> (A. P. Herbert, *Uncommon Law*)

'in the written work one could hear even the weaker students straining to the best of their ability'.

> (An external examiner's report)

TIMES are hard in higher education. A key priority of many universities and colleges is to find less labour-intensive means of delivering instruction. The purpose of this chapter is to supplement teaching resources by offering study guidance. It is hoped that the material will be useful to all students of Organization Behaviour though it is especially intended for those with only limited access to tutorial support. The issues which are addressed by this chapter include:

Key Issues

- How to study effectively.
- How to approach the task of essay writing.
- How to prepare for examinations.

11.1 How to Study Effectively

ONE of the challenges of studying Organization Behaviour is that unlike subjects in science and technology there are no correct answers. Organization behaviourists place relatively small emphasis upon exact knowledge. While it may be necessary to describe a particular concept, theory or idea, the skills required are very different from, say, applying a formula in order to calculate the correct dosage of a particular drug, or the time required to drain a storage tank. Nor does the study of Organization Behaviour call for detailed categorization in the way that a civil engineer might classify different types of road junctions.

Although the subject requires some memory training (what are the principal correlates of job satisfaction, for example? (see section 3.3)) the ability to memorize is a means to an end. The 'end' lies in the student's ability to discuss concepts, theories and ideas intelligently.

Intelligent discussion requires the student to approach the subject in an analytical and reflective frame of mind. Studying Organization Behaviour also requires a high tolerance of role ambiguity (see section 8.3.2) as there are no absolutes. For example, the same essay title can be interpreted and approached in many different ways. Such freedom can make study interesting but it can also be stressful. Requirements cannot be specified precisely. Time is inevitably short. The student may strive for perfection, but perfection is unattainable. There is always more that could be done.

The literature is vast and some of it difficult. Study involves extracting material from a range of sources. It requires skill in identifying what is central, and the self-discipline to disregard the tangential, however interesting it seems. Effective study is about making best use of scarce resources including lectures, seminars, access to tutors and, not least, the student's own time.

11.1.1 Getting started

The key to effective study is to work backwards. Most courses culminate in a written assessment and/or an examination. The student's first task is to obtain an overview of requirements. Proceed as follows:

1. Scan reading lists and course material to gain an overview of the course content.
2. Skim-read one or two textbooks to gain a feel for the material.
3. Obtain details of assignments and past examination papers.

Done properly, this is an extremely powerful technique because it establishes the foundations for study and enables the student to direct their efforts productively from the start. To be forewarned is indeed to be forearmed.

11.1.2 Making good use of lectures

The lecture was a medieval solution to book shortages before printing was invented. In those days 'textbooks' were handwritten and almost as expensive as they are now. The medieval tutor read from the text, hence the university grade of 'Reader'.

Some academics argue that the lecture is redundant as it merely repeats textbook material, and that there are more cost-effective means of teaching. This is not the place to pursue the debate. Suffice it here to suggest that attending lectures is usually a good use of time as most lecturers aim to do more than recite the contents of text books. More specifically the lecture typically serves to:

1. Highlight a particular tutor's approach to the subject.

2. Communicate key information and ideas.
3. Stimulate interest and awareness.

Since there are many different ways of approaching Organizational Behaviour, it is important to grasp early on a particular tutor's approach to the subject. For example, some tutors are apt to emphasize the psychological aspects of the subject. Some may be more interested in the sociological dimension. Others may aim to strike a balance between disciplines. Some tutors may stress the practical aspects of the subject. Others may be more interested in concepts and theories for their own sake.

It also useful to learn how the tutor sees their role, and how they interpret course requirements. While only a weak student will rely upon the tutor to explain the basic subject matter, the student can use the lecture to check their understanding.

The most important function of the lecture is to stimulate interest. Tutors attempt to achieve this in two ways. First by communicating their own enthusiasm for the subject to an audience. Second, by offering insights and asides which are not available in textbooks and journal articles. For example, the tutor may have recently returned from a conference where new developments in research were discussed which have yet to be published.

Effective use of lecturers depends upon:

■ preparation,
■ effective note taking, and,
■ systematic follow up.

Effective *preparation* involves familiarizing yourself with the lecture topic beforehand. Aim to skim at least one textbook chapter on the subject in advance of the lecture. Better still, arrive with a skeletal outline of the material. Such preparation minimizes the burden of note taking and facilitates listening and the development of understanding.

Effective note taking involves listening out for key points and for asides and insights. Divide the page into two and fill the left hand side with notes made before the lecture. Reserve the right hand side for notes taken during the lecture. Figure 11.1 shows a specimen page of notes compiled in preparation for a lecture on the topic of organization commitment. Note how the student has obtained a basic grasp of the subject beforehand leaving them free to listen out for cues for issues surrounding the topic and further reading.

11.1.3 Following up the lecture

A page of lecture notes soon becomes meaningless without an effective system of follow up. Effective follow up involves:

1. Ordering the material.
2. Expanding upon each point while the material is still fresh in your memory.
3. Compiling and executing a private study plan (see below).

Figure 11.1 A specimen page of notes

ORGANIZATION COMMITMENT

Definition: process whereby individuals come to think about and evaluate relationship with an organization.

Key components: loyalty, willingness to work hard, acceptance of organization goals and values.

See also Allen and Meyer (1990) on needing, wanting, and feeling one ought to remain in organization as different forms of commitment.

Antecedents: age, central life interest, education, early employment period, role conflict, role ambiguity, peer relations, organizational characteristics — e.g., autonomous work groups.

Correlates: commitment associated with motivation, job involvement, stress, occupation, union commitment, job satisfaction.

Consequences: commitment may affect job performance and withdrawal behaviours.

Further reading: Becker (1960), on 'side-bets' and golden handcuffs; Mathieu and Zajac (1990) and Meyer and Allen (1997) reviews of literature. Randall (1987) on dysfunctional aspects.

The objective is to generate notes that will facilitate the tasks of revision and extraction of information for essays and other forms of assessment. The more accessible and comprehensive the notes (typed if possible) the easier the student's task later. Even the best organized student will discover that some reorganization of the material is invariably required. It is a mistake to try and write down everything that is said during a lecture. A more effective technique is to make a note of the points and expand upon it later while it is still fresh in the student's memory. The more detailed the notes, the better.

It is advisable to follow up additional reading immediately after the lecture—otherwise it becomes a case of tomorrow and tomorrow. It is a chore copying papers and chapters. Once complete, however, the student can concentrate upon study. Dilatory colleagues begin to scramble for the same. A small notebook is a useful investment. Not only does it reduce the risk of forgetting an important reference, but locating all outstanding work in one place can enable the student to use the odd half-hour productively.

11.1.4 Making good use of seminars and tutorials

The purpose of seminars and tutorials varies from institution to institution. Sometimes they are basically lectures by another name, especially where large groups are involved. Alternatively they are used to complement lectures through group discussion, presentation of papers and case studies. Sometimes seminars and tutorials are based upon a hybrid model, combining formal lecturing with interactive participation.

Ideally, seminars and tutorials will prompt discussion and reflection and encourage students to think for themselves. They may focus upon applying theory to practice through analysis of case studies and other exercises. Seminars and tutorials are also a potential platform for rehearsing essays and other assessments. Seminars and tutorials depend to a large extent upon student preparation and participation for their success. Although students may not be formally assessed upon the quality of their contributions, conscientious, responsive individuals and analytically minded students are noticed by tutors. Conversely, the larger the group, the more difficult it is for tutors to draw the more diffident students into the discussion.

The requisite level of note taking depends upon the purpose of the session. Where seminars and tutorials comprise a taught component the same guidance as for lectures applies. Otherwise, make a brief note of anything which seems useful or proves thought provoking. For example, I once led a seminar on motivation. A student from Nepal said, 'How can you talk about motivation? Our people are starving. They have to be forced to work.'

That comment prompted me to think about the extent to which the Organization Behaviour literature is culturally specific. It also raises a contradiction, that is, people starving and yet having to be forced to work. The image seems inconsistent with Maslow's theory of human needs (see section 3.2.1).

11.1.5 Making good use of facilities for individual tuition

Most tutors set aside time each week for private consultations with students. Although the amount of time available per individual tends to be extremely limited, a few minutes discussion with a tutor can save a student hours of time. More specifically, the tutor can normally be expected to:

- guide the student's reading,
- act as a sounding board for ideas,
- explain requirements, and,
- provide feedback.

A typical textbook chapter on Organization Behaviour may contain upwards of fifty references. Rarely can a student follow up more than a handful of these. The tutor can help the student by identifying potentially profitable lines of research. The tutor may also offer advice upon how to approach written work and examinations and act as a sounding board for the student to test out essay plans and examination tactics. Some may be willing to peruse draft essays and specimen exam answers and to provide extended feedback upon assessed work. Individual discussions can also yield ideas and information which have not been mentioned in lectures or tutorials.

The best way to approach a busy tutor is to be clear, brief, and prepared. Explain what you want from the discussion and stand by to take notes. Do not expect the tutor to read your mind. Above all, be mindful of the squeaky wheels analogy (see section 7.2). Those who seek attention receive it. The diffident student, the student who is reluctant to make demands upon a tutor's time simply loses out.

11.2 Planning Private Study

PRIVATE study is the most vital element of a student's workload. The student who relies upon lecture notes is destined to achieve, at best, a borderline pass and risks failing. Conversely, private study is the gateway to high marks.

The purpose of engaging in private study is to deepen knowledge and understanding by building upon lecture material. The student's biggest enemy is time. This is particularly true of subjects such as Organization Behaviour which call for extended reading and reflection and maturing of ideas. Time becomes all the more pressing where single semester courses are involved, especially where examinations follow soon after a course ends. Crowded libraries, busy computer facilities, short loan restrictions, vandalism to books and journals add to stress.

> **Golden rule**
> Make effort pay.

Time management is of paramount importance, therefore. Although we may be critical of the notion of added value when it comes to organizations, (see section 4.5) there is no harm in applying the precept for conducting private study. To recapitulate:

waste is any operation which does not add value.

Value lies in reading, contemplation and writing. Waste includes searching for books, queuing for access to a library catalogue or computer, and photocopying. Although such activities are unavoidable, the aim should be to plan work in order to minimize lost time. For example, plan visits to libraries and computer facilities to coincide with relatively quiet times such as early morning and late evening. Why spend half an hour queuing at lunch time when you could be doing something more productive? Why make four separate trips when the same materials could be gathered during one visit?

It is important that all expenditure of time, effort and money is made to pay. Only results count in the end. Time spent on reading which is subsequently forgotten or in making notes which are then lost counts for nothing. If planning to read a chapter or a paper insist that the effort pays dividends.

11.2.1 Prioritizing work

On some courses students are furnished with lists of required and/or recommended reading. Sometimes, tutors supply long lists and leave it to the student to select what to read. While the latter can make study interesting, it can also be daunting. Either way the student is also faced with the problem of deciding whether to follow up references contained in the books and articles listed.

In the absence of tutorial guidance prioritize reading according to the following criteria:

1. Availability,
2. Relevance,
3. Interest.

Concentrate upon materials which are available in the library. Few institutions expect students on taught courses to apply for a battery of inter-library loans. The most relevant articles are those which seem likely to expand the student's knowledge of central issues. There is something to be said for reading primary source materials. For example, although Deming's (1986) *Out of the Crisis* is a long book (see section 4.1) it is very readable. Moreover, parts of the text are repetitive and can be skimmed.

Theoretical essays and discussion papers are extremely useful. For example, while it may be sufficient to note that the Hawthorne studies are controversial, you will be able to write and speak with more authority if you have read Carey's (1967) exposé. Likewise, consider the following potential essay/examination question: 'Why is it important for organizations to foster high levels of commitment?' While it may be adequate to note that commitment can be dysfunctional, the student who has read Randall's (1987) discussion will be able to explain why this may be so and why an organization might wish to guard against employees becoming overly committed. Reading the article will enable the student to write three or four informed paragraphs whereas the student who has relied on basic sources will at best be able to manage a paragraph of generalities.

Recent reviews of research are another valuable source of information as they usually combine a wealth of descriptive material with critical discussion of the issues, and an overview of research. See Cordes and Dougherty (1993) on burnout, Staw (1996) and Drummond (1996) on escalation, and Bryman (1996) on leadership, for example.

Articles comprising research reports require special discrimination. While the introductory and concluding sections can contain useful background information, many are highly specialized dealing with only a tiny aspect of a particular topic. The student is well advised to use such materials in a highly selective fashion and to avoid becoming embroiled in methodological issues or abstruse mathematical analysis unless there is particular reason to do so.

Acquiring depth does not necessarily make study more difficult but easier.

This because the student obtains more material to work with. Academic research is subject to the laws of diminishing returns, however. To mix metaphors it is rather like working a drift mine. The further you dig, the more specialized the material becomes. Effective study depends upon knowing where to stop. For instance, a reading of Braverman's (1974) thesis will provide an interesting and substantial critique to Taylorism (see section 2.1.2). Yet it may not be necessary to read the whole book nor to delve into critiques of Braverman's work (Knights and Willmott 1990). Instead it may be more useful to consult two or three articles dealing with modern-day applications of Taylor's ideas, such as those contained in Blyton and Turnbull's (1992) edited collection (Delbridge and Turnbull 1992), and/or to consider Taylor's ideas in relation to other topics in Organization Behaviour. For example, Taylor largely ignores the impact of culture and politics in organizations, and implicitly favours the more instrumental styles of leadership.

The student's own interests are another important criteria in deciding what to read. If something excites your curiosity, why not follow it up provided some self-discipline is required to prevent oneself becoming distracted? For example, we saw in section 8.8 it is almost thirty years since Alvin Toffler's (1970) *Future Shock* was published. How many of Toffler's predictions have materialized? Is the impact of change as dramatic as Toffler implies? Intellectual pleasure apart, such research can yield important benefits in the longer run. For instance, a reading of Kieser's (1987, 1989) accounts of medieval monasticism and craft guilds may provide an idea for a dissertation topic or even a subsequent research degree.

11.2.2 Effective reading

Figure 11.2 sets out a method for approaching the task of reading in an effective manner. Scanning enables the student to ensure an item is worth reading and to prioritize it. Should you decide not to read the work then make a note that you have seen the reference in order to avoid duplication of effort. Stages two and three are intended to facilitate comprehension and act as a final check upon relevance.

Figure 11.2 A method of effective reading

1. Scan the material.

2. Read the introductory and concluding parts.

3. Skim–read the remainder of the material.

4. Jot down one or two objectives or questions to focus the reading.

5. Read the material and highlight important sections.

6. Make a summary note.

7. Compile more detailed notes if appropriate.

8. Check whether objectives have been achieved or questions answered.

9. Note the reference in full and identify key words.

10. File notes and, if possible, a copy of the source material.

Much of the Organization Behaviour literature is far from user friendly. Psychologists are sometimes accused of telling people what they already know in language they do not understand. Many sociologists are just as obscurant, using long words and tortuous phrases to say very little. It may be necessary to read some texts several times in order to understand them. The trick of comprehension is to remember that most academic works, however long or complex they may appear, are usually built around one simple idea.

> **Golden rule**
>
> Ask yourself:
>
> 'What is the simple idea behind all of this?'

For example, Becker's (1960) paper on entrapment is based upon the simple idea that unforseen extraneous commitments can prevent people from changing direction in an optimal manner. Etzioni's lengthy book entitled *Complex Organizations* rests upon the simple idea that organizations can be classified according to the type of power used to control the lower echelons.

Having grasped the central idea, the next task is to identify the subsidiary points and supporting evidence. This exercise requires discrimination.

The trick is to extract enough to demonstrate that you have done your homework without becoming submerged in a morass of detail.

Setting yourself a question or objectives will help you to maintain a sense of perspective and force you to make an effort to understand the material. Again the important thing is to remember that most texts contain only six or seven simple subsidiary points.

It is obvious if a student has read only the summary of a research article. (Academics are often equally guilty though with less excuse). Although a summary is better than nothing, more detailed reading is usually rewarding. For example, in summary, Ackroyd and Crowdy's (1990) ethnography of a slaughterhouse suggests that elements of organizational culture are beyond managerial control (see section 9.6). The article is worth reading in its entirety because it contains a wealth of detail which could not be included in the present text because of space constraints. Likewise Bowen's (1987) discussion of information poverty brings alive the nature of decision dilemma, and provides a strong counter-balance to the psychological literature with its emphasis upon decision 'error' as distinct from 'mistake' (see section 7.9.3).

Copying huge chunks of text is the least effective means of making notes. A much more powerful technique is to read the material, highlight key passages, and then try and summarize the contents in your own words, preferably without looking at the text. Although this method is taxing it enables the student to acquire a real grasp of the subject and reduces the amount of revision required.

> **Golden rule**
> Never wait until you feel like working.

Self-discipline is vital. If you wait until you feel like working, you will probably never start and almost certainly never finish. F. W. Taylor had some good ideas. There is no substitute for a task-orientated approach to study especially on a course involving severe time constraints. The student should identify regular times for study and adhere to these regardless.

Academic study almost invariably involves some tedium. Note taking and summarizing notes, for example, can be extremely laborious. One way of minimizing boredom is to work on the principle of 'a little often', say about an hour and a half's concentrated effort followed by a reward upon completion. Another self-motivating technique is to divide the work into short-cycle subtasks. Head the list with a few easy jobs and cross them out as they are accomplished. Item number one might be 'access computer file' or 'fill fountain pen'!

11.2.3 How much reading is enough?

The amount of reading in a subject such as Organization Behaviour is potentially limitless. Much depends upon the level of course, the time available and the student's resources. As a guide:

try and do more than seems necessary.

Reading provides the material for the construction of essays and examination answers. To a point, therefore, the more the better.

That said, too much reading can be nearly as harmful as too little if it means there is insufficient time left to assimilate what has been read.

> **Golden rule**
> It is not what you have that counts, but what you do with it.

Reading alone is not enough. You have to make your material work for you.

- Either the student masters the material, or,
- the material masters the student.

Mastery is not just about understanding theories, concepts and insights. Above all, it is the ability to bend the material to your purpose. The literature can be seen as pile of fencing panels which have to be shaped, hammered and coaxed into place. The skill in utilizing material lies in learning to link ideas. It is this ability which is the hallmark of the outstanding student. Note, for example, how Pfeffer (1982) invokes equity theory and the Hawthorne studies in a discussion about organizational politics. Likewise, Etzioni (1975) links compliance theory to leadership styles (section 5.2.1). Etzioni implies that transformational leadership (see section 3.5.5) is inappropriate in utilitarian organizations. (You would need to read the relevant sections of Etzioni's work to muster the requisite detail). Likewise, in what ways could themes of organizational culture and politics be linked?

Study is not just about reading but also:

interpretation.

Another sign of distinction is the ability to see familiar things differently. For example, Alvesson and Willmott (1996), and Alvesson and Billing (1997) utilize familiar materials but interpret these in a very different way from managerialist writers. Likewise, Trist and Bamforth's (1951) study of coal-mining is normally grouped in the socio/technical literature. Yet it could be used as material for an essay on organizational culture. Braverman's (1974) influential thesis (see section 2.1.2) basically rests upon probing the surface meaning of Taylor's ideas—a contribution made possible by conscientious reading of primary sources and thinking what no one else had thought.

This is where time really does become an enemy because the process of linking ideas and using material creatively requires reflection, and ideally, rehearsal and development.

The more successful students are often those who make a little go a long way.

Although such students may not be the most deserving, they earn their marks by displaying a good grasp of the basic subject matter and by engaging in intelligent discussion to the limits of their material. This may explain why the best students are sometimes the least confident. Their extended reading has made them aware of the limits of their knowledge, unlike their colleagues living in the bliss of ignorance.

11.3 Essay Writing

Most institutions require the student to submit one or more pieces of written work for assessment. Written assignments may range from brief exercises intended as basic checks of the student's understanding of the subject matter, to longer pieces requiring significant independent research.

Figure 11.3 contains a plan of action for the student to follow. Many institutions

Figure 11.3 Writing an essay

1. Ascertain requirements.

2. Compile an initial research plan.

3. Decide the approach.

4. Check the proposed approach with the tutor.

5. Finalize the research plan and execute.

6. Organize the material.

7. Write the first draft.

8. Review the first draft.

9. Write the final version.

10. Proofread the work.

publish their assessment criteria in order to reduce role ambiguity. It is important to study the rules and plan your work accordingly. For example, some institutions place considerable emphasis upon reading. Others are more concerned with the student's ability to relate theory to practice. Likewise, what weighting is given to presentation? How are the criteria applied in practice?

11.3.1 Compiling a research plan

The next step is to compile an initial research plan. This task should involve more thought than action. How might the question be answered, and, what type of material might be useful? For example, the student faced with the question, 'What is an organization?' might begin by scanning the relevant sections of a few organization theory and organization behaviour texts. That corpus of literature may suggest that organizations are distinguishable by factors such as goals, social structure, and continuity (Hall 1987). The student may then skim Morgan's (1996) *Images of Organization* and realize the extent to which organizations are potentially a figment of imagination.

Step three involves deciding the approach. The student might consider whether to base the essay on the more traditional approach to the question, or to base it around Morgan's ideas, or to try and incorporate both schools of thought. This is an important decision because the student is basically determining what 'angle' to take. At this stage it may be helpful to map out two or three alternative approaches as a kind of feasibility test and to gain some feel for what additional research is likely to be required. Figure 11.4 shows what the opening paragraph of a first attempt might look like.

Before making a final decision, the student would be well advised to discuss the possibilities with the tutor. For instance, would an essay which focused upon one or other perspective be regarded as too narrow? Alternatively, could an essay which attempted to embrace both perspectives achieve the requisite depth?

Figure 11.4 First-draft opening of an essay

'WHAT IS AN ORGANIZATION?'

According to Gareth Morgan (1996) an organization can mean different things to different people. Morgan suggests that organizations are not just 'machines' or 'systems' but can be all sorts of things including 'brains' and 'psychic prisons'. Of course an organization is not really a 'psychic prison'. What Morgan means is that we can think about organizations as prisons. . . .

For the purposes of our discussion we will assume that the student has decided to base the essay upon Morgan's thesis. The next step involves finalizing and executing the research plan. For example, the student may decide to consult Morgan's (1980, 1983) two papers in the journal *Administrative Science Quarterly* which explain the epistemological foundations of his work. Reading the 1983 paper, the student realizes that Morgan's idea provoked a controversy. Curiosity prompts the student to read Pinder and Bourgeois's (Bourgeois and Pinder 1983, Pinder and Bourgeois 1982, see also section 1.6.2) contribution to the debate. The student then realizes that it may be possible and indeed necessary to incorporate the more conventional material. Figure 11.5 shows the essay becoming more sophisticated.

The student might also consider whether Mangham's (1996) critique of Morgan as locking organization theory into eight single metaphors should be incorporated and whether it is appropriate to highlight links between metaphoric thought and notions of paradox and contradiction in organizations (see section 1.4.2).

A good way of learning essay technique is to study theoretical articles in leading journals. In particular note how authors start from a simple idea and how they build their argument and substantiate it with evidence.

11.3.2 Writing the first draft

It is a mistake to begin writing before the research and preliminary organization of material are complete. Organizing essay material requires discrimination and reflection. Avoid the temptation to incorporate tangential material simply because you

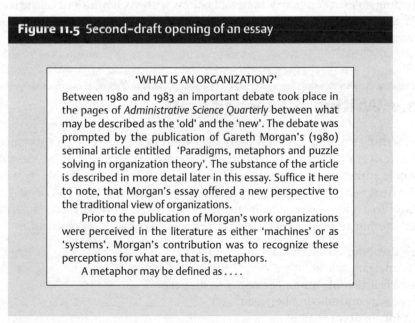

Figure 11.5 Second-draft opening of an essay

'WHAT IS AN ORGANIZATION?'

Between 1980 and 1983 an important debate took place in the pages of *Administrative Science Quarterly* between what may be described as the 'old' and the 'new'. The debate was prompted by the publication of Gareth Morgan's (1980) seminal article entitled 'Paradigms, metaphors and puzzle solving in organization theory'. The substance of the article is described in more detail later in this essay. Suffice it here to note, that Morgan's essay offered a new perspective to the traditional view of organizations.

Prior to the publication of Morgan's work organizations were perceived in the literature as either 'machines' or as 'systems'. Morgan's contribution was to recognize these perceptions for what are, that is, metaphors.

A metaphor may be defined as . . . .

have taken the trouble to research it. If an essay seems better for omitting a particular section then omit it—no one will miss it. Conversely, an inconsistency in your essay will stick out like the proverbial sore thumb.

The real test is writing the first draft. Skeleton outlines are useful for envisaging the structure of an essay. In theory, a well-researched and well-planned essay should virtually write itself. In practice it is only when the student tries to write, however, that the limitations (also the potential) of ideas become apparent.

11.3.3 Reviewing the first draft

It is important to allow time for work to mature. Mistakes, repetition, erratic constructions, and weak sections are easier to spot if some time has elapsed between writing the first draft and rereading it. Many students make the first draft the last, thus depriving themselves of the opportunity to earn significant additional marks by spending an afternoon polishing their work.

The principal signs of an unpolished and even noncomprehending student are:

- wholesale reliance upon texts,
- excessive use of quotations, and,
- poorly integrated material.

Tutors are quick to recognize the student who has basically copied from a book, and then altered the ordering of the text and played with the wording. Quotations should be used sparingly. More than 10 per cent is excessive. For example, nothing is gained by opening an essay on power in organizations with six definitions of the concept of power if each of those definitions are basically identical, or if no attempt is made to discuss the significance of different definitions.

11.3.4 Writing the second draft

When writing the first draft it is more important to concentrate on substance rather than style. It is a waste of time to worry about how a particular sentence sounds when the whole paragraph may be deleted later. Aim for clarity and simplicity when writing the final version. What you say is more important than how you say it. However, it is wise to avoid slang and colloquialisms in written work as these undermine the writer's authority. It is better to confine yourself to conventions such as:

- 'this theory/proposition assumes . . . '
- 'it is unclear . . . '
- 'there is little/only limited evidence to support . . . '
- 'there is a contradiction between . . . '
- 'A is inconsistent with B'

- 'significantly . . . '
- 'it is doubtful whether . . . '
- 'this claim/theory/idea is questionable because . . . '
- 'The evidence is conflicting . . . '
- 'Conceivably', 'arguably,' 'potentially', 'generally speaking', 'specifically', 'alternatively . . . '
- 'one possible explanation is' . . . 'another plausible hypothesis is . . . '

Well-presented work always makes a good impression—recall the theory of anchoring adjustment discussed in section 7.6.3. If possible, type your essay, even if the institution will accept handwritten work. Although paper is expensive, wide margins and double spacing and the use of one side only make the marker's task much easier, thus predisposing them to the student. Likewise, be as generous with headings and other forms of 'sign-posting' as the material and line of argument allow. Allow time for proofreading in order to eliminate spelling mistakes, and 'typos' which occur inevitably, and which also undermine the authority of your work if left uncorrected.

11.4 Preparing for Examinations

Golden rule
Technique, technique, technique.

THE student who has prepared well should not find examinations too stressful. Examination technique is also important, however. Figure 11.6 summarizes the components of good examination technique.

Leading from strength is the most important element of examination technique.

Figure 11.6 The elements of examination technique

1. Lead from strength.

2. Train your memory.

3. Practise by preparing specimen answers under examination conditions.

4. Answer the question.

Most institutions offer students a choice of questions. It is important to remember that:

what counts is what appears on the examination script.

The remainder of the student's knowledge (or lack of it) is irrelevant. It is important, therefore, to choose questions which enable you to capitalize upon your abilities. The eminent physicist Stephen Hawking recounts that his undergraduate days were largely spent drinking beer. He obtained a first-class honours degree because he chose examination questions which required problem solving ability rather than specific knowledge (White and Gribben 1992).

Although examinations require recall they need not involve prodigious feats of memory. The key to success lies in reducing your knowledge into skeletal form. The ultimate revision tool is a small piece of card for each topic listing key points. Figure 11.7 shows a specimen revision card of a student intending to answer a question on the topic of escalation in decision making.

Note how knowledge has been reduced to seven key points. The student's first task in the examination hall is to jot these down on the script before list the details.

Figure 11.7 Specimen revision card

ESCALATION

1. *Definition:* persistence with investment decision beyond an economically defensible point, e.g., Taurus, Euro–Disney, BSE controversy.
2. *Causes:* social-psychological pressures; organizational factors, information poverty, economic constraints.
3. *Social–psychological pressures:* responsibility, information biasing, framing effects, social binding.
4. *Organizational factors:* politics, administrative inertia, 'decision–less decisions', 'non-decisions'.
5. *Information poverty:* i.e., time taken for failure to become apparent.
6. *Economic constraints*: refers mainly to prohibitive closing or switching costs, e.g., Sheffield's tramline system; in careers, Becker's notion of 'side–bets'.
7. *Preventing escalation*: review projects frequency — expectations still realistic? change decision makers, reduce fear of failure, avoid becoming involved in questionable projects, set limits, take decisive action.
8. *Other issues*: what constitutes 'objective' success and failure as social construction, mental budgeting and risks of premature de–escalation?

11.4.1 The psychology of success

Answering an examination question is rather like taking a driving test. In theory, a driving test involves performing a series of actions correctly. In reality, the trick is to make the examiner feel safe being driven by you. Much the same applies in examinations. In Organization Behaviour 'safety' involves convincing the examiner that you *understand* the subject matter. Understanding is evidenced by the student's ability to direct the material to the question, to engage in analysis and discussion, and by the use of examples over and above those suggested in class.

It is essential to answer the question which the examiner has set, and not the one you wished they had set. It is *vital* to read the question paper slowly and carefully. A paper which *seems* familiar can contain differences of emphasis. It is a good idea to plan *all* answers before writing. Jotting down key points not only facilitates recall, but also prompts cross-fertilization. Cross-fertilization is particularly important in a subject like Organization Behaviour where themes and ideas can be usefully inter-related; for example, the notion of metaphor, and information and decision making, (see section 1.2.3) and interpretations of power and stress in organizations (see section 5.7.1). Planning also builds confidence as the student sees outline answers emerging.

A common failure is to write down everything you know about a particular topic without making any attempt to relate the material to the question. For example, in the hands of a weak student the question, 'Do organizations need managers?' becomes an opportunity to recite Mintzberg's (1973) research upon how managers spend their time. While that material is relevant to the question, by itself it cannot answer it. Pages of description unrelated to the question create unease in examiners because they suggest an uncomprehending student.

11.4.2 Decoding examination questions

Examination questions vary according to the level of the course. An important task involves decoding the requirements. The most basic question is that which requires the student to *describe* or to *explain* something. Figure 11.8 contains some examples.

The style of questioning shown in Figure 11.8 basically calls for a descriptive answer. Such questions offer limited scope for discussion and analysis. The student can, however, earn marks for a well-organized and well-presented answer. Figure 11.9 shows how such a question might be approached.

The easiest question to answer is the one styled 'Write brief notes . . .' Such questions allow the student to make the best of shallow material. Unsurprisingly, they are sometimes known in the profession as, 'the raft upon which marginal students float to safety!'

More advanced questions typically require the student to combine description with

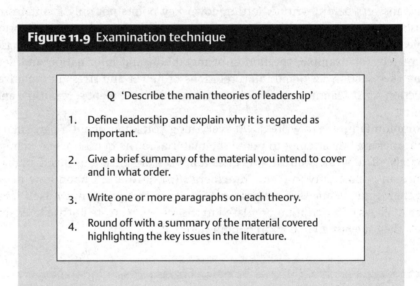

Figure 11.8 Basic–level examination questions

1. Explain the main theories of leadership.

2. Describe the main theories of leadership.

3. What are the main theories of leadership?

4. Write brief notes upon three theories of leadership with which you are familiar.

Figure 11.9 Examination technique

Q 'Describe the main theories of leadership'

1. Define leadership and explain why it is regarded as important.

2. Give a brief summary of the material you intend to cover and in what order.

3. Write one or more paragraphs on each theory.

4. Round off with a summary of the material covered highlighting the key issues in the literature.

some form of analysis or critical discussion. Figure 11.10 contains examples of such questions.

Such questions aim to strike a balance between offering the student a challenge while avoiding making unfair demands. Although each question is phrased differently, all basically require the student to combine description with analysis and discussion.

One option is to approach such questions in an integrated fashion whereby description and discussion are mingled. Another possibility is to answer the question in two parts, that is, with a description of the relevant theories followed by a discussion. Both techniques imply risks. An integrated approach can descend into a 'sandwich' style of answer, that is, a descriptive paragraph with a few lines of commentary tacked on, giving the work a shallow and disjointed appearance. The risk with

Figure 11.10 More advanced examination questions

1. *Critically discuss* the main theories of leadership.

2. *Compare and contrast* 'new' and 'old' theories of leadership.

3. *Comment* upon the suggestion that all leaders are also led.

4. *Describe* the main theories of leadership.
   How useful are they to the practising manager?

separating description and discussion is that the analytical requirements of the task are forgotten altogether or dealt with in a few lines of commentary at the end. Another problem is avoiding repetition of the first half of the essay in the second half. One way of acquiring the skill of distinguishing analysis from description is to read law reports. Note how judges state the facts of the case thoroughly and in plain and simple language before considering the issues.

11.4.3 Displaying critical ability

Examination questions often require the student to display critical ability. Figure 11.11 contains some possible points of focus.

Organization Behaviour ultimately amounts to words. Concepts, and measures of concepts such as job satisfaction and organization commitment do not exist in any absolute sense. They are basically metaphors which are human inventions and therefore open to critical scrutiny. For example, how far is Maslow's definition of 'self-actualization' satisfactory? Is it just another way of saying 'I do not know?'

The Organization Behaviour is riddled with inconsistencies. For example, Ray (1986) suggests that one attraction of cultural control to organizations is cheapness because transaction costs are lower than bureaucratic control (see section 2.1.3). Contrast this suggestion with Adler and Adler's (1988) study of team building and the intense commitment of resources required to maintain loyalty.

All theories and ideas are based upon assumptions. For example, we saw in Chapter 3 that the behavioural approach to management assumes that 'happy' workers are more productive and that 'more is better' when it comes to motivation, job satisfaction and so forth. Likewise, leadership theory is egocentric, emphasizing the power of the individual (see section 3.6.2).

Figure 11.11 Focusing an answer

1. Definition and vagueness in theories and ideas.

2. Overlap with other theories and ideas.

3. Inconsistencies or contradictions within the theory itself.

4. Assumptions upon which an idea or theory rests.

5. Quantity and quality of empirical evidence.

6. The question itself.

7. The ideological basis of the question.

Another possibility is to challenge the question itself. Does it miss the point, for example? If so, what issues does it fail to raise? For example, much of the literature on the topic of workplace stress ignores ideological issues of domination, focusing more upon treating the symptoms of stress than reflecting upon its underlying causes. Likewise, the managerialist literature on corporate culture ignores the existence of counter-cultures and the subtle dynamics of resistance. Whatever approach is taken, the important thing is to discipline your thoughts and direct your response in a coherent manner. Do remember:

there are no wrong answers, only weak answers and strong answers.

Sometimes a question is structured in two parts. It is essential to answer *both* elements of the question in full and equal measure. Part one requires the student to *describe* a particular area of the literature. Part two calls for some commentary or discussion. It is a serious error to neglect the second part because it means that the student has not answered the question and may therefore be at risk of failing. It is better to write a few paragraphs however intellectually feeble they may seem than to do nothing at all. Making some attempt to address the issues can mean the difference between passing and failing because it enables the examiner to justify a pass even though the discussion is weak.

Incidentally, as far as possible, observe a similar standard of presentation in the examination is in essays. Although tutors make allowances for examination conditions, a well presented script is always welcome.

Golden rule
Never despair.

Finally, never leave the examination hall in despair, however hopeless things may seem. If you feel unable to answer even a single question, doodle for a while or write nonsense. You may be surprised by what comes back to you. However doubtful you may feel about what you write, carry on. It may be better than you think.

Chapter 12
Writing and Researching Dissertations in Organization Behaviour

> Discovery consists of seeing what everybody has seen and thinking what nobody has thought.
>
> (Albert von Szent-Gyorg)

THE purpose of this chapter is to assist the student faced with completing a dissertation or similar project in a topic related to Organization Behaviour. Although the precise requirements of the exercise vary between institutions, the dissertation usually involves conducting independent research, and a report ranging from 8,000 to 20,000 words.

For many students writing a dissertation is just one more task and one which they could do without. Yet at very least, the dissertation is a factor determining the degree, and may significantly affect the student's final mark. Moreover, when there is little to choose between job candidates, evidence of a meticulously executed dissertation can be decisive. Likewise, the experience of writing a dissertation is useful preparation for professional life which often involves research and report writing. This experience may prove invaluable in selection tests. So, if the dissertation has to be done, let it be done well.

This chapter aims to highlight potentially fruitful directions for research and to offer basic guidance in writing the dissertation. The student is advised to consult specialist texts for detailed advice upon methodology and presentational techniques (Bryman 1988, Denscombe 1998). Many university libraries also produce their own short guides on literature searching and report writing. These have the added advantage of being available free of charge. The issues which are addressed by this chapter include:

Key Issues

- How to choose a topic.
- How to turn an interest into a research topic.
- How to formulate a research question.
- How to write the dissertation.

12.1   How to Choose a Topic

Most universities allow the student considerable freedom when it comes to selecting a topic. While this can make study exciting, the range of possibilities can be daunting. Moreover, timescales and other resource constraints restrict the scope for experimentation. The student must ensure a particular topic is feasible before embarking upon extensive reading and data gathering.

The first point to consider in choosing a dissertation topic is that there are two types of research problem. These are:

1. Problems that are interesting, and;
2. Problems that are researchable.

It is essential that the topic is researchable. It also helps if it is interesting.

Research, by definition, involves venturing into the unknown. Part of the art of selecting a topic is to minimize risk. Figure 12.1 lists the attributes of a good dissertation topic. It can be used as checklist for assessing the feasibility of potential topics. Each of the points listed in Figure 12.1 is now discussed in turn.

12.1.1   Choosing a topic that interests you

Bearing in mind the caveat about choosing a researchable topic, a good way to get started is to ask yourself:

what interests me?

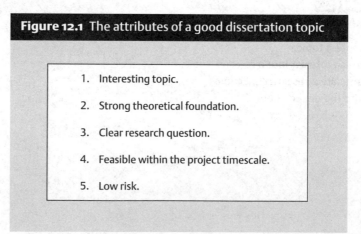

Figure 12.1 The attributes of a good dissertation topic

1. Interesting topic.

2. Strong theoretical foundation.

3. Clear research question.

4. Feasible within the project timescale.

5. Low risk.

A topic which interests the student is far more likely to motivate than one which is perceived as soul destroying. At this stage, concentrate upon identifying as many ideas as possible without worrying about the practicalities. Let curiosity run riot. For example, I have always wondered:

- Why dentists never seem bored doing the same things day after day.
- Why there are not more cases of food poisoning given the state of many restaurant kitchens.
- Where infant teachers get the energy.

It does not matter how silly or irrelevant the question seems. It may not even be immediately related to Organization Behaviour. For example, during my periodic visits to Leeds market (see pages 3–4) I have often wondered:

- What happens to the fish heads and other waste from the fish market?
- Who buys the fired doughnuts?
- How do stalls selling nothing but eggs survive especially as no one ever seems to buy?
- Why is there no oyster bar?

What matters is that the question interests you.

The next stage is to consider how a particular interest might be turned into a viable research project. For example, the question about dentists might become a study of job satisfaction. The question about food hygiene might translate into a study of how food safety laws are observed. The third question might focus upon older teachers. How do they cope as their energy levels decline with age? The question on egg stalls might translate into a topic on social-constructionism (see section 6.4.6). For example, many so-called 'free range eggs' come from farms with stocks in excess of 25,000 birds—far removed from the farmyard image depicted by the producers. The literature on critical marketing might inform such a project (Alvesson and Willmott 1996).

12.2 How to Turn an Interest Into a Research Topic

As we have seen, ideas for dissertations can come from almost anywhere. Other potential sources include:

- the course material itself,
- aspects of Organization Behaviour not covered by the course material,
- the student's experience.

Any element of the taught course which the student finds interesting is worth exploring. The student is also at liberty to browse beyond the course material, or to pursue an issue which was mentioned only briefly on the course. For example, the student may have been interested by a paragraph in a textbook on white collar crime in organizations. The next step might be to conduct a preliminary literature search in order to assess the possibilities for a dissertation topic. Likewise the student fascinated by the absence of oyster bars in the city market (see section 12.1.2) might begin by examining the literature on social class.

The student's own life experience can be a source of inspiration and data. Work experience, paid or voluntary, might be written up as a case study. For instance, the student who is involved with a mountain rescue group or volunteer railway might have the opportunity to observe normative commitment (see section 5.2.1) and even over-commitment (see section 3.6.1), or decision making—to name only a few possibilities. Alternatively, work experience might provide the student with access to people willing to be interviewed or answer questionnaires.

Hobbies can also suggest ideas for a dissertation. Membership of an amateur dramatics group might facilitate a study of the metaphor of management as theatre (Mangham 1990, see also Chapter 1), or might muse on the relationship between organizational politics and decisions about who gets parts. The student active in sports might be interested in the symbolic aspects of leadership (Pfeffer 1977, see also section 12.2), or the creation of commitment (Adler and Adler 1988).

Postgraduate students and students on joint degree courses might capitalize upon their wider knowledge. For example, engineers might interest themselves in the social and behavioural implications of concurrent engineering or business process re-engineering. Environmental scientists might focus upon human attitudes to risk. Theologians might apply their knowledge of symbolism to Organization Behaviour.

The student's daily experience can also suggest possibilities. An article in a newspaper or professional journal may suggest an issue for research. Publications in other disciplines can suggest possibilities. Half an hour browsing in a university bookshop amid subjects as diverse as medicine, nursing, software engineering, hospitality management, equine studies and archaeology combined might stimulate ideas. For example, unlike say building a bridge, in software engineering there is nothing to see. What power does that place in the hands of software engineers and how do they use it?

Shops and supermarkets can present rich possibilities. For instance, a shop such as 'Office World', might be analysed as text (see section 10.7.1) with Morgan's image of organizations as psychic prisons (see section 1.2.4) as part of the theoretical context. For example, note the proportion of items dedicated to facilitating tidiness. What does that suggest? Can so-called 'Post It' stickers be interpreted as a manifestation of unconscious anxiety? Likewise, how do supermarket cashiers behave? What proportion seem bored or lost in day dreams? Are they mainly older or younger staff who seem disinterested, or is age irrelevant?

12.2.1 The importance of choosing a topic with a strong theoretical foundation

The level of theoretical content in a dissertation will vary according to the requirements of the institution and the choice of topic. The advantage of choosing a topic with a strong theoretical foundation is that it provides a context for the research.

There should be little difficulty where the topic obviously relates to a social sciences concept, such as power, technology, job satisfaction, bureaucracy, and stress.

Defining a theoretical framework is more difficult if the student starts from a topic which is not immediately related to the Organization Behaviour literature. The tutor has a particular role to play here. The student can also help themselves by considering what aspects of the literature might be relevant. For instance, an interest in the Internet could be transformed into a study examining the implications for organization structure or a study of communication in organizations. (See also the problem of under-focusing below.)

12.2.2 The importance of defining a clear research question

The research question is the focal point of the dissertation. Defining a research question can be difficult, even for experienced researchers. The student may be tempted to plunge ahead with a topic and see what emerges. While this strategy can work, it is extremely risky. At very least it is likely to involve extra work later on as the student struggles to focus the reading and data collection. Worse: the project can descend into aimlessness. It is much safer and ultimately quicker to wrestle with the problem early on.

> **Golden rule**
>
> Keep asking yourself:
>
> 'What is the research question?'

The student can anticipate one of two problems in attempting to define a research question. These are:

- under-focusing, or,
- over-focusing (Howard and Sharp 1983).

The *under-focused* question is one which is too broad to be researchable. The problem usually arises where the topic relates to a vast literature such as decision making. The task with an under-focused dissertation is to narrow the topic.

The easiest way to explain this process is to take a hypothetical problem of under-focusing. Let us assume that the student is starting from the question, 'What are the causes of stress?'

As it stands, the question either implies a textbook essay on the subject of stress, or, an extensive literature search. The former may not meet the requirements for a dissertation. The latter is unlikely to be feasible within the project timescale.

12.2.3 Re-engineering a research question

One way of narrowing a topic is to revert to first principles and ask yourself:

what is it about the topic that interests?

In this case, the student's interest stemmed from seeing a friend suffer the effects of exposure to stress. The friend happens to be a junior hospital doctor. This insight enables the student to narrow the focus as 'stress' becomes 'stress and the medical profession'. The task of conducting a literature search is already more manageable.

Next the student conducts a preliminary scan of the literature. The scan reveals that there is actually a significant amount of research into the effects of stress on junior doctors. This discovery enables the student to further narrow the topic. 'Stress and the medical profession', now becomes 'stress and junior doctors'.

This still leaves the problem of an actual research question. Again the student reverts to first principles. The student now asks:

'What is it about A (stress) and B (junior doctors) that interests me?

For example, is it the impact of long hours, or is it the contrast between expectations and reality? The student realizes that it is the experience of stress that interests. That is, what it feels like to be a junior hospital doctor working eighty hours a week.

The final twist in defining the topic is that the student decides to base the dissertation upon a single case study of their friend's experience. Single case studies make good dissertation projects because they limit the risks involved in data collection, and facilitate depth (Dyer and Wilkins 1991). Incidentally, the fact that the respondent is a friend (or a close relative) is no impediment to research. (See, for example, Mintzberg's (1979) impassioned article on the subject).

The dissertation might be entitled, 'Stress: a junior doctor's experience' or 'The experience of stress: the case of a junior doctor'. The important point is that the student keeps focused upon the research question and ultimately produces an answer.

By contrast, the *over-focused* topic is one which is too narrowly defined to meet requirements. For example, the student may have an interest in the semi-conductor industry but no idea of how to link it to a dissertation in Organization Behaviour. Or, the student may have been fascinated by a visit to the zoo and want to capitalize upon the experience in some way.

Whereas the over-focused topic requires narrowing down, the under-focused topic requires expansion. Expansion usually involves identifying a body of theory to underpin the topic. A good knowledge of the Organization Behaviour literature can help. For example, one of the problems currently faced by the semi-conductor industry is over-supply. Escalation theory (see section 7.9) might be relevant here. The student interested in zoos might focus upon the tension between educational objectives and commercial viability. Du Gay and Salaman's (1992) analysis of the 'cult' of the customer informs the theoretical context of such a study (see section 4.6). Etzioni's (1975) compliance theory (see section 5.2) might also be relevant.

Sometimes it is easier for the under-focused student to think of an alternative topic. For instance, I was once asked to supervise a dissertation based on a petrol station in India comprising a solitary pump. The answer may be obvious to some, but I am still wondering how to turn the idea into a researchable topic.

12.3 How to Formulate a Research Question

EVEN a well focused student can find it difficult to formulate a research question. Figure 12.2 contains a list of different styles of question which might be employed. Organization Behaviour lends itself well to questions which focus upon *how* a particular phenomenon is experienced. The student can utilize this approach to explore a

Figure 12.2 Styles of research question

1. *How* is a particular phenomenon experienced?

2. *What* is the relationship between A and B?

3. *How* has X affected Y?

4. *What* causes A?

5. *How* did A occur?

6. *How* can problem A be solved or prevented?

7. *How* relevant is X to Y?

8. *How* does A differ from B?

9. *What* similarities exist between A and B?

10. *What* does X signify?

wide range of phenomenon including stress, (mentioned earlier) or specific stressors such as role ambiguity, role overload, and sexual harassment (see section 8.3). Other possibilities include job satisfaction, motivation and the experience of work generally. A foundational theme might be Alvesson and Willmott's (1996) suggestion that management theorists overemphasize the significance of motivation (see section 3.6).

Questions styled 'what is the relationship between A and B?' might imply a correlational study. For example, the student may undertake a questionnaire survey of relationship between organizational commitment and professional commitment, or other work attitudes utilizing one of the standard psychometric measures (Allen and Meyer 1990, Bartram 1997, Bartram et al. 1995, Cook and Wall 1980, Warr, Cook and Wall 1979). Note, however, that certain psychometric tests can only be administered under supervision, and some are restricted to specially trained personnel.

Questions styled 'how has X affected Y?' might imply a study of change. For example, the student may compare and contrast, 'before' and 'after'. Topics likely to lend itself to this approach include:

■ the impact of new technology,
■ the impact of a merger or organizational restructuring,
■ the impact of a specific managerial intervention, for example, an attempt to change the culture of an organization, or a change of policy.

Question 4 in Figure 12.2 implies a causal investigation. Projects requiring sophisticated research designs and analytical techniques may be beyond the scope of a short dissertation. There are many other possibilities. For instance, government inquiries into disasters and organizational failures can make an interesting subject for study. Moreover, the reports are usually stocked by university libraries or are easy to obtain on inter-library loan. The incident need not necessarily be a recent one. For example, the inquiry into the collapse of the Bank of Credit and Commerce International (BCCI) concludes that the culture of supervision was a significant factor in the Bank of England's failure to detect fraud (Inquiry into the Supervision of the Bank of Credit and Commerce International 1992).

Question 5, 'how did A occur?' differs from a causal investigation as analysis focuses upon the sequence of events from one state of affairs to another. Military history is rich in potential case studies for this purpose. Question 6 'how can problem A be solved or prevented?' implies a dissertation with a practical focus. For example, the student might investigate how organizations can prevent collusive fraud, product abuse, sabotage, or some other organizational problem.

Questions concerning the relevance of X to Y imply a critical examination. For example, Guest (1990) suggests that the so-called Human Relations School has never really been taken seriously by managers in the UK (see section 3.6). Knights and Willmott's (1992) insightful study into the realities of leadership (see section 3.6.4) might inform part of the theoretical framework. Another possibility might be to interview managers and/or employees for their views. Another option is to focus upon training needs. For example, to what extent do vocational courses in law, architecture, engineering, surveying, nursing, and so forth, prepare students for practice?

Questions 8 and 9 imply questions such as how does the culture in office A differ from that in office B, or, in what ways is the Church similar to a modern corporation? A nice twist to such questions is to look for:

- similarities between things which appear different, and/or,
- differences between things which appear similar.

Question 10, '*what* does X signify?' implies an interpretive study, for example, the 'Office World' project referred to earlier. Other options include studying rites, ceremonial, the use of coded language and the expression of status differences in organizations. The works of Ackroyd and Crowdy (1990) and Collinson (1988, 1992), Trist and Bamforth (1951), might suggest ideas for how such research can be conducted. For example, it may be possible to replicate Collinson's study of masculine values in a male orientated environment. Alternatively, Collinson's study could serve as template for studying a female dominated environment.

12.3.1 The importance of conducting a feasibility exercise

In addition to being academically acceptable, the dissertation topic must be feasible given timescales and other constraints. It is important to remember that research reported in leading academic journals is typically the result of two or three years of work, long experience, financial sponsorship, and considerable redrafting. A student on a taught course may have little or no previous experience. Resources for postage, travel, and specialist items of equipment are likely to be limited. The timescale for completion is likely to be measured in months or even weeks.

There are two ways of determining the feasibility of a project. These are:

- as you go along, or,
- before you start.

The first strategy has *nothing* to commend it. Research may be a journey of discovery. Yet to discover midway through a project that a critical data base or software package cannot be utilized as expected, or, that interview data does not make sense, not only means wasted time and money, it also casts an ominous shadow over the student's prospects.

> **Golden rule**
> Think ahead.

12.3.2 How to conduct a feasibility exercise

Conducting a feasibility study involves making an imaginative leap and conducting pilot work. The questions which should be asked at this stage include:

1. *Exactly* what literature is available on a particular topic?
2. *Exactly* what information does a report or suite of documentation contain?
3. Where *exactly* can a specific group of respondents be located?
4. How *exactly* will X be measured, analysed or interpreted?

Note the emphasis upon the word 'exactly'. Vague proposals such as:

- 'I will measure the motivation of managers using a questionnaire',
- 'I will interview employees about stress,' and,
- 'I will find information in books,'

will not do.

The student must be able to define exactly what information is to be sought and where it is to be found, exactly who is to be interviewed, and how access will be obtained, exactly what psychometric scale is to be used, and so forth.

Figure 12.3 contains an outline checklist which the student can utilize to hammer out the details. It is one thing to say, 'I will conduct fifty interviews,' It is another thing to actually specify 'who' will be interviewed, 'where' those interviews are to be conducted, 'when' they will take place and 'how' they will be conducted. For example, will the student use a structured approach?

The last question 'why?' is potentially the most important of all. In my experience, students are apt to burden themselves needlessly because they fail to check their assumptions about what is required. For example, the student may assume that a

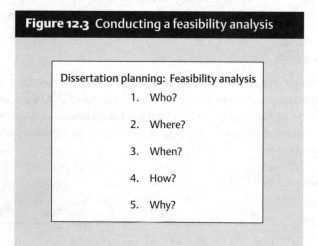

Figure 12.3 Conducting a feasibility analysis

Dissertation planning: Feasibility analysis

1. Who?

2. Where?

3. When?

4. How?

5. Why?

dissertation in business and management precludes studying a voluntary group or an extremist political sect. Likewise, why fifty interviews? One in-depth account might well suffice. When planning research remember:

It is not the problem that impedes a solution so much as the assumptions you make about the problem. (De Bono 1977, 1990, Watzlawick, Weakland and Frish, 1974)

Conducting a feasibility analysis can be a painful exercise because it forces the student to confront vague assumptions, to see the difficulties involved, and to test the practicality of their ideas. The student who is tempted to skip it and trust to luck should be mindful of Francis Bacon's axiom:

If a man will begin with certainties, he shall end in doubts; but if he will be content to begin with doubts, he shall end in certainties. (*The Advancement of Learning* (1605) Bk. 1, Ch. 5, sect. 8)

12.3.3 The importance of choosing a low risk topic

All research involves risk. No matter how carefully the student plans the project, there are no guarantees. It helps, therefore, to choose a topic involving minimal risk.

> **Golden rule**
> The fewer dependencies, the lower the risk.

Very simply, the more the student depends upon others in order to complete the project, the greater the risk. In my experience, the biggest risk factor in student dissertations usually centres upon the data collection. The proposals which sound alarm to me include:

- 'I have a friend who can *maybe* arrange for me to interview So-and-So.'
- 'My friend has *promised* to sent XYZ reports from Brazil/Thailand/Tanzania . . . '
- 'If I write to the firm's head office *perhaps* they will let me have some information.'
- '*Maybe* I can make an interview with . . . '

The sooner words like 'maybe', 'promised' and 'perhaps' disappear from the student's plans, the better. If critical dependencies are unavoidable then be sure to make contingency plans should your arrangements for securing access to data break down. For example, the person who offers help in November may have changed jobs by March. Likewise, the person who offered to access data may retract their promise when they discover that commercially sensitive information is involved or that the research involves them in undue work. The student may wait weeks or even months for a report to arrive only to discover that the information it contains does not enable the student to answer the research question.

12.3.4 How to choose a low risk topic

The least risky option is to utilize data which is in the public domain. The most obvious option is turn the dissertation into a literature search. The primary advantage of a literature search, assuming adequate library facilities, is that it poses fewest problems of access.

Focusing a topic can be difficult, however. Even the most seemingly obscure subject may be the subject of several hundred articles while the more popular topics such as leadership can generate thousands of references.

Set out below are some possibilities for narrowing a literature search:

1. Focus upon a specific element of a topic. For example, instead of researching stress, consider narrowing the research to a stressor such as role ambiguity, sexual harassment, or shift work.
2. Focus upon a specific country, industry, organization or occupational group.
3. Limit the search to a specific time frame, or to studies utilizing a specific methodology. For instance, the student may decide to concentrate upon the most recent research, or examine qualitative contributions in a field dominated by quantitative studies or vice versa.
4. Some combination of points 1, 2 and 3.

Where a highly specialized topic is involved, some lateral thinking (De Bono 1977, 1990) may be required. For example, the student may be interested in how organizations protect themselves against the risks of terrorism. Unfortunately a preliminary scan of the literature reveals that although the literature upon terrorism is extensive, comparatively little exists on the subject of terrorism and organizations. Instead of abandoning the project the student reverts to first principles and asks:

what is it about the topic that interests me?

The student then realizes that their primary interest is terrorism. Why not study the literature on terrorism and write a dissertation on its implications for organizations? The research question thus becomes, 'What are the implications of terrorism for large-scale organizations?'

12.3.5 More low risk options

There are plenty of other low risk options for writing a dissertation. The key is to remember that:

data are everywhere.

The entrepreneur sees a business opportunity where others notice only a rubbish site.

The same goes for identifying potential research topics. For example, many university libraries stock the *Harvard Business Review* back to 1922. Why not design a project which involves comparing older and newer editions? For instance, what evidence is there to suggest that the so-called 'human factor' has become more important in recent years? Has the proportion of articles devoted to Organization Behaviour and Human Resources Management increased? Has the approach to those subjects changed, and if so, how? Many university libraries retain old textbooks. The student might address the research question by comparing and contrasting old and new.

Business biographies are another possibility. For example, could Nicola Horlick's (1997) *Can You Have It All?*—be analysed as a case study to generate insights into the lives of modern professional women? Company reports are another possibility. One option might be to compare and contrast a sample of chairman's statements of companies which have performed well with those which have performed badly. If escalation theory is correct (see section 7.9) we can expect good performance to be attributed to the management team and bad performance to be attributed to exogenous causes such as currency fluctuations.

Another possibility is to utilize other sections of the library. For instance, Shakespeare's play *Macbeth* could be rewritten as a study in office politics. Likewise, the film *The Full Monty*, could be analysed as a case study of how unemployment is experienced. The themes depicted by the film include stress (one of the characters becomes impotent), marital breakdown, and major life transition as the balance of power between men and women reverses. History too, is replete with possibilities. The Norman Conquest of England might be rewritten as a company takeover bid. The term 'bunker mentality' refers to Hitler's isolation from reality as the Reich crumbled. The student might utilize accounts of Hitler's behaviour in order to generate insights into how 'bunker mentality' develops, how it is sustained, and what finally breaks it.

Research involving unobtrusive data gathering is another low risk option. For example, poor diet can contribute to stress (see section 8.3.1). A city centre at lunchtime is a good data site for studying eating habits. What sort of people visit sandwich bars, and what do they buy? The technically literate student might pose as a customer interested in buying a computer or some other sophisticated product in order to test the product knowledge of sales staff in high street stores.

The next least risky option is to utilize data sources which are easily accessible. Again, the possibilities abound. Surveys undertaken in public places are a relatively low risk option. For example, people can be stopped in the streets and asked about their attitudes to work. The unemployed may be willing to answer questions as they emerge from the Job Centre. It may be possible to conduct a survey of attitudes to risk by questioning shoppers about buying patterns of foods which have been linked to BSE and other dangers. Morgan (1996) links the BSE crisis to the metaphor of organizational flux and transformation. It might be possible to analyse subsequent developments utilizing this metaphor (most university libraries stock back issues of newspapers on compact disc). The forthcoming publication of the results of the government enquiry on BSE might suggest other ideas for research. The literature on politics and decision making might also inform the theoretical context. Fellow students are also potentially sympathetic subjects for research.

Another possibility is to try a novel approach to a familiar question. Weick (1989) has argued that organizations are poor sites for theory testing because of the myriad of confounding factors. Weick suggests that researchers invoke 'disciplined imagination' in order to identify more reliable methods. For instance, says Weick, a good way to test the theory that motivation increases as a person nears their goal, is to observe behaviour on escalators. If the theory is correct, says Weick, people should start running as they near the top.

12.4   How to Write the Dissertation

THE requirements for writing up the dissertation vary between universities and according to the demands and constraints imposed by a particular topic. Generally speaking, however, dissertations are structured as follows:

1. Introduction or executive summary.
2. Theoretical context and research question.
3. The method employed.
4. Presentation of the findings.
5. Discussion and conclusions.
6. List of references and appendices.

Each of these points is now discussed in turn.

12.4.1   How to write the introduction or executive summary

Golden rule

When reporting research:
1. Begin by telling the reader what you are going to tell them.
2. Tell them.
3. End by telling them what you have already told them.

The introduction or executive summary is the place to tell the reader what you are going to say. More specifically, this section should:

- define the research topic,
- identify the research question,

- explain why the issue is important,
- indicate how the work was approached, and,
- state the key findings.

The purpose of the introduction or executive summary is to enable the reader to obtain an overview of the dissertation. Brevity is the hallmark of this section. Each component part should occupy no more than a paragraph.

> **Golden rule**
>
> Explain your findings in one sentence.

Explaining the key findings can be difficult. The better focused student, the easier it is. Yet even the well focused student can become submerged in a morass of detail, unable to see the wood for the trees. One way of overcoming this problem is to imagine that you are being interviewed by a journalist or radio presenter. They will not be interested in all the 'ifs' and 'buts' and 'maybes' surrounding the research. Journalists are apt to focus upon the pith, that is:

- what was the research *question*, and,
- what is the *answer*?

For example, the student who began with the question, 'How do junior doctors cope with working long hours?' emerges with the answer, 'It is not the long hours which are stressful but the hostile way in which patients react when they are kept waiting.'

12.4.2 How to write the opening chapters

The aim of the section describing the *theoretical context and research question* is to set the dissertation in context. The selection of material should be dictated by the research question. Generally speaking, the more academically orientated the dissertation, the greater the need for theoretical underpinning.

> **Golden rule**
>
> Move from the general to the specific.

For example, a study of a re-engineering project might have a *general* chapter on Taylorism and the 'total quality management literature', followed by a more *specific* account of the re-engineering literature.

The emphasis in a more practically orientated dissertation is likely to be upon providing background information rather than academic theory. For example, a dissertation focusing upon the training needs of sales staff in a drugs company would probably require a section describing recent changes in the health service. It may be appropriate to divide the material into two chapters. The first chapter might comprise a *general* description of recent changes in the health service. The second might focus *specifically* upon those changes with direct implications for purchasing arrangements.

The incorporation of theoretical material in a practically based dissertation can lend the work additional authority. For example, the training needs dissertation referred to earlier might incorporate a theoretical section entitled, 'What is selling?' Likewise, the study of hygiene violations in a restaurant might draw upon the literature on fraud, resistance or sabotage.

It is a mistake, however, to force material into the dissertation simply because you have taken the trouble to read it. Early reading, in particular, is apt to become redundant. For example, the student who began with an interest in social relations at work may have a lot about the so-called 'Human Relations School' and its derivatives before deciding to focus upon the problems of social isolation experienced by people who work from home. The human relations material is still relevant but must be pruned and utilized adroitly. For instance, detailed descriptions of the Hawthorne experiments (see section 3.1.1) are not required, though these might have been relevant in another context.

12.4.3 How to write the method section

The method section explains how the research was conducted. The student should explain:

- *what* was done,
- *how* it was done, and,
- *why* it was done in a particular way.

The general rule in reporting research is that enough detail should be supplied to enable another person to replicate the study. This rule is less relevant where the data collection involves mainly observation and/or unstructured interviewing. Even so, the student should supply a reasonably informative picture of the research. For example, what sort of questions were asked? When and how were the observations conducted? What types of people were interviewed, and how many?

If possible, try and paint a picture which enables the researcher to visualize the context. For example, what was the restaurant kitchen like? Describe the sounds, the smells, the colour, and the atmosphere. It may also be appropriate to mention the background to the research and how you became interested in the topic. For example, here is an account of one episode in a day in the life of a hospice nurse:

John (aged sixty-six) was admitted for symptom control of his Dyspnoea (breathlessness). On the day of his discharge he was laughing and joking all morning. He even bought me a 'thank-you' card and a box of chocolates 'for being his mate'. After lunch, I was doing the medis (*sic*) when John began to cough violently. An auxiliary nurse went over to tend to him but screamed and rushed to draw the curtains around him. I immediately went in to find John haemorrhaging massive amounts of blood which covered him, his bed, and the surrounding area. Within about ninety seconds, surrounded by a team of stunned doctors and nurses, John was dead. . . . I remained composed until about five minutes from the end of my shift when the floodgates opened. . . . I think the sobs came from my boots. . . . I think it was the shock of such a horrendous sight, the cruelty of it all when he was looking forward to going home but mostly because I think he was fully aware of what was happening because he was conscious up until he died. (Wilson-Owens 1998, p. 36)

The vital point in explaining why a particular approach was adopted is to ensure that:

the relationship between the research question and the techniques employed is clear.

For example, if the research question centres upon how stress is experienced, then interviewing people about their experiences is appropriate because the technique can illuminate the actual experience of stress. If the aim is to trace the sequence of events a documentary analysis is appropriate because it allows the researcher to do precisely that.

12.4.4 How to present the results

This section basically reports the results of the research. The format will vary according to the topic. For example, this section may contain statistical tables with accompanying textual explanation, or the substance of a case study.

The important points to remember in presenting the results are:

- discipline, and,
- clarity.

Clarity flows from discipline. It is important to structure the report in a manner calculated to enable a reader unfamiliar with the subject to understand the key findings with ease. Where statistical data are employed, again move from the *general* to the *specific*. This means beginning with an overall picture first, followed by sub-analyses. Where textual material is involved, the key is to tell the story but in a disciplined fashion. For example, analysis might reveal five or six (more or less) theoretically significant themes in the data. The student might present material relating to each theme under a separate heading.

12.4.5 How to write the discussion and conclusions

The purpose of the discussion section is to explain the significance of the findings. The basic difference between the results section and the discussion and conclusions is as follows:

- Results Section: 'Here is what the findings *say*'.
- Discussion and Conclusions: 'Here is what the findings *mean*.'

In the discussion and conclusions section the student interprets the results and answers the research question. Figure 12.4 shows how this section might be structured.

For instance, the student who studied behaviour upon an escalator might have expected that people would start to run about two thirds from the top. The student may have discovered that the data are broadly consistent with this proposition. (Incidentally, data are rarely neat and tidy). If so, the student may conclude that the theory that motivation increases as the goal becomes nearer is potentially correct. Alternatively the student may discover that, broadly speaking, there are two categories of people who use escalators, that is, those who are in a hurry and those who are not. The student notes that it is mainly people in a hurry who run as they near the top of the stairs. The student thus concludes that the theory depends upon the perceived importance of the goal.

The discussion section should relate the results of the research back to the theoretical context. Sometimes, however, it is necessary to invoke additional literature in order to explain the findings. In the case of the hospice nurse, referred to in section 12.4.3 the student discovers that joking and horseplay are a feature of organizational behaviour:

There are a few nurses here who I really love working with. We wind each other up something rotten. I have locked someone in the fridge in the morgue with three other bodies and ran away screaming laughing. I have hidden in empty rooms and pressed the patient call bell, (suggesting a ghost) and jumped out almost giving them heart attacks . . .   (Wilson-Owens 1998, p. 41)

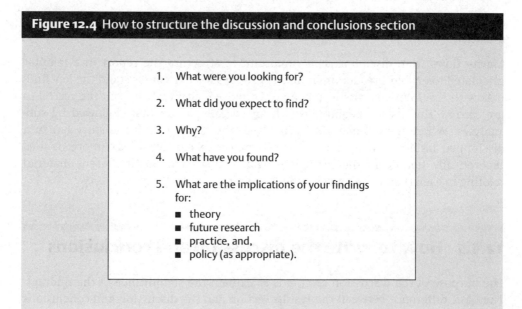

Figure 12.4 How to structure the discussion and conclusions section

1. What were you looking for?

2. What did you expect to find?

3. Why?

4. What have you found?

5. What are the implications of your findings for:
   - theory
   - future research
   - practice, and,
   - policy (as appropriate).

This raises a question. Does horseplay mitigate the effects of stress and burnout, or, does the cultural theory of stress (see section 8.8.2) suggest that claiming stress and burnout justify horseplay?

It may also be appropriate to discuss the implications of the dissertation for policy and practice. For example, the student may have discovered that few high street staff have adequate technical knowledge. What are the implications of this discovery? For instance, how do staff feel when they are unable to answer questions? Likewise, what are the implications for customer satisfaction?

Likewise, the student may have expected violations of food safety regulations to be more frequent when the restaurant is busy, that is, when staff are working under pressure. The student discovers, however, that the opposite is true. Staff are more likely to re-use old coffee, reheat dishes and so forth when the restaurant is quiet. What can be inferred from that discovery?

> **Golden rule**
> If the research no longer fits the research question: try changing the question.

It is when the student attempts to write the discussion and conclusions section that the importance of a clear research question and contextual material becomes apparent. A well conceived, well planned, and well executed study should not give rise to many problems. Yet even the most meticulously planned study can go awry. Besides, research is a creative process. The student may discover that the ground has shifted, that is, the data and literature search no longer answer the research question. If that happens, there are two options. The first and most preferable course of action is to refocus the study. This usually involves reformulating the research question. Supposing, for example, that the student discovers that it is actually very difficult to tabulate behaviour on an escalator. (This problem would probably have been avoided had the student conducted a pilot study. Remember: interesting questions and researchable questions). Faced with this problem, the student might recast the project into a methodological study. The research question thus becomes, '*What* are the difficulties involved in applying Weick's (1989) idea?'

The dissertation still makes a useful contribution because another researcher would want to refer to it before embarking upon a similar exercise.

The alternative is to make the best of the work as it stands. Where undergraduate and taught masters dissertations are concerned, process is usually more important than outcome. While this should not be taken to imply that 'anything goes' it does afford the student some protection against inconclusive results or a project which fails to work out as planned. The most important criteria are that the student demonstrates that what was done:

- was done carefully,
- for good reason, and,
- that something has been learned from the exercise.

Writing the conclusions basically involves telling the reader what you have already told them. The student should be able to achieve this in a paragraph.

> **Golden rule**
> Check: have you answered the research question?

The student might begin with a sentence or two recapitulating the general area of the research, followed by a brief restatement of the specific topic and the research question. The answer to the research question, that is, the conclusions, may be implicit from the preceding discussion. The dissertation should end, however, with a clear, but brief, statement of the study conclusions.

12.4.6   How to compile the list of references and appendices

Bibliographic techniques are beyond the scope of this chapter. The important points to note are:

1. Keep bibliographic records of reading as you go along—it saves time hunting for references later.
2. The Harvard system of referencing is by far the easiest to use.
3. Unless otherwise directed, avoid footnotes. These make referencing complicated. If it is worth saying, say it in the text.
4. Whatever citation system is used, be consistent.

When presenting results, it can be difficult to know what material to include and what to omit. Intelligent use of appendices can help to solve this problem. Appendices enable the student to demonstrate due diligence without distracting or confusing the reader with extraneous material.

Generally speaking, any material which is not central to the discussion and conclusions should be placed in an appendix. For example, the student may have conducted sub-analyses to check for exceptions to a general pattern. The analyses may not affect the study conclusions but it is important that the reader knows that this possibility has been checked. Likewise, interview data usually has to be used selectively in order to eliminate repetition and extraneous material. The student might show the entire transcript in an appendix so that the reader can see for themselves what has been excluded, and what emphasis has been accorded to particular passages and how specific quotations appear in context.

If in doubt whether to include something in an appendix, include it. Ultimately:

- it is not what you have done that counts, but,
- what you are seen to have done.

'Is there no way out of the mind?'
(Sylvia Plath, 'Apprehensions')

Bibliography

Abrahams, P. (1998) 'Toshiba Soars as Deep Restructuring Bites,' *Financial Times*, 9 November.

Acker, J. (1992) 'Gendering Organizational Theory', in A. Mills and P. Tancred (eds.) (1992) *Gendering Organizational Analysis*, London, Sage.

Ackroyd, S., and Crowdy, P. A. (1990) 'Can Culture be Managed? Working with Raw Material: The Case of English Slaughtermen', *Personnel Review*, 19, 3–13.

Adams, C. (1998) 'On the Safe Side', *Financial Times*, 29 January, 25.

Adams, J. S. (1963) 'Toward an Understanding of Inequity', *Journal of Abnormal and Social Psychology*, November, 422–36.

—— (1965) 'Inequity in Social Exchange', in L. Berkowitz (ed.), *Advances in Experimental Social Psychology*, New York, Academic Press, 267–99.

Adler, M. E., Boyce, T., Chesney, M. A., Cohen, S., Folkman, S., Kahn, R. L., Syme, S. L. (1994) 'Socio-economic Status and Health', *American Psychologist*, 49, 15–24.

Adler, P. A., and Adler, P. (1988) 'Intense Loyalty in Organizations: A Case Study of College Athletics', *Administrative Science Quarterly*, 33, 401–17.

Adler, P. S. (1993) 'Time and Motion Regained', *Harvard Business Review*, 71, January/February, 97–108.

Allen, N. J. and Meyer, J. P. (1990) 'The Measurement and Antecedents of Affective, Continuance and Normative Commitment', *Journal of Occupational Psychology*, 63, 1–18.

Allison, G. T. (1971) *Essence of Decision: Explaining the Cuban Missile Crisis*, Boston, Little Brown & Co.

Alpert, G. P. (1978) 'Prisons as Formal Organizations: Compliance Theory in Action', *Sociology and Social Research*, 63, 112–130.

Alvesson, M. and Willmott, H. (1996) *Making Sense of Management*, London, Sage.

Alvesson, M. and Billing, Y. D. (1997) *Understanding Gender and Organizations*, London, Sage.

Anderson, J. C., Manus, R. and Schroeder, R. G. 'A Theory of Quality Underlying the Deming Management Method', *Academy of Management Review*, 19, 472–509.

Appelbaum, S. H. and Hughes, B. (1998) 'Ingratiation as a Political Tactic: Effects Within the Organization', *Management Decision*, 36, 85–95.

Ashford, S. J. and Black, J. S. (1996) 'Proactivity During Organizational Entry: The Role of Desire for Control', *Journal of Applied Psychology*, 26, 199–214.

Assad, T. (1987) 'On Ritual and Discipline in Medieval Christian Monasticism', *Economy and Society*, 16, 159–203.

Aven, F. F., Parker, B. and Mcevoy, G. M. (1993) 'Gender and Attitudinal Commitment to Organizations: A Meta Analysis', *Journal of Business Research*, 26, 63–73.

Bacharach, P., and Baratz, M. S. (1963) 'Decisions and Non-decisions: An Analytical Framework', *American Political Science Review*, 56, 947–82.

—— (1970) *Power and Poverty: The Theory and Practice*, New York, Oxford University Press.

Bacharach, S. B. and Lawler, E. J. (1980) *Power and Politics in Organizations*, London, Jossey Bass.

Bagaloni, A. J., and Cooper, C. L. (1988) 'A Structural Model Approach to the Development of a Theory of the Link Between Stress and Mental Health', *British Journal of Medical Psychology*, 61, 87–102.

Baker, A. J. (1982) 'The Problem of Authority in Radical Movement Groups: A Case Study of a Lesbian Feminist Organization', *Journal of Applied Behaviour*, 18, 323–41.

Barley, S. R. (1983) 'Semiotics and the Study of Occupational and Organizational Cultures', *Administrative Science Quarterly*, 28, 393–413.

Barley, S. R. and Knight, D. B. (1992) 'Toward a Cultural Theory of Stress Complaints', in B. Staw and L. L. Cummings *Research in Organization Behavior*, 14, 1–48.

Barnard, C. (1938) *The Functions of the Executive*, Cambridge Mass., Harvard.

Barton, J. (1994) 'Choosing to Work at Night: A Moderating Influence on Individual Tolerance to Shift Work', *Journal of Applied Psychology*, 79, 449–54.

Bartram, D. (1997) *Review of Ability and Aptitude Tests*, (Level A), Leicester, British Psychological Society.

Bartram, D., Anderson, N., Kellett, D., Lindley, P. , Robertson, I. (1995) *Review of Personality Assessment Instruments for Use in Occupational Settings* (Level B), Leicester, British Psychological Society.

Bass, B. M. (1985) *Leadership and Performance Beyond Expectations*, New York, Free Press.

—— (1990) *Bass and Stogdill's Handbook of Leadership: Theory Research and Applications*, New York, Free Press.

Bauman, Z. (1989) *Modernity and the Holocaust*, Cambridge, Polity Press.

Bazerman, M. H. (1984) 'The Relevance of Kahneman and Tversky's Concept of Framing to Organization Behaviour', *Journal of Management*, 10, 333–43.

—— (1998) *Judgement in Managerial Decision Making*, New York, John Wiley.

Becker, H. S. (1960) 'Notes on the Concept of Commitment', *American Journal of Sociology*, 66, 32–40.

Becker, T. E. (1992) 'Foci and Bases of Commitment: Are They Distinctions Worth Making?' *Academy of Management Journal*, 35, 232–44.

Begley, T. M., and Czajka, J. M. (1993) 'Path Analysis of the Moderating Effects of Commitment on Job Satisfaction, Intent to Quit, and Health Following Organizational Change', *Journal of Applied Psychology*, 78, 552–6.

Belbin, M. (1981) *Management Teams*, London, Heinemann.

Berg, P. O., and Kreiner, K. (1990) 'Corporate Architecture: Turning Physical Settings into Symbolic Resources', in P. Gagliardi (ed.), *Symbols and Artifacts: Views of the Corporate Landscape*, Berlin, de Gruyter, 41–67.

Berger, J. (1972) *Ways of Seeing*, Harmondsworth, Penguin.

Berger, P. T. and Luckman T. (1966) *The Social Construction of Reality*, New Jersey: Doubleday.

Bettleheim, B. (1943) 'Individual and Mass Behaviour in Extreme Situations', *Journal of Abnormal and Social Psychology*, 38, 417–52.

Bevan, K. (1995) 'Business Travel: How to Attract Lucky Dragons', *Financial Times*, 2 October, 18.

Beyer, J., and Trice, H. (1987) 'How an Organization's Rites Reveal its Culture', *Organizational Dynamics*, 15, 5–23.

Bierstedt, R. (1950) 'An Analysis of Social Power', *American Sociological Review*, 15, 730–8.

Blackburn, J. D. (ed.) (1991) *Time-Based Competition*, Homewood, Irwin.

Blake, R. R., and Mouton, J. S. (1985) *The Managerial Grid*, Gulf, Houston.

Blau, P. M. and Scott, R. W. (1963) *Formal Organizations: A Comparative Approach*, London, Routledge.

Bloch, H. A. (1947) 'The Personality of Inmates of Concentration Camps', *American Journal of Sociology*, 52, 335–41.

Bourgeois, V. W. and Pinder, C. C. (1983) 'Contrasting Philosophical Perspectives in Administrative Science: A Reply to Morgan', *Administrative Science Quarterly*, 28, 608–13.

Bowen, M. G. (1987) 'The Escalation Phenomenon Reconsidered: Decision Dilemmas or Decision Errors', *Academy of Management Review*, 12, 52–66.

Bower, T. (1992) *Maxwell: The Outsider*, London, Mandarin.

—— (1996) *Maxwell: The Final Verdict*, London, HarperCollins.

Bowles, M. L. (1989) 'Myth, Meaning and Work Organization', *Organization Studies*, 10, 405–21.

Boyle, J. (1973) *A Sense of Freedom*, Harmondsworth, Penguin.

Braverman, H. (1974) *Labour Monopoly Capital*, New York, Monthly Review Press.

Breach, I. (1998) 'Sobering Facts about Booze in the Workplace', *Financial Times*, 18 December, 16.

Brockner, J. (1992) 'The Escalation of Commitment to a Failing Course of Action: Toward Theoretical Progress', *Academy of Management Review*, 17, 39–61.

Brockner, J., Tyler, T. R. and Cooper-Schneider, R. (1992) 'The Influence of Prior Commitment to an Institution on Reactions to Perceived Unfairness: The Higher They are, the Harder They Fall', *Administrative Science Quarterly*, 37, 241–61.

Brown, W. (1960) *Exploration in Management*, Harmondsworth, Penguin.

Brown, R. H. (1977) *A Poetic for Sociology*, Cambridge, Cambridge University Press.

—— (1989) *Social Science as Civic Discourse*, Chicago, University of Chicago Press.

Brown-Humes, C. (1998) 'Investors Hope Halifax's New Chief Keeps his Eye on the Ball', *Financial Times*, 20 November, 28.

Bryman, A. (1996) 'Leadership in Organizations', in S. R. Clegg., C. Hardy, and W. Nord (eds.) *Handbook of Organization Studies*, London, Sage, 276–92.

—— (1992) *Charisma and Leadership in Organisations*, London, Sage.

—— (1998) *Doing Research in Organizations*, London, Sage.

Burns, J. M. (1978) *Leadership*, New York, Harper and Row.

Burns, L. R., Andersen, R. M., Shortell, S. M. (1990) 'The Effect of Hospital Control Strategies on Physician Satisfaction and Physician–Hospital Conflict', *Health Service Review*, 25, 527–60.

Burns, T. and Stalker, G. M. (1961) *The Management of Innovation*, London, Tavistock.

Burrell, G. (1984) 'Sex and Organizational Analysis', *Organization Studies*, 5, 97–118.

—— (1998) *Pandemonium: Towards a Retro Organization Theory*, London, Sage.

Burrell, G. and Morgan, G. (1979) *Sociological Paradigms and Organizational Analysis*, Chicago, University of Chicago Press.

Burrell, I. (1997) 'How Stress Distorts a Healthy View of Life', *The Independent*, 13 June, 18.

Caldwell, D. F., and O'Reilly, C. A. (1982) 'Responses to Failures: the Effects of Choices and Responsibility on Impression Management', *Academy of Management Journal*, 25, 121–36.

Calivino, I. (1978) *The Castle of Crossed Destinies*, trs. by W. Weaver, London, Pan.

Cameron, K. S. and Quinn, R. E. (1988) 'Organizational Paradox and Transformation', in R. E. Quinn and K. S. Cameron (eds.) *Paradox and Transformation: Toward a Theory of Change in Organization and Management*, Cambridge, Mass: Ballinger.

Cappelli, P. and Rogovsky, N. (1995) 'What do New Systems Demand of Employees?' *Financial Times: Mastering Management*, 24 November, II.

Carey, A. (1967) 'The Hawthorne Studies: a Radical Criticism', *American Sociological Review*, 32, 403–16.

Cartwright, D. (1973) 'Determinants of Scientific Progress', *American Psychologist*, 28, 222–31.

Cartwright, S. and Cooper, C. L. (1994) *No Hassle: Taking the Stress Out of Work*, London, Century.

—— (1995) 'Why Suitors Should Consider Culture', *Financial Times*, 1 September, 8.

—— (1997) *Managing Workplace Stress*, London, Sage.

Champy, J. (1995) *Reengineering Management: The Mandate for New Leadership*, New York, Harper Business.

Chia, R. (1996) 'Metaphors and Metaphorization in Organizational Analysis: Thinking Beyond the Thinkable', in D. Grant and C. Ostwick (eds.) *Metaphor and Organizations*, London, Sage.

Chow, E. N. L. and Grusky, O. (1980) 'Productivity Aggressiveness and Supervisory Style', *Sociology and Social Research*, 65, 23–36.

Clark, A., Oswald, A. and Warr, P. (1996) 'Is Job Satisfaction U-Shaped in Age?' *Journal of Occupational and Organizational Psychology*, 69, 57–81,

Clark, T. and Salaman, G. (1996) 'The Management Guru as Organizational Witchdoctor', *Organization*, 3, 85–107.

Clegg, S. R. (1979) *The Theory of Power and Organization*, London, Routledge.

—— (1989) *Frameworks of Power*, London, Sage.

—— (1994) 'Power Relations and the Constitution of the Resistant Subject', in J. M. Jerimer, D. Knights, and W. R. Nord (eds.), *Resistance and Power in Organizations*, London, Routledge.

Clegg, S. R., and Dunkerly, D. (1980) *Organization, Class and Control*, London, Routledge.

Clegg, S. R. and Gray, J. (1996) 'Metaphors in Organizational Research: of Embedded Embryos, Paradigms and Powerful People', in D. Grant and C. Ostwick (eds.) *Metaphor and Organizations*, London, Sage.

Cohen, M. D., March, J. G., and Olsen, J. P. (1972) 'A Garbage Can Model of Organizational Choice', *Administrative Science Quarterly*, 17, 1–25.

Cohen, N., Denton, N., Sharpe, A., Urry, M., Waters, R., and Wighton, D. (1995) 'The Takeover of S. G. Warburg: Year that Killed the Global Dream', *Financial Times*, 22 May, 20.

Collinson, D. (1988) 'Engineering Humour: Masculinity, Joking and Conflict in Shopfloor Relations', *Organization Studies*, 9, 181–99.

—— (1992) *Managing the Shopfloor: Subjectivity, Masculinity and Workplace Culture*, Berlin, De Gruyter.

—— (1994) 'Strategies of Resistance: Power, Knowledge and Subjectivity in the Workplace', in J. M. Jerimer, D. Knights, and W. R. Nord (eds.), *Resistance and Power in Organizations*, London, Routledge.

Conlon, D. E. and Garland, H. (1993) 'The Role of Project Completion in Resource Allocation Decisions', *Academy of Management Journal*, 36, 402–13.

Cook, J. D. and Wall, T. D. (1980) 'New Work Attitude Measures of Trust, Organizational Commitment and Personal Need Non-fulfilment', *Journal of Occupational Psychology*, 53, 39–52.

Cooper, C. L., Cooper, R. D. and Eaker, L. H. (1988) *Living With Stress*, London, Penguin.

Cooper, C. L., Davidson, M. and Robinson, P. (1982) 'Stress in the Police Service', *Journal of Occupational Medicine*, 24, 30–6.

Cooper, C. L., Makin, P. and Cox, C. (1993) 'Managing the Boss', *Leadership and Organization Development Journal*, 19, 28–32.

Cooper, C. L., Mallinger, M. and Kahn, R. (1978) 'Identifying Sources of Occupational Stress Among Dentists', *Journal of Occupational Psychology*, 51, 227–34.

Cooper, C. L. and Payne, R. (1988) *Causes, Coping and Consequences of Stress at Work*, Chichester, Wiley.

Cooper, C. L., and Sadri, G. (1991) 'The Impact of Stress Counselling at Work', *Journal of Social Behaviour and Personality*, 6, 411–23.

Cooper, C. L. and Smith, M. J. (1985) *Job Stress and Blue Collar Work*, London, John Wiley.

Cordes, C. L., and Dougherty, T. W. (1993) 'A Review and Integration of Research on Job Burnout', *Academy of Management Review*, 18, 621–56.

Cordon, C. (1995) 'Ways to Improve the Company: What are Re-engineering, Bench Marking and Continuous Improvement?' *Financial Times: Mastering Management*, 10 November, xiii.

Cox, T. (1980) 'Repetitive Work', in C. L. Cooper and R. Payne, (eds.) *Current Concerns in Occupational Stress*, Chichester, Wiley.

Crainer, S. (1995) 'Management Dressed to Obsess', *Financial Times*, 19 July, 12.

Crick, B. (1976) *In Defence of Politics*, Harmondsworth, Penguin.

Cummings, T. and Cooper, C. L. (1979) 'A Cybernetic Framework for the Study of Occupational Stress', *Human Relations*, 32, 395–419.

Cunnison, S. (1963) *Wages and Work Allocation*, London, Tavistock.

Curphey, M. (1998) 'Brokers Dress up as the Markets Tumble Down', *The Times*, 1 September, 44.

Dahl, R. A. (1957) 'The Concept of Power', *Behavioural Science* 2, 201–18.

Dalton, M. (1948) 'The Industrial Ratebuster', *Applied Anthropology*, 7, 5–18.

Daily, R. L. (1986) 'Understanding Organization Commitment for Volunteers: Empirical and Managerial Implications', *Journal of Voluntary Action Research*, 15, 671–89.

Dandridge, T. C. (1986) 'Ceremony as Integration of Work and Play', *Organization Studies*, 7, 159–70.

Dandridge, T. C., Mitroff, I. and Joyce, W. F. (1980) 'Organizational Symbolism: a Topic to Expand Organizational Analysis', *Academy of Management Review*, 5, 77–82.

Davenport, T. (1993) *Process Innovation*, Boston, Mass., Harvard Business School Press.

Dawson, P. and Webb, J. (1989) 'New Production Arrangements: The Totally Flexible Cage?' *Work, Employment and Society*, 3, 221–38.

Deal, T. and Kennedy, A. (1988) *Corporate Cultures: The Rites and Rituals of Corporate Life*, Harmondsworth, Penguin.

De Bono, E. (1977) *Lateral Thinking: A Textbook of Creativity*, Harmondsworth, Penguin.

—— (1990) *Lateral Thinking for Management*, Harmondsworth, Penguin.

—— (1995) *Parallel Thinking*, Harmondsworth, Penguin.

—— (1997) *Textbook of Wisdom*, Harmondsworth, Penguin.

Delbridge, R., and Turnbull, P. (1992) 'Human Resource Maximisation: The Management of Labour Under just-in-time Manufacturing Systems', in P. Blyton and P. Turnbull (eds.) *Reassessing Human Resource Management*, London, Sage.

Deming, E. (1986) *Out of the Crisis*, Cambridge, Cambridge University Press.

—— (1993) *The New Economics for Industry*, Cambridge, Mass., Cambridge University Press.

Denison, D. R. (1996) 'What is the Difference Between Organizational Culture and Organizational Climate? A Native's Point of View on a Decade of Paradigm Wars', *Academy of Management Review*, 21, 619–54.

Denscombe, M. *The Good Research Guide*, Open University, Buckingham.

Dias De Oliveira, E. T. V. (1996) 'The Development and Inter-relations of Organizational and Professional Commitment: An Empirical Study of Solicitors in Large Law Firms', Ph D thesis, University of Liverpool, UK.

Dickens, C. (1989) *Hard Times*, Oxford, Oxford University Press.

Doise, W. (1969) 'Intergroup Relations and Polarization in Individual and Collective Judgements', *Journal of Personality and Social Psychology*, 12, 136–43.

Downs, A. (1967) *Inside Bureaucracy*, Boston, Little Brown & Co.

Drucker, P. F. (1954) *The Practice of Management*, New York, Harper and Row.

Drummond, H. (1991) *Power: Creating It, Using It*, London, Kogan Page.

—— (1992) 'Triumph or Disaster: What is Reality?' *Management Decision*, 30, 29–33.

—— (1992) *The Quality Movement*, London, Kogan Page.

—— (1995) 'Beyond Quality', *Journal of General Management*, 20, 68–77.

—— (1995) De-escalation in Decision Making: A Case of a Disastrous Partnership', *Journal of Management Studies*, 32, 265–81.

—— (1996) *Effective Decision Making*, London, Kogan Page.

—— (1996) *Escalation in Decision Making: The Tragedy of Taurus*, Oxford, Oxford University Press.

—— (1996) 'The Politics of Risk: Trials and Tribulations of Taurus', *Journal of Information Technology*, 11, 347–57.

—— (1997) 'Giving it a Week and then

Another Week: A Case of Escalation in Decision Making', *Personnel Review*, 26, 99–113.

Drummond, H. (1998) 'Go and Say "We're Shutting": Ju-jitsu as a Metaphor for Analysing Resistance', *Human Relations*, 51, 1–19.

Drummond, H. and Chell, E. (1992) 'Should Organizations Pay for Quality?' *Personnel Review*, 21, 3–11.

Drummond, H. and Kingstone-Hodgson, J. (1996) 'Something Fishy: Heavy Industry and Women's Employment', *Work Study*, 45, 21–3.

—— 'The Chimpanzees' tea-party: A New Metaphor for IT Project Management', unpublished mimeo, University of Liverpool.

DuBrin, A. (1978) *Winning at Office Politics*, New York, Ballantine.

Du Gay, P. and Salaman, G. (1992) 'The (Cult)ure of the Customer', *Journal of Management Studies*, 29, 615–33.

Durham, K. (1992) *The New City*, London Macmillan.

Durkheim, E. (1934) *The Division of Labour in Society*, London, Macmillan.

Dyer, G. (1995) *The Missing of the Somme*, Harmondsworth, Penguin.

Dyer, W. G. Jr. and Wilkins, A. L. (1991) 'Better Stories, Not Better Constructs to Generate Better Theory: A Rejoinder to Eisenhardt', *Academy of Management Review*, 16, 613–19.

Ebbessen, E. B. and Konecni, V. J. (1980) 'On the External Validity of Decision-Making Research: What do we Know About Decisions in the Real World?' In T. S. Wallsten (ed.), *Cognitive Processes in Choice and Decision Behaviour*, Hillsdale, NJ, Erlbaum, 21–45.

Eisenberg, P. and Lazarsfeld, P. F. (1938) 'The Psychological Effects of Unemployment', *Psychological Bulletin*, 35, 358–90.

Eisenhardt, K. E. and Bourgeois, L. J. (1988) 'Politics of Strategic Decision Making in High-velocity Environments: Toward a Mid-range Theory', *Academy of Management Journal*, 31, 737–70.

Eisenhardt, K. M. and Westcott, B. J. (1988) 'Paradoxical Demands and the Creation of Excellence: The Case of just-in-time Manufacturing', in R. E. Quinn and K. S. Cameron (eds.) *Paradox and Transformation: Toward a Theory of Change in Organization and Management*, Cambridge, Mass., Ballinger.

Etzioni, A. (1959) 'Authority Structure and Organizational Effectiveness', *Administrative Science Quarterly*, 4, 43–7.

—— (1965) 'Dual Leadership in Complex Organizations', *American Sociological Review*, 30, 688–98.

—— (1965) 'Organizational Control Structure', in J. G. March (ed.) *Handbook of Organizations*, Chicago, Rand McNally.

—— (1975) *A Comparative Analysis of Complex Organizations*, London, Collier Macmillan.

—— (1989) 'Humble Decision Making', *Harvard Business Review*, July/August, 122–26.

Farkas, C. M. and Wetlaufer, S. (1996) 'The Ways Chief Executive Officers Lead', *Harvard Business Review*, May/June, 110–22.

Festinger (1957) *A Theory of Cognitive Dissonance*, New York, Harper and Row.

Fiedler, F. E. (1967) *A Theory of Leadership Effectiveness*, New York, McGraw Hill.

Fiedler, F. E. and Garcia, J. E. (1987) *New Approaches to Leadership: Cognitive Resources and Organizational Performance*, New York, Wiley.

Financial Times, 'After Taurus: City Lessons', 23 March 1993, 21.

Fineman, S. (1996) 'Emotion and Organizing', in S. R. Clegg., C. Hardy, and W. Nord (eds.) *Handbook of Organization Studies*, London, Sage, 543–64.

Fisher, S. (1993) 'The Pull of the Fruit Machine: A Sociological Typology of Young Players', *Sociological Review*, 41, 446–74.

Fisher, R. and Ury, W. (1983) *Getting to Yes*, London, Hutchinson.

Fourcher, L. A. (1975) 'Compliance Structures and Change within Mental Health Service Organizations', *Sociology of Work and Occupations*, 2, 246–56.

Fox, F., and Staw, B. M. (1979) 'The Trapped Administrator: The Effects of Job Insecurity and Policy Resistance Upon Commitment to a Course of Action', *Administrative Science Quarterly*, 24, 449–71.

French, J. R. P. and Caplan, R. D. (1972) 'Occupational Stress and Individual Strain', in A. J. Marrow (ed.) *The Failure of Success*, New York, Amacom, 31–66.

French, J. R., and Raven, B. (1968) 'The Bases of Social Power', in D. Cartwright and A. Zander (eds.), *Group Dynamics*, New York, Harper and Row.

Friedman, M. and Rosenman, R. H. (1974) *Type A Behaviour and Your Heart*, New York, Knopf.

Friedman, S. D., Christensen, P. and Degroot, J. (1995) 'Developing a Work/Life Balance', *Financial Times: Mastering Management*, November 10, v.

Frone, M. R., Russell, M. and Cooper, M. L. (1997) 'Relation of Work–Family Conflict to Health Outcomes: A Four Year Longitudinal Study of Employed Parents', *Journal of Occupational and Organizational Psychology*, 70, 325–35.

Funder, D. C. (1987) 'Errors and Mistakes: Evaluating the Accuracy of Social Judgement', *Psychological Bulletin*, 101, 75–90.

Gagliardi, P. (1986) 'The Creation and Change of Organizational Cultures: A Conceptual Framework', *Organization Studies*, 7, 117–34.

—— (1996) 'Exploring the Aesthetic side of Organizational Life', in S. R. Clegg, C. Hardy, and W. R. Nord, *Handbook of Organization Studies*, London, Sage.

Galbraith, J. K. (1984) *The Anatomy of Power*, London, Hamish Hamilton.

Gantt, H. (1919) *Organizing for Work*, New York, Harcourt Brace.

Ganster, D. C., Fusilier, M. R. and Bronston, T. M. (1986) 'Role of Social Support in the Experiences of Stress at Work', *Journal of Applied Psychology*, 71, 102–10.

Gapper, J. and Denton, N. (1996) *All that Glitters: the Fall of Barings*, Harmondsworth, Penguin.

Garfunkel, H. (1956) 'Conditions of Successful Degradation Ceremonies', *American Sociological Review*, 61, 420–24.

Garud, R., and Kotha, S. (1994) 'Using the Brain as a Metaphor to Model Flexible Production Systems', *Academy of Management Review*, 19, 671–98.

Gents, J. and Maare, V. V. (1980) 'The Experience of Workplace Politics', *Academy of Management Journal*, 23, 237–51.

Gephart, R. P. (1978) 'Status Degradation and Organizational Succession: An Ethnomethodological Approach', *Administrative Science Quarterly*, 23, 553–81.

Gerth, H. H. and Mills, C. W. (eds.) (1991) *From Max Weber: Essays in Sociology*, new Preface by Bryan S. Turner, London, Routledge.

Giddens, A. (1979) *Central Problems in Social Theory*, London, Macmillan.

Gilbert, M. (1994) *Winston S. Churchill, 1914–1916*, Companion vol. iii, London, Heinemann.

—— (1994) *In Search of Churchill*, London, Harper Collins.

Gilberth, F. B. (1908) *Field System*, New York, Myron Clark.

Gilberth, F. B. and Gilberth, L. (1916) *Fatigue Study*, New York, Sturgis and Walton.

Gioia, D. A. and Pitre, E. (1990) 'Multi-paradigm Perspectives on Theory Building', *Academy of Management Review*, 15, 584–602.

'Goldman team steps closer to windfall', (1998) *The Times*, p. 21.

Goffee, R. (1997) 'Cultural Diversity', in Bickerstaffe, G. (ed.) *Mastering Management*, London, Pitman, 240–46.

Gouldner, A. W. (1954) *Patterns of Industrial Bureaucracy*, Glencoe, Free Press.

—— (1957) 'Cosmopolitans and Locals: Towards an Analysis of Latent Social Roles', *Administrative Science Quarterly*, 2, 281–306.

Graham, G. (1999) 'Scientific Certainties have taken a Beating', *Financial Times*, 29 January, Survey of Global Investment Banking, 3.

Graham, L. (1993) 'Inside a Japanese Transplant: A Critical Perspective', *Work and Occupations*, 20, 147–93.

Grant, D. and Oswick, C. (1996) 'Getting the Measure of Metaphors', in D. Grant and C. Ostwick (eds.) *Metaphor and Organizations*, London, Sage.

Grey, C. and Mitev, N. (1995) 'Re-engineering Organizations: A Critical Appraisal', *Personnel Review*, 24, 6–18.

Griffin, R. W. (1991) 'Effects of Work Re-design on Employee Perceptions, Attitudes and Behaviours: A Long Term Investigation', *Academy of Management Journal*, 34, 425–35.

Guest, D. E. (1990) 'Human Resource Management and the American Dream', *Journal of Management Studies*, 27, 377–97.

Hackett, R. D. and Bycio, P. (1996) 'An Evaluation of Employee Absenteeism as a Coping Mechanism Among Hospital Nurses', *Journal of Occupational and Organizational Psychology*, 69, 327–38.

Hackman, J. R. (1976) 'Group Influences on Individuals', in M. D. Dunnette (ed.) *Handbook of Industrial and Organizational Psychology*, Chicago, Rand Mcnally, 1455–525.

Hackman, J. R. and Oldham, G. R. (1980) *Work Redesign*, Reading, Mass., Addison Wesley.

Hackman, J. R. and Wageman, R. (1995) 'Total Quality Management: Empirical, Conceptual and Practical Issues', *Administrative Science Quarterly*, 40, 309–42.

Hall, R. H. (1987) *Organizations: Structure, Processes, Outcomes*, Englewood Cliffs, Prentice Hall.

Hammer, M. (1990) 'Reengineering Work: Don't Automate Obliterate', *Harvard Business Review*, 67, 104–12.

Hammer, M. and Champy, J. (1993) *Reengineering the Corporation: A Manifesto for Business Revolution*, New York, Harper Business.

Hammer, M. and Stanton, S. A. (1995) *The Reengineering Revolution: A Handbook*, New York, Harper Business.

Hardin, G. (1968) 'The Tragedy of the Commons', *Science*, 162, 1243–8.

Hardy, C. (1985) 'The Nature of Unobtrusive Power', *Journal of Management Studies*, 22, 384–99.

Hatch, M. J. (1997) 'Irony and Social Construction of Contradiction in the Humor of a Management Team', *Organization Science* 8, 275–88.

—— 'Exploring the Empty Spaces of Organizing: How Improvisational Jazz Redescribes Organizational Structure', *Organization Studies* (forthcoming).

Hatch, M. J. and Ehrlich, S. B. (1993) 'Spontaneous Humour as an Indicator of Paradox and Ambiguity in Organizations', *Organization Studies*, 14, 505–26.

Hawking, S. (1988) *A Brief History of Time*, London, Bantam.

Hayes, J. (1984) 'The Politically Competent Manager', *Journal of General Management*, 10, 24–33.

Hayes, J. and Nutman, P. (1981) *Understanding the Unemployed*, London, Tavistock.

Hedberg, B., and Jonsonn, S. (1977) 'Strategy Formulation as a Discontinuous Process', *International Studies of Management and Organization*, 7, 88–109.

Heider, F. (1958) *The Psychology of Interpersonal Relations*, New York, Wiley.

Herzberg, F. (1968) 'One More Time, How do you Motivate Employees?' *Harvard Business Review*, January/February, 53–62.

Herzberg, F., Mausner, B. and Snyderman, B. B. *The Motivation to Work*, New York, Wiley.

Hickson, D. J., Hinings, C. R., Lee, C. A., Schneck, R. H., Pennings, J. M. (1971) 'A Strategic Contingencies Theory of Intra-organizational Power', *Administrative Science Quarterly*, 16, 216–19.

Hingley, P. and Cooper, C. L. (1986) *Stress and the Nurse Manager*, London, John Wiley.

Hobbs, D. (1988) *Doing the Business*, Oxford, Clarendon.

Hochschild, A. R. (1983) *The Managed Heart: Commercialisation of Human Feeling*, London, University of California.

Hofstede, G. (1980) *Culture's Consequences: International Differences in Work Related Values*, Beverly Hills, Sage.

—— (1994) *Culture in Organizations*, London, HarperCollins.

Holmes, T. H. and Rahe, R. H. (1967) 'The Social Readjustment Scale', *Journal of Psychomatic Research*, 11, 213–18.

Horlick, N. (1997) *Can You Have It All?*, Harmondsworth, Penguin.

Houlder, V. (1998) 'Keeping the Body in Mind', *Financial Times*, March 19, 16.

House, R. J. (1971) 'A Path-goal Theory of Leader Effectiveness', *Administrative Science Quarterly*, 16, 321–8.

House, R. J. and Mitchell, R. R. (1974) 'Path Goal Theory of Leadership', *Journal of Contemporary Business*, 3, 81–97.

Howard, K and Sharp, J. (1983) *The Management of a Student Research Project*, Aldershot, Gower.

Howard, S. (1998) 'Avoid Getting Fired Because you don't Fit', *The Sunday Times*, 1 November, 20.

Huczynski, A. and Buchanan, D. (1991) *Organizational Behaviour*, London, Prentice Hall.

Inquiry into the Supervision of the Bank of Credit and Commerce International (1992) (Bingham Report) London, HMSO.

Ishikawa, K. (1985) *What is Total Quality Control? The Japanese Way*, Englewood Cliffs, Prentice Hall.

Ivancevich, J. M. and Matteson, M. T. (1980) *Stress at Work*, Glenview Ill., Scott Foresman.

Ivancevich, J. M., Matteson, M. T. and Richards, E. P. (1985) 'Who's Liable for Stress on the Job?' *Harvard Business Review*, March/April, 60–72.

Izraeli, D. M. and Jick, T. J. (1986) 'The Art of Saying No: Linking Power to Culture', *Organization Studies*, 7, 171–92.

Jackson, B. G. (1996) 'Re-engineering the Sense of Self: The Manager and the Management Guru', *Journal of Management Studies*, 33, 571–90.

Jackson, S. E. (1983) 'Participation in Decision Making as a Strategy for Reducing Job Related Strain', *Journal of Applied Psychology*, 68, 3–19.

Jackson, S. E., Schwab, R. L. and Randall, R. S. (1986) 'Toward an Understanding of the Burnout Phenomenon', *Journal of Applied Psychology*, 71, 630–40.

Jackson, T. (1995) 'Copperplate v the Computer', *Financial Times*, 10 April, 13.

—— (1998) 'New Style Quality is Just a Fiddle', *Financial Times*, 29 December, 12.

Janis, I. L. (1972) *Victims of Groupthink*, Boston, Houghton Miflin.

—— (1989) *Crucial Decisions: Leadership in Policy and Crisis Management*, New York, Free Press.

Janis, I. L. and Mann, L. (1977) *Decision Making*, New York, Free Press.

Jaques, E. (1952) *The Changing Culture of a Factory*, London, Tavistock.

Jay, A. (1993) *Management and Machiavelli*, London, Century.

Jelinek, M., Smircich, L., and Hirsch, P. (1983) 'Introduction: A Code of Many Colours', *Administrative Science Quarterly*, 28, 331–8.

Jenkins, R. (1998) 'Hounded Man Defeats His Woman Boss', *The Times*, 2 September.

Johanasson, H. J., McHugh, P., Pendlebury, J. A., and Wheeler, W. A. (1993) *Business Process Engineering: Break-Point Strategies for Market Dominance*, Chichester, John Wiley.

Jones, F. and Fletcher, B. (1996) 'Taking Work Home: A Study of Daily Fluctuations in Work Stressors, Effects on Moods and Impacts on Marital Partners', *Journal of Occupational and Organizational Psychology*, 69, 89–106.

Judge, T. A., Locke, E. A., and Durham, C. C. (1997) 'The Dispositional Causes of Job Satisfaction: A Core Evaluation Approach', in B. Staw and L. L. Cummings (eds.), *Research in Organizational Behavior*, San Francisco, Jossey Bass, 151–88.

Juran, J. M. (1974) *The Quality Control Handbook*, New York, McGraw Hill.

—— (1988) *Juran on Planning for Quality*, New York, Free Press.

Kanner, A. D., Coyne, J. C., Schaefer, C. and Lazarus, R. S. (1981) 'Comparison of Two Models of Stress Management: Daily Hassles and Uplifts Versus Major Life Events', *Journal of Behavioural Medicine*, 4, 1–39.

Kahneman, D. and Tversky, A. (1979) 'Prospect Theory: An Analysis of Decision Under Risk', *Econometrica*, 47, 263–91.

—— (1982) 'The Psychology of Preferences', *Scientific American*, 246, 162–70.

Katz, F. W. (1982) 'Implementation of the Holocaust: The Behaviour of Nazi Officials', *Comparative Study of Society*, 24, 510–29.

Katz, D. and Kahn, R. L. (1966) *The Social Psychology of Organizations*, New York, Wiley.

Kegan, J. (1993) 'Churchill's Strategy', in R. Blake and W. R. Louis (eds.), *Churchill*, Oxford, Oxford University Press, 327–52.

Kets De Vries, M. (1996) 'Leaders Who Make a Difference', *European Management Journal*, 14, 486–93.

Kets De Vries, M. F. R., and Miller, D. A. (1987) 'Interpreting Organizational Texts', *Journal of Management Studies*, 24, 233–48.

Kieser, A. (1987) 'From Asceticism to Administration of Wealth. Medieval Monasteries and the Pitfalls of Rationalization', *Organization Studies*, 8, 103–23.

—— (1989) 'Organizational, Institutional and Societal Evolution: Medieval Craft Guilds and the Genesis of Formal Organizations', *Administrative Science Quarterly*, 34, 540–64.

Kim, S. H. and Smith, R. H. (1993) 'Revenge and Conflict Negotiation', *Negotiation Journal*, 9, 37–43.

Kipnis, D. (1976) *The Powerholders*, Chicago, University of Chicago Press.

Klein, J. A. (1991) 'A Re-examination of Autonomy in the Light of New Manufacturing Processes', *Human Relations*, 44, 21–38.

Knights, D. and Roberts, J. (1982) 'The Power of Organization and the Organization of Power', *Organization Studies*, 3, 47–63.

Knights, D. and Willmott, H. (1990) (eds.) *Labour Process Theory*, London, Macmillan.

—— (1992) 'Conceptualizing Leadership Processes: A Study of Senior Managers in a Financial Services Company', *Journal of Management Studies*, 29, 761–82.

Kobasa, S. C. (1979) ' Stressful Life Events, Personality and Health; An Enquiry into Hardiness', *Journal of Personality and Social Psychology*, January, 1–11.

Kobasa, S. C., Maddi, S. R., and Kahn, S. (1982) 'Hardiness and Health: A Prospective Study', *Journal of Personality and Social Psychology*, January, 168–77.

Korda, M. (1976) *Power!*, New York, Ballantine.

La Nuez, D. and Jermier, J. M. (1994) 'Sabotage by Managers and Technocrats: Neglected Patterns of Resistance at Work', in J. M. Jerimer, D. Knights, and W. R. Nord (eds.), *Resistance and Power in Organizations*, London, Routledge.

Lakoff, G. and Johnson, M. (1980) *Metaphors We Live By*, Chicago, University of Chicago Press.

Lam, A. (1996) 'Engineers, Management and Work Organization: A Comparative Analysis of Engineers' Work Roles in British and Japanese Electronics Firms', *Journal of Management Studies*, 33, 183–212.

Lammers, C. J. (1988) 'The Inter-organizational Control of an Occupied Country', *Administrative Science Quarterly*, 33, 438–57.

Langer, E. J. (1975) 'The Illusion of Control', *Journal of Personality and Social Psychology*, 33, 311–28.

Langer, E. J. (1989) *Mindfulness*, Reading Mass., Addison-Wesley.

Langley, A., Mintzberg, H., Pitcher, P., Posada, E., and Saint-Macary, J. (1995) 'Opening up Decision Making: The View From the Black Stool', *Organization Science*, 6 (3), 260–79.

Larsen, J., and Schultz, M. (1990) 'Artifacts in a Bureaucratic Monastery', in P. Gagliardi (ed.), *Symbols and Artifacts: Views of the Corporate Landscape*, Berlin, de Gruyter, 41–67.

Lasswell, H. D. (1963) *Politics: Who Gets What, When, How*, New York, McGraw-Hill.

Lawler, E. E. (1994) 'Total Quality Management and Employee Involvement: Are They Compatible?' *Academy of Management Executive*, 8, 68–76.

Lee, R. T. and Ashforth, B. E. (1996) 'A Meta-analytic Examination of the Correlates of the Three Dimensions of Job Burnout', *Journal of Applied Psychology*, 81, 123–33.

Lewis, M. (1990) *Liar's Poker*, London, Coronet.

Lincoln, J. R. (1989) 'Employee Work Attitudes and Management Practice in the U.S. and Japan: Evidence from a Large Comparative Survey', *California Management Review*, 32, 89–106.

Lindblom, C. E. (1959) 'The Science of "Muddling Through"', *Public Administration Review*, Spring, 79–88.

Locke, E. A. (1976) 'The Nature and Causes of Job Satisfaction', in M. D. Dunnette (ed.) *Handbook of Industrial and Organizational Psychology*, Chicago, Rand McNally.

Locke, E. A. and Latham, G. P. (1990) *A Theory of Goal Setting and Task Performance*, Englewood Cliffs, Prentice Hall.

Lopes, L. L. (1981) 'Decision Making in the Short Run', *Journal of Experimental Psychology*, 7, 377–85.

Lukes, S. (1974) *Power: A Radical View*, London, Macmillan.

Lupton, T. (1963) *On the Shopfloor: Two Studies of Workplace Organization and Output*, Oxford, Pergamon.

Luthans, F., McCaul, H. S., and Dodd, N. G. (1985) 'Organizational Commitment: A Comparison of American, Japanese and Korean Employees', *Academy of Management Journal*, 28, 213–19.

Mackintosh, J. (1998) 'Net Gain could be a Threat', *Financial Times*, 9 November, Private Banking (*Financial Times* Survey), 4.

Makin, P., Cox, C., and Cooper, C. L. (1988) *Managing People at Work*, London, Routledge.

Mangham, I. L. (1990) 'Managing as a Performing Art', *British Journal of Management*, 1, 105–15.

—— (1996) 'Some Consequences of Taking Gareth Morgan Seriously', in D. Grant and C. Ostwick (eds.,) *Metaphor and Organizations*, London, Sage, 21–36.

March, J. G., and Simon, H. A. (1958) *Organizations*, New York, Wiley.

Marsh, R. M. and Mannari, H. (1973) 'Japanese Workers: Responses to Mechanization and Automation', *Human Organization*, 32, 85–93.

Martin, J. and Siehel, C. (1983) 'Organizational Culture and Counter-Culture: An Uneasy Symbiosis', *Organizational Dynamics*, Autumn, 52–64.

Martin, R. (1977) *The Sociology of Power*, London, Routledge.

Marx, G. (1995) *The Groucho Letters*, London, Abacus.

Marx, K. (1967) *Capital*, vol. 1, Harmondsworth, Penguin.

Marx, K. and Engels, F. (1967) *A Communist Manifesto*, Harmondsworth, Penguin.

Maslow, A. H. (1954) *Motivation and Personality*, New York, Harper and Row.

Mathieu, J. E. and Zajac, D. (1990) 'A Review and Meta Analysis of the Antecedents, Correlates, and Consequences of Organizational Commitment', *Psychological Bulletin*, 107, 171–94.

Maule, J. A., Hockey, G. R. J., Clough, P. J., and Bdzola, L. (1998) 'An Experimental Investigation of Mood on Risk Taking: The Relation Between State, Risk-Propensity and Strategy', unpublished mimeo, University of Leeds.

McGregor, D. M. (1960) *The Human Side of Enterprise*, New York, McGraw-Hill.

Mechanic, D. (1962) 'Sources of Power of Lower Participants in Complex Organizations', *Administrative Science Quarterly*, 7, 349–64.

Meek, V. L. (1988) 'Organizational Culture: Origins and Weaknesses', *Organization Studies*, 9, 453–73.

Melamed, S., Ben-Avi, I, Luz, J. and Green, M. S. (1995) 'Objective and Subjective Work Monotony: Effects on Job Satisfaction, Psychological Distress, and Absenteeism in Blue Collar Workers', *Journal of Applied Psychology*, 80, 29–42.

Meyer, J. P. and Allen, N. J. (1997) *Commitment in the Workplace: Theory Research and Application*, London, Sage.

Meyer, J. W. and Rowan, B. (1978) 'Institutionalized Organizations: Formal Structure as Myth and Ceremony', *American Journal of Sociology*, 83, 340–63.

Meyerson, D. E. (1994) 'Interpretation of Stress in Institutions: The Cultural Production of Ambiguity and Burnout', *Administrative Science Quarterly*, 39, 628–53.

Meyerson, D. E. and Martin, J. (1987) 'Cultural Change: An Integration of Three Different Views', *Journal of Management Studies*, 24, 623–47.

Miller, J. D. B. (1962) *The Nature of Politics*, London, Duckworth.

Mills, A. J. (1988) 'Organization, Gender and Culture', *Organization Studies*, 9, 351–69.

Mills, A. J. and Tancred P. (eds.) (1992) *Gendering Organizational Analysis*, London, Sage.

Mills, C. W. (1951) *White Collar*, New York, Oxford University Press.

Mintzberg, H. (1973) *The Nature of Managerial Work*, New York, Harper.

—— (1985) 'The Organization as Political Arena', *Journal of Management Studies*, 22, 133–54.

—— (1994) *The Rise and Fall of Strategic Planning*, New York, Free Press.

Mintzberg, H. A., Raisingham, D., and Thoeret, A. (1976) 'The Structure of Unstructured Decision Processes', *Administrative Science Quarterly*, 21, 146–75.

Mitchell, T. R. (1997) 'Matching Motivational Strategies with Organizational Contexts', in B. Staw and L. L. Cummings (eds.), *Research in Organizational Behavior*, San Francisco, Jossey Bass, 57–149.

Morel, J. (1983) *Pullman*, David and Charles.

Morgan, G. (1980) 'Paradigms, Metaphors and Puzzle Solving in Organization Theory', *Administrative Science Quarterly*, 25, 605–22.

—— (1983) 'More on Metaphor: Why We Cannot Control Tropes in Administrative Science', *Administrative Science Quarterly*, 28, 601–07.

—— (1990) 'Paradigm Diversity in Organizational Research', in J. Hassard and W. Pym (eds.), *The Theory and Philosophy of Organizations*, London, Routledge.

—— (1993) *Imaginization*, London, Sage.

—— (1996) *Images of Organization*, London, Sage.

—— (1996) An Afterword: Is There Anything More to be Said about Metaphor?' in D. Grant and C. Ostwick (eds.), *Metaphor and Organizations*, London, Sage.

Morgan, G., Frost, P. J., and Pondy, L. R. (1983) 'Organizational Symbolism', In Pondy, L. R., Frost, P. J., Morgan, G., and Dandridge, T. C. (eds.) *Organizational Symbolism*, London, JAI, 3–35.

Morris, W. (1934) *Selected Writings*, Glasgow, Glasgow University Press.

Mowday, R. T. (1991) 'Equity Theory Predictions of Behaviour in Organizations', in R. M. Steers and L. W. Porter (eds.) *Motivation and Work Behaviour*, Chicago, St Clair, 111–30.

Mowday, R. T., Porter, L., and Steers, R. H. (1982) *Employee–Organization Linkages, the Psychology of Commitment, Absenteeism and Turnover*, London, Academic Press.

Mulford, C. L. (1978) 'Why They Don't Even When They Ought to: Implications of Compliance Theory for Policy Makers', *International Journal of Comparative Sociology*, 19, 47–62.

Mumby, D. K. and Putnam, L. L. (1992) 'The Politics of Emotion: A Feminist Reading of Bounded Rationality', *Academy of Management Review*, 17, 465–86.

Muringham, J. K. and Conlon, D. E. (1991) 'The Dynamics of Intense Work Groups: A Study of British String Quartets', *Administrative Science Quarterly*, 36, 165–86.

Murphy, W. P. (1980) 'Secret Knowledge as Property and Power in Kpelle Society: Elders Versus Youth', *Africa*, 50, 193–207.

Murray, C. (1995) 'Structural Unemployment, Small Towns and Agrarian Change in South Africa', *Journal of African Affairs*, 20, 33–57.

Murray, S. (1998) 'For Better and For Worse', *Financial Times*, 16 October, Mergers and Acquisitions Survey, 6.

Muscovici, S. and Zavalloni, M. (1969) 'The Group as a Polarism of Attitudes', *Journal of Experimental and Social Psychology*, 12, 125–35.

Neale, M. A., Bazerman, M. H., Northcraft, B. G., and Alpèrson, C. A. (1986) ' "Choice Shift" Effects in Group Decisions: A Decision Bias Perspective', *International Journal of Small Group Research*, 2, 33–42.

Near, J. P. (1989) 'Organizational Commitment among Japanese and US Workers', *Organization Studies*, 10, 281–300.

Near, J. P. and Miceli, M. P. (1995) 'Effective Whistle Blowing', *Academy of Management Review*, 20, 679–708.

Northcraft, G. B. and Wolfe, M. A. (1984) 'Dollars Sense and Sunk Costs. A Life Cycle Model of Resource Allocation Decisions', *Academy of Management Review*, 9, 225–34.

Northouse, P. (1997) *Leadership: Theory and Practice*, London, Sage.

Nyerere, J. (1973) *Freedom and Development*, Dares Salaam, Oxford University Press.

Ogbonna, E. (1992) 'Organization Culture and Human Resource Management: Dilemmas and Contradictions', in P. Blyton and P. Turnbull (eds.), *Reassessing Human Resource Management*, London, Sage.

Ohno, T. with Mito, S. (1988) *Just-In-Time For Today and Tomorrow*, Cambridge Mass., Productivity Press.

Ollard, R. (1984) *Samuel Pepys*, Oxford, Oxford University Press.

O'Reilly, C. A., and Caldwell, D. F. (1979) 'Informational Influence as a Determinant of Perceived Task Characteristics and Job Satisfaction', *Journal Of Applied Psychology*, 64, 157–65.

Ouchi, W. G. (1980) 'Markets, Bureaucracies and Clans', *Administrative Science Quarterly* 25, 129–41.

Overell, S. (1998) 'Bishops and Clerics Prepare for Battle', *Financial Times*, 13 November, 13.

'Oxbridge Men Dominate FTSE 100 Companies', (1998) *Financial Times*, 25 November, 33.

Partnoy, F. (1997) *F.I.A.S.C.O*, London, Profile.

Pascale, R. T. and Athos, A. G. (1982) *The Art of Japanese Management*, Harmondsworth, Penguin.

Pauchant, T. and Mitroff, I. (1992) *Transforming the Crisis-Prone Organization: Preventing Individual, Organizational, and Environmental Tragedies*, Jossey-Bass.

Pearson, C. L. and Chong, J. (1997) 'Contributions of Job Content and Social Information on Organizational Commitment and Job Satisfaction: An Exploration in a Malaysian Nursing Context', *Journal of Occupational and Organizational Psychology*, 70, 357–74.

Perrow, C. (1979) *Complex Organizations: A Critical Essay*, Illinois, Scott Foreman.

Peters, T. J. (1978) 'Symbols Patterns and Settings: An Optimistic Case for Getting Things Done', *Organizational Dynamics*, 9, 3–23.

—— (1988) *Thriving on Chaos*, New York, Knopf.

Peters, T., and Waterman, R. H. (1982) *In Search of Excellence: Lessons from America's Best-Run Companies*, New York, Harper and Row.

Pettigrew, A. (1973) *The Politics of Organizational Decision Making*, London, Tavistock.

Pettigrew, A. M. (1979) 'On Studying Organizational Cultures', *Administrative Science Quarterly*, 24, 570–640.

Pfeffer, J. (1977) 'The Ambiguity of Leadership', *Academy of Management Review*, 2, 104–12.

—— (1981) 'Management as Symbolic Action', in L. Cummings and B. Staw (eds.) *Research in Organizational Behaviour*, Greenwich, Conn., JAI Press.

—— (1982) *Power in Organizations*, Boston, Pitman.

—— (1992) *Managing with Power in Organizations*, Boston, Harvard Business School.

Pfeffer, J. and Langton, N. (1993) 'The Effect of Wage Dispersion on Satisfaction, Productivity and Working Collaboratively: Evidence from College and University

Faculty', *Administrative Science Quarterly*, 38, 382–407.

Pinder, C. C. (1984) *Work Motivation: Theories, Issues, Applications*, Glenview, Scott Foresman.

Pinder, C. C. and Bourgeois, V. W. (1982) 'Controlling Tropes in Administrative Science', *Administrative Science Quarterly*, 27, 641–52.

Podsakoff, P. M. (1982) 'Determinants of Supervisors Use of Reward and Punishment: A Literature Review and Suggestions for Future Research', *Organizational Behaviour and Human Performance*, 29, 58–83.

Podsakoff, P. M. and Schriesheim, C. A. (1985a) 'Leader Reward and Punishment Behaviour: A Methodological and Substantive Review', in B. Staw and L. L. Cummings (eds.), *Research in Organizational Behaviour*, San Francisco, Jossey Bass.

—— (1985b) 'Field Studies of French and Raven's Bases of Power: Critique, Re-analysis and Suggestions for Future Research', *Psychological Bulletin*, 97, 387–411.

Pollock, E. J. (1998) 'As Corporate Climate Turns Stormy, Workers get Worried about Security', *Wall Street Journal Europe*, 20 October, 4.

Pretzlick, C. (1999) 'Hanson Throws Out Old Image', *Financial Times*, 20 January, 23.

Quaid, M. (1993) 'Job Evaluation as Institutional Myth', *Journal of Management Studies*, 30, 239–60.

Quick, J. C. and Quick, J. D. (1984) *Organizational Stress and Preventative Management*, New York, McGraw-Hill.

Quinn, R. E. (1977) 'Coping with Cupid: The Formation, Impact, and Management of Romantic Relationships in Organizations', *Administrative Science Quarterly*, 22, 30–45.

Quinn, R. E. and Cameron, K. S. (1988) 'Paradox and Transformation', in R. E. Quinn and K. S. Cameron (eds.) *Paradox and Transformation: Toward a Theory of Change in Oganization and Management*, Cambridge, Mass., Ballinger.

Rafaeli, A. (1989) 'When Cashiers Meet Customers: An Analysis of the Role of Supermarket Cashiers', *Academy of Management Journal*, 32, 245–73.

Randall, D. M. (1987) 'Commitment and the Organization Man Revisited', *Academy of Management Review*, 12, 460–71.

Raphael, A. (1995) *Ultimate Risk*, London, Corgi.

Raven, B. H. (1974) 'A Comparative Analysis of Power and Power Preference', in J. T. Tedeschi (ed.), *Perspectives on Social Power*, Chicago, Aldine.

Raven, B. H. and Kruglanski, A. W. (1970) 'Conflict and Power', in P. Swingle (ed.) *The Structure of Conflict*, New York, Academic Press.

Ray, C. A. (1986) 'Corporate Culture: The Last Frontier of Control', *Journal of Management Studies*, 23, 287–99.

Reich, C. (1980) 'The Confessions of Seigmund Warburg', *Institutional Investor*, March, 167–201.

Reichers, A. E. (1985) 'A Review and Re-conceptualisation of Organizational Commitment', *Academy of Management Review*, 10, 465–76.

Reynolds, D. (1993) 'Churchill in 1940: The Worst and Finest Hour', in R. Blake and W. R. Louis (eds.), *Churchill*, Oxford, Oxford University Press, 241–56.

Reynolds, S., Taylor, E. and Shapiro, Z. (1993) 'Session Impact in Stress Management Training', *Journal of Occupational and Organizational Psychology*, 66, 99–113.

Rice, R. and Kelly, J. (1998) 'Arthur Andersen Pulls out of City Law Firm Takeover', *Financial Times*, 4 June, 1998.

Rickert, E. *Chaucer's World*, Oxford, Oxford University Press.

Riley, P. (1983) 'A Structurationist Account of Political Culture', *Administrative Science Quarterly*, 28, 414–37.

Ritzer, G. (1993) *The McDonalization of Society*, London, Sage.

Robert, R. J. (1974) *Winston S. Churchill: His Complete Speeches 1897–1963*, vol. vi, London, Chelsea House.

Roberts, J. (1984) 'The Moral Character of Management Practice', *Journal of Management Studies*, 21, 287–302.

Roberts, R. (1973) *The Classic Slum*, Harmondsworth, Pelican.

Robinson, J. (1998) *The Laundrymen*, London, Pocket Books.

Roethlisberger, F. J. and Dickson, W. J. (1939) *Management and the Worker*, Cambridge, Mass., Harvard University Press.

Rorty, R. (1989) *Contingency, Irony, and Solidarity*, Cambridge, Cambridge University Press.

Rosen, M. (1985) 'Breakfast at Spiro's: Dramaturgy and Dominance', *Journal of Management*, 11, 31–48.

—— (1988) 'You Asked for it: Christmas at the Bosses' expense', *Journal of Management Studies*, 25, 463–80.

Rosenman, R. and Friedman, M. (1971) 'The Central Nervous System and Coronary Heart Disease', *Hospital Practice*, 6, 87–97.

Ross, J. and Staw, B. M. (1986) 'Expo 86: An Escalation Prototype', *Administrative Science Quarterly*, 32, 274–97.

Roy, D. F. (1952) 'Quota Restriction and Goldbricking in a Machine Shop', *American Journal of Sociology*, 57, 427–42.

Roy, D. (1954) 'Efficiency and "The Fix": Informal Group Intergroup Relations in a Piecework Machine Shop', *American Journal of Sociology*, 60, 3, 255–66.

Russell, B. (1938) *Power: A New Social Analysis*, London, Allen & Unwin.

Russell, D. W., Altmaier, E., and Van Velzen, D. (1987) 'Job Related Stress, Social Support and Burnout Among Classroom Teachers', *Journal of Applied Psychology*, 72, 269–74.

Russell, R. (1995) 'Property: How to Buy a Happy Home', *Financial Times*, 16 December, ix.

Salancik, G. R., and Pfeffer, J. (1978) 'A Social Information Processing Approach to Job Attitudes and Task Design', *Administrative Science Quarterly*, 23, 224–53.

Salancik, G. R. and Pfeffer, G. R. (1974) 'The Bases and Uses of Power in Organizational Decision Making: The Case of a University', *Administrative Science Quarterly*, 19, 462–63.

Sancton, T. and MacLeod, S. (1998) *Death of a Princess*, London, Orion.

Sanna, L. J. and Pusecker, P. A. (1994) 'Self-efficacy, Valence of Self-evaluation and Performance', *Personality and Social Psychology Bulletin*, 20, 82–92.

Sauter, S., Hurrell, J. T., and Cooper, C. L. (1989) *Job Control and Worker Health*, Chichester, John Wiley.

Schaubroeck, J. and Williams, S. (1993) 'Type A Behaviour Pattern and Escalating Commitment', *Journal of Applied Psychology*, 5, 862–67.

Schein, D. (1980) *Organizational Psychology*, New Jersey, Prentice Hall.

Schein, E. H. (1992) *Organizational Culture and Leadership: A Dynamic View*, San Francisco, Jossey Bass.

—— (1996) 'Culture: The Missing Concept in Organization Studies', *Administrative Science Quarterly*, 41, 229–40.

Scherkenbach, W. W. (1986) *The Deming Route to Quality and Productivity*, London, Mercury.

Shingo, S. (1988) *Non-Stock Production*, Cambridge, Mass., Productivity Press.

Schneider, K. T., Swan, S. and Fitzgerald, L. F. (1997) 'Job-related and Psychological Effects of Sexual Harassment in the Workplace: Empirical Evidence from Two Organizations', *Journal of Applied Psychology*, 82, 401–15.

Schon, D. A. (1993) 'Generative Metaphor: A Perspective on Problem-setting in Social Policy', in, A. Ortony (ed.), *Metaphor and Thought*, Cambridge, Cambridge University Press.

Schonberger, R. J. (1982) *Japanese Manufacturing Techniques: Nine Hidden Lessons in Simplicity*, New York, Free Press.

—— (1986) *World Class Manufacturing: The Lessons of Simplicity Applied*, New York, Free Press.

Schoorman, F. D. (1988) 'Escalation Bias in Performance Appraisals: An Unintended Consequence of Supervisor Participation in Hiring Decisions', *Journal of Applied Psychology*, 73, 58–62.

Schuler, R. S. and Jackson, S. E. 'Managing Stress Through PHRM Practices: An Uncertainty Interpretation', in K. Rowland

and G. Ferris (eds.), *Research in Personnel and Human Resources Management*, vol. 4, Greenwich, JAI Press, 183–224.

Schwartzman. H. (1986) 'The Meeting as Neglected Form in Organizational Studies', in B. M. Staw and L. L. Cummings (eds.), *Research in Organizational Behavior*, 8.

Schwenk, C. R. (1986) 'Information, Cognitive Biases and Commitment to a Course of Action', *Academy of Management Review*, 11, 290–310.

Sewell, G. and Wilkinson, B. (1992a) 'Someone to Watch Over Me: Surveillance, Discipline and the JIT Labour Process', *Sociology*, 26, 271–89.

—— (1992b) 'Empowerment or Emasculation? Shop Floor Surveillance in a Total Quality Organization', in P. Blyton and P. Turnbull (eds.), *Reassessing Human Resource Management*, London, Sage, 97–115.

Selye, H. (1974) *Stress Without Distress*, New York, Lippincott.

Shaw, M. E. (1981) *Group Dynamics*, New York, McGraw-Hill.

Simmel, G. (1950) 'The Secret and the Secret Society', in K. H. Wolff (ed. and trs.) *The Sociology of Georg Simmel*, New York, Free Press, 307–76.

Simon, H. (1960) *The New Science of Management Decision*, New York, Harper.

Simonian, H. (1998) 'Daimler-Chrysler deal in final stages', *Financial Times* 19 September, p. 17.

Sims, H. P. (1980) 'Further Thought on Punishment in Organizations', *Academy of Management Review*, 5, 133–8.

Sims, H. P. and Manz, C. C. (1984) 'Observing Leader Verbal Behaviour: Toward Reciprocal Determinism in Leadership Theory', *Journal of Applied Psychology*, 69, 222–32.

Smircich, L. (1983a) 'Concepts of Culture and Organizational Analysis', *Administrative Science Quarterly*, 28, 339–58.

—— (1983b) 'Organizations as Shared Meanings', in Pondy, L. R., Frost, P. J., Morgan, G., and Dandridge, T. C. (eds.) *Organizational Symbolism*, London, JAI, 55–65.

Smircich, L. and Morgan, G. (1982)

'Leadership: The Management of Meaning', *Journal of Applied Behavioural Science*, 18, 257–73.

Smith, A. (1983) *The Wealth of Nations*, Harmondsworth, Penguin.

Smith, C. G. W. and Hepburn, J. R. (1979) 'Alienation and Prison Organizations: Comparative Analysis', *Criminology*, 17, 251–62.

Smith K. K. and Simmons, V. M. (1983) 'A Rumpelstiltskin Organization: Metaphors on Metaphors in Field Research', *Administrative Science Quarterly*, 28, 377–92.

Spriegel, W. R. and Myers, C. E. (eds.) (1953) *The Writings of the Gilbreths*, Homewood Ill., Irwin.

Stalk, G. (1988) 'Time: The Next Source of Competitive Advantage', *Harvard Business Review*, 66, 41–51.

Stalk, G. and Hout, T. M. (1990) *Competing Against Time*, New York, Free Press.

Stalk, G. and Weber, A. M. (1993) 'Japan's Dark Side of Time', *Harvard Business Review*, July/August, 93–103.

Starbuck, W. H., Greve, A. and Hedberg, B. L. T. (1978) 'Responding to Crises', *Journal of Business Administration*, 9, 111–37.

Staw, B. M. (1981) 'The Escalation of Commitment to a Course of Action', *Academy of Management Review*, 6, 577–87.

—— (1986) 'Organizational Psychology and the Pursuit of the Happy/Productive Worker', *California Management Review*, 28, 40–53.

—— (1996) 'Escalation Research: An Update and Appraisal', in Z. Shapira (ed.) *Organizational Decision Making*, Cambridge, Cambridge University Press.

Staw, B. M., Sandelands, L. E., Dutton, J. E. (1981) 'Threat-rigidity Effects in Organizational Behaviour: A Multi-level Analysis', *Administrative Science Quarterly*, 26, 501–24.

Staw, B. M. and Ross, J. (1987) 'Behaviour in Escalation Situations: Antecedents, Prototypes and Solutions', in, L. L. Cummings and B. M. Staw, (eds.), *Research* in *Organization Behaviour*, London, JAI Press, 9, 39–78.

Stephenson, T. (1985) *Management: A Political Activity*, Basingstoke, Macmillan.

Sterba, R. L. A. (1978) 'Clandestine Management in the Imperial Chinese Bureaucracy', *Academy of Management Review*, 3, 67–78.

Stockdale, J. E. (1991) 'Sexual Harassment at Work', in J. Firth-Cozens and M. A. West (eds.), *Women at Work: Psychological and Organizational Perspectives*, Philadelphia, Open University Press.

Stogdill, R. M. (1974) *A Handbook of Leadership: A Survey of Theory and Research*, New York, Free Press.

Stoner, J. A. F. (1968) 'Risky and Cautious Shifts in Group Decisions: The Influence of Widely Held Values', *Journal of Experimental Social Psychology*, 4, 442–59.

Taguchi, G. (1981) *On-Line Quality Control During Production*, Nagoya, Central Japan Quality Control Association.

—— and Wu, Y. (1985) Introduction to Off-Line Quality Control, Nagoya, Central Japan Quality Control Association.

—— and Clausing, D. (1990) 'Robust Quality', *Harvard Business Review*, January/February 65–102.

Tannen, D. (1995) 'The Power of Talk', *Harvard Business Review*, September/October, 138–48.

Taylor, F. W. (1947) *Scientific Management*, New York, Harper and Row.

Teger, A. I. (1980) *Too Much Invested to Quit*, New York, Pergamon.

Tett, G. (1998) 'Bank Puts Brave New Face on the Future', *Financial Times*, 4 May, 5.

Thomas, D. A. and Ely, R. J. (1996) 'Making Differences Matter: A New Paradigm for Managing Diversity', *Harvard Business Review*, September/October, 79–99.

Thompson, E. P. (1967) 'Time, Work Discipline and Industrial Capitalism', *Past and Present*, 38, 55–97.

Thompson, P. and McHugh, D. (1995) *Work Organizations: A Critical Introduction*, London, Macmillan.

Tjosvold, D. (1985a) 'The Effects of Attribution and Social Context on Superior's Influence and Interaction with Low Performing Subordinates', *Personnel Psychology*, 38, 361–78.

—— (1985b) 'Power and Social Context in Superior Subordinate Interaction', *Organizational Behaviour and Human Decision Processes*, 35, 281–93.

Toffler, A. (1970) *Future Shock*, London, Pan.

—— (1992) *Powershift*, London, Bantam.

Totterdel, P., Spelten, E., Smith, L., Barton, J., and Folkard, S. (1995) 'Recovery From Work Shifts: How Long Does it Take?' *Journal of Applied Psychology*, 80, 43–57.

Trevor-Roper, H. (1972) *The Last Days of Hitler*, London, Pan.

Trice, H. M. and Beyer, J. M. (1984) 'Studying Organizational Cultures Through Rites and Rituals', *Academy of Management Review*, 9, 653–69.

—— (1992) *The Cultures of Work Organizations*, Englewood Cliffs, Prentice Hall.

Trist, E. L. and Bamforth K. W. (1951) 'Some Social and Psychological Consequences of the Longwall Method of Coal-getting', *Human Relations*, 4, 3–38.

Tsoukas, H. (1991) 'The Missing Link: A Transformational View of Metaphors in Organization Science', *Academy of Management Review*, 16, 566–85.

—— (1993) 'Analogical Reasoning and Knowledge Generation in Organization Theory', *Organization Studies*, 14, 323–46.

Turner, B. A. (1986) 'Sociological Aspects of Organizational Symbolism', *Organization Studies*, 7, 101–15.

—— (1990) 'The Rise of Organizational Symbolism', in, J. Hassard and W. Pym (eds.), *The Theory and Philosophy of Organizations*, London, Routledge, 13–29.

Turner, M. (1996) *The Literary Mind*, New York, Oxford University Press.

Tversky, A. and Kahneman, D. (1973) 'Judgement Under Uncertainty; Heuristics and Biases', *Science*, 185, 1124–31.

—— (1981) 'The Framing of Decisions and

the Psychology of Choice', *Science*, 211, 453–63.

Uchino, B. N., Cacioppo, J. T., and Kiecolt-Glaser, J. K. (1996) 'The Relationship Between Social Support and Physiological Process: A Review with Emphasis on Underlying Mechanisms and Implications for Health', *Psychological Bulletin*, 119, 488–531.

Ury, W. (1991) *Getting Past No*, London, Century.

Van Maanen, J. (1973) 'Observations on the Making of Policemen', *Human Organization*, 32, 407–18.

Vestey, M. (1998) 'Keep on Listening', *The Spectator*, 19/26 December, 100.

Vidal, J. (1997) *McLibel: Burger Culture on Trial*, London, Pan.

Voss, C. (ed.) (1987) *Just in Time Manufacturing*, London, IFS.

Vroom, V. (1964) *Work and Motivation*, New York, Wiley.

Waldman, D. A. (1994) 'The Contributions of Total Quality Management to a Theory of Work Performance', *Academy of Management Review*, 19, 510–36.

Wallace, J. E. (1993) 'Professional and Organizational Commitment: Compatible or Incompatible?' *Journal of Vocational Behaviour*, 42, 333–49.

Warr, P. (1983) 'Work, Jobs and Unemployment', *Bulletin of the British Psychological Society*, 36, 305–11.

Warr, P. B. (1987) *Work, Unemployment and Mental Health*, Oxford, Oxford University press.

Warr, P. and Wall, T. (1975) *Work and Well-Being*, Harmondsworth, Penguin.

Warr, P., Cook, J., and Wall, T. D. (1979) 'Scales for the Measurement of Some Work Attitudes and Aspects of Psychological Well Being', *Journal of Occupational Psychology*, 52, 129–48.

Waterman, R. H. (1987) *The Renewal Factor*, London, Bantam.

Watson, T. (1994) *In Search of Management: Culture Chaos and Control in Managerial Work*, London, Routledge.

Watson, T. (1995) *Sociology Work and Industry*, London, Routledge.

Watts, M. and Cooper, C. L. (1992) *Relax: Dealing with Stress*, London, BBC Books.

Watzlawick, P. (1988) *Ultra-solutions: How to Fail Most Successfully*, New York, Norton.

Watzlawick, P., Weakland, J. H., and Frish, R. (1974) *Change: Principles of Problem Formation and Resolution*, New York, Norton.

Weber, M. (1947) *The Theory of Economic and Social Organization*, (A. M. Henderson and T. Parsons, eds. and Trs.) New York, Oxford University Press.

Weick, K. (1976) 'Educational Organizations as Loosely Coupled Systems', *Administrative Science Quarterly*, 21, 1–18.

Weick, K. E. (1989) 'Theory Construction as Disciplined Imagination', *Academy of Management Review*, 14, 516–31.

Weiss, A. M. and Cropanzano, R. (1996) 'Affective Events Theory: A Theoretical Discussion', in B. Staw and L. L. Cummings (eds.), *Research in Organizational Behaviour*, San Francisco, Jossey Bass.

Weisse, C. S. (1992) 'Depression and Immunocompetence: A Review of the Literature', *Psychological Bulletin*, 111, 475–89.

White, M. and Gribben, J. (1992) *Stephen Hawking—A Life in Science*, Harmondsworth, Penguin.

Whyte, D. H. (1957) *The Organization Man*, London, Jonathan Cape.

Whyte, W. F. (1949) 'The Social Structure of the Restaurant', *American Journal of Sociology*, 54, 302–10.

Whyte, G. (1986) 'Escalating Commitment to a Course of Action: A Re-interpretation', *Academy of Management Review*, 11, 311–21.

—— (1989) 'Groupthink Reconsidered', *Academy of Management Review*, 14, 40–56.

Wilkins, A. L. (1983) 'Organizational Stories as Symbols Which Control the Organization', in Pondy, L. R., Frost, P. J., Morgan, G., and Dandridge, T. C. (eds.), *Organizational Symbolism*, London, JAI, 81–92.

Wilkins, A. L. and Ouchi, W. G. (1983) 'Efficient Cultures: Exploring the Relationship Between Culture and Organizational Performance', *Administrative Science Quarterly*, 28, 468–81.

Willmott, H. (1993) 'Strength is Ignorance; Slavery is Freedom: Managing Culture in Modern Organization', *Journal of Management Studies*, 30 (5), 515–52.

—— (1994) 'Business Process Reengineering and Human Resource Management', *Personnel Review*, 23, 34–46.

Wilson-Owens, R. (1998) 'Occupational Stress: The Case of a Hospice Nurse', unpublished MBA dissertation, University of Liverpool, UK.

Winner, E. and Gardner, H. (1993) 'Metaphor and Irony: Two Levels of Understanding', in A. Ortony (ed.,) *Metaphor and Thought*, Cambridge, Cambridge University Press.

Wisdom, J. (1965) *Paradox and Discovery*, Oxford, Blackwell.

Wood, L. (1995) 'Worthwhile and Diverse Companies Need to Make their Culture Family-friendly if they are to Attract Women Who Will Stay', *Financial Times*, Survey of Engineering in Action, 4.

Wortman, C. B. and Linsenmeiier, J. A. (1977) 'Interpersonal Attraction and Techniques of Ingratiation in Organizational Settings', in B. M. Staw and G. R. Salancick (eds.), *New Directions in Organization Behaviour*, Chicago, St Clair.

Wright, R. M., George, J. M., Farnsworth, S. R., and McMahan, G. C. (1993) 'Productivity and Extra-role Behaviour: The Effects of Goals and Incentives on Spontaneous Helping', *Journal of Applied Psychology*, 78, 374–81.

Wrong, D. H. (1979) *Power, Its Forms, Bases and Uses*, Oxford, Basil Blackwell.

Yamba, C. B. (1997) 'Cosmologies in Turmoil: Witchfinding and AIDS in Chiawa, Zambia', *Africa*, 67, 200–23.

Young, E. (1989) 'On the Naming of the Rose: Interests and Multiple Meanings as Elements of Organizational Culture', *Organization Studies*, 10, 187–206.

Yukl, G. (1989) 'Managerial Leadership: A Review of Theory and Research', *Journal of Management*, 15, 251–89.

Zahn, G. I. and Wolf, G. (1981) 'Leadership and the Art of Cycle Maintenance: A Simulation Model of Superior Subordinate Interaction', *Organizational Behaviour and Human Performance*, 28, 26–49.

Zander, A. (1982) *Making Groups Effective*, San Francisco, Jossey Bass.

Index